WORKS ISSUED BY
THE HAKLUYT SOCIETY

————

THE *ITINERÁRIO* OF JERÓNIMO LOBO

SECOND SERIES
No. 162

Indian painting of a Jesuit

THE *ITINERÁRIO* OF JERÓNIMO LOBO

Translated by
DONALD M. LOCKHART

From the Portuguese Text Established and Edited by
M. G. DA COSTA

With an Introduction and Notes by
C. F. BECKINGHAM

THE HAKLUYT SOCIETY
LONDON
1984

© The Hakluyt Society 1984

ISBN
0 904180 15 8

Printed in Great Britain by the
University Press, Cambridge

Published by the Hakluyt Society
c/o The Map Room
British Library Reference Division
London WC1B 3DG

CONTENTS

CONTENTS

PREFACE

The manuscript of Lobo's travels, generally known as the *Itinerário* and long thought to have been lost, was found by Padre M. G. da Costa in 1947 in the Public Library at Braga[1], where it is MS. n. 813. He made known his important discovery five years later in his diocesan journal *A Voz de Lamego*, and in 1971 published an annotated edition along with those other writings of the author which had either not been printed at all or had appeared only in translation. It is obvious that the book would have been revised before publication. Composition and style leave much to be desired. There is some repetition and the syntax of the meandering sentences sometimes collapses. P. da Costa's is not a diplomatic edition but he naturally did not revise his text. He did, however, divide it into chapters and supply headings for them. These have been included in Dr Lockhart's translation but, like anything else that is not in the original, they have been placed within square brackets.

Except for a few familiar names of cities or countries the translation preserves the original spellings of proper names, inconsistent as they often are. In the notes I have used freely but selectively, and have supplemented, the annotations to the Portuguese edition, and I have profited from a number of suggestions made by Dr Lockhart. I have tried to include all variations and additions of any importance to be found in the French version published by Le Grand in 1728.

Readers will notice some inconsistency in the spelling of Portuguese names. In the seventeenth century the same family name might be written to end in *-es* or *-ez* indifferently. It is now customary to spell all names in accordance with the rules of the reformed orthography so that the author whose name was printed Tellez on the title-page of his book in 1660 is now called Teles, while Páez has become Pais. The transliteration of Ethiopian names and words presents peculiar and intractable problems. The script used for Ethiopic (Ge'ez), Amharic and Tigrinya includes a number of letters which do not represent different sounds and which may be used interchangeably. Besides, the script has

---

[1] Now the Library of the University of the Minho. Except for some corrections and additions the MS. is not in Lobo's own hand.

two deficiencies. It cannot record the gemination of consonants, so that there is no difference in writing between, e.g., Abay and Abbay, and it makes no distinction between a 'furtive' vowel (the so-called sixth order)[2] and no vowel at all, so that the same name may be read as Susenyos or Susneyos. In these circumstances it did not seem justifiable to resort to all the typographical monstrosities that have been devised to represent Ethiopian spellings with precision. Ethiopian and other oriental names have been spelt in the notes without diacritical points. Words, when quoted by Lobo, have been given in forms which it is hoped will be sufficiently exact to enable anyone to find them in the dictionaries of the languages concerned.

In the course of the work we have incurred many obligations. The extent of our debt to Professor Francis M. Rogers is explained in the Introduction. It was from him that I first learnt of P. da Costa's discovery of the manuscript, and it was through his intervention that the Gulbenkian Foundation enabled the three of us to meet and plan our work. My own greatest obligation has been to Professor Edward Ullendorff. For many years now he has given me the benefit of his profound knowledge of Ethiopian culture and of the Semitic languages and literatures of Ethiopia. He has taken great trouble to answer some specific questions. Dr Richard Pankhurst has been of great assistance both in his capacity as Librarian of the Royal Asiatic Society, and in allowing me to draw upon his long and intimate experience of Ethiopia. I am especially grateful to him for the protracted loan of a valuable book from his private library and for his advice in choosing illustrations. The Rev. Professor Henry Chadwick kindly traced a patristic reference for me. Professor P. José Geraldes Freire of the University of Coimbra provided us with the explanation of a local toponym. Several friends and former colleagues at the School of Oriental and African Studies have given generous help with linguistic difficulties, Professor B. W. Andrzejewski for Somali and Galla (Oromo), Dr Hazel Carter and Mr David Rycroft for Bantu languages, Dr R. J. Hayward for Afar, Dr A. K. Irvine for Ethiopic, and Sheikh Yahya Omar for Swahili. In trying to identify fauna and flora I have had much help from Mrs Margaret Speak of the staff of the International Commission on Zoological Nomenclature. On specific questions I have sought the advice of Dr Humphrey Greenwood, Miss Bernice Brewster and Mr I. R. Bishop of the British Museum (Natural History), of Mrs Warr, formerly of the staff of the same museum, and of Dr David L. Harrison,

[2] For convenience it is represented by ĕ, but it is not necessarily short in pronunciation.

with whom I discussed the unicorn. My indebtedness to the books and conversation of Professor C. R. Boxer will be as obvious as it is pervasive.

Dr Lockhart wishes to acknowledge the financial support of the Research and Publications Committee of the University of Norwich, Northfield, Vermont. I have made heavy demands on the staffs of the British Library, especially of the Map Room, and of the libraries of the School of Oriental and African Studies and the Royal Asiatic Society. I have been particularly grateful for the patient help of Mr C. Perkins, Curator of Maps at the School.

For the illustrations we are indebted to the National Museum, Delhi, the Royal Geographical Society, The British Library, Mrs Edward Ullendorff and the South African Embassy in London.

C. F. B.

LIST OF ILLUSTRATIONS

LIST OF MAPS

BIBLIOGRAPHY OF BOOKS AND ARTICLES MENTIONED IN THE FOOTNOTES

ABBADIE, Antoine d'. *Dictionnaire de la langue amariñña*, Paris, 1881.

ALBUQUERQUE, Afonso de. *The commentaries of the great Afonso Dalboquerque*, 4 vols. London, 1875–84. (Hakluyt Society, 1st series, nos. 53, 55, 62, 69.)

ALMEIDA, Manoel de. See BECCARI, C.

ALVARES, Francisco, *The Prester John of the Indies*, 2 vols. Cambridge, 1961. (Edited by C. F. Beckingham and G. W. B. Huntingford, Hakluyt Society, 2nd series, nos. 114, 115.)

ARISTOTLE. 'De inundatione Nili', *Aristotelis qui ferebantur librorum fragmenta*, Lipsiae, 1886.

BABINGER, F. 'Contraffazioni ottomane dello zecchino veneziano nel XV secolo', *Aufsätze und Abhandlungen zur Geschichte Südosteuropas und der Levante*, 3 vols. München, 1962–76.

BARRADAS, M. See BECCARI, C.

BARROS, João de. *Asia*, 4 vols. Lisboa, 1945, 46.

BECCARI, C. *Rerum aethiopicarum scriptores occidentales inediti*, 15 vols. Roma, 1905–17. (Includes the histories of Pedro Páez (Pêro Pais), Almeida, Barradas, and Mendes.)

BECKINGHAM, C. F. 'A note on the topography of Aḥmad Grãn's campaigns in 1542', *Journal of Semitic Studies*, IV, no. 4 (Oct. 1959).

BECKINGHAM, C. F. *The achievements of Prester John*, London, 1966.

BECKINGHAM, C. F. 'The quest for Prester John', *Bulletin of the John Rylands University Library of Manchester*, LXII, no. 2 (Spring 1980).

BECKINGHAM, C. F. and HUNTINGFORD, G. W. B. *Some records of Ethiopia, 1593–1646*, London, 1954. (Hakluyt Society, 2nd series, no. 107.) Cited as *SRE*.

BEST, Thomas. *The voyage of Thomas Best*, London, 1934. (Edited by Sir William Foster. Hakluyt Society, 2nd series, no. 75.)

BLAKE, J. W. *Europeans in West Africa, 1450–1560*, 2 vols. London, 1942. (Hakluyt Society, 2nd series, nos. 86, 87.)

BOCARRO, António. *Livro das plantas de tôdas as fortalezas, cidades e povoações do estado da India Oriental*, Bastorá, 1937.

BOXER, C. R. *The Tragic History of the Sea, 1589–1622*, Cambridge, 1959. (Hakluyt Society, 2nd series, no. 112.)

BOXER, C. R. *Further selections from the Tragic History of the Sea, 1559–1565*, Cambridge, 1968. (Hakluyt Society, 2nd series, no. 132.)

BRUCE, James. *Travels to discover the source of the Nile*. 3rd edition. 8 vols. Edinburgh, 1813.

BUDGE, E. A. Wallis. *The Book of the Saints of the Ethiopian Church*. 4 vols. Cambridge, 1928.

BUDGE, E. A. Wallis. *A history of Ethiopia*. 2 vols. London, 1928.

CABREYRA, Joseph de. *Naufragio da nao N. Senhora de Belem*, Lisboa, 1636.

CARLOS I, King of Portugal. *A Pesca do atum no Algarve em 1898*, Lisboa, 1899.

CARRÉ, Abbé B. *The travels of the Abbé Carré*. 3 vols. London, 1947, 48. (Hakluyt Society, 2nd series, nos. 95, 96, 97.)

CASTANHOSO, Miguel de. See WHITEWAY, R. S.

CASTRO, Dom João de. *Obras completas de D. João de Castro*. 2 vols. Coimbra, 1968, 71. (Edited by Armando Cortesão and Luís de Albuquerque.)

CERULLI, Enrico. *Somalia. Scritti vari editi ed inediti*. 3 vols. Roma, 1957–64.

CESPEDES Y MENESES, Gonçalo de. *Primera parte de la Historia de D. Felippe el IIII*, Lisboa, 1631.

CHEESMAN, R. E. *Lake Tana and the Blue Nile*, London, 1936.

CORTESÃO, A. and TEIXEIRA DA MOTA, A. *Portugaliae monumenta cartographica*. 6 vols. Lisboa, 1960.

CRAWFORD, O. G. S. *Ethiopian itineraries*, Cambridge, 1958. (Hakluyt Society, 2nd series, no. 109.)

CRAWFORD, O. G. S. *The Fung Kingdom of Sennar*, Gloucester, 1951.

DALGADO, S. R. *Glossário Luso-Asiático*. 2 vols. Coimbra, 1919, 21.

DUFFY, James. *Shipwreck and Empire*, Cambridge, Mass., 1955.

FONSECA, J. N. da. *An historical and archaeological sketch of the city of Goa*, Bombay, 1878.

FOSTER, William. *The English factories in India 1622–1623*, Oxford, 1908.

FREEMAN-GRENVILLE, G. S. P. *The East African coast*, Oxford, 1962.

FREEMAN-GRENVILLE, G. S. P. *The Mombasa rising against the Portuguese, 1631*, London, 1980.

GEORGE, Wilma. 'The bestiary: a handbook of the local fauna', *Archives of Natural History*, 10 (1981).

GESNER, Conrad. *Historia animalium*, 5 vols. Tiguri, 1551–87.

GOLD, Joel J. 'Johnson's translation of Lobo', *PMLA*, LXXX (1965).

Guida dell'Africa Orientale Italiana, Milano, 1938.

GUIDI, Ignazio. *Vocabolario amarico-italiano*, Roma, 1901.

GUIDI, Ignazio. *Storia della letteratura etiopica*, Roma, 1932.

HAIR, P. E. H. 'Portuguese contacts with the Bantu languages of the Transkei, Natal, and southern Mozambique 1497–1650', *African Studies*, 39, no. 1 (1980).

HARRISON, D. L. *The Mammals of Arabia*, 3 vols. London, 1964–72.

História trágico-marítima. 3 vols. Lisboa, 1735– ? (The date of publication of the third volume is uncertain.)

Hobson-Jobson. Edited by H. Yule and A. C. Burnell. New edition by W. Crooke. Reprint, London, 1968. Cited as *HJ*.

HOROWITZ, J. 'Das äthiopische Maccabäerbuch', *Zeitschrift für Assyriologie*, XIX, Heft 3/4 (1906).

HUNTINGFORD, G. W. B. *The Galla of Ethiopia*, London, 1955.

IRENAEUS. *Adversus Haereses*, in MIGNE, *Patrologia Graeca*, tom. VII, Lutetiae Parisiorum, 1857.

JOSEPHUS. *Flavii Josephi opera*. Edited by B. Niese. 7 vols. Berlin, 1885–95.

KITTEL, F. *A Kannaḍa-English Dictionary*, Mangalore, 1894.

LANE, E. W. *An Account of the manners and customs of the modern Egyptians*. 3rd edition. London, 1842.

LE GRAND, Joachim. See LOBO, J.

LEITÃO, Humberto and LOPES, J. Vicente. *Dicionário da linguagem de marinha antiga e actual*, Lisboa, 1963.

LEWIS, I. M. *The modern history of Somaliland*, London, 1965.

LOBO, Jerónimo. *Itinerário e outros escritos inéditos*. Edição crítica pelo P.ᵉ M. Gonçalves da Costa. Barcelos, 1971.

LOBO, Jerónimo. *A Short Relation of the River Nile, of its source and current; of its overflowing the Campagnia of Ægypt, till it runs into the Mediterranean and of other curiosities: written by an eye-witness, who lived many years in the chief kingdoms of the Abyssine Empire*. Translated by Sir Peter Wyche. (Lobo's name does not appear.) London, 1669.

LOBO, Jerónimo. *Voyage historique d'Abyssinie, du R. P. Jerome Lobo de la Compagnie de Jesus*. Traduite (*sic*) du Portugais, continuée & augmentée de plusieurs Dissertations, Lettres & Memoires. Par M. Le Grand. Paris, La Haye, 1728.

LOBO, Jerónimo. *A voyage to Abyssinia, by Father Jerome Lobo a Portuguese Jesuit*. (Translated from Le Grand by Samuel Johnson.) London, 1735.

LOCKHART, D. M. 'The fourth son of the Mighty Emperor: the Ethiopian background of Johnson's Rasselas', *PMLA*, LXXVIII (1963).

LUDOLF, J. *Historia Æthiopica*, Francofurti ad Moenum, 1681.

MACKWORTH-PRAED, C. W. and GRANT, C. H. B. *Birds of eastern and north eastern Africa*. 2nd edition. 2 vols. London, 1957, 60.

MACLEOD, N. *De Oost-Indische Compagnie als Zeemogendheid in Azië*, 2 vols. Rijswijk, 1927.

MENDES, A. See BECCARI, C.

NESBITT, L. M. *Desert and Forest*, London, 1934.

ORHONLU, Cengiz, *Habeş eyaleti*, Istanbul, 1974. (In Turkish)

ORTA, Garcia da. *Coloquios dos simples, drogas he cousas medicinais da India*, Goa, 1563.

PAIS, Pêro *História da Etiópia*. 3 vols. Porto, 1945, 46. See also BECCARI, C. (Páez).

PARKYNS, Mansfield. *Life in Abyssinia*. 2 vols. London, 1853.

PIMENTEL, MANUEL. *Arte de navegar de Manuel Pimentel*. Comentada e anotada por Armando Cortesão, Fernanda Aleixo e Luís de Albuquerque. Lisboa, 1969.

PRITCHARD, J. B. (ed.). *Solomon and Sheba*, London, 1974.

PYRARD, François. *The voyage of François Pyrard de Laval.* 3 vols. London, 1887–90. (Hakluyt Society, 1st series, nos. 76, 77, 80.)

Red Sea Pilot, London, 1883.

Red Sea and Gulf of Aden Pilot, London, 1955.

RÜPPELL, E. *Reise in Abyssinien.* 2 vols. Frankfurt a. M., 1838, 40.

SANDOVAL, Alonso de. *Tratado primeiro de instauranda Aethiopum salute*, Madrid, 1647.

SEEMANN, B. *Popular history of the Palms and their allies*, London, 1856.

SILBERMAN, L. H. 'The Queen of Sheba in Judaic tradition', in J. B. PRITCHARD, *Solomon and Sheba*.

SILVA, A. de Moraes. *Diccionário da lingua portugueza.* Nova edição. 2 vols. Rio de Janeiro, 1889, 91.

SKELTON, R. A. 'An Ethiopian embassy to western Europe', in CRAWFORD, O. G. S., *Ethiopian itineraries*.

TELLEZ, B. *Historia geral de Ethiopia a alta*, Coimbra, 1660.

THEODORET. *Graecarum affectionum curatio*, in MIGNE, *Patrologia Graeca*, tom. lxxxiii, Lutetiae Parisiorum, 1859.

TIBBETTS, G. R. *Arab navigation in the Indian Ocean before the coming of the Portuguese*, London, 1971.

TOSTADO, Alfonso, *Opera omnia*, 13 vols. Coloniae Agrippinae, 1613.

TRIMINGHAM, J. S. *Islam in Ethiopia*, London, 1952.

ULLENDORFF, Edward. 'Hebraic-Jewish elements in Abyssinian (Monophysite) Christianity', *Journal of Semitic Studies*, I, no. 3 (July 1956).

ULLENDORFF, Edward. 'The Queen of Sheba in Ethiopian Tradition' in PRITCHARD, J. B., *Solomon and Sheba*.

ULLENDORFF, E. and BECKINGHAM, C. F. *The Hebrew letters of Prester John*, Oxford, 1982.

VALENTIA, Lord. *Voyages and travels to India, Ceylon, the Red Sea, Abyssinia and Egypt.* 3 vols. London, 1811.

VARTHEMA, L. *The travels of Ludovico de Varthema*, London, 1863. (Hakluyt Society, 1st series, no. 32.)

WHITEWAY, R. S. *The Portuguese expedition to Abyssinia, 1541–3*, London, 1902. (Hakluyt Society, 2nd series, no. 10.) (Includes the narratives of Castanhoso and Bermudes.)

WILSON, John. *The Lands of the Bible visited and described*, 2 vols. London, 1847.

Yosippon (Ethiopic text). *Geschichte der Juden*...herausgegeben von Murad Kamil. New York, 1937.

Yosippon (English translation of the Hebrew). *A compendious and moste marveylous History of the later times of the Jewes commune weale*, London, 1561.

ABBREVIATIONS

Amh. Amharic
Eth.   Ethiopic (Ge'ez)
HJ   *Hobson-Jobson.* Edited by H. Yule and A. C. Burnell. New edition by W. Crooke. Reprint, London, 1968.
SRE C. F. Beckingham and G. W. B. Huntingford, *Some Records of Ethiopia, 1593–1646*, London, 1954. (Hakluyt Society, 2nd series, no. 107)

INTRODUCTION

Life of Lobo[1]

Jerónimo Lobo was born not later than the first quarter of 1595. He was the third of at least five sons and six children of Francisco Lobo da Gama, Governor of Cape Verde, who was related to the Counts of Sarzedas. His mother was D. Maria Brandão de Vasconcelos; for a time, at the instance of his superiors, he was to use the name Brandão instead of Lobo.[2] He entered the Society of Jesus as a novice at the earliest possible age, fourteen, at Coimbra in 1609. When he had completed the course in Arts he spent two years at the college of São Paulo at Braga, then returned to Coimbra to study theology. While he was at a farm belonging to the College outside the town he suddenly received an order to go to India. The *Itinerário* begins with this incident.

The book records the adventurous life he led for the next eighteen years. Ordained sub-deacon, deacon and priest on three successive days, he sailed for India the following week with the newly appointed Viceroy. The departure of the fleet had been delayed until dangerously late in the season and the voyage was unsuccessful. After having reached the Gulf of Guinea it was decided to return to Portugal. Next year another attempt was made but this time the ships were involved in a battle with the Dutch and English near Moçambique. When the fight was broken off, the incompetence of the pilots wrecked the Portuguese fleet and Lobo did not arrive in Goa till December 1622. He spent a year there in theological studies and was then accepted for the Ethiopian mission. The labours of Pedro Páez, who died in 1622, had culminated in the conversion of the Emperor Susenyos to the Roman Catholic faith. Though, therefore, assured of a welcome when they arrived, it was by no means easy for the missionaries to reach the country. The Christian Ethiopians had no effective control over any part of the coast, the population of which was Muslim, and the most convenient port,

---

[1] The following account is greatly indebted to P. da Costa's introduction to the Portuguese edition, where he has recorded what is known of Lobo's life. Some corrections are made in the review by P. J. Pereira Gomes in *Archivum historicum Societatis Iesu*, XLIII (1974), 192–5. [2] See p. 197.

xxi

Massawa, was held by the Ottoman Turks. Lobo made an astonishing journey from Pate to the mouth of the Juba in Somalia in the hope of ascending the river to Ethiopia. After the understandable failure of this project he returned to India. He finally arrived at the Jesuit headquarters at Fremona in 1625, by way of the little port of Bailul and a journey across the Danakil desert.

He was to spend nine years in Ethiopia, principally in the north and in the neighbourhood of the source of the Blue Nile; he does not seem ever to have been in Shoa. During these years opposition to the teachings and still more the practices of the Roman Church increased. The Ethiopians resented not only the repudiation of the Monophysite dogma which they had accepted from, and shared with, the Coptic Church of Egypt, but the condemnation of many of their rites, such as male circumcision, the observance of the Sabbath as well as of the Christian Sunday, Judaic dietary laws, and the annual commemoration of the Feast of Kings in a way which the Jesuits considered to be re-baptism. They were also virtually, though not technically, poly-gamous. As P. da Costa has noted, the opposition of high-born Ethiopian ladies was particularly determined, and none of them was converted. There can be no doubt, too, that some of the nobility feared that the Emperor might introduce Portuguese troops to reinforce his sometimes uncertain authority. Susenyos eventually restored the Ethiopian Church to its former position and died soon afterwards, in September 1632. His son and successor Fasiladas banished the Jesuits, first to Fremona, then from the country altogether. They sought help from friendly chiefs, but one of these betrayed them, accepting an important appointment from the Emperor and handing them over to the Turks. They were taken first to Massawa, then to Suakin, and Lobo recounts the extortions from which they suffered. He left Suakin in August 1634 and arrived in Goa in the following December.

In February he sailed for Portugal, entrusted with important business. He was to report to the authorities, religious and secular, on the collapse of the Ethiopian mission and to urge upon the governments in Lisbon and Madrid the desirability of sending a military expedition which would ensure liberty of action for the missionaries. The voyage, like so many other Portuguese voyages from India at this time, ended in shipwreck on the coast of Africa, perhaps near St John's. The survivors built two small boats and one of them sailed round the Cape, an astonishing achievement, reaching Luanda in Angola in March 1636. There being no ship leaving for Portugal Lobo embarked with the retiring Governor, who was taking a cargo of slaves to Cartagena. When near the Spanish Main the ship was captured by the famous Dutch admiral Houtbeen. He released his captives on an island and they contrived to make their way to Cartagena. Here Lobo met the Rector of the Jesuit College, Alonso de Sandoval, whose preoccupation was the conversion and religious instruction of the numerous African slaves who were unloaded there. In the second and much enlarged edition of his book *De instauranda Æthiopum salute* he cites Lobo several times as an authority on India and Ethiopia.[1]

From Cartagena he sailed to Havana, where he embarked on the Spanish treasure fleet for Europe. He landed at Cadiz in November 1636 and travelled by way of Seville to Lisbon. Here he had an audience with Margaret of Savoy, the widowed Duchess of Mantua and Vicereine of Portugal on behalf of Philip IV of Spain, who was also King of Portugal until 1640. Lobo next went to Madrid, and then by way of Barcelona, Genoa and Tuscany to Rome. The *Itinerário* ends with his return to Lisbon. He tells us little of the negotiations with which he had been entrusted but it is obvious that he had only very limited success. This is in no way surprising. It would have been both difficult and costly for the Portuguese to have maintained a garrison at Massawa with such long and precarious lines of communication. Internal opposition in Ethiopia would have been vigorous and there was no obvious political or commercial advantage to be obtained from such an expensive undertaking. Above all, resources were needed to defend Portuguese interests, not against the Ottomans, but against the Dutch. While Lobo was in Italy they, in alliance with the King of Kandy, captured Batticaloa and, in the following year, Trincomalee. What to some appeared the belligerence of the Jesuits was ill-timed.

It is at this juncture that the *Itinerário* stops. It seems that Lobo spent most of the year 1639 in Lisbon and he presumably worked on the first draft of his book. In March 1640 he left for India again and arrived in Goa in September, shortly before the revolution which terminated the union of crowns with Spain and made João IV King of Portugal. Lobo became Father Superior of São Paulo o Velho in Goa, then Rector of São Paulo in Bassein, and finally Prefect of the Casa Professa at Goa. We do not know exactly when he entered upon these offices, but in 1647 he was designated in Rome as Father Provincial. He had, however,

[1] In spite of the Latin title the book is in Spanish. The first edition (1627) is sometimes catalogued as a different work, as it is entitled *Naturaleza, policia sagrada i profana, costumbres i ritos, disciplina i catechismo evangelico de todos etiopes*. It is, however, referred to by the Latin title in the licence to publish.

become involved in a bitter and protracted quarrel with the Viceroy, Dom Filipe Mascarenhas, who prevented him from exercising this function. In May 1648 he was forcibly confined in a Franciscan convent, accused of having Spanish sympathies and of complicity in the hanging of an effigy of the Viceroy to which pasquinades had been attached. In spite of the support of his old companion in Ethiopia, the Patriarch Afonso Mendes, he was kept a prisoner till the end of 1652, when he was freed by a new Viceroy, Dom Vasco Mascarenhas. Next year Lobo's friend Dom Bras de Castro forcibly removed the Viceroy and took his place. Lobo was restored to his position as Prefect of the Casa Professa and became Vice-Provincial. In August 1655 a new Viceroy with proper authority arrived from Portugal, Dom Rodrigo Lobo da Silveira. Dom Bras was imprisoned and his protégé relegated 'to the South'; it was presumably at this time that he visited Ceylon and Malacca, as he says he did in his treatise on the palm-tree. The Society was divided into factions and its standing was adversely affected. Eventually, in 1657 he was persuaded to return to Europe. Next year he was in Rome again to report on the state of the mission. At some time he visited Rouen; he was for a while Rector of the College at Coimbra; in 1660 he became Vice-Prefect of the Casa de São Roque. He was removed from office two years later, but spent the rest of his life there. He came into contact with the British envoy Sir Robert Southwell, who was in Lisbon most of the time from early in 1666 till August 1669, and gave him two short manuscripts about Ethiopia which were translated into English and published in London in 1669. He also had some correspondence with the Secretary of the Royal Society. He died on 29 January 1678, the last survivor of the Ethiopian mission. His funeral is said to have attracted a large crowd.

The Itinerário

The *Itinerário* is Lobo's only book of any length and its history is almost as adventurous as its author's. When he died he was the greatest living authority on Ethiopia and it was known that he had written an account of his travels. Sandoval, in the second edition of his book *De instauranda Æthiopum salute*, published in 1647, mentions him several times and, in his description of the provinces and peoples of 'Ethiopia Oriental', there is a marginal reference to the authority of 'P. Geronimo Lobo, historia Indica' (p. 123). In 1660 Lobo's fellow-student and friend, the Jesuit Balthasar Tellez, published at Coimbra a book entitled *Historia geral de Ethiopia a alta.* It was partly an abridgment and partly a revision of Manoel de Almeida's unpublished *Historia de Ethiopia*, itself a revision of Pedro Paéz's work of the same name, also then unpublished. Lobo was deputed by the Jesuit authorities to examine the book before publication and his approbation is printed in it under his name. It appears, moreover, from a letter he wrote to Henry Oldenburg, the Secretary of the Royal Society of London, in 1668, that he had assisted in the composition of the book. Ethiopia had now become very difficult of access; geographical obstacles were reinforced by Ethiopian suspicion of foreigners and Ottoman supremacy in the Red Sea. At the same time there was considerable interest in the country, and in the years 1661 to 1698 Ludolf was publishing a series of books which laid the foundations for the scholarly study of its languages, history and institutions. There was naturally great curiosity about whatever it was that Lobo was believed to have written.

The *Itinerário* first appeared in French. In 1692 the Abbé Joachim Le Grand arrived in Portugal as secretary to the ambassador, the Abbé d'Estrées. As he says 'les négotiations n'étoient pas fort vives entre la France & le Portugal' during the five years he spent in Lisbon, and he devoted much time to searching out and examining Portuguese records of exploration, conquest and missionary work in Africa and Asia. He had been made aware of the existence of Lobo's book by Thévenot who believed he had seen and published part of it himself, though in this he was mistaken, as we shall see. Le Grand had despaired of finding it when the Count of Ericeira produced it for him. His translation, with the addition of a number of relevant essays and documents, was published at Paris and The Hague in 1728 under the title *Voyage historique d'Abissinie, du R. P. Jerome Lobo, de la Compagnie de Jesus. Traduite* [sic] *du Portugais, continuée & augmentée de plusieurs Dissertations, Lettres & Memoires.* We do not know, and for reasons that will appear it is possible that we shall never know, to what extent Le Grand abridged and adapted the text before him.

It is Le Grand's French version which was translated into English by Samuel Johnson and published in London in 1735 as *A voyage to Abyssinia, by Father Jerome Lobo a Portuguese Jesuit.* It was his first publication and his name did not appear in the original edition. He did the work, for which he was paid five guineas, while staying with his surgeon friend Hector at the house of a Birmingham bookseller called Warren. He is said to have dictated the translation to Hector from his bed. Over thirty years later, when Boswell brought him a copy, he told him to ignore it. 'Sir,' protested Boswell, 'your style is much improved since you translated this.' 'Sir,' retorted Johnson, 'I hope it is.' Professor J. J. Gold has shown that in places Johnson abbreviated or altered Le Grand's text.[1] Dr D. M. Lockhart has published a careful analysis of the relation of this work to *Rasselas*[2]

Bruce's colourful narrative of his travels, first published in 1790, excited interest in Ethiopia. It contained several insulting and grossly inaccurate comments upon Lobo and the other Jesuits, whose works Bruce knew only from the English version of Tellez, published in 1710. No one knew, however, what had become of Lobo's own book and it was often assumed that it had perished in the great Lisbon earthquake of 1755. However, on 1 December 1829 at a session of the Academia Real das Sciencias de Lisboa, Manoel José Maria da Costa e Sá 'presented the autograph of the travels of our well-known Padre Jeronymo Lobo, which are missing in Portuguese though they are in print in other languages'.[3] Scholars subsequently tried to find the manuscript in the Academy's library, failed, and concluded that it had been lost after 1829. This is stated, for example, in the *Grande Enciclopedia Portuguesa e Brasileira*. However, the word 'presented', *apresentou*, does not necessarily imply that the manuscript was given to the Academy, but merely that it was displayed at the session in question. The list of acquisitions for the year in question does not include it, and we must conclude that Costa e Sá showed it to the academicians and then took it away with him.

In 1947 P. Manuel Gonçalves da Costa, then the parish priest of Lalim in the diocese of Lamego, was searching for unpublished philosophical dissertations in Portuguese libraries when he came upon a manuscript of the *Itinerário* in the Biblioteca Pública at Braga. It was not, however, until 1952 that he announced his discovery in a short article in his diocesan gazette, *A Voz de Lamego*. This attracted no attention from scholars until 1964, when it came to the notice of Professor Francis M. Rogers who was visiting Portugal. He at once went to Lalim and was soon satisfied that the manuscript was indeed the long-lost *Itinerário*. On his way to Portugal he had passed through London where we had met and talked about Lobo. He had told me of the existence of another short work in the possession of the Duke of Palmela, which Dr Lockhart was then examining as part of his

[1] 'Johnson's Translation of Lobo', *PMLA*, LXXX (1965).
[2] '"The Fourth Son of the Mighty Emperor": the Ethiopian Background of Johnson's *Rasselas*', *PMLA*, LXXVIII (1963).
[3] *Historia e Memorias da Academia Real das Sciencias de Lisboa*, X, pt 2 (1830), xiv.

doctoral research; I told Professor Rogers of the Lobo material in the library of the Royal Society and explained why I did not believe that the Lisbon Academy of Sciences had lost, but on the contrary had never possessed, the manuscript. Professor Rogers now invoked the help of the Gulbenkian Foundation which sponsored a meeting in Lisbon between P. da Costa, Dr Lockhart and myself. The first result of this meeting was the publication in 1971 by P. da Costa of an edition, not only of the *Itinerário* but of such other writings by Lobo as could be traced, including those belonging to the Duke of Palmela and those in the library of the Royal Society. It was envisaged from the beginning that there should be an English translation of the *Itinerário*. This was undertaken by Dr Lockhart and accepted for publication by the Hakluyt Society.

The complicated textual history of the *Itinerário* has been reconstructed by P. da Costa. Not every episode can be proved beyond doubt but what he has suggested is the most plausible explanation of such evidence as we have. This evidence is specified in his introduction to the Portuguese edition. We can be sure that Lobo had written some part of his travels before his first return to Europe. Not only is it inconceivable that the whole narrative should have been recorded from memory, but we have Sandoval's reference to his 'Historia Indica'. Moreover, Cabreira, who commanded the ship in which Lobo sailed and which was wrecked on the African coast, wrote and published his own account of the disaster. In this he alludes to the fact that Lobo had written a more detailed and more elegant description. It seems certain that the *Itinerário* was completed during its author's stay in Lisbon before his return to India in 1640, and that the manuscript remained in the Casa de São Roque after his death. P. António Franco, a historian of the Society in Portugal, in a book published at Evora in 1719, entitled *Imagem da virtude em o noviciado de Coimbra*, cited Lobo's own narrative as his source for the brief biography of him which he included: 'He composed an extensive narrative which I have at my disposal...from which I have gathered enough to give some account of this ardent missionary'. The subsequent fate of the manuscript is not known for certain. P. da Costa suggests that it stayed at São Roque until 1761 when, following the suppression of the Jesuits in Portugal by Pombal, the contents of the library were transferred to the Casa da Misericórdia. From time to time this institution sold items to raise money for charitable purposes. Among those who purchased manuscripts from the Casa was Sir Joseph Banks, who is known to have acquired in this way a copy of Páez's history and a volume of letters of the missionaries in Ethiopia; it is not known, but is obviously possible, that he also obtained the *Itinerário*. In 1789 António de Araujo de Azevedo, first Count da Barca, passed through London on his way to take up an appointment as ambassador at The Hague. He was introduced to Banks who gave him some of his Portuguese manuscripts including those relating to Ethiopia. When Napoleon's armies overran Portugal and the court fled to Brazil the Count da Barca accompanied it, and his library accompanied him. Much of it passed to, and was later sold by, his brother and heir, and became the property of the National Library in Rio de Janeiro. The manuscripts, however, returned to Portugal and were later acquired by a Dr Manuel de Oliveira. On his death they came to the Public Library in Braga, where P. da Costa was to find the manuscript of the *Itinerário* in 1947.

This manuscript, however, cannot have been the one lent to Le Grand by the Count of Ericeira, if it was in the Casa de São Roque at the time. It is known that, after his second return from the East, Lobo was working on his book. On 6 March 1668 the British envoy Sir Robert Southwell wrote that 'the good old Jesuite Hieronimo Lobo...is himself writing his Travels'. On 1 October of the same year Lobo wrote to the secretary of the Royal Society of London, Henry Oldenburg, saying that he was preparing for the press a full account of the wonders he had recorded in his travels. This revised version was, P. da Costa believes, what Le Grand saw. In April 1724 Francisco de Xavier de Menezes, fourth Count of Ericeira, began a series of communications to the Royal Academy of History on the contents of the library of the Counts of Vimieiro, who had acquired the very valuable collection of the great antiquary, Manuel Severim da Faria. In the reports of the session of 4 June 1728 P. da Costa has found references to 'huma larga Relação da Ethiopia' and to a 'Relação diffusa da Ethiopia'. He concludes that, as this was the Count who made a manuscript of Lobo available to Le Grand, this must have been the manuscript that Le Grand used.[1]

The library of the Counts of Vimieiro was indeed lost in the earthquake of 1755, so we shall probably never know to what extent

[1] P. da Costa informs me that, in an article entitled 'Jerónimo Lobo e o seu Itinerário', published in the Lisbon magazine *Panorama* in March 1972, Senhora Maria Antonieta S. de Azevedo has inferred that the Braga MS. was the one used by Le Grand. His letters, preserved in the Collection Clairambault, prove that the manuscript he borrowed included an account of Lobo's return journey at least as far as Angola. However, some of the additions and variants in Le Grand's version are difficult to explain if he was working from the Braga MS.

Le Grand altered or abridged the text before him. The differences between his printed version and the Braga manuscript are considerable. For example, the description of the first two voyages is much abbreviated in the *Voyage historique*, and all that follows Lobo's departure from India in 1635 is reduced to one sentence. Of course this may be because Le Grand thought these detailed narratives irrelevant to his subject, which was Ethiopia. There are, however, a few passages which seem to indicate deliberate revision by Lobo himself, e.g. pp. 54, 102, 103.[1]

If, though, he was preparing his book for publication, as Southwell reported, why was it not printed? There is no obvious answer. P. da Costa has suggested three considerations that may explain this. Lobo's style is clumsy, and in his time the rhetorical canons of the Renaissance humanists were still highly respected in Portugal; his allusions to important personages are on occasion more critical than may have been prudent; his relations with his superiors in the Society, both in India and after his return, were not without difficulty. This is true, though it has been claimed by P. J. Pereira Gomes in his review of P. da Costa's edition that there is no reason to suppose that, except for one passing incident, the authorities of the Society showed any hostility to Lobo in his last years. His case is, however, not unique. It is curious that the works of the Jesuits of the Ethiopian mission, Páez, Almeida, Mendes, and Barradas as well as Lobo, should have remained unpublished until this century, except for the revised version of Almeida's history which was prepared by Tellez with Lobo's help. In this way a vast amount of geographical, historical and anthropological information was withheld from public knowledge for over two centuries while far inferior books were gaining acceptance. The other Jesuit narrations became available in the first two decades of this century in Beccari's great corpus, but even so their contents have been only partially assimilated by historians of Ethiopia.

Lobo's other writings

The *Itinerário* was by far the longest, but not the only, work of Lobo's, and one short book by him appeared in an English translation in his lifetime. It has been mentioned that in his later years he was in touch

[1] However, whether it is the fault of Lobo himself, or a copyist, or the printer, there are about a dozen places where Le Grand's text has a reading obviously inferior to what is in the Braga MS., e.g. p. 25 n. 2, p. 123 n. 2, p. 133 n. 2.

with the Royal Society of London. In 1669 a little book was published in London under the title *A Short Relation of the River Nile, of its source and current; of its overflowing the campagnia of Ægypt, till it runs into the Mediterranean and of other curiosities: written by an eye-witnesse, who lived many years in the chief kingdoms of the Abyssine Empire. Translated by Sir Peter Wyche.* The author's name does not appear in the book, but it is stated on the page opposite the title-page: 'These Discourses...were there by curious Sir Robert Southwell procured from an inquisitive and observing Jesuit of Lisbon'. Southwell was, like Wyche, a Fellow of the Royal Society, of which he was later President. At this time he was a Clerk to the Privy Council. He arrived in Lisbon early in 1666 to supplement the efforts of the ambassador in Madrid, the Earl of Sandwich, in arranging a treaty of peace between Spain and Portugal. It is possible that he had been asked by the Royal Society to seek out Lobo and put specific questions to him. The treaty was concluded in February 1668 and Southwell then returned to England. He was back in Lisbon in June and remained until August 1669. The book consists of tracts on five topics: the river Nile, its source, and its annual flood; the unicorn; the reason why the Abyssinian Emperor was called Prester John; a description of the Red Sea and an explanation of its name; a discourse on the palm-tree and its uses. The last occupies about half the book. The original manuscripts are still in the library of the Royal Society. Wyche's translation was reprinted in 1673 and again, no doubt because of the interest in Ethiopia occasioned by Bruce's book, in 1791 and 1798; Lobo's name appears in the last two. It was translated, from Wyche's translation, into German, French, Italian and Dutch.

Three short works exist in manuscript in the library of the Duke of Palmela, a short description of Massawa, some notes on Dom João de Castro's cosmography of Ethiopia, and another tract on the source and annual flood of the Nile. These were first made known by Gabriel Pereira on the occasion of a cartographical exhibition at Lisbon in 1903; they were intensively studied by Dr Lockhart in his doctoral dissertation at Harvard in 1958. In 1966 P. da Costa discovered in the Ajuda library at Lisbon another short treatise by Lobo entitled *Breve Noticia e Relação de Algumas Cousas Novas Curiosas Certas nao vulgares, e dignas de se saberem, escritas e* [sic] *instancia de Curiosos.* It is concerned with four of the topics of the *Short Relation*, omitting the discourse on the palm-tree. All these minor works merely repeat, summarize, or expand slightly what he writes on the same subjects in the *Itinerário*, which is why we have not translated them here. In addition, there exists a memorial which he submitted to King Philip IV in Madrid in February 1637; it presents the arguments for seizing Massawa and establishing a fort there. Like all of his writings mentioned so far it is in Portuguese. Three letters survive from his correspondence with Henry Oldenburg, the secretary of the Royal Society; one is from Lobo, two are from Oldenburg; all three are in Latin. Oldenburg's letters are dated 13 April 1668 and 8 June 1669, Lobo's reply to the first is dated 1 October 1668. He presented to the Society an inscribed copy of Tellez's book, and the Society sent him spectacles and a magnifying glass. The original of Lobo's letter, copies of Oldenburg's, and the book are preserved in the Society's library. These letters, as well as all the minor writings, were included by P. da Costa in his edition.

Lobo's reputation; qualities of his book

The Jesuit writers on Ethiopia have been both maligned and neglected. As we have seen, apart from what Tellez published in 1660 and Le Grand in 1728, their major works remained in manuscript until this century. Even after Beccari had made them accessible they were often ignored, and the immense amount of careful observation and recording which they undertook has been little used in the increasing number of books written about Ethiopian history. Lobo, if only because a version of his book was available in French and English, was less neglected, but he was more unfairly abused than his companions. His most famous and influential detractor was, of course, Bruce. His *Travels to discover the source of the Nile* is an exhilarating book to read, and in some respects it is a valuable source of information, but he was, as Johnson said to Boswell, 'not a distinct relater'. He was both careless and prejudiced. He detested Catholics and Jesuits in particular; he at once detested and despised the Portuguese. He referred to Lobo as 'a grovelling, fanatic priest', and to his book as 'a heap of fables, and full of ignorance and presumption; and I confess myself disappointed that it has come from so celebrated a hand as the translator, so very little amended, if indeed it can be said to be amended at all'. Yet if one compares his description of the source of the Nile or of the falls at Tisisat with Lobo's, and then with Cheesman's very careful accounts, it is obvious that he was less accurate. How reckless he could be in his hostility to the Jesuits is shown by his comment on the execution of some Capuchin missionaries in Ethiopia in 1714. He found it strange that Tellez did not mention them. It would have been much stranger if he had done. His book was published in 1660.

One further instance of Bruce's irresponsibility will suffice. 'Lobo', he writes, 'is said to have sailed from the peninsula of India, and, being bound for Zeyla, to have embarked in a vessel going to Caxume, or Axum, capital of Tigre...it is inexplicable, how a ship going to Zeyla should choose to land 300 miles beyond it; and still more so, how, being once arrived at Axum, they should seek a ship to carry them back again to Zeyla, 300 miles eastward, when they were then going to Gondar, not much above a hundred miles west of Axum. This seems to me absolutely impossible to explain'. The explanation is that Caxume is Qishn on the south coast of Arabia.

Johnson, who came to doubt whether Bruce had been in Ethiopia at all, gave a just assessment of Lobo as a travel writer. In the preface to his translation he wrote:

The Portuguese traveller...has amused his reader with no romantick absurdities or incredible fictions: whatever he relates, whether true or not, is at least probable; and he who tells nothing exceeding the bounds of probability, has a right to demand that they should believe him who cannot contradict him.

He appears, by his modest and unaffected narration, to have described things as he saw them, to have copied nature from the life, and to have consulted his senses, not his imagination. He meets with no basilisks that destroy with their eyes; his crocodiles devour their prey without tears; and his cataracts fall from the rock without deafening the neighbouring inhabitants.

The reader will here find no regions cursed with irremediable barrenness, or blest with spontaneous fecundity; no perpetual gloom or unceasing sunshine; nor are the nations here described either devoid of all sense of humanity, or consummate in all private or social virtues: here are no Hottentots without religion, polity, or articulate language; no Chinese perfectly polite, and completely skilled in all sciences: he will discover what will always be discovered by a diligent and impartial inquirer, that wherever human nature is to be found, there is a mixture of vice and virtue, a contest of passion and reason; and that the Creator doth not appear partial in his distributions, but has balanced in most countries their particular inconveniences by particular favours.

In his account of the mission, where his veracity is most to be suspected, he neither exaggerates over-much the merits of the Jesuits, if we consider the partial regard paid by the Portuguese to their countrymen, by the Jesuits to their society, and by the Papists to their church, nor aggravates the vices of the Abyssinians.

If Lobo was a more modest and more careful narrator and a more accurate observer, it has to be admitted that he was a less engaging writer. His style, at least in this version of the *Itinerário*, is often inelegant, sometimes obscure, occasionally ungrammatical, and rarely as easy to read as the outcome of Bruce's impatient dictation to his unlucky amanuensis. Yet for the modern reader he is in some ways a more sympathetic author than the other Jesuits who wrote about Ethiopia. His book is more anecdotal and includes more picturesque details. His own experiences and opinions are much more prominent. The difference is obvious if one compares, say, Páez's description of his journey through Wadi Hadramaut to San'a, or the Patriarch Mendes's account of his crossing of the Danakil desert. One cannot imagine any of the others giving such details as Lobo does about the games played by the sailors with captive sharks, mentioning his own unwillingness to obey his superiors by using his mother's surname, or telling the story of the converted devil who was reluctant to be circumcised. At times he seems to belong to a later generation than his own. When I first read the French version I suspected that it must have been adapted to commend it to the taste of the Parisian public of the age of Louis XV. P. da Costa's discovery has proved that, whatever liberties Le Grand may have taken with the text before him, he had no need to do this. Indeed, in his robust contempt for superstition, in his curiosity about fauna, flora and natural phenomena, and in the personal character which his narrative sometimes assumes, Lobo recalls not so much Páez, Almeida, Mendes and Barradas, as his own calumniator James Bruce of Kinnaird.

CHRONOLOGY OF LOBO'S LIFE

1636, April	Sails from Luanda for Cartagena
1636, August	Leaves Cartagena for Havana
1636, September	Leaves Havana for Europe
1636, November	Arrives in Cádiz
1636, December	Arrives in Lisbon
1637, January	Leaves for Madrid Returns to Lisbon
1637, October	Leaves for Rome
1638, May	Arrives in Rome
1639	Returns to Portugal
1640, March	Sails for India
1640, September	Arrives in Goa
1648, May	Confined by order of the Viceroy
1651	Released. Returns to the Casa Professa
1655	Relegated to 'the South'
1657	Returns to Portugal
1658	Visits Rome
1660–1662	Vice-Prefect of São Roque
1678, 29 January	Dies at S. Roque

Plate I. The first page of the MS. of the *Itinerário*

Account from the time I left Portugal and the voyages and travels I made, experiences I had, lands I saw and the remarkable things I noticed in them.

CHAPTER I

[How I set out for the first time for India and was forced to return to Lisbon]

I was informed in Coimbra of my assignment to the India mission on the Friday before Low Sunday, April 16, 1621. The order had made its way from Lisbon to Coimbra at the rate of 20 leagues per day, the mail arriving at the College at eight o'clock in the morning; and I was called to the College from a farm where I was staying. I was notified at a quarter to ten, and at three in the afternoon of the same day I left the College and began my journey. On the following Monday at midnight I arrived at the main door of S. Antão.[1] On Tuesday morning I was ordained a subdeacon by the Inquisitor-General, Dom Fernão Martinz Mascarenhas.[2] On Wednesday and Thursday, Dom Jeronimo de Gouvea[3] ordained me a deacon and priest. On the following Sunday I said my first Mass; and, although on the following Wednesday the weather was foul and it was raining heavily at nightfall and it had already been decided in the Council that the fleet could not leave that year since it was already the end of April, from midnight onwards the weather improved so much that at dawn the flagship[4] began to fire the signal-guns for the fleet's departure. It was a beautiful day: clear skies, a north-east wind – an opportunity not to be missed. What with the great agitation of the people and the still greater desire for the voyage felt by the prospective voyagers and by the authorities on land as well, it was felt that a day so long awaited should not be lost. Between eight and nine o'clock in the morning, the flagship cut cable and set sail followed by the rest of the fleet, which had been waiting more than a month to cross the bar; it was indeed a great moment, but our sanguine desires and hopes were, unfortunately, not to be answered by the event.

[1] The Jesuit college in Lisbon, on the site of the present Hospital of S. José.

[2] 1548–1628, Bishop of the Algarve, 1594, Grand Inquisitor, 1616.

[3] Bishop of Ceuta and Tangier, 1600–2, and subsequently confessor to the Empress Maria, widow of Maximilian II. After her death in 1603 he became Chaplain-General to the convents of the Orphans and Catechumens.

[4] *Capitania*, the ship in which the Captain-Major, the commander-in-chief of the fleet, sailed.

I

On that day, the 29th of April, all the carracks departed with the same tide. The fleet consisted of five sails: four carracks and one galleon, in addition to the caravel carrying the watersupply and many other vessels which were sailing, as is the custom on such occasions, for various ports of the Portuguese conquests. The five ships were as follows: that of Viceroy Dom Afonso de Noronha[1] called the *Conceição*; the *Pataqueira*,[2] or the *São Carlos*, with Dom Rodrigo Lobo as captain; the *S. Thomé* with Nuno Pereira Freire as captain; the *S. Joseph*, with Dom Francisco Enriques as Admiral,[3] to return as Captain-Major; and accompanying the fleet, a galleon,[4] with Gonçalo Rodriguez da Cunha as captain. The Viceroy's flagship was captained by Dom Francisco Lobo, who had returned to Portugal the previous year in the same carrack.[5]

The sailing was smooth and the weather was all that could be desired. From such auspicious beginnings one would surely have predicted for the whole fleet a much better fate than it afterward experienced. With a fresh, favourable breeze we were soon well out to sea so that we lost sight of land, the sea playing its usual tricks on those new to it and even on many who had sailed many times before. In the fleet were travelling many people, fidalgos accompanying the Viceroy and other captains as well as soldiers and nobility. In a few days we saw the island of Tanarifa, one of the Canaries, as well known for being a sure land-mark as it is for its famous high peak which forms the greater part of the island and is a beautiful sight to behold. We sailed to the leeward of it and closer to the coast of Africa than was reasonably required for an evening passage, according to what those experienced in these matters said and what actually resulted; for, as we went between the island and the mainland, the currents so forced us toward the coast of Africa that they carried us to the shoals of Santa Anna, where we were brought to ruin, as I shall presently relate; and this was the whole cause for our return to Lisbon.[6]

The time we were at sea was notable for a variety of reasons. First, we saw land in each of the five months and eight days we sailed, going and returning: in April we saw Lisbon, our place of departure; in May,

[1] Governor of the Algarve. He had been to India as Captain-Major of the fleet in 1597.
[2] A game of chance so-called, or perhaps 'The trollop'; ships were sometimes given such nicknames.
[3] I.e. deputy commander under the Captain-Major.   [4] The *São Simão*.
[5] Le Grand adds: 'It was a long time since so many nobles had embarked for the Indies'.
[6] Ships were recommended to sail eight or ten leagues to the west of Palma, or at most between Grand Canary and Tenerife, keeping seventy or eighty leagues from the coast of Africa, because of the winds and currents forcing them towards the land.

Tanarifa; in June, the shoals of Santa Anna, the land of that coast; in July, Cape Verde; in August, another land; in September, the Berlengas; in October the bar of Lisbon, when we entered. We had varied weather, but more bad than good. And as we were sailing so close to the coast of Africa, toward which we were being driven by the sea because it was the monsoon and the waves were moving in the direction of the semicircular bay or inlet of São Thomé and the coast of Malagueta,[1] it was incredible how rapidly they carried us and pushed us in that direction. On several occasions we verified the extraordinary speed with which the water carried whatever was upon it, by throwing a board on the sea, which would immediately dart away from us with remarkable speed, with the carrack following it, although more slowly because of its greater weight.

The closeness of the coast of Guinea caused us to experience more of its excessive heat and disagreeable rainstorms. Our discomfort was also greatly increased by the fact that we were already sailing very close to the Equator. The rainstorms are frequent and particularly heavy because they are accompanied by the trade winds. Although at times we experienced them at night as well as in the daytime, they never caught our sails, as the saying goes. It was thus the usual experience of mariners not to be visited by the particular trade wind they so much desired. Only once did it turn its face to us, to our great joy, for a period of up to two hours. It soon departed, however, leaving us, on its departure, with a sadness even more intense than the joy we had felt when it arrived. The rains, normal for these latitudes, were hot, heavy, and noisome; for, as they fell on one's skin, they made sores, and in woollen clothing they bred noxious white worms. We could penetrate no further south than to a point five degrees north of the Equator; and when we had the opportunity to take the altitude of the sun, after a few days of not being able to do so, we found ourselves nine degrees north of the Equator, to which point we had been pushed back by the current. The reason for this was that the great hulk of the carrack, receiving no driving force from the wind, was thoroughly becalmed and was carried willy-nilly by the sea-currents.

We travelled for two and a half months in these equatorial latitudes, and as we were very close to the coast of Guinea, we were the more

[1] The Malagueta coast was properly the coast of West Africa from Sierra Leone to Cape Palmas, but the term was sometimes used to refer to the coast as far as Elmina. The name was derived from Malagueta pepper, also known as Guinea grains, or grains of Paradise, extracted from the shrub *Aframomum malagueta*; J. W. Blake, *Europeans in West Africa, 1450–1560* (London, 1942), p. 40.

affected by its climate and by the burning of the sun which scorches it so and which afflicted us sorely, especially because this trouble was of such long duration; so that the people began to fall sick, as was to be expected under such conditions, and, of the nearly nine hundred persons who had embarked on the carrack, few remained who did not experience the force of the disease. The malignant fevers were of such a nature that in four or five days, the list of dead had become substantial. There were several reasons for the rapid spreading of this disease. The first and principal reason was our long detention in these latitudes and their unhealthy climate. The second was the fact that the very large number of people who had embarked were packed into a carrack already infected with disease from the preceding year when, because of inexperience, nearly all aboard had fallen sick and more than three hundred persons had died, apparently leaving the air inside the carrack extremely foul, and the foulness was now intensified by the nature of the climate. The third and most urgent reason was the spoiled, rotten food. The pork meat was such that whole pipes of it were thrown overboard as soon as they were opened because it was rotten and mouldy; and the people claimed this was caused by its being salted when not dry, so that the pork would weigh more, by which it was all lost. In the same way, the wine was spoiled so that the taps were opened and whole pipes-full were poured through the scupper holes into the sea. I saw rice thrown on the deck so rotten and altered that I thought it was lime, and I should have certainly believed so if I had not been assured it was rice. Because most of the people lived on this king's ration, not taking any other, this was a further cause of hardship, since the sickness, running rampant among the poorest, passed also to the others because it was so contagious, and I was no exception; for, going to hear confession in the gunroom where there were many sick, and because we were very close together, I had to hear the penitent at very close range, and confessions always occurred in the morning before the place was cleaned up. I later felt shaky, and the day after I fell ill and the disease very tenaciously stayed with me for more than a month. But God was served in that my illness responded to the remedies, especially to the very effective and universal remedy of scarification and application of cupping-glasses for the purpose of relieving the head of the blood which rises to it with the intensity of the fever. After several blood-lettings, as the disease soon gains great force, on the fourth or fifth day, relief is brought to it by the cupping-glasses, then by the bezoar-stone, the effect of which is to cause sweating.[1] But if the disease is not alleviated by this, it is expedient to supply the remedy of a blood-letting from the head in order to avoid the brain-fever caused by the blood going to the head. When, unfortunately, even this is not enough, in a few hours the patient dies.

The fire that burns inside one's body with these fevers is excessive and is fed by many causes: the food, due to both the curing and quantity, there being none to refresh and whet the appetite; the living conditions, lying on a cot suspended in the air or on four foul-smelling tarred pine boards in a very cramped space; the confusion and early rising of crowds of people; and not a cup of cool water to encourage you, all of it being warm; few medicines, such as they are, when there are any – everything, in short, favours the progress of the disease, few or no comforts contributing to health. Being on the water, in this condition, has many advantages over being on land, where the rigours of the disease are much greater. I had occasion to learn this later through personal experience.

As long as the height of the disease lasted a priest was at the foot of my bed day and night giving me water in as great quantity and as often as I asked, which was very often indeed. Experience demonstrated that this was not a bad antidote to the force of the unaccustomed and harmful heat. The doctors on the carrack, two in number, consented to this although so little used in our homeland where they so strictly and methodically prohibit giving water to those who are at the height of the fever or when their fever is rising. Those who reasoned best argued in favour of taking water, and their arguments were as follows:—
Since the heat of the fever and the extreme heat of the climate both served to drain essential moisture from the body, it was necessary to give those two enemies a substance to feed upon, something which would also aid and support the essential moisture. That substance, they argued, would be a great quantity of water, which could cause only one difficulty, namely that the patient at the end of the illness might be more or less constipated, a condition certainly preferable to death, which was the result of consumption of the body's essential moisture by fever. This is how the illnesses and remedies for them were handled, the sick taking all the water they could obtain. One of them, whom I frequented most because I had already known him as a soldier, about twenty-four years of age, was so gripped by the illness and fever that

[1] Le Grand adds 'Our physicians and surgeons, though they were clever, took a long time to recognize the disease; their first remedies made it worse and killed the patients instead of curing them, until they decided to bleed their heads and cup them. This is what saved me and many others.'

his whole battle being by means of water and more water, he not only drank his own ration, the water we gave him, the water others brought him, and the water he could take from his companions, but also all he could buy with all of his clothing; and even so he died of the heat and fever. The heat of his body was so intense that after he was dead some vital spirits could be felt in his pulse and in the area of his heart and an extreme heat in the chest which sustained them; and it continued this way from nightfall, when he died, through most of the night. This illness caused and causes many to lose their minds, giving way to wild delirium and, even when cured, remaining crack-brained for a long time. I met one such person on the deck coming out of the hatch-way of the gun-room, the infirmary for the whole carrack. The poor fellow, burning with heat, was so far out of his mind that, when I asked him where he was coming from, he answered, nonsensically, that he was coming from that limekiln. When I asked him further where he was going, he answered that he was bound for Alcántara, which must have been where he was from or a place with which he had some connection. But as this was on the coast of Guinea, when I asked him what way he planned to go, he replied, looking at the sea through the gangway which was open, that he was going through that field. And he doubtless would have thrown himself into the water, so feverish was he as he came out of that place, if he had not been held back and confined. I heard of many such cases; some extremely pitiful, mention of which I omit in the interest of brevity and in order not to frighten further the reader of this narrative, in case, perhaps, he plans to see and experience for himself these happenings so typical of the India voyage. The number of deaths was remarkably low considering the great number of sick. Our Lord certainly favoured the extensive care afforded the sick, both from the King's medical stores, through two doctors, a surgeon, and barbers who were on the carrack, and through the generosity with which the Viceroy ordered that everything necessary be given at his own expense to all who asked, so that the dead were fewer than twenty in number.

At this time and place, I saw one day a phenomenon we have heard about so often and almost disbelieve so long as we have not witnessed it, namely, the cloud that gathers in or sucks up water from the sea. It was on a cloudy Sunday afternoon and it was raining lightly. A small cloud lowered a sort of column, called a water-spout, and as the foot of it reached the water, we saw that the whole cloud kept increasing uniformly in size and, after it was well filled and fat, it raised the foot it had in the sea and, spreading out in the air, it emptied itself and poured down on us the water it had gathered up, which was as sweet and pleasant as it had been salty when taken from the sea.[1]

Other novelties we saw in the remaining months of voyaging were few, beyond the usual ones such as a variety of large and small birds of many colours and shapes. The reason for our seeing so many birds was that, usually to our detriment, we were not far from the shore. The fish called flying fish were at times countless, filling the air as far as one could see. They were pursued by other fish underwater which fed on them, the pursuers being bonitos, *cachorras*, albacores and others.[2] The tunnyfish forced them to behave unnaturally and seek safety outside of their element but, even so, they could not escape because their pursuers swam after them; and when they either touched the water to wet their wings (as they commonly do in order to fly better) or, thinking themselves in safety, took refuge in their natural element, they were again attacked by the enemies following them or by others equally bent on catching them, the quantity of these fish being very great. Attacking them furiously with great leaps from the water, the tunny fish snatch them, and the sight of this chase affords some amusement. And we happened to find in the bellies of some of the tunnyfish we caught a number of flying fish, some intact and others half-digested according to the time elapsed since they had been eaten. One afternoon, there were so many of these flying fish filling the air in greater quantity than ever, and as the pilot brought two tame pigeons on the stern, they flew from the carrack and flew among the flying fish as if they were of the same species, but making several flights among them and not recognizing them, came back again to the carrack. These fish have the shape of a horse mackerel[3] or a river barbel and are approximately one palm in length.[4] They have four wings shaped like those of a grasshopper. They fly over a large area as long as their wings are wet, and they would have flown much further if the wetness had lasted; and in order to replenish the moisture on their wings, they touch the water from time to time, rising immediately to continue their flight,

[1] Le Grand adds: 'It surprised us all the more as it is difficult to understand how it could lose the salt in such a short time'.

[2] *bonites, cachorras, albicoras.* The Ocean bonito, *Sarda sarda* (Bloch), *Euthynnus thunnina* (Cuv. and Valenc.), *Euthynnus quadripunctatus* (E. Geoffroy Saint-Hilaire). The names *bonito* and *albacora* are sometimes applied to other fishes of the families Thunnidae (tunas) and Scombridae (mackerels). On the distribution of these fish in the Atlantic and the Mediterranean, and on their nomenclature, see D. Carlos de Bragança (King Carlos I of Portugal), *A Pesca do Atum no Algarve em 1898* (Lisboa, 1899).

[3] *carapao*, the horse mackerel or scad, *Trachurus trachurus* (L.).

[4] They differ in shape.

7

unless, as is often the case, they are snatched by the enemies pursuing them; for, as soon as the tunnyfish see them touch the water, they seize them with remarkable agility.

In these latitudes and on these occasions of our being becalmed as well as all other such occasions during our whole voyage, the fish that accompanied us most and bothered us at the time were large and small sharks as well as other larger, fiercer fish called tiger sharks. Since these creatures appear only when the sea is calm, which unfortunately for our voyage was most of the time, we had occasion to see many of them, which served as a diversion relieving the many hardships and misfortunes which the latitude, location, and hot sun caused the poor sailors. They passed the time catching sharks, which they threw on the deck; and, putting out their eyes, they used them as substitutes for bulls in mock bullfights.[1] No one got close to them for fear of their teeth, which were as sharp as razors. They tied several well-stoppered jugs to the tail-fins of some of them, and, throwing them back into the sea, enjoyed watching them struggle to swim without being able to sink. These creatures are very carnivorous. Anything they find outside the ship cannot escape them, and they dismember even dead bodies floating on the water and with one snap cut in two the arm or leg which they seize. One poor soldier had let his meat ration ride in the water at the end of a rope so as to unsalt it. It was all taken in one bite by the shark, which subsequently paid for it, however, since someone volunteered another piece of meat for the soldier to use as bait so that he could avenge himself for not having been able to recover what he had just lost; and, throwing it to the shark on a rig consisting of a very heavy, sharp hook attached to a *covado* length of heavy chain,[2] so that the shark could not cut it with its teeth, and with all this tied to a line of thin cordage, he threw it to the shark, as I have said, so successfully that he caught it, brought it on board ship, and opening it up, recovered his ration, which he found still intact; and the shark thus paid for the snack with his life. Some fish called pilot-fish,[3] as small as sardines and very much striped on their back always swim close to the shark's mouth, so much so that it is a wonder they are not caught, though from time to time some are. But as they are small and quicker, they swiftly flee whenever the shark turns or attacks. Their desire for the food they get from what the shark does not eat makes them run such a risk. Another

---

[1] P. da Costa cites an earlier instance of this practice from the voyage of the *São Francisco* in 1596.

[2] 1 *covado* = 66 cm.

[3] *romeiros, Naucrates ductor* (L.).

advantage for the pilot-fish is that they are protected, in the shadow of this lion of the sea, from the other fish who are afraid of the shark and stay away from it. The pilot-fish would doubtless be a staple of the diet of these other fish if they did not have recourse to this natural way of keeping separated from them.

We had only two perilous experiences. One was of no great consequence since it was only that our main top-yard broke as we were sailing with a brisk wind. No one was hurt. The other was extremely perilous and could have meant total destruction for us all if God's mercy had not intervened in our great heedlessness and ignorance of the danger we were in; for, not knowing for certain how close to land we were sailing and unaware of the force with which the sea was carrying us toward land, in the dead of night, after the second watch had been relieved, as we were sailing with a very useful brisk wind, our main-topsail sheet broke. The sailors soon afterward had it repaired; but the wind, still blowing while the sailors were working, died down completely as soon as the work was finished and the sail hoisted. We were, of course, much distressed by this, for we had such a good wind at our disposal on so few occasions, and this one turned out so badly and left us very sorrowful both because of what had happened to the sheet and because of the total disappearance of the wind which we thought was the trade-wind we wanted so much. It had seemed that we had only to unfurl the sail in order to place ourselves in a better latitude and to make the safety of the voyage more assured than it was at that time. We remained becalmed for the rest of the night, the carrack moving only with the sea-current. At dawn, however, we realized how Our Lord had favoured us by taking the wind away from us; for by the light of day the topman made out some things that looked like sails and, he informed us that he saw one, then two, three, and four. The curiosity that made us investigate the number and nature of the supposed sails led us to the conclusion that they were rocks in the shoals of Santa Anna,[1] so perilous and so greatly feared, where before dawn, if the wind had lasted, we could not have avoided running aground and, quite obviously, the destruction of all on board, the nature of these shoals being such that no one could escape alive; and even if someone by a miracle were to reach land, the barbarous people who populate it would not spare those spared by the sea. The previous year, this same carrack, with Dom Francisco Lobo as captain, who was on the present occasion captain of the same ship, now carrying the Viceroy,

[1] In the Bay of Sta Ana de Chaves on the N.E. side of the island of São Tomé.

9

found itself in similar peril in this same place where the rapid sea-currents brought it to a stop, and it reached a point so close to danger that they could see the people on land. And as that bay cuts in very deeply and the pull of the currents that go into it is strong, it was correspondingly more difficult for the carrack to get out of danger than it had been effortless for it to fall into it. But God willed that we should not experience the miserable shipwreck with which we were obviously threatened. The wretched people, especially those who had been informed of the dire circumstances we were in, were showing their affliction in their anxious faces and changed colour caused by the shock of the news when, in the greatest danger and when hope had been all but given up, a land-breeze sprang up, a gentle breeze but enough to counteract the force of the currents, by which little by little we emerged from the danger and continued our voyage, thanking Our Lord for sparing us; for the danger to our lives, according to those best versed in the sea, had been extreme.

[How it was decided that we would return to Lisbon]

By this time we had already used up much of the sailing time [available for the India voyage] since leaving Lisbon, and as people had been talking for days about returning to Lisbon in view of the fact that the monsoon season was over and we were so far from the Cape and in an area from which only the best of circumstances would permit us to extricate ourselves, it was again and more earnestly a question of returning to Lisbon, although the Viceroy, to his credit, and especially Dom Francisco Lobo, the Captain, raised many objections to the return. Yet, considering it necessary, the Viceroy ordered the captains and officers to come from the other ships. After discussing the matter at great length in a council meeting, which took place on the Viceroy's balcony, they all agreed that we should return, a memorandum of the decision was drawn up and signed by all, and we immediately changed course for Lisbon. As soon as the return was announced, and the troubled sailors learned that we were actually putting it into effect, the joy was so great with which those most sick and tired of the sea, who were the majority, celebrated it that the joy they would show if they were arriving in the port of destination where they wished to anchor could be no greater. I do not cast blame on such inclinations and demonstrations because as the sea prepares so many hardships and we had certainly experienced them in so long a time of sailing, and being becalmed, everyone was so annoyed and disgusted with the sea that it was quite natural they they should want so desperately to reach land as soon as possible, except for those interested in the trip either because of the cargo they were carrying or because of profitable business ventures. Having made our decision, we continued our homeward course, and in the rest of our voyage we had only one furious storm, which assailed us off the Treseiras Islands.[1] The storm was all the more fearful because it came in the middle of the night. The wind was strong,

---

[1] The central group of the Azores, comprising Terceira, Graciosa, São Jorge, Pico and Faial.

the rain heavy, and the disorder equal to the confusion and darkness
in which we were all moving, and our anxiety was increased by the
fierceness of the wind roaring in the upper rigging of the ship. The
sea was stirred up and tumultuous, so that the sailors were busy attend-
ing to necessary tasks while the rest remained in their cabins and berths,
fearful of what they were experiencing, especially those for whom this
was a new experience. Suddenly, the boatswain, a respected old man
who from his place on the poop deck was issuing orders appropriate
to the emergency, blew his whistle and shouted with great emotion,
as sailors do when they see this, for them to see and pay reverence to
the corposant, which had appeared at the top of the flag. And as all
present affirmed that they saw it, and falling on their knees at the second
urging of the boatswain who first set the example for great devoutness,
they gave it a salvo of shouts, saying, 'Hail corposant of the sea of the
islands', for that was our location at that time. With this the religious
fervour, confidence, and curiosity of the seamen increased, each one
observing things seen or imagined, and there were those who claimed
they saw what they call Our Lady's crown, which turns out to be many
such lights together, which they say are stars. And, as for the appearance
of one of these, although on this occasion I did not see it, on another
occasion — one of many such occasions in which I found myself — I saw
it very clearly and distinctly when I was with the fleet coming [to Spain]
from the Indies in 1636 during one raging storm, among others, which
persecuted us for many days on that voyage; for, as they lasted or kept
coming one after the other, in the one that gave us most trouble because
of its raging unabated for an excessively long time, a similar apparition
occurred, which the Spaniards call St Elmo and we call corposant. This
is nothing other than a light like that of a candle whose flame is not
very clear, possibly because it is so high and because of heavy wind
and rain ordinarily present when it appears. It can be seen, however,
very distinctly. The corposant which appeared on the ship, from whose
story I have digressed momentarily, soon descended to the top of the
yard-arm of the main-yard on the starboard side and from there was
soon seen on the top of the mizzen-sail, whence, whether the same one
or another, descending on the Captain's cabin (located at the bottom
of the poop-deck on the port side), it disappeared there; and with its
disappearance the storm soon ended, leaving the seamen confirmed and
obstinate in their superstitious piety and the others amazed and with
something to talk about and to lighten their work for the remainder
of the night. They were disabused of their erroneous belief that it is

an infallible sign of total destruction or of a worsening of the storm, with obvious peril to lives, when the exhalation, for that is all that people see, descends to the low places, as it did here, and the storm ended, the sea becoming calm immediately. And daylight came and delighted the souls and bodies tired and disturbed from the work and danger they had undergone all through the night. Some who prided themselves on their philosophy, concerning what had happened in the night, tried to discourse on the matter and show, by philosophical reasonings, the reality of what was seen. Their efforts were in vain, however, and they had to break off and stop their discourse, being unable to counteract the stubbornness with which the seafaring people and maritime authors defended their opinions, fervour, and imagination.[1]

From our position off the Islands we made our course for the bar of Lisbon. However, since we had reached a very high latitude and we had gone too far from land into the neighbourhood of the Sargasso Sea we spent more days than we wished, much to the exasperation of all those aboard who were so anxious to reach land. The Sargasso I mentioned is a seaweed that grows at the bottom of the sea, and, uprooted by the motion of the water, rises and floats on the water; and one sees so much of this seaweed on the water that the ship goes cutting through it. They say that a distillation of this seaweed is an excellent remedy for gallstones. And since by now we were sick and tired of so long and difficult a time at sea and the return to port, the delay in reaching land became all the more painful for us. We were comforted in these troubles by the first signs of land, a seaweed called *curriolas*,[2] two or three *varas*[3] long and less than an inch thick with only stalks for leaves, because of the assurance they gave of the nearness of land.

However on the day before we caught sight of land, a remarkable thing happened to us, remarkable because of its circumstances, unfortunate for the one who experienced it and pitiful for those of us who saw it, which I relate because it was the last that happened to us in this ill-fated voyage and so that it may serve as a good warning for anyone who might wish to profit from it. We had aboard as an artillery soldier, a man newly married who, they say, had with him a goodly

[1] Le Grand adds: 'The danger was not big enough to stop me from laughing at the grimaces and attitudes of most of the officers and sailors, and the way that others were talking who thought themselves to be cleverer.'

[2] *Convolvulus arvensis* (L.). Le Grand has *Verriola*.

[3] 1 *vara* = 1.096 m.

capital for India both in borrowed money and in his wife's dowry, all of which he had converted into *patacas*[1] for the voyage because this was good for trading in India but risky in the possession of gamblers such as he. After a few days' voyage he began to put some money from his supply on the gaming table, at first in moderation, winning and losing according to the fortunes of the game. As he was getting more angry since he was now losing, he would come out onto the deck with his cap full of *patacas* which he would bet by the handful at each cast of the dice, usually with bad luck and with less patience than was reasonable, for it was another loss to break out in swearing and blasphemies unworthy of a Christian. It happened that a Father was passing near that place when the poor man was losing not only his money but, much more importantly, his soul, with swearing and execrations. Moved by this, the Father approached him discreetly saying to him, 'Brother, you are losing your fortune but don't lose your soul also with such blasphemy and swearing, and remember that you are a Christian and that God is not to blame for your losses for you to offend him with such blasphemous talk.'

At sunrise on a Monday, the fourth of October, we sighted land which we could later identify as the Rock of Sintra. The excitement with which everyone received the news was greater than can be imagined. Since the wind abated for us we would have had time to enter the harbour that very day, and a fishing boat did come to reconnoitre us. We did not, however, go very close to shore. Our rowboat went out to it to obtain news from the fishing boat and to give news of who we were so that pilots would come from land to bring us inside the bar. The only refreshment found there was a single apple that a sailor brought to the ship. No one dared to eat it but everyone breathed in its aroma with great longing and devotion. On the following day we also had little wind, and we still could not sail into the harbour. At sunset on that day we saw coming in our wake the carrack *São Thomé* which had separated from us in June in the latitude of Cape Verde and which, trying to continue its voyage and being unable to make further headway, decided to turn back just as we had done and found us at this place. On the same day a carrack sailing from India came to wait with us, captained by Gaspar de Mello

---

[1] An old Castilian silver coin. According to Manoel de Almeida (d. 1646) it was worth a gold *dirham*; the weight and value of a *dirham* varied greatly but was usually less than three grams. See C. F. Beckingham and G. W. B. Huntingford, *Some Records of Ethiopia, 1593–1646* (London, 1954), p. 44.

and the companion vessel of the ship which on the following Monday was burned by the Moors or was burned while fighting with them.[1] That night between Tuesday and Wednesday we were still outside, entering on Wednesday and anchoring between Casquais and the tower of São Joam.[2]

In this place we were in great danger, because suddenly as we were sailing in with our sails full, the strong wind to which we had set our sails and by which we were entering the harbour suddenly changed and drove the sails against the masts so that it was impossible to strike them as quickly as necessary and we came to within a stone's throw of Cabeça Seca;[3] and as the space was so narrow between the reefs and Cabeça Seca the anxiety and murmuring of those aboard were commensurate with the danger. But with the sails thrown down and an anchor cast to the bottom, the ship was for the moment safe from danger but not from the dread that we could have at night when, if the wind became stronger, because Cabesa Seca was so close and the passage at Alcaseva[4] had narrowed by fifty fathoms because of the sand which had been washed down from the mountain by the heavy rains which had begun immediately following our departure from Portugal and had continued for a long time, our ship was obviously in danger of drifting toward the shoals if a brisk wind were to come up again at night. As a precaution against this possibility, the sailors put down two anchors apeak in anticipation of any misfortune which might befall the ship during the night; but it pleased God our Lord that we passed the night without any sudden change in weather.

On this occasion there were ten French galleys at Passo d'Arcos.[5] They were on their way to bring aid to their King who was laying

---

[1] The carrack *Conceiçao* attacked and burnt by Moors near Berlengas.

[2] I.e. between Cascais and the tower of S. Julião da Barra. Cascais is a well-known place on the north shore of the estuary of the Tagus. S. Joam is a mistake for S. Julião. Probably Lobo abbreviated this to S. Gião, as he did on p. 396 below, and it was misread by the copyist. The tower was a fortification between Cascais and Oeiras, commanding the entrance to the inner part of the estuary.

[3] There are two shoals at the bar of the Tagus, known as the Cachopo Norte and the Cachopo Sul. The head of the second is sometimes above the water and this is presumably what is meant by the Cabeça Seca or 'Dry Head'.

[4] Because of the shoals mentioned in the preceding note there are two channels. They were known as the Carreira de S. Julião and the Carreira de Alcácer or Alcáçova. The latter is the name used by D. João de Castro in his 'Roteiro de Lisboa a Goa', *Obras Completas de D. João de Castro*, ed. A. Cortesão and L. de Albuquerque (Coimbra, 1968, 71), I, 125. Manuel Pimentel, Cosmographer Major, ?1679–1719, writes 'Barra de Alcaceva de Lisboa', *Arte de Navegar*, ed. Cortesão, Aleixo and Albuquerque (Lisboa, 1969), p. 300.

[5] They had been sent from Marseille to help with the siege of La Rochelle and had reached Lisbon on 29 September 1621. Paço d' Arcos is on the northern shore about two miles NE of S. Julião.

siege to Rochela. Because of the lateness of the season they could not continue the voyage and were taking shelter for the winter in this friendly port. The captains of these galleys in their skiffs came to see the ship from the outside, and since two of them towing us for the distance of a stone's throw would have been enough to remove us from danger, Dom Afonso de Noronha, seeing the captains next to the ship, went to the side of the ship and asked them to order the towing so that the ship would not be lost because of the risk it was undergoing. They, however, did not behave as they should, saying that they did not have an order from their king for such towing, whereupon they rowed away, leaving us as worried as before. Our worry was somewhat alleviated by the people who came presently from shore. One of the first of these was the Padre Procurador of India, who begged us to let him take us ashore with him.[1] However, since the Viceroy was remaining on the ship we did not want to seek safety so hastily. Although this was a very appropriate courtesy, it was possible that it might be very costly for us, and if we were later to repent of it our repentance would be late and of no avail.

Although the night was spent in watchfulness and anxiety there was no danger. The rising sun cheered us with a beautiful day, and presently fresh provisions began to arrive from shore – fruit, fresh water and fresh bread, which was what we needed most. The first to receive their provisions shared them with the rest, and as ours were among the first and best, including much late fruit, dark pears, very poor melons, some of the worst grapes in existence, and good bread, we shared them with the Viceroy and the other fidalgos. All of these refreshments seemed to us and were as pleasing to us as if they were the best fruit from the Lisbon orchards in their most abundant season, when in reality they were scarcely fit for horses. But to us they were the equal of the best fruit grown in Chamusca.[2] Although the grapes were of the variety called 'chokes'[3] they seemed to us the sweetest, ripest muscatel or black grape. Only the sweet apples and bread were excellent since everything else was out of season. Nevertheless we ate it all.

Something happened to us which, although rather funny, shows how miserable the occasion of returning from an abortive voyage can be. It was about ten o'clock in the morning. All the ships were anchored close together, one of them being the one that had come from India.

[1] P. António Colaça.

[2] A small town on the Tagus about 14 miles NE of Santarem; the neighbourhood is very fertile and is famous for fruit-growing.

[3] *esgana*, a variety of small, white grape.

A boat came out from land with four rowers and a woman who was steering at the stern. The boat was laden with every refreshment covered with crinkled cloths. Since our ship, being the Viceroy's, was the largest, the huckstress thought it was the one coming from India and she brought the refreshment to it in order to make a good profit. Arriving on board she ordered the cloths to be removed and as the boat was seen to be loaded with beautiful grapes apparently saved for that occasion and because they were such and the ones which drew our attention the most, the sight of all that fresh fruit invited everyone on board to buy some refreshment, each one thinking that he would have a feast then and there and get rid of the seasickness, disgust, and revulsion with which he had been consumed for so many months on the sea. But when she inquired where the ship was coming from and learned that it was returning from an abortive voyage and seeing that it was not bringing back a cargo and that she could not expect so much profit from it as she was seeking, she ordered her men to cover the grapes again and to row to the ship from India. Paying no attention to the many pleas of those aboard our ship, she passed before our eyes and sold to the other ship leaving us with our mouths watering and so rueful that they wanted to throw stones at her, and they would have done all they could, such was the feeling that remained with them. They became reconciled to it, however, because of their unfortunate lot as people who had turned back, and also because they were so close to going ashore where they could make up for the loss and relieve the pain, need and appetite caused by the sight of that feast.

At two o'clock in the afternoon as the tide began to rise, we weighed anchor to enter the harbour, but with so little success that we put to sea again three times because the fury of the waves and our misfortune carried us with such force against the shoals of the bar just as if our course were in that direction. However, even with our turning back, we made a little more headway into the harbour with each attempt; and little by little we were out of danger and were escaping the shoals until finally they were completely behind. us. We continued on our way, with the rest of the ships following in our wake until we anchored opposite São Paulo[1] on a Thursday, the seventh of October, five months and eight days after passing the bar on another similar Thursday, the twenty-ninth of April of the same year.

[1] 'The recently organized parish of St Paul, just outside the medieval walls, was a district largely populated by sailors, shipwrights, and other maritime personnel at this period', C. R. Boxer, *Further Selections from the Tragic History of the Sea 1559–1565* (Cambridge, 1968), p. 153, n. 4.

If the fleet had not gone out on that day, we would not have been attempting to reenter the harbour on this day in the same year with such poor results from our voyage; for the day on which we departed was the only one with a favourable wind and was followed by a resumption of stormy weather at sea, which immediately closed in and proved to be continuous; the Council, furthermore, had already concluded that it was so late in the season that the ships should not leave. Would to God that the Council had acted upon its decision; but the fleet was unfortunately unable to leave during the period of almost two months during which it lay at anchor waiting for a good day, which misfortune was the cause of many others to follow. The worst trouble was that at many times there is not even a single galley available to tow any ship to mid-channel whence it could leave the harbour in safety. That entire fleet suffered for lack of a galley. One day at ten o'clock, when all ships of the fleet had been ready to leave for a long time, a violent storm struck the fleet so hard that the ships were about to be wrecked over the cables which held them in position against the storm. They were forced to seek shelter so close to land that when a favourable wind finally came and they wanted to depart they were unable to do so because of their proximity to the shore. They therefore not only lost the voyage but also ensured their later necessity of returning to port after an abortive voyage, with all its attendant loss of life and property. All of these troubles could have been avoided if there had been a galley on that occasion to tow the ships further away from shore, where they could have availed themselves of the wind and could have had a successful voyage. The most serious loss that ensued, however, is the one which has been the subject of much consideration and analysis in intelligent discourse: if the Viceroy had been able to leave port at the time when he was ready to do so if the galley had helped him avail himself of the favourable winds – which he could not do because there was no galley – he would have arrived in India in October at the latest, whence he could have come to the aid of Ormuz, which had been under siege for some time and would not have been lost the following May as it was,[1] God permitting our reversal to occur, using this means to punish us for our sins in the loss of Ormuz, when that fortress should have been helped and relieved of the siege it was enduring with the arrival of the fleet and of such a Viceroy.

[1] Le Grand: 'The Persians, helped by the English, besieged that stronghold from the month of October in this year 1621 and took it in May of the following year'. In fact Ormuz (Hurmuz) surrendered to the English on 23 April/3 May 1622.

Although I emerged from the voyage in reasonably good health, I still had some symptoms of the illness I had, there coming out all over my body painful large boils, which, although they caused me uneasiness, were actually good for my health and may even have saved my life, nature alleviating in this way the bad humours caused by the sea and some intermittent fevers, not many but very high, so that the illness was finally purged. I had them almost until Christmas which I went to observe in Coimbra where I stayed semi-convalescent until the middle of February, at which time I again went to Lisbon to embark with the fleet of the Conde da Vidigueira,[1] which departed in the month of March following, as I shall presently relate.

[1] Fourth Conde da Vidigueira and great-grandson of Vasco da Gama. He had already served as Viceroy from 1597 to 1600. In the Portuguese edition, p. 170 n. 1, the date of his death is misprinted 1623, for 1632.

CHAPTER 3

[How I departed a second time for India with the Conde da Vidigueira, Viceroy of India]

In dispatching this second fleet, the members of the Council tried to avoid the earlier mistakes. Since the new Viceroy, the Conde da Vedigeira, replacing Dom Afonso, who did not wish to return to India,[1] had so much experience in this voyage because of having already been Viceroy of India, and also because of the many years he was a member of the Council of India and the Council of State, the ships were prepared more energetically, so that on the eighteenth of March four carracks and a galleon were ready to make the voyage.[2] The following were the captains of the carracks: Dom Felippe Lobo, captain of the Viceroy's ship, the *Santa Tereza*; Dom Francisco Mascarenhas, Admiral, captain of the *S. Joseph*; Dom Francisco Lobo, on the *S. Carlos*; and Nuno Pereira Freire, on his carrack the *San Thomé*. The captain of the galleon was Gonçalo de Siqueira.[3] On the eighteenth of March we set sail from the bar of Lisbon with good weather, the entire fleet going out on the same tide; and since the wind was fresh and favourable, we soon were out to sea and lost sight of land in a few hours, the sea in the meantime causing the usual seasickness among the voyagers. I had my full share of it, becoming so ill that I thought I was also losing my life; and although the pangs and suffering were great it was very beneficial in preserving the good health God granted me throughout the voyage. Seasickness is extremely troublesome and painful and at times can be fatal. It has no other remedy than patience and it seems that there is no other illness so violent and which will lay low any robust constitution. Seasickness is without chills or fever, and one cannot specify a particular part of the body that hurts but rather one complains of suffering mortal agonies everywhere. One is so weary and disgusted with everything as to abhor life itself; if this suffering

---

[1] P. da Costa notes that the appointment of D. Afonso de Noronha had not been well received and that the King was advised to take the opportunity to nominate someone else.

[2] Some accounts mention two galleons and two pinnaces, *patachos*, in addition to the four carracks.

[3] His galleon was the *São Sebastião*. Le Grand wrongly calls its captain Figueira.

Plate II. Dom Francisco da Gama, fourth Conde da Vidigueira

were to last for a long time it would be fatal. It ordinarily does not last long however, although, varying with the constitution and nature of the sufferer, it may last for days. There have already been instances of some who have died from this sickness alone and others who have been afflicted with it for the entire voyage to India. But there are also many whom the sea does not affect at all, even on their first voyage.

Our navigation was as prosperous, as long as it lasted, as it was unfortunate at the end, as I shall relate in its proper place. In a few days we caught sight of the Canaries, recognizing the famous island of Tanarifa which we passed to leeward. As we were sailing better because of the latitude and the course we were following farther out to sea, our early departure with the monsoon favouring us, and because it was the time always considered the most suitable for the voyage to India, we were making it without any difficulty whatever. We passed the Equator with few calms, and we can say that we were off the coast of Guinea only three days. The few rains we experienced began at that time along with the winds called trade winds, which stayed with us for the rest of the voyage; and this explains why we did not have many illnesses, although some began to spread, and why so few people died, not more than seven. Making a course for the Cape and sailing at its latitude after reaching it we wasted more days there than we thought we would because the winds had weakened, but, thanks be to God, at the end of May we had signs of having passed it.

The infallible signs of this passage, so much desired, have been observed by sailors. They are that, as the point called the Cape of Good Hope, well known and feared by those who pass it — and we saw the sharp, high, black, frightful rocks, as rough and irregular as they were beaten by the furious waves and blackened by the force of the storms — as this famous point of land is at a latitude of thirty-four and a half degrees south, there is another, at thirty-five degrees called Cape Agulhas, from the point of which, from north to south and in the same direction as the Cape, there extends a shelf more than fifty leagues long and as much as thirty leagues wide.[1] This place and all the rest of the coast from the Cape inward, is frequented by certain birds the size of ganders, their bodies white all over, their feet and beaks yellow, and their wings all black, for which reason they are called velvet sleeves.[2] They are easily recognized from a distance by their manner of flapping their wings hurriedly in flight as well as by other peculiarities. They are more

[1] The latitude of the Cape of Good Hope is 34° 20′ S., and of Cape Agulhas 34° 50′ S.
[2] *manga de veludo*, the wandering albatross, *Diomedea exulans*.

prevalent in this area than in any other from the Cape outward. We know of no other birds more certain to be found only here, since the shelf is shallower than the open sea that runs close to the coast. The sight, then, of these birds is very much desired by those who sail for the Cape. And since they are seen in this place alone, not going far from shore, when any appear it is a sure sign of the ship's having passed the desired Cape. We had been sailing for the Cape for several days, hoping every hour to hear the happy news. God be thanked that one morning a few days into the month of June, a sailor shouted that he saw a 'velvet sleeve'; and, as the fact was verified not only by the sight of this first one but by several others that soon appeared, everyone aboard was filled with joy, asking for rewards which the Viceroy and many noblemen gave liberally, congratulating themselves on the good success of the voyage and on the certainty of no longer having to fear a reversal, but rather in hopes for equal and better success in the remainder of the voyage.

It is the custom on the occasion of such news for the first ship that sees the sign to fire a cannon, and the other ships then do the same so that the joy may be shared by all. And this is what our flagship did, taking in sail and heaving to in order to throw out the sounding-line, as did all of the ships. It is the custom on this occasion for the sounding-line to be laden with fish hooks; and, when the line is pulled up, to find many fish on it as was the case now when we were in a depth of less than seventy fathoms. We spent the rest of the day and all night in this place catching many fish; for the sailors were very well prepared for this occasion: hake, gurnards and what the sailors call *requeimes* are the fish caught here.[1]

And since I have spoken of this famous and most delightful fishing of the whole voyage, I shall also speak of the ordinary fishing that is done during the voyage. As there are so many fish following the ship because of the delicacies that fall from it, six varieties are ordinarily the ones that are caught: bonitos, a bad fish; *caxoras*, better (they look like mackerel but are shorter and fatter); *albacores*, excellent fish shaped like a tunnyfish,[2] *esmargal*, shaped like a shad but longer and thinner, a little better fish than those already mentioned;[3] pompanos,[4] like small grey

---

[1] *pescadas, cabrinhas, ruivos, a que os mariantes chamão requeimes.* The second and third words are often synonymous and are applied to species of gurnard found off the Portuguese coast; *requeime* is the name of several fishes of the genus *Serranus*, in particular *Serranus scriba* L. [2] On these fishes see above p. 7 n. 2.

[3] A fish of the Indian Ocean that is mentioned in early narratives but not described with sufficient precision to enable it to be identified.

[4] *pelometas*, now usually written *palombeta*.

mullets;[1] dorados, the best of all, so called because under the water they display on certain parts of their body the colour of gold – an excellent fish with very white, tasty, wholesome meat.[2] Not many are caught, however, nor are many *esmargais* or *pelometas* caught. They cast a hook to the fish with some bait of good meat like chicken or fresh fish and they fish for it by sight because the fish swim very near the surface of the water. The albacores, *cachorras* and bonitos are caught in a different way. Tying to the hook a bundle of white feathers, they put a streamer on the line so that with the wind it will carry the hook on top of the water and will not let it sink. And since this fishing is ordinarily done where there is a good wind and the ship is moving at a good clip, a greater quantity of these fish following it then, when they see the hook with the feathers skipping over the water, thinking it is a flying fish, they throw themselves out of the water to snatch it and as they adroitly pursue their quarry, thinking they are making a catch they are caught themselves. And it happens that there are so many of these fish in the ship that people are surfeited with them, although not everyone can partake of them in abundance. The first ones caught, of whatever species, are sold to the highest bidders for the benefit of some confraternity or charity, and it often happens that fish worth only a few *reales*[3] are bought for many *patacas* because of the spirited bidding; and I have seen twenty *patacas* paid for fish worth only one *pataca* when there are many available.

After finishing our fishing at Cape Agulhas and secure in the knowledge that the Cape of Good Hope was now behind us, on the next day we continued our course toward the island of São Lourenço.[4] In few days we entered the fearful sea of the land called Natal, which begins at 32 degrees and ends at 28 degrees.[5] The carrack was made ready, as is the custom, to withstand the violent storms experienced in this area because ships ordinarily pass through it either at the beginning or at the height of winter when storms are at their worst. And because the carrack, what with the fury of the winds and the fury and weight of the waves, strains a great deal so as not to break up, they make for it three or four lashings which they call cables with thick rope in three places from one side to the other over the forward spar-deck; for, since the carrack is weakest here it runs greater danger

---

[1] *tainhas.*   [2] *dourados.*
[3] The *real* was money of account. 100 reals (*reales*, *reis*) were worth about 2½d. in contemporary English money. The *pataca* was worth 320 reals.
[4] Madagascar.
[5] The present province of Natal is almost contained between 27° S and 31° S.

and they thus secure the prow. And it even happens that they encircle it all around the outside with a few lashings of the cable for greater security. In this manner we were entering that fearful sea, experiencing the threatening weather with which the sky is always darkened, gloomy, covered with black clouds, the seas rough, the nights dreadful and dismal, the rains violent and heavy, the winds strong and impetuous. At times, the storms attacked us with great fury but did not last very long, but in any case they are still much to be feared, especially by people new to the sea. Heavy thunderstorms are quite usual here and all the more dangerous since the ship has no protection against so much force. If the lightning were to touch the gunpowder, pitiful destruction would be assured. We did not escape a taste of some of these misfortunes; for in July, on the octave of the Feast of Saints Peter and Paul[1] between nine and ten o'clock in the morning, all of the ships having their sails furled in a thunderstorm in a medium to heavy sea with no wind at all, the sky all clouded over and a kind of mist in the air, a single thunderclap rang out accompanied by a bolt of lightning that hit our carrack at the masthead where the flag was and came down to the foot of the mast, splitting off from it fifteen splinters the size of a man's arm. And although all of the people on the ship were on the spar-deck and in the half-deck, it pleased God that it did no more harm to anyone than to knock down two soldiers: one, who was near the door of the galley on the spar-deck, something burning him on the left cheek without any other harm; the other was hurt on the head from the blow, and his wound later became infected and he was in a serious condition. Although the bolt of lightning zigzagged several times among the people on the half-deck, frightening everyone, it did not touch anyone, but going out to sea through a porthole for bombards it was seen skipping along the surface of the water. A search was made with all possible diligence to see if the lightning bolt had left any damage or had started a fire in the wood, but nothing was found. And since God's mercy was so evident, in thanksgiving we made a procession singing all the litanies. At an altar that we had prepared on the Viceroy's quarterdeck[2] there was a sermon and it fell to me to give it. I was advised to admonish those present to mend their ways in whatever way necessary so that we all would not receive the effective punishment of the Lord our God, deserved by some, of which until then we had seen only the threat.

With the difficulties of these thunderstorms we were leaving this area,

---

[1] June 29.   [2] *tolda.*

so ill-boding and infested with disastrous happenings, setting our course
for the Cabo de São Romão[1] on the famous island of São Lourenço,
which we soon saw at daybreak; and, using this landmark to get our
bearings, we set our course for India by the inner way, as they say,
that is, between the island and the mainland forming the seacoast
between Çofala and Mosanbique. And because in this area are located
first the famous and perilous shoals of Judia, justly feared, and further
on the shoals of João da Nova, we watched for them for several days;[2]
and, with due regard for each in its respective latitude, we came out
of danger and headed for another still greater which was awaiting us
without our knowing it and for our miserable shipwreck near the bar
of Mosambique. In a few days we sighted land on a Thursday with
greater joy than we later experienced as we approached it; for such
are the pleasures of life wont to be. We were sailing along the coast,
and after we had passed the shoal of Sofala, those familiar with this
voyage were aware that the land was close to the island of Mosambique.
By this time the whole fleet was reduced to a company of three carracks
and the galleon; for the S. Thomé had become separated from us long
before we reached the Cape of Good Hope, and although, after we
had passed the line,[3] Sancho de Tovar[4] joined us with some galleons
and hulks[5] in whose company he had departed from the bar of Lisbon
shortly after we did, those vessels, being much smaller than our
carracks, could not withstand the storms of the Cape, and so they
separated from us, since they could do nothing else, one very stormy
night.[6]

As I was saying, our three carracks and the galleon were sailing along
the coast and on a Friday afternoon we reached a point less than 20
leagues from Mosambique. Since we expected to reach port on the next
day, which undoubtedly would have been the case if our bad fortune
had not prevented it, toward evening we put the launch in the water

---

[1] Now Cape Andavaka.

[2] The shoals of Judia, now known as the Bassas da India (sic) in the channel between
Madagascar and the east coast of Africa, originally named Judia after the ship that discovered
them. See C. R. Boxer, The Tragic History of the Sea 1589–1622 (Cambridge, 1959), p. 62,
n. 1. The island, now usually called Juan de Nova, is also in the Moçambique channel some
400 miles further north, and is surrounded by dangerous shoals. In Le Grand the name
is misprinted Mova.

[3] The Tropic of Capricorn.

[4] Sancho de Tovar was in command of five galleons.

[5] urcas, store-ships.

[6] The Spanish historian Gonçalo de Cespedes y Meneses, Primera parte de la Historia de
D. Felippe IIII (Lisboa, 1631), p. 252, records a rumour that the S. Tomé and Tovar's
galleons had deliberately deserted the fleet, fearing that the Viceroy would send them to
the relief of Hurmuz, which was besieged by the Persians and English.

with a few sailors in it to carry messages to the other carracks concerning the Viceroy's orders with respect to procedures for disembarkation. Meanwhile the large launch[1] was being elaborately decorated because the Viceroy was going to go ashore in it to visit the fortress in accordance with the order he had received from His Majesty that he sail directly to that island and that he order certain things to be done there in His Majesty's service.[2] Night fell on these preparations, and the night seemed very long to us because of our desire to set foot on land, since it had been four months and five days since we had left Lisbon; for that much time had elapsed from our departure on the 18th of March until the 23rd of July when we were wrecked on the same bar for which we were heading.

[1] *batelão*.
[2] There was concern that Moçambique might be attacked by the Anglo-Dutch fleet, Cespedes, 1631, p. 252.

[Naval battle with the Dutch and how we were wrecked at the bar[1]]

At dusk the Viceroy and most of the fidalgos on board went onto the ship's balcony for the usual relaxation at the end of the day, some to gamble, others to converse. After long hours, doubtless after ten o'clock at night, when we were still ten or 12 leagues from the fortress, the Viceroy was informed that a *pangaio* had been sighted. (They call *pangaio* the boats that navigate that coast, small, fragile, sewn with coir and without any nails at all.) The news was received with great joy and there were many people who gave a reward of several *reales* to the bearer of the news, as was the custom. They would doubtless have given more willingly if that *pangaio* had not appeared or had not been what we afterward found out; for, as all aboard were running to the bow wanting to see new, strange people and to hear news of land, but with the light afforded by the moonlight at that time and in the calmness of the night they could see another one, which, being the second, did not yet cause the slightest suspicion of what it was. However, the rejoicing of the people was abruptly interrupted when after the second they saw the third and then the fourth, which, as they came near our bow were clearly seen to be large ships which were crossing from land to the sea. Since they were all heading for the open sea they began to exchange signals whereby we clearly recognized them as warships, especially when one of them leaving the others behind made directly for us in order to observe us. At this time everyone was on the foredeck, and as the ship kept coming and we did not know what its intentions were, the captain ordered two cannons to be made ready for any eventuality.[2] Since they had been ready for days, they

---

[1] I have not seen Professor C. R. Boxer's article, 'Dom Francisco da Gama, Conde da Vidigueira e a sua viagem para a India no ano de 1622. Combate naval de Moçambique em 23–25 de julho de 1622', *Anais do Club Militar Naval* (May–June 1930). Professor Boxer has, however, drawn my attention to the account of the battle by Cespedes, 1631, p. 252. Further details will be found in W. Foster, *The English Factories in India 1622–1623* (Oxford, 1908), and N. MacLeod, *De Oost-Indische Compagnie als zeemogendheid in Azië* (Rijswijk, 1927), I, 275–8.

[2] The Viceroy was under general instructions to try to avoid fighting during the voyage, Cespedes, 1631, p. 252.

pointed both of them through the porthole to greet the strangers according to their intention which we soon knew on seeing that it was also preparing its artillery as was revealed by the light that appeared from time to time in the portholes. The ship was approaching us with this intent, and when it was beside us we fired a shot overhead to which it courteously replied in kind. Since it was now at our stern quarter, a cannon at that same location fired a second shot and trained on its hull, the effect of which we did not know, only that it did not reply with a second shot because it had already separated from us. The other carracks and the galleon that were following us did so, however, exchanging shots because the ships in our company, seeing the reception we gave the stranger, treated him in the same way. The admiral had the worst of it because, being the last[1] and receiving three or four cannon shots, it responded only with one because it was not ready with its upper artillery and the Admiral was very sick. The challenge was thus issued and the naval battle engaged and we now recognized the *pangaios* for the Dutch ships that they were, whose admiral had come to reconnoitre us, that being its only purpose in coming near us. We later learned that a month earlier six ships, three Dutch and three English, had cast anchor in Mosambique harbour, sent from Jacatra,[2] in their New Holland as they call it and which they possess in the southern parts, for the purpose of doing battle with the carracks that might come from the Kingdom – and they consider it certain that they would have to come to that port – and even if they should not gain all the success they desired they would at least succeed in disturbing the pleasure and diminishing the forces with which the Viceroy came to India. For this purpose they had waited a whole month in that place raising anchor in the mornings with the wind from the land and putting out to sea to find it, and with the evening breeze they came back to anchor in the same port, the Dutch and English alternately flying the flag of the command-ship, each doing so for a week at a time.[3] The English, however, were unfortunate, for in the week of their

---

[1] The *S. Joseph* was well behind the rest and it was understood that this was because of a lack of understanding between Mascarenhas and the Viceroy, Cespedes, 1631, p. 252.

[2] Jakarta.

[3] The ships belonged to the Anglo-Dutch so-called Defence Fleet. It was commanded by Jacob Dedel, flying his flag in the *Goede Fortuijn*. The other Dutch ship was the *Suijt Hollandt*. The second-in-command was the Englishman Michael Green, elected to replace Humphrey Fitzherbert, who had died at sea. Green commanded the *Royal Exchange*. The other English ships were the *Royal Anne* and the *Diamond*. The Dutch had, against the protests of the English, detached two ships, the *Noort Hollandt* and *'t Wapen van Seelandt*, and sent them to the Red Sea to buy slaves. They were supposed to rejoin the fleet at Mayotte in the Comoros, but did not have time to do so. The English were resentful of

command appeared a *pangaio* coming from the island of São Lourenço with meat and raw hides, and because the route they follow is the Cuama river's,[1] thinking that this strategem might be employed and that it was carrying the usual large quantity of gold, they made every effort to prevent it from escaping them. To this end the English flagship closest to it was so hotly in pursuit of it that, because it was keeping so close to the shore, it was forced to sail over a shallow place that was a large shelf. As the English ship was sailing furiously, greedy for the spoils without realizing the danger, it ran aground on the rocky bottom and was stranded so that it remained there with no way of extricating itself.[2] The people, artillery and goods, however, were saved. Setting fire to what was left of the ship, they destroyed what had been the most beautiful ship in the convoy. And it was no small blessing from God that they were so diminished in strength; for, considering the desperate plight to which they afterward reduced us, it is obvious that our plight would have been all the worse if that ship had not been kept from adding to their strength, in view of the fact that the five remaining ships soon gave us so much trouble. Since we were sailing so close to land and were already so close to the place where the enemy ships lay at anchor, we almost did not see them nor they us; for, as they were in the shadow of the shore we could not see them because our full sails were on the landward side with the wind coming from the open sea, so that it was they who first spied us. And even though they could have come out that evening, they were unwilling to do so because they did not want to do battle with us in the open sea where they would have been at a disadvantage, preferring to meet us near land where, because of the great currents, our carracks, being so heavy, would be in great danger and where they might have some stroke of good fortune, as it afterward happened, in punishment of our sins, so much to their desire that, even if they had arranged the events themselves, the outcome could not have been more favourable for them.

With the visit and reply we had from the Dutch admiral, now sure of the future combat, the happiness we had on seeing land was exchanged for new cares and tasks in preparation for war. All the rest of the night the carrack prepared itself for battle very laboriously, and

this, claiming that, if the other Dutch ships had been present, the whole Portuguese fleet would have been captured, and they £100,000 richer. Foster, 1908, pp. 130, 132, 194.

[1] The Zambesi.

[2] The ship, *'t Hert*, was not English, but Dutch. As it was old and leaky, it was stripped, set on fire and abandoned. Foster, 1908, pp. 2, 5.

with much confusion because of the impedimenta that a carrack bound for India carries, the carelessness with which we had come, and the resolve that we knew the enemy had for combat. The half-decks and cabins of all kinds were in a state of disorder, everything was put in order, all the storerooms and the deck were cleared, the artillery was made ready, the commanders and soldiers were distributed in the stern-castle and the forecastle to drag the cannon into position and help in everything necessary along with their officers who assisted them. We religious who were aboard also did our duty according to our profession. We admonished the people to make their peace with God, exhorting them to their duty, primarily insofar as their souls were concerned, and we heard confessions of almost all on board, which probably amounted to more than seven hundred persons.

When everything aboard ship was ready for battle, the Viceroy assigned himself a position at the bottom of the mast as is the custom; for, having asked what position his father-in-law Rui Lourenço de Tavora[1] had on a similar occasion on returning from India to the Kingdom, and having been told that at the bottom of the mast a scuttle had been opened for him over the hatchway, he ordered the same to be done and placed himself in it. The Captain Dom Felipe Lobo was on the foredeck to ascertain what was being done and what the enemy's plan was, and to order what was required in the battle. Meanwhile dawn was beginning to break and in dim light we saw the enemy ships coming to meet us, all of them displaying red pennants, the flagship in front, the admiral behind, the three ships of lesser tonnage in the middle, all of the ships in a line, sounding their war trumpets, which, were they not a signal of war and of the determination with which they were coming, could serve as a happy morning serenade more pleasant than the one we had. The enemy flagship carried twenty-four guns on each side. The others carried as many as twenty-five, some using twenty-eight-pound cannon-balls. Our flagship carried twenty-four beautiful guns, as did the other two carracks. The pinnace[2] was also fitted out with artillery but it was prepared in such a way and fitted out in such a way for fighting that it was no help to us. It fired not one shot during the two days the battle lasted. The admiral in which Dom Francisco Mascarenhas was travelling, because the captain was so ill and many of the fidalgos and other people were in the same state,

---

[1] Rui Lourenço de Távora, Viceroy 1608–12, had been attacked by English and Dutch ships on his return voyage in 1613. His daughter, D. Leonor Coutinho, was the second wife of D. Francisco da Gama.   [2] *pataxo*.

was also unable to prepare adequately; for, if the captain were in good health, his ship favoured by the presence of such a captain with the personnel and guns that it carried, his ship alone would have sufficed to contend with the power of all the enemy ships. However it was our misfortune that it was in such a state at a time when there was the most need for its assistance, when only the Viceroy's ship and that of Dom Francisco Lobo, the *São Carlos*, were prepared to offer resistance and fight wherever the enemy ships wished to attack them. They came to meet us arranged as follows: the flagship came to do battle with ours, in which the Viceroy was travelling, and the four others divided two for each one of the carracks, paying no attention to the galleon, for they immediately understood how little it could contribute and that they had nothing to fear from it.

When they came within cannon-range, they received our volley of cannon-shot which we very willingly gave them first. But as it was a little far away, the damage was not great. After that, they came very close to us and made use of their artillery much to their pleasure, and did us some damage with it, but more in the shrouds, sails, and yards than among the people. And the first volley they fired being on the starboard side, going around to the port side, they received and gave another, going around the flagship in this way giving and receiving volleys as skilful and swift, darting in and out wherever and whenever it wished, as if it were a well-trained horse. The four other ships did the same, fighting our two ships. And although the ship commanded by Dom Francisco Lobo, a brave soldier and expert captain, fought boldly, the admiral could not adequately respond to the volleys the enemy ships gave it because of the state of the ship and its captain. The Captain, in bed as he was and half-mad from the force of the fever, impelled by his natural courage which, even in so weakened and delirious a state, stirred him to do his duty, ordered himself to be carried to the deck, where he assisted. Since the enemy ships sensed so much weakness and so little resistance in this ship, they concentrated their bombardment on it in order to reduce it completely, killing many people there – grief and damage that also came to the other ships, although the admiral felt them to a greater extent. Nor were the enemy ships free from trouble, for our artillery also killed many people, as was afterwards evident to us. The reason for this was that our guns, being larger and more furious than theirs and being used on the body of the ship which, because theirs were weaker and slenderer, offered less resistance to the force of the cannon-balls, wreaked havoc among the people, whereas we received our damage primarily in the rigging, masts and yards, on which they especially concentrated their fire because of the great strength of the sides of our ships in resisting the fury of their cannon-balls, even though some passed through and broke open casks and cannons[1] where they happened to hit them, intending also to wreck our masts and rigging so that the force of the currents of Sofala, in which we were located, would carry us along and run us aground; and it was for this reason that they concentrated their bombardment from the side of the open sea.

The battle continued with this rigour and contention until noon when we separated at no great distance, all ships having much to complain of, but especially our admiral in which the enemy had killed many people and had partially stripped the masts and rigging. We must have spent two or something less than three hours, on both sides, preparing ourselves for the second battle and repairing part of the damage from the first, when one of the smallest enemy ships was seen approaching us stealthily on the starboard side at the rear quarter of our ship, placing itself so cleverly that it was not far enough forward for our guns at that location to hit it, nor was it far enough back for it to fear damage from our guns at the stern. And as there were many people in the stern-castle unaware of such a deceitful or bold move, discussing the events of the morning and the determination of this little ship and the others, it came so close to us that, touching off one of its guns, it shot at the stern-castle where there were more than thirty of us; and if the shot had not been high because of the bombardier's poor aim and had been accurate, it certainly would have killed many of us who were there, very unmindful of what could have happened to us. But since it had come only to make that one attempt and it was very light, it turned to leeward so quickly that, even though we did the same thing after it in order to repay it in kind, the heavier weight of our carrack allowed the lighter ship to seek safety so rapidly that we were unable to catch up with it.

Soon however we were fighting again with the same furiousness on both sides as we had done in the morning, the battle lasting in full fury for a good three hours. The admiral at this time going ahead, as we let it pass, all of the enemy ships fell upon her and from all sides treated her in such a way that soon neither yards nor ropes and few pieces of sails were to be seen on her, the mast, from many cannon-shots, was about to fall; many people were killed, and the enemy ships were

[1] *canoens.* Perhaps a mistake for *canos*, 'pipes'.

32

attacking her so furiously that if Dom Francisco Lobo had not come to her aid, they doubtless would have defeated her and sent her to the bottom; for she was already taking in much water. Since it was then nearly night-time, when night came the enemy ships withdrew further out to sea; and we remained closer to the land, communicating with one another by messages, which were delivered by small boats, concerning the condition of each ship. The Admiral's ship was the worst, and in the most wretched condition imaginable, so that, the other ships not being able to help her because they had so much to do and repair and fear on their own ships, she was forced to turn to the shore and run aground with the current where she could in order to avoid going straight to the bottom. The two other carracks, the Viceroy's and Dom Francisco Lobo's, were repairing the damage they had received, Dom Francisco's being greater than ours, and were preparing for the events of the following day. Work continued all night, there being very little opportunity for rest and eating.

With the break of day and in the increased daylight, when we were awaiting the coming of the enemy ships, we saw them at a distance out to sea, close together and within hearing distance of one another. We also saw our admiral run aground, which was a continual source of grief for us as we saw the enemy ships all ready for battle and realized that we were lacking so important a one and that this was reviving the courage of the enemy and made them believe in their own good fortune and our bad fortune. They spent all morning in that discussion without attacking us, nor did we have enough presence of mind to enter our port in the three hours which would have sufficed, considering the short distance there was; but there was only a weak breeze which was nothing for the size and weight of our ships but enough for the enemy ships to come in and go out. The action they decided upon, as we learned from what they later did, was to fight us as far as the entrance to the port, attacking us always from the direction of the sea so that we would go along the shore where there are many shallow places, with the intention that we might possibly run aground on one of them. With this intent, our ships being in this order: the galleon first, next the carrack *São Carlos*, and that of the Viceroy bringing up the rear, all five of the enemy ships came to attack us with fierce determination, pelting our ship on all sides with metal cannon-shot, some piercing the side, showing the fury and size of their artillery. With the continual rain of cannon-balls they tormented the side of the ship and at the same time attacked the rigging and masts with some iron crowbars used as cannon-balls, which did great damage. With some with diamond points they pierced the ship, and with ordinary round ones, but weighing many pounds, they passed through the weakest parts destroying and breaking up everything inside the ship. Many volleys of these were given and received all afternoon, the whole armada, both ours and that of the enemy, fighting bravely, six men having been killed in our ship, none of importance, and a few wounded, of whom one, a brave soldier, died after being struck such a blow by a splinter caused by a cannon-ball that he died a few days later on land. There was another, half of whose leg was taken off, and no matter how much one tried to help him – I even tore up most of my shirt to stop the flow of blood for lack of anything else at hand – the wound was so large that all diligence was in vain. In the last volleys, the enemy admiral had made a special effort to fire upon us, which we returned in usual measure. And wishing to fire upon her with the gun located at the front quarter because that gun was large and very powerful – I named it São Tiago so that it would be under the protection of that saint, since his day was the 25th of July – we fired a shot that was so direct and so well-timed that the ship received great damage from the blow to which the carrack *São Carllos* immediately added another with the same cannon with such good teamwork that, hitting almost in the same place, it opened up a large breach with which the ship would have gone right to the bottom if it did not careen itself, leaving the battle for the sea, leaning over on one side. And since we thought it was irreparably doomed to go to the bottom, we gave a great hue and cry, ringing a bell we had at the stern of the ship; but for the moment the sea did not take it; shortly, however, after those aboard saved all they could from it, as we afterward learned, it did go to the bottom. At this time it was almost sunset and we were not far from our fortress. And since Dom Francisco Lobo was a valiant soldier, he wanted to end the battle with a bit of gallantry, which was to cost him his life. Loading all his artillery and going in front of us, he hove to, turning towards the enemy ships, which soon encircled him and, keeping him in the middle, fired on him vigorously, to which Dom Francisco responded so bravely that he made them depart and not return to the battle, going back out to sea. Dom Francisco Lobo, however, was mortally wounded by a cannon-ball which, entering through a porthole, made a ricochet on the deck and, bouncing up, struck him in the back of the thigh, giving him a terrible blow which went so far into his leg that it caused internal injuries from which he died in a few days, which was a great loss because of his bravery and personal and soldierly qualities as well as many other excellent qualities with which he was endowed. After the departure of the enemy ships, we were following our course, being at that time less than two leagues from the bar, from where *almadias*[1] came out to receive us, which was the origin of the pitiful event that I am about to relate.

Rid of the enemy ships as we were and relatively unscathed as we felt ourselves to be with the small number of dead and wounded, the enemy having fought so bravely and obstinately, and we having expended on them, according to our count of the missing cartridges of gunpowder, one hundred and eighty shots on the first day and two hundred and twenty on the second, being certain of the great quantity fired by Dom Francisco, since we were witnesses of it, we began to catch our breath, setting aright what had been damaged or disordered aboard ship, all of us rejoicing, and hastening to have something to eat in peace – something we had not done for two days. The soldiers vied with one another to be knighted by the Captain, as is the custom on such occasions. The Viceroy sat on a chair in the stern-castle. The pilots' *almadia* arrived bringing two pilots, a Portuguese and a Muslim, who, welcoming the Viceroy, then went off with his approval to lead the way into the port. Since we were now so near the bar and since the place where we were sailing was full of reefs, the carrack's officers were on the starboard yards and cathead dropping the plumb line to find out the number of fathoms in which the ship was navigating. The number of fathoms kept diminishing rapidly as the numbers twenty, fifteen, thirteen, eleven, ten, nine were called out. When a certain person[2] heard the number nine being called out he hurried out of the cabin where he was and warned that they should order the anchor to be dropped, but we were already in no more than seven fathoms, and, because there was great noise and confusion aboard and everyone was thinking only of the excitement of being so close to land, we soon found ourselves in a depth of four fathoms when we would have thought that there was still depth for the ship to navigate in. This disastrous turn of events must have come about either because we suddenly went into a shallow area that was there or because they were falsifying the number of fathoms by saying ten when there were eight; for, when seven was being repeated we found ourselves in four as the carrack made the first hit against the bottom. And as others followed immediately since we

[1] A canoe, often a dugout.
[2] Le Grand reads 'un Religieux'. P. da Costa concludes that it was Lobo himself.

were over rock, we very fearfully became aware of our danger and misfortune, which increased with the repeated multiplication of the blows causing the carrack to open up and receive much water, to which was added the fact that the tide was ebbing, leaving us in even less water. They hurried to cut the main mast in order to relieve the ship of the weight of it, but this did not cause the ship to come up at all. On the contrary, because the quantity of water kept decreasing, the keel settled on the rock and the carrack leaned over on its port side, tipped over so far that the water came in over the sail yards, flooding almost all of the deck.

Realizing how little could be done to save the ship and certain of its doom, each person aboard tried to salvage his own affairs amid all the confusion caused by the event. The Viceroy, who until then was in the stern-castle, went below, taking me with him, to remove his papers and something of value that he handed over to me in a writing-case. And since his presence there was now unnecessary, nor were lives in danger since the ship was stationary and near land and there were many *almadias* beside the ship, enough for everyone, which had come for a task quite different from that which our misfortune offered them, i.e. taking the people to safety. However, since one misfortune is almost always accompanied by another, it happened that the people aboard the carrack *São Carlos*, sailing in our wake, were in such a state of distraction or confusion that they failed to observe our predicament, even though they could easily have observed it because of the very short distance between the two ships, the bowsprit of the *S. Carlos* almost touching our stern. Although we made signals for them to turn aside, first by extinguishing the signal-light, then by firing a cannon, and also by shouting to them from the stern, nothing was enough to prevent them from coming between us and the island of Santo Antonio,[1] going even closer to the shore than we were, where, with equal if not greater misfortune than ours, they ran aground because of failure to heed our warnings. With the same fright that we had experienced, they immediately sought ways to save the ship; but, since the Captain was in a very bad condition from the cannon-ball

---

[1] Evidently the rocky islet on which there stood at one time a fort called Santo António. It was at the south-western corner of the island of Moçambique. It is marked, but not named, on the map of the island by Pêro Barreto de Resende, reproduced from the British Library MS. Sloane 197, opposite p. 164 in the Portuguese edition of Lobo's text. The name of the fort is marked on the illustration in the Bibliothèque Nationale copy, reproduced in the printed edition of Bocarro's *Livro das plantas de tôdas as fortalezas, cidades e povoações do estado da India Oriental*, I (Bastorá, 1937), p. 4. Bocarro says the fort had been abandoned, p. 12. It is now called São Lourenço.

that had struck him a few hours earlier and from which he soon died, this event threw them into confusion and did not permit them to do what they were capable of doing and what they would doubtless have done if the Captain had been present on that occasion.

The Viceroy, with eight other persons, was offered a boat in which he left for shore, the Captain, Dom Felipe Lobo, remaining on board and tending to everything necessary. What was most to be feared was the return of the Dutch, but, with God's special favour, it had been more than an hour and a half since they had departed from us, despairing of being able to do us any more harm, not being able to imagine the sad condition we were in, determined to descend at dawn upon the carrack *São Jozeph*, which was aground on the reefs of Mogincali,[1] as we had seen all that day; for, if they had had news of our misfortune or if they had been nearby at the time it happened, they doubtless would have had greater booty and good fortune than they could ever have wished for. The seriously crippled state, however, in which they too found themselves, for they departed so, with many dead and their ships damaged, and the good condition in which they left us, with the joy of going into port and recovering on land, caused them to depart so quickly, greedy for the booty from the stranded carrack, and caused us to enter the harbour at that time without suspicion of the ill-fated experience we were to have and could fear on that bar and location which was so dangerous.[2] But the joy and heedlessness with which we ventured to enter so perilous a bar at such a time did not let us recover in any way. Our misfortune was caused especially by our using pilots from land, and even though others ill-advisedly and without foundation attribute to fear what was pure heedlessness, the fact remains that we had had nothing of which we could have been afraid for more than an hour and a half, and we were not so routed and dazed that we feared things no longer in sight, since there was no vestige of the enemy coming after us.

[1] Mogincual.

[2] The Viceroy reported to Lisbon that the Dutch had taken from the stranded carrack some crew members, some money and the orphan girls under the protection of the Crown. The latter were 'respectable girls of marriageable age, provided with dowries in the form of colonial government posts for whoever would marry them after their arrival in India' (Boxer, 1959, p. 21). According to the English sources 68,553 reals of eight and about 100 prisoners were taken from the *S. Joseph*; the money was divided equally between the English and Dutch. There was also some private plunder. They thought some 300 Portuguese had been killed and about 150 drowned. Three Portuguese girls were taken, one of whom married the Dutch factor at Surat. Green was accused of having kept the other two for a year, refused a ransom of 600 reals for them at Moçambique, given them costly clothes and eventually left them at Jakarta. The English lost only five or six men. The Portuguese saved forty chests of reals from the *S. Joseph*, Foster, 1908, pp. 16, 15, 132, 155, 194.

I was one of the eight who accompanied the Viceroy in the boat when he went to the fortress. And since it was night-time, even though the fortress was no farther than half a league and there was moonlight, and as the oarsmen were not familiar with that place, we missed the bar and were going along the island continually hitting the many boulders underwater near the shore. And as we did not hit upon the channel we should have followed, confused in this uncertainty, we continued in a state of great perplexity, not because of the danger, which was small or non-existent, but because of the place, with which we were totally unfamiliar. And as we were going along close to the shore, we noticed people in a palm grove. A soldier immediately leaped into the sea, beating the water vigorously because of the many sharks there, which cut off one's leg or arm with one bite and carry off everything they take hold of. He went ashore and from a nearby palm grove brought a negro who by signs showed us the fortress, which was behind us; whereupon we immediately turned back and recognized it more easily because of the many *manchuas*[1] and *almadias* with their accustomed music of the rowers, who do not row without it, and because of the great noise of people flocking to the ships. At the foot of the fortress and in the narrowest part of the entrance to the harbour is a chapel of the Virgin Our Lady, called the Chapel of the Fortress, a place where, because there are many rocks, caves and hollow places which the boisterousness of the sea has fashioned there, the sea always runs high, entering and going out of those caves boisterously and with huge waves. And as we were going very close to shore, when we reached this place we found ourselves in the greatest danger; for, going into the midst of the waves which were very high and with a very strong undertow, the boat was immediately caught up by these and thrust sideways into the crashing waves, so that we were all in obvious danger of perishing; but the help of Our Lady and the strength of the oars with which we were provided caused us to escape danger and reach land at the gate of the fortress, where the occupants and inhabitants of the town came to receive the Viceroy and give him their condolences for such a great misfortune. The Viceroy withdrew into the fortress, and I and the other Fathers went away toward our college.

That night and the two following days were spent in evacuating our

---

[1] 'A large cargo-boat, with a single mast and a square sail' (*Hobson-Jobson*). Boxer, 1959, p. 62, n. 2, quotes Peter Mundy, who describes them as 'small vessels of recreation... pretty handsome things resembling little frigates; many curiously carved, gilded and painted, with little beak-heads'.

carrack, where most of the goods were under water, saving from it what could be saved. The carrack *São Carlos* had better luck, because, as it remained upright and the tide was rising, it began to float, and, with the same force of water came to run aground at the foot of the fortress on the side facing the sea, where it was unloaded of everything, everything aboard being saved, even the nails in the keel. On the third day we saw three carracks were coming toward the bar and toward our carrack that was run aground, and we soon recognized them as the enemy carracks. The day before at dawn, they had descended upon the carrack *São Joseph*. Although the *São Joseph* had had time to unload most of the goods aboard, and, although they had taken a goodly quantity, it was not as much as they could and should have taken in the two nights and one whole day, which was the time available to them, the reasons for this being that there were great numbers of sick and wounded, their carrack was a great distance from land, their small boat was damaged, and, above all, their Captain was very sick. For all these reasons, they were unable to hurry the evacuation of the main part of the goods which were carried in the carrack. And as the enemy ships arrived quickly, they found some people still on the ship, all of the Orphans of the King, who certainly should have been the first ones to leave for land, a certain part of the King's money which usually comes in *patacas*, along with the rest of the goods they had been unable to carry off in the few boat-loads they had taken. After the enemy ships had plundered what they found on the ship, knowing what had happened to ours, they came to put into the harbour. And as they appeared and were recognized, the Viceroy ordered that our carrack be set afire. It burned to the water as the weather prevented the enemy ships from reaching it any sooner for lack of wind. In this way they derived no gain from it. They did, however, derive credit and great joy from seeing the loss of three beautiful carracks, of which they were the major cause. They must be given all the more credit for this since any one of ours by itself, under ordinary circumstances, would have sufficed to contend with all of theirs at once. Our affliction was increased by the sight of their victorious carracks so free of damage and ours so wretchedly destroyed. The enemy ships remained in the harbour for a few days, on one of which they hoisted a white flag as a signal that they wanted to come to talk. The request was answered by an experienced man from Mosambique, who went to the ship in a boat. But when he went aboard and asked them what they wanted the reply was vague. They stated finally that they were sailing for India and would meet us again in some harbour there.[1] Whereupon, after the boat had withdrawn, they set sail, leaving us on that island in want of many things, all the more because of the difficulty in transporting so many people to India. A start was made in this as the Viceroy ordered the majority of the people in the fleet to embark in the galleon, sending them from there to Mascate[2] for the dual purpose of involving them in some military manoeuvres at that fortress, providing it with a large number of able people, and relieving the island of so many people, which it was incapable of sustaining.

[1] The Defence Fleet returned to the Comoros and in August sailed for India. After refitting at Swally it blockaded Goa from December 1622 to March 1623. There was much mutual recrimination. The Dutch accused the English of abandoning the fight to loot the *S. Joseph*, but are said to have praised Goodall's 'verie valiant stout performance' in the *Royal Anne*, Foster, 1908, pp. 151, 183.

[2] Muscat.

[Concerning the voyage from Moçambique to Goa]

During the time we remained on the island, we ministered to the wounded, some dying, others falling sick because the climate was not very healthy. The moonlight, especially that of September, is so harmful that it causes mortal illnesses in those who stay out in it. Its ill effects are such that it damages even the bronze bells and cannon, causing them to crack. For this reason they are kept covered with straw, and men walking in the streets at night wear hats and take greater care against being touched by moonlight and night air than they would against the sun's rays in the greatest heat of the day, against which they also protect themselves; for the moonlight is more harmful. Of the vessels that were in the harbour and others which had come from outside since the enemy ships had left it, the Viceroy selected three or four pinnaces and a galiot, in which he prepared for his passage to India, selecting the galiot for his own person as being lighter and less cumbersome and having the capability of using oars in case of emergency; and twenty-eight good sailors were put aboard to man them. On the day before Our Lady of September[1] all four of our vessels left the harbour; and as it was already late because of the tide, night falling as we were near the entrance to the harbour, we then were caught in such currents that we were all driven off course in such a way that at dawn we had almost lost sight of one another and certainly could not distinguish one another, as one of the pinnaces disappeared, which had no choice but to let the sea take it where it would. It was carried to the island of Ceylon, where it put in and gave news of our loss. The three other vessels were able to re-enter the harbour, recover and await a better tide and wind, which we had on the next day and with which we went out to sea, bound for the coast of India with the intention of landing at the first fortress where we could put into port, even though we had planned our course for Cochin, but with some apprehension because, since it was such a well known harbour, we could

[1] September 7. Le Grand says that they sailed on the evening of 8 September.

reasonably fear that some of the enemy ships would be lying in wait for us there, and a very small number would suffice to spoil our joy at the successful voyage and sight of land, and they could do us much harm in the state we were in.

After we left Mosambique, our voyage was good with no bad weather except for a few calms which did not fail to cause us uneasiness as we passed the Equator, after which, continuing with favourable winds, already near the coast of India, we caught sight of land one morning between eight and nine o'clock, the lookout in the crow's-nest shouting that he saw it dead ahead. Our joy was as great as our desire to be there. And as the vessel had a good wind when it was sailing southward, not only were we able to learn that it was not the mainland but rather one of the Mamalle islands,[1] but also we found ourselves meeting land head on, a beautiful mountain all covered with thick foliage. And because we wanted to reconnoitre more than we should have, we soon found ourselves between two arms of a string of shoals which extended outward from the island far into the sea, leaving in the middle a very large inlet, which we were entering and from which we would not have been able to extricate ourselves readily in the event of a need to escape. If we entered further, the danger was especially great because, at about two or three o'clock in the afternoon, the sun appeared surrounded by a large halo similar to that often seen surrounding the moon, which on the sun is a sign of stormy weather. In the place and circumstances in which we were, this turned out to be extremely dangerous because the halo surrounding the sun opened partially, leaving us with a contrary wind, and as the sea was all bursting in foam the pilots and sailors were very fearful and were shouting that we should immediately fall to leeward, which we did very cautiously because we had gone far inside the two arms. We got out however, passing very close to the point of the reef and setting our course once again for the coast of India, which we saw two days later. The Viceroy's galiot was then accompanied by only two pinnaces, for, of the two others, one had gone off course and had set its course for the island of Ceylon the first night of our departure from Moçambique and the other landed at Coulão,[2] twenty-five leagues from Cochim toward the south and Cape Comorin; and the reason for veering from course in

---

[1] The Laccadives. They were sometimes given this name by the Portuguese after the famous Cananor merchant whom they knew as Mammale Mercar and who monopolised the trade of the Laccadives and Maldives in the early sixteenth century, *The Voyage of François Pyrard of Laval*, tr. and ed. Albert Gray (London, 1887–90), I, 323, n. 1.
[2] Quilon.

this way was that we were fearful of meeting the Dutch on the coast of India and in the harbour of Cochim, according to what they had given us to understand, for which place we were heading. The Viceroy ordered this pinnace to be three or four leagues forward and, on catching sight of the enemy ships, to signal with fire at night and with cannon in the daytime, turning either to the north or to the south, whichever would be better for it, so that we would take the opposite course from the one it had taken in order thus to deceive the enemy who, on seeing it, would doubtless give chase, leaving the way clear for us. This was good reasoning if there were only one ship, but if there were more there was enough work for all. In any case, this was the procedure that was followed.

With this intent the pinnace sailed, following the same course as we except that shortly before dark it suddenly allowed the wind to change its course by two quarter-points of the compass and since we were following her, we did the same. Our pilots, however, who were experienced and more certain of their latitude and course, from which they concluded that they were heading straight toward the harbour of Cochim, as indeed they were, did not wish to follow the pilot of the other pinnace, but rather returned to their original course, understanding full well the intent and whim of the other, which was changing course because of their belief that our pilots were steering an erroneous course for the harbour of Cochim and they wanted to correct it in that way. They corrected it so well that they went to the harbour of Coulam. Continuing our course, we saw land on the next day and arriving there recognized it as the coast of Porqua,[1] twelve leagues below Cochim, which leagues we lost in that short space of time when we changed course, and even though we tried to correct the error it was no longer possible to do so because of the strong southerly current along the coast, the winds also being contrary, which impeded not only sailing but also rowing. The people on shore immediately recognized us as friends and they visited us, bringing many kinds of food – fresh fish, chicken, bread, fruit, fresh water – all of which brought us much comfort, weary as we were from so many months' voyage. From here we spent twelve days before we reached Cochim at a distance of twelve leagues, paying well for the calm seas we had experienced from Moçambique to this point. For, after one day at anchor, during which we enjoyed serene weather and beautiful bright sunlight, the fine weather lasting until the setting of the moon, there descended upon us such a great

[1] Porakad (Porca, Porcatt).

storm of wind, rain, thunder and lightning, the whole sea swelling in such a way, that we could consider ourselves doomed. We threw out three or four anchors to support the galiot, which continued to suffer from these torments for as many more hours, during which time our lives were in greater peril. When the storm was over we had calm weather until the next day at the same time, and in this way we continued on the other days until, little by little, by rowing and with some sailing when the sea breeze came, we were approaching our destination. As we neared Cochim, where news of the Viceroy's arrival had been received, the people of the city came out to greet us, with great celebration, in many boats called *manchuas, empalegas, tones, balões*,[1] with a concert of shawm trios[2] and with much food. Everyone was celebrating, playing musical instruments for greater rejoicing, which was much greater for us. In one of these boats, which was a beautiful *balão* covered with an awning and well fitted out, came our Fathers to receive us and take ashore the two of us who came in the company of the Viceroy. The other two were taken to Coullão in the pinnace which went there, having taken an erroneous course. Our *manchua* accompanied that of the Viceroy who also was going ashore. We all went to the beach which was covered with an infinite number of people who had come to see, receive and celebrate the arrival of the *reinoes*, the name they use in reference to new arrivals from Portugal during the first months after their arrival in India. Some keep this name longer, and even all their lives, according to their deserts and the occasions which they may give for this. For among the Indians or those born in those parts or who had been from these parts[3] and have been living in India for a long time, this name *reinol* means novice, the people designated by it not being considered very astute; for they so consider all who go from here as long as they do not adopt the weapons and trickery of those of India, a land where trickery comes long before the use of reason in children and in older people is refined to the highest degree, whether the earlier appearance of these characteristics and their communication among the *reinois* are because of the air, climate and

---

[1] *manchua*, see above, p. 38 n. 1; *empalega*, a Malabar canoe; *tone*, an oriental cargo ship, those used for carrying pepper being about 11 yards long with very convex ribs; *balão*, a small, light rowing boat, the bottom of which was made from a single piece of wood, H. Leitão and J. V. Lopes, *Dicionário da Linguagem de marinha antiga e actual* (Lisboa, 1963), and for the last *H.J.*, 'baloon'.

[2] *ternos de charamellas*.

[3] Dr Lockhart notes that Lobo here uses *aquellas partes* for India and *estas partes* for Portugal, an indication that he was writing this part of the book after his return from the East.

nature of the land or whether it is because of their association with the natives who are past masters in them and from whom they learn this behaviour which is so prevalent.

We two of the Company, whom they called *reinois*, taking the road to our College, were being led in the midst of all the Fathers of the College who had come out to receive us, as is the custom. As we proceeded, we were also surrounded by a huge crowd of people who came to us and followed us, and the windows of the houses were filled with people as on a day of great celebration or when people gather to see some curiosity; and more attention was called to our procession and the applause increased because of the people attracted by the sound of a trio of shawm players who preceded us, playing skilfully and most harmoniously. They purposely led us through the principal streets of the city, and as we were recognized by our dress, the colour of our faces and state of our health, in addition to the fact that our companions formed single files on either side of the street, leaving us in the middle as the main figures in the act, we gave everyone occasion for great joy and applause, all well-intentioned, as they threw upon us a thousand blessings and gave us a hearty welcome. Some were weeping, commiserating with the suffering they knew we had endured; others were sorry for us because of the common things that are always suffered on so long a voyage; others were giving thanks to God because they saw us safely arrived from so far, with all the other demonstrations of kindness that women are wont and know how to give on these occasions – all of which was of great mortification for the poor *reinois* that we were, walking in the middle of the street in such a procession, so embarrassed and timid that we would have gladly exchanged the celebration for some great penance. We were walking, however, to our Jesuit house and the crowd was continually growing larger. As we arrived at the door of the church the seminarians with some more Fathers and a fine choir were waiting for us. The church, which is very beautiful, was bedecked with holiday decorations as if for one of the principal holidays of the year. We entered the church as the *Benedictus Dominus* was being sung, the whole hymn being sung in polyphony. And after giving the thanks due to God Our Lord for having brought us to that place after nearly seven months, from the eighteenth of March to the fourth of October on which we went ashore in the city of Cochim, having received the embraces of the Fathers and Brothers who gave them to us with affection and true joy, we went into the College, where the first action is a bath in hot water in a large wooden tub, certainly necessary because of the filth, pitch, tar and all the bad luck we accumulated from the sea and the ship. Even so, this is not sufficient to get rid of it all, for it seems that there is no bilge stench or other filth spawned by the sea with which we were not covered, or at least they considered us so. The greatest demonstration of kindness is in clothing, for the people of India are extremely fastidious and pride themselves on cleanliness, being squeamish about everything, especially the *reinois*, for whom they reserve the name *bag of lice*.[1] And there surely are more or fewer lice according to the care each person takes of himself, but in any case there are many lice on all new arrivals. I emerged from the tub, having shed a coating of dirt from head to foot, and at one point I had been about to shed my skin also because they inadvertently and boldly threw water at me that was too hot, some of which splashed on me, much to my chagrin.

These kindnesses lasted a few days and continued until the time for our departure, which was the Day of the Feast of the Presentation of Our Lady;[2] for our heading for that city was by way of correction of error, our direct course having been to Goa. There arrived from Goa a beautiful fleet, of the best there was in India, to receive the Viceroy and take him to Goa. The Viceroy embarked on a fine ship, which along with the others formed a fleet of more than two hundred, all with oars, many of them warships, the rest merchant ships, which were also impressive, many noblemen bringing ships at their own expense to accompany the Viceroy with greater pomp.

We set sail on the day of Our Lady of the Pleasures and, although it is not more than a hundred leagues from Cochim to Goa, we spent twenty-six days in the voyage because some of the days there was a contrary wind and on others we stopped sometimes at anchor because of not being able to continue, at other times in various places and fortresses on that coast. Despite this loitering we reached Goa at a place called Cabo de Rama.[3] Several of the warships which were guarding the harbour came to meet us, informing us that eleven Dutch carracks had been anchored in the harbour for days (which must have been to fulfil the promise that they had given us in Mosambique to go and wait for us at the mouth of the harbour), and for greater entertainment they were bringing more companions. The news of the visitors and

---

[1] Le Grand reads: 'It is true that most of our Europeans are much less careful about washing themselves and keeping clean than the Indians are'.
[2] November 21. It is also known as the Feast of Our Lady of the Pleasures. In the Portuguese edition, p. 214, n. 1, the month is misprinted September.
[3] Cape Ramas, to the south of Goa.

their arrival with so many large carracks did not fail to cause some delay in our entering the harbour, even though, if there had been greater resolve and less fear and faint-heartedness caused by our misfortune at Moçambique, the ships in our fleet were sufficient in number and power to attack them and give them a well deserved drubbing. Rejecting this good or bad advice, however, if perchance it entered his mind, the Viceroy ordered the warships to be divided into three groups, one to stand off to sea as if acting as a rear guard, another to take the lead in the direction of the enemy, the other with the whole throng of merchant vessels to accompany the Viceroy. With this appearance and arrangement, we doubled the shelf of sand of Our Lady of the Cape which juts out under water far into the sea.[1] To avoid it the whole fleet had to make a wide swing out to sea and come well within range of the enemy's guns. In a situation such as this it was always to be feared that the enemy, either trusting in its power or arrogant because of our misfortune at Moçambique, might entertain us with some guns. However, whether it was because they feared the many ships they saw and the order in which they were divided or whether they were unwilling to pick a quarrel with us because they did not know how we would take it and how we would respond, they remained in their positions; and the triumphant attitude they flaunted before our eyes, for they they had us virtually surrounded in the mouth of our harbour with the new Viceroy and such forces, contrasted sharply with the abjectness with which we chose to enter the harbour when we could have repaid them very well indeed.

The celebration of our arrival as *reinois* at Goa was similar to what we had experienced at Cochim. It was, however, more elaborate in proportion to the greater facilities in the three houses that we have in Goa and a beautiful seminary of many students, thus permitting more elaborate celebrations and receptions, such as this one, which took place on a Saturday, the sixteenth of December, the day before the Feast of Our Lady of the O.[2]

---

[1] Nossa Senhora do Cabo. The Cabo is the western promontory of the island of Goa, 15° 28′ N. 73° 47′ E. There are shoals to the W and SW of the cape. A chapel and hermitage dedicated to Our Lady were built there and later incorporated in the fortress, J. N. da Fonseca, *An historical and archaeological Sketch of the City of Goa* (Bombay, 1878), p. 4; C. R. Boxer, 1959, p. 68.

[2] The Feast of the Expectation of the birth of the Holy Child, celebrated in Spain and Portugal on 18, not 17, December.

[How I tried to enter Ethiopia by way of Malindi]

I stayed in Goa for a little more than a year finishing my theological studies. At that time letters came from Ethiopia in which the Fathers of that mission asked for many Jesuits because of the conversion of Emperor Seltan Segued, who had received Communion and had professed himself a Roman Catholic.[1] Because of this and because of the many new converts to our holy faith, more labourers were needed to carry forward the good beginnings set in motion by that Christian mission. Although the Father of the mission, as I say, asked for many, it was not possible at the time to send them more than eight, for entering and leaving Ethiopia was necessarily by way of the Red Sea and the island of Maçua, which were in the hands of the Turks, and there was the obvious danger that they would not allow them to pass and would capture them all.[2] And there was even doubt that as many as eight would be sent, so we made good use of a letter written by the converted Emperor to the Father Provincial of India asking him for many Fathers and informing him that they could go through the kingdom of Dancali, whose inhabitants, although Muslim, were his vassals and friends.[3] The secretary, however, had erroneously written Zeila instead of Dancali, little dreaming how much this word was to cost two Jesuit Fathers, my companions, for it was the cause of their losing their lives, and the same would have happened to the other two, of whom I was one, as I shall presently relate. Of the eight chosen for this mission and undertaking, four were ordered to enter Ethiopia by the ordinary way via Macuá.[4] These soon left and successfully entered

---

[1] His personal name was Susenyos, which, because of the ambiguity of the Ethiopic script, can also be read Susneyos. His throne name was Seltan Sagad, or Malak Sagad. He came to the throne in 1607, professed the Roman Catholic faith in 1621, restored the practices of the Ethiopian church in 1632, and died in September of that year.

[2] Massawa and a varying extent of territory in northern Ethiopia had constituted a province of the Ottoman Empire since 1555.

[3] The Danakil (Afar), a Muslim people inhabiting the saline depression between the Ethiopian plateau and the Red Sea, sometimes owed a vague allegiance to the Emperor.

[4] These four were Manoel Lameira, Thomé Barneto, Gaspar Paez and Jacinto Francisco. The last was an Italian, properly called Giacinto Franceschi.

the empire even though the Baxa of the Turks, taking advantage of the opportunity, refused to let them pass unless the Emperor first sent him a wild ass of a species called zebra, as large as a good mule, the most beautiful animal I have seen and of which I shall make further mention.[1] When the zebra was brought and delivered, the Fathers left. The other four, of whom I was one, were to enter by way of Zeila, a new and risky way, vouched for only by the Emperor's letter, and we were totally unaware that the information contained in it was in error and, of course, were unable to foresee the dire outcome. Since we wanted to find a new, safe way to enter that empire in order to avoid the tyranny of the Turks which we always experienced upon entering their ports and falling into their hands, there began to be a rumour that by way of the coast of Melinde, penetrating that interior, one could find an easy, safe way. There were even people who gave news of such a way, indicating a river that could be navigated and lands and peoples to deal with and to civilize; and as this way was new and risky, even though there was a great desire to discover it, the superiors were unwilling to risk individuals except when there were volunteers. And as there were already four of us who had volunteered for a similar task via Zeila, although there were more of these later, and since I was of the opinion that there was very little difference between the two as far as risk was concerned, another Father and I decided to be the pioneers in this undertaking of discovery.[2] So the four of us divided, two to go via Zeila, and two to enter via the coast of Melinde.

All of us prepared for the voyage according to the route that each of us was to follow.[3] The two who were going by way of Zeila sailed for Caxem in a ship belonging to Muslims whose king was an old and loyal friend to the Portuguese, lord of the island of Socotorá in addition

[1] The Pasha was probably Ahmed Pasha. See the list of governors of the Ottoman province of Habesh (Abyssinia) in Cengiz Orhonlu, *Habeş eyaleti* (Istanbul, 1974), p. 183. The Fathers were delayed at Massawa for two and a half months until the arrival of the zebra. See C. F. Beckingham and G. W. B. Huntingford, *Some Records of Ethiopia 1593–1646* (London, 1954), p. 192.

[2] Francisco Machado and Bernardo Pereira attempted to go by Zeila, Lobo himself and a Spaniard, Juan de Velasco, by Malindi. This second route had been tried, unsuccessfully, in the reverse direction by António Fernandez and the Ethiopian envoy Fequra Egzi'e in 1613–14. See Almeida's account of their journey in *SRE*, pp. 143–171, and the same, pp. 191–202 for his account of Machado and Pereira.

[3] A letter of Velasco, printed in C. Beccari, *Rerum aethiopicarum scriptores occidentales inediti* (Roma, 1905–17), vol. xii, p. 77, says that Lobo collected information from merchants who frequented the Somali coast, in particular Estevão Leitão. Le Grand adds: 'We asked advice from everyone and listened to all who were willing to offer it...The country was watered by several navigable rivers;...in short, they made a frightful desert into a fertile and delightful country...We went to seek our superiors and begged them to allow us to try the Melinde route'.

to the state of Caxem in Arabia Felix.[1] He received them very kindly and, preparing a boat for them, sent them to Zeila as they had requested, in which port the *Xeque*[2] of the port (*Xeque* is the name given to the captain or lord) received them with words and demonstrations of feigned benevolence, immediately sending a message to his king, who was inland, informing him of the prize that had come into his hands. The king ordered the Fathers to go to his court, called Auxa,[3] where he received them with good words and soon with evil deeds. He ordered them stripped of the poor possessions they carried with them and put them in a harsh prison on the pretext that the Emperor of Ethiopia had caused an envoy of his to be killed while the alleged victim was travelling with the Emperor's court. The truth of the matter, however, was that the envoy died a natural death and the king's cruel treatment of the Fathers was really motivated by greed and an inherited hatred of Catholics, particularly the Portuguese. The Emperor of Ethiopia was fully aware of these predispositions on the part of the King of Zeila, so that, upon receiving the news from India that the Fathers had separated into two groups and that two Fathers were going by way of Zeila, he immediately gave them up for dead. He made every effort to save them, however, sending many messages and presents and promising the tyrant great rewards if he would send him the Fathers. Yet all these efforts were to no avail; for the Muslim's hatred for the Catholic faith and for the very name 'Portuguese' was too deeply ingrained in him. The soldiers of Dom Christovão da Gama had killed his great-great-great-grandfather, dispossessing him of the whole empire of Ethiopia which the latter had usurped for fourteen years.[4] The motivation provided by this ancient inherited enmity was reinforced by the machinations of a cruel rebellious Ethiopian heretic who nullified the Emperor's efforts by advising the Muslim king to kill those Fathers in order to prevent them from going to Ethiopia to preach the Roman faith. The Ethiopian heretic ensured the success of

[1] Caxem is Qishn on the south coast of Arabia. The Mahri Sultan of Qishn was often at war with the Kathiri Sultan of Shihr and was relatively friendly to the Portuguese. Socotra had been subject to him since about 1480, except for the Portuguese occupation of the fort, 1507–1511. Le Grand says the ruler of Qishn was lord of a part of Socotra. The princelings of south Arabia tended to conciliate the Portuguese whenever they felt their independence threatened by the Ottomans. The name is misprinted Qish in the Portuguese edition, p. 219, n. 3.

[2] Arabic *shaikh*.

[3] Aussa, an oasis in the Danakil desert. It had been the capital of a Muslim state since 1577, J. S. Trimingham, *Islam in Ethiopia* (London, 1952), p. 97.

[4] The rulers of Aussa at this time belonged to the family of Ahmad Grañ, who had been killed by one of the Portuguese contingent at the battle of Wayna Dega in 1542.

his scheme by promising the Muslim great wealth for his trouble, which in itself was reason enough for him to kill them. The result of all these influences was that he ordered their heads cut off one night, and he would have done the same to us if we had been with them.

After these good Fathers had left, we discussed our route and journey into unknown territory, and because those who were experienced in the region advised us concerning what we should take with us to gain the good will of those savages with whom we necessarily had to deal, we brought some pieces of painted cotton, which also served as money where necessary, red caps, small glass beads and other trinkets of this kind. And we fitted ourselves out with clothing in the Moorish style, turban, tunic[1] over the underclothing, but shirts made with wide sleeves in the Arabian style, like those of the habit worn by the Bernadine monks, a sash instead of a belt, tight breeches in the Moorish style down to the ankle-bone, which could serve as a Devil's costume for a carnival; shoes, also in the Moorish style, pointed and turned up at the end. With these provisions and equipment, the other Father and I set out for whatever might befall us, exposed to whatever God had in store for us, heading for the coast of Melinde. And truly there were few among those who said farewell to us who could promise us long lives. For the undertaking was extremely risky, never before attempted or imagined; the lands were unknown, and the people were savage and had never before dealt with Portuguese people; the road, when such existed, could not fail to have an infinite number of mishaps in store for two foreigners with white skin penetrating the interior of Africa where everyone's skin was the colour of coal; and the culture, food, mountain ranges, wildernesses and deserts were the last of our concerns. The problem of language was particularly troublesome, especially since, as we learned afterward, there is a different language in almost every district. In view of the barbarity, ferocity, greed and faithlessness of the people, with whom we afterward became acquainted, it was certain that they would not let us go for many days' journey or live many days. And even though all or at least the most important of these difficulties were present in our minds, the desire to discover the way, because of the great benefits that could be hoped for, made these and greater difficulties, if there should be such, easier to bear. We took with us, for the language in which he could serve as an interpreter, an Abyssinian, a good and faithful young man, with whom, on the twenty-sixth of January, 1624, we set sail from the harbour at Goa,

---

[1] *cabaia*, a tunic or long surcoat. See *H.J.*, 'cabaya'.

setting out to cross the Indian Ocean that lies between the coast of India and the coast of Africa called Melinde. The galiot was Portuguese and it was bound for Mosambique. By order of the Viceroy it was to let us off at Pati,[1] a Muslim city on the coast of Melinde where there is a factory of Portuguese under the authority of the Captain of Monbaça. The voyage was an extremely fortunate one, for in eleven days we saw the so-called Land of the Desert which stretches from the Cape of Goardafui to Magadoxo,[2] without having any of the usual rough seas and stormy weather, which was not a small gift from God. In the afternoon of our fourth day of sailing along that coast, we came so close to shore that we could speak with the barbarous, savage natives who had come to see us. However, since they understood neither our signals nor what we said, we were unable to learn from them where we were or how far Pati was from there, Pati being the place we were seeking. Unfortunately we found ourselves among shoals and rocks so visible that if the ship had not been small we could not have got out of there, and if the wind had freshened we would have been in great danger. The galiot's crew were unacquainted with the port so that it was necessary to go in, the fact being that we were right upon it and almost in the mouth of the harbour.

At sunset we reached land, and seeing a mouth and inlet that the sea made in it, we took in our sail and launched our small boat with two men in it. They made for the mouth in the hope of discovering some news of the port of Pati which we were seeking. They entered by one mouth and came out afterward by another which we did not see, with only the news that they had found in there a large bay, had seen no boat there, nor any trace of people on land. And, as we afterward learned, there were few people in this locality beyond some wretched black people of the Muslim faith who lived inland. And because darkness was upon us as the small boat returned, we had to sleep overnight there at anchor, and, thanks be to God, we anchored at the only spot in the vicinity where the galiot could float. For in the dead of the night we saw that water was lacking in that whole vicinity as the tide went out and left mud and pebbles where formerly there had been a spacious sea. Since we were worried that the galiot might also be left stranded, the sailors jumped to the ground and surrounded the ship with many struts,[3] which are supports kept in readiness for

[1] Pate, a city on an island of the same name in the Lamu archipelago off the coast of Kenya some hundred miles north of Malindi.

[2] Mogadishu in Somalia.

[3] *gadamos.*

such contingencies. Our situation was better than expected because the spot occupied by the galiot was a depression as long and wide as the boat itself in which there was always enough water to keep the galiot afloat, all of the rest of the surrounding area being dry until, as the tide came in again, we found ourselves once again on a beautiful sea. Since the galiot had to stop at Mosambique and we did not know the location of Pati harbour, which we were seeking, even though we were actually anchored in it, seeing the anguish of the people aboard and the little hope we had of finding what we wanted, we resolved to continue the voyage as far as Mosanbique with the intention of returning during the same monsoon in another boat but sailing slowly in the same vicinity and having complete information about what we were looking for. But as it was morning already, before setting sail, we performed the last task which was to fire a cannon, a signal which ships give so that pilots will come to them from land, for if by chance that was the port of Pati we were seeking, pilots would come to find us. This task accomplished and seeing for some space of time that people were not coming, we set sail, still, however, keeping a close watch on the shore, whence we saw an *almadia* coming toward us, and as we awaited it with our sails hauled close to the wind, it soon reached us. The pilots informed us that that was the port of Pati we were seeking and that they were pilots who were coming to bring us into the harbour, which they did in a few hours. The galiot anchored, however, at a league's distance from shore in order to remain in sufficient depth of water because of the great distance the tide goes out there and the dryness of all that space when the tide is out.

As there was little time left that day, we had to disembark so that those on the galiot could continue their voyage and course, as they did on the following day, leaving us on land in the company of an Augustinian monk, who was serving as vicar on that coast. Living at a good two leagues' distance from there, as soon as he learned of our arrival he came to meet us and took us to his house with much charity and benevolence since he was overflowing with these and other virtuous qualities, for which he was revered as a saint even by the Muslims and pagans. He had his house and church, where he was alone, in the city of Ampasa[1] on the same island of Pati, which island being four leagues in length had as many towns and as many kings, one for each town. The first one is the town of Lamo,[2] more toward

[1] Faza, See G. S. P. Freeman-Grenville, *The East African Coast* (Oxford, 1962), p. 203, map 4.
[2] The town of Lamu is on the island of the same name, not on Pate; it is further to the south.

Mosambique; the second is the town of Pati, the largest and the one with the largest population and trade with a factory of Portuguese in it; the third is the town of Cio,[1] not much to speak of, but abounding in civet;[2] the fourth town is Ampaza, small but pretty, with its port and trade, with more Portuguese in it, although not more than eight, but more highly esteemed, containing the church and residence of the friar, so that the Christians and Portuguese who made their living by trading along that coast often came there.[3]

The monk had us carried in some *machilas*;[4] each one of us was in one on the shoulders of two men called *amal*,[5] which means sedan-chair-man or porter. After they tied the pointed ends of the afore-mentioned netting on a stout pole, we stretched out on it like corpses. Each one of the men then took an end of the pole on his shoulder and walked very rapidly. But it is not possible for a person to travel in this way unless he is lying down well settled as if for sleeping.[6] As it was our intention to discover the way, so much desired, to that empire of Ethiopia we tried immediately to obtain information. We learned that in Jubo,[7] forty leagues beyond Ampasa there was a river of the same name and that there had arrived at that place an army of savages called Gallas, a people well known in Ethiopia.[8] With the idea that they were now more civilized because of the time they had dealt with our people since arriving there, we thought that through them we might be able to discover what we wanted to find, and it was also possible that they might take us and serve as guides on the journey. These savages, as we learned afterwards were from the interior of that vast hinterland, had left their lands which they called Manoagem,

---

[1] Siu.

[2] *algalia.*

[3] The Franciscan Gaspar de S. Bernadino visited Ampaza in 1606 and found an Augustinian, who was the only priest in the town, Freeman-Grenville, 1962, p. 161.

[4] A hammock of netting used as a palanquin, H.J., 'Muncheel, manjeel'.

[5] Arabic *ḥammāl*, porter.

[6] Le Grand adds: 'Though the hammock was soft and comfortable, we should have preferred to go on foot, so as to be able to study the places through which we passed, and enquire whether what we had been told about the country of Melinde was true, whether we should find navigable rivers forty leagues from Ampasa, whether one could negotiate with the Gallas, and whether they would supply us with guides'.

[7] The country traversed by the Juba river.

[8] A Hamitic people who appear to have originated in northern Somaliland. By the twelfth century a series of migrations began in which they were pressed S and SW by the Somali. By the early seventeenth century they occupied much of the territory between the Webi Shabelle and the Juba. Many of them had invaded Ethiopia in the previous century and the Somali eventually separated those in Jubaland from those further north. The former either crossed the Tana river into Kenya or were subjugated and mostly assimilated by the Somali, I. M. Lewis, *The Modern History of Somaliland* (London, 1965), pp. 22, 23, 28.

the tribe being called Grazede,[1] for all the people of these lands are divided up into tribes or families with distinctive features by which they are known, as I shall relate further on in my narrative. They had left their homeland to settle new lands and they had come destroying and consuming everything they found until they reached the sea, doing the same all along that coast, terrorizing and intimidating all the people there.

With our minds made up that we should go and deal with these people, it appeared to us that it was not a good thing to risk both of us but that it would be better for one to remain behind to remedy any misfortune that might occur and so that the negotiation could be carried out with greater dissimulation. Of the two of us, it fell to my companion to stay in the company of the monk while I left with a Portuguese who was well informed concerning the region where I was going. We took also an Abyssinian who served us. We had decided that if we found the way we would send a message to the Father and that if we did not find it we would return or, in the case of our dying at the hands of the savages, we would not be risking both members of our expedition as well as the discovery and the information about what we had discovered. I left the little city of Ampaza in the garb of a religious. I carried with me, however, two other sets of clothing. One was that of a Portuguese layman, in order to disguise my person and profession, for that whole coast was frequented by Portuguese soldiers and merchants. The other was an Arabian costume to serve me when I found myself with people for whom this would be

---

[1] The complicated movements of peoples in the Horn of Africa in the sixteenth and seventeenth centuries are inadequately documented. It seems that some Galla groups moved along the coast, being displaced, absorbed or subdued in their turn by the Somali. The Grazede are now the Gardyed who have moved into the Tana region of Kenya, Cerulli, 1959–64, I, 59. Velasco's letter calls them Garzedas and Gargedas. For Manoagem he has Manoaya. This may be connected with Munjiya near Merka, once the scene of conflict between the Galla and Somali, Cerulli, I, 96, and with 'Rēr Mānyo', the name given to small groups of seafaring people found in certain towns along the coast, including Mogadishu and Brava. Velasco, however, locates it near Cape Delgado 'or lower' (abaixo). This is ambiguous. It might mean either further down the African coast, i.e. further south, or in a lower latitude, i.e. nearer the Equator and so further north. The Portuguese may have confused it with the name of one of the states or regions of the interior, such as Manyisa in the hinterland of Maputo (Lourenço Marques), on which see Boxer, 1959, 72, n. 4. Velasco says the king of Manoaya sent his son Beiramo with 3000 Gallas to fight the Emperor. Beiramo probably represents Birmaji, the name of one of the age-sets, luba. The Galla certainly did not come from the interior of Moçambique or Tanzania. Velasco may have confused them with the WaZimba, who erupted from the lower Zambesi and moved north devastating the settlements and massacring the inhabitants until they were stopped at Malindi in 1593. They practised cannibalism and this may explain Lobo's mistaken statement in the following note.

[2] Le Grand states that they were cannibals.

appropriate and whose language I was learning. I had to make the journey or voyage partly by sea and partly by land. The provisions were few – only a few loaves of bread and some flour, a few days' supply, the land of Jubo where I was going being at a distance of forty leagues. The boat I took was a small boat with a crew of eight Muslims. It is called a *pangaio*. It has no nails whatever but the boards are sewn together with a thin rope as if with a needle; the sail is made of reed matting; and the ropes are weaker than ropes made of esparto grass. And since these boats are so weak, the load that this one carried was correspondingly small, consisting only of ourselves, millet for the sailors,[1] and our poor victuals with a small basket containing the necessary equipment for saying Mass.

The people along that coast are of various tribes, each of which has its king. The first king we met was that of the *Abunhes*,[2] a great thief rowing stark naked in a small boat with no other indications of royalty than a very old straw hat on his head and the courtesy of my companion who called him 'Highness', a shameful use of the term for such a person. Nor did he place much value on it, paying much more attention to a piece of fried fish and a piece of bread that we gave him and which he ate immediately, and which he owed to his arriving at a time when we were having dinner. The journey took more days than we thought and was therefore difficult not only because of the lack of victuals but much more because of the inconvenience of every kind in the lands through which we were travelling. We slept on the ground, and when we had sand on which to throw our bodies when very tired it was no small treat. The open night air served us as a blanket, some stone or bundle of grass was our usual pillow. The worst thing was that our sleep was sometimes disturbed by our being soaked by the rain that visited us at night. And since the land was populated only by poor, rustic Muslims, we seldom chose their miserable villages for shelter, preferring the open country. Within a distance of little more than four leagues, we found ten or twelve kings,[3] each one having little more jurisdiction than the place occupied by his small village, which was at the same time court, kingdom, and all its extent. This locality and its people did not permit me to continue wearing the costume of a

[1] Le Grand says they took a little honey, 'miel', for the sailors. Is this a mistranslation of *milho*, 'millet'?

[2] Le Grand, Abagnes. Bon is the name given to the low castes living among the Hawiyya Somali. It was originally the name of a hunting people of whom there are remnants on the lower Juba and along the Kenya frontier, Enrico Cerulli, *Somalia. Scritti vari editi ed inediti*, II (Roma, 1959), pp. 283–4.

[3] Le Grand: 'I counted up to ten or twelve of them in less than four leagues'.

religious, so that, for greater deception for the purpose of reaching the goal for which I was striving, it was necessary for me to change into the secular costume loaned to me by a Portuguese merchant and soldier who went with me. Part of the way we had to go on land; for, since we were going along the coast and the boat was very small, two or three extra persons getting into it made a fatal load which it could not carry without obvious danger when crossing places where it had to go out to the open sea to go around some points of land, where the waves were large. Because of this we left the boat and travelled on land, walking sometimes through undergrowth and rugged lands, sometimes along the beach; and as the tide left it covered with slime and various shells and shellfish, barefooted as we were because of the water and slime, our feet were treated very roughly indeed. And as we had to make several days' journey in this manner – longer than the harshness of the terrain warranted – the suffering was continually great, which also increased because of our lack of provisions, and there was no place where we could buy any to our taste. At times we would rise in the morning and travel without having anything for dinner or any sure hope of our finding anything. The same also happened for supper when God supplied something for our dinner, both meals often being extremely meagre, as I experienced and suffered when I had none. God Our Lord came to our rescue at times with some boat of Muslims, wretched fishermen carrying fish, from whom we bought some in exchange for tobacco. We boiled it in water and ate it without any other spices or seasoning, not even bread, than the healthy appetite we had and the necessity in which we found ourselves. If the journey had lasted more days, the lack of preparation of the food would have bothered me more, but even so it bothered me God knows how much. And it is certain that, as I was inexperienced in such voyages, although I was better able to endure the hardship, I was never able to accustom myself to it or to drive from my mind how much it had pained me, at least for a time following the first few days, which is when the hardship is felt the most. To make things even worse, water was not plentiful nor of very good quality, but rather in places was very bad. Necessity, however, made it seem excellent, and, although we usually had enough, we sometimes felt the lack of it, so that it was necessary for us to travel carrying water on our backs in a sort of leather bottle called *chiquel*,[1] both to have available in places where there was no water and to alleviate the weariness and dryness caused by the travelling and

---

[1] A leather water-bottle for carrying at the saddle-bow.

by the sun along that coast. On the last day of our journey, which came to an end almost at sunset, as we had travelled all that day along a long, scorching, unprotected stretch of sand, we necessarily suffered, especially because of not being used to it. I carried my *chiquel* with as much as a *canada*[1] of water with which I kept quenching my thirst and combating the heat, both of which were extreme, by drinking from time to time until there was only a very small quantity of water left. The last of it, which I was saving in case of extreme need, since I could no longer stand the thirst, I drank; and with the knowledge that I did not have any other water nor any place to get any since the nearest town was more than two leagues away, I confess that I saw myself, with this thought and with the thirst and the oppressive heat, in a state which would have been certain to bring me severe misfortune if I had not stirred myself to exert all the strength of which my constitution was capable and had not been buoyed by the hope of arriving soon; and because there was much good water in the town, with these hopes I was able to overcome the hardship which was to come to an end when we finally arrived, just before sunset, in the town of Jubo.[2]

This land is just below the Equator. It is populated by Muslims and has its own king whose authority extends over little more territory than the one I left behind. They are vassals of the King of Portugal, and the Portuguese frequent that coast and land because of the trade and profit they find there, obtaining from their trading much ivory, an abundance of which is got from the many elephants found there, much amber of three types: a black type called *arevessado* [vomited], which is the type vomited by the whale, a gray type called *ameixueira*, and a white type called *gris*.[3] These last two types are of the kind which grows at the bottom of the sea, where the whale eats them. The black type is of the least value, the grey better, and the white most highly esteemed. The land also yields some gold, Maldive coconuts which grow on palm trees on the bottom of the sea and are so highly esteemed and of such medicinal value that they are worth their weight in silver.[4]

[1] Approximately 3 pints.
[2] Presumably the modern Jumbo, or a site nearby.
[3] Lobo refers to ambergris, not amber. The same opinion concerning the relative merits of ambergris of different colours is expressed by Garcia da Orta, the second of whose *Coloquios dos simples e drogas he cousas medicinais da India* is devoted to this substance. Among theories of its origin were that it was vomited or excreted by whales, that it issued from the bottom of the sea, and that it was produced there in the way that fungi grow on rocks and trees.
[4] The Double Coconut, *Lodoicea seychellarum*, the product of a palm growing only in the Seychelles, cast up on the shores of the Indian Ocean, especially of the Maldives. 'Great Virtues as medicine and antidote were supposed to reside in these fruits and extravagant

These coconuts, like amber, are thrown up by the sea onto the beach, and, rightly or wrongly, they belong to the king of that land or beach where they are deposited. The subjects however take most of them and the best ones. Also good slaves are bought in this land, especially some called *maracatos*, which are a certain tribe of Muslims, who live inland at a distance of one or two days' journey from the sea, extending many tens of leagues forming a belt along that whole coast behind the Muslims who live closer to the water.[1] The *maracatos* are people of good facial features, not very black in colour, with handsome bodies, and the men are active and tall. They oblige the women not to allow themselves to be deprived of their virginity until they are married, because it is a great affront among them to have in their tribe an unmarried woman who has lost her virginity. In order to avoid the danger of this, they sew them up when they are born in such a way as to make any defloration impossible. When a woman is to go to the house of her husband she first submits to an operation by knife.[2] Although they take such great precautions in this particular, the custom not being too barbarous or typical of savage people, they still deserve some shadow of praise for the obscure veneration they pay to the noble, sacred virtue of chastity. They are, in other respects, as perfidious, treacherous, and malicious as the snakes with which this coast is so infested, as it is with all kinds of wild, ferocious animals which the whole of Africa has in very great abundance, such as: elephants, lions, tigers, monkeys (so large and bearded that they resemble a large bullock), deer, gazelles, and a thousand other breeds of these animals, which are countless.[3] From the elephants they obtain much ivory from the two large tusks that each one has, like two beams. Only the males grow them, and in order to obtain them they kill them; for the *aleans*,[4] which are the females, do not have any of these large tusks which are valued so highly. Every year there depart from this coast a great number of

prices were paid for them...The old belief was that the fruit was produced on a palm growing below the sea', *HJ*, 'Coco-de-mer, or double coconut'.

[1] Perhaps the Marrehaan, a Somali tribe of the Sadda group of the Daarood, occupying, though not now continuously, a belt of inland territory extending from the north of the former Italian protectorate into Jubaland. The form of the name in Portuguese may have been influenced by the place-name Merka, near Mogadishu, which is at least as old as the twelfth century.

[2] Clitoridectomy and infibulation are generally practised by the Galla and Somali.

[3] There are no tigers in Africa; Lobo probably refers to leopards. The error was common among the Portuguese who seem to have spoken of 'lions and tigers' rather as we speak of 'dogs and cats' or 'rats and mice', and to have assumed that they were always found together, *SRE*, p. 51, n. 3. Several species of monkeys have beards, though none of them are as large as bullocks. There are no deer in Africa.

[4] Elephants without tusks, whether male or female.

ships, laden especially with this merchandise which the merchants buy from the natives in exchange for pieces of cloth like coarse sheets of sack-cloth, which serves them for their clothing and bedding; and there are tusks which, because of their weight and size, are worth from forty to seventy of these pieces of cloth. They are called *gadubos*.[1] Of the snakes there is a variety the thickness of a man and which proportionately must be more than fifteen palms long. These have in their heads a stone like a bezoar-stone the size of an egg, which has great powers, especially against poison. Others have such a stone in their stomachs, but these snakes are smaller, and the stones are the size of a nut.[2]

[1] I am indebted to Sheikh Yahya Omar of the School of Oriental and African Studies for detecting in this word Swahili *jidovu*, a big elephant.

[2] It was widely believed that a stone which was an antidote to snake-bite was obtainable from the head or stomach of snakes. See quotations from Tavernier and Tenreiro respectively, *HJ*, 'Snake-stone' and 'Bezoar'.

CHAPTER 7

[Information is presented concerning the Gallas and how we returned to Diu]

I stayed in this village and locality for some time for the purpose of discovering the way, especially through the pagan Gallas, two thousand of whom were living at a place three leagues inland. They had taken up residence there because of the suitability of the land to their manner of living, particularly to their raising various tame and wild animals which they breed and on which they live. This pagan tribe came from very remote lands and, although small in number, destroyed and subdued everything in their path. They were able to do this more because of the fear they inspired in others with their cruelty and ferocity rather than because of the quantity of people they brought with them. With them comes the king, whom they elect every eight years called *Luba*.[1] They bring their women with them, and they pay little attention to a neighbour or friend occupying their homes; nor do they pay attention to children if any are born to them while they are soldiers; for they order them to be thrown into the forest to the wild beasts, nor can anyone rescue them without undergoing the death penalty. However, when they lay down their arms and make peace, they recognize the children they produce after this and rear them as such. All of them dress in leather, the men as well as the women. They do not have a distaste for half-cooked beef, so that they do not use much firewood in preparing it. With the blood they anoint their faces, chests and arms, making certain signs. With the intestines that are left over they make small ribbons which they wear around their necks in the form of chains as a thing of elegance. They give them to their women after they are tired of wearing them, by which time they are not very fragrant.

Some of these people came to the town where I was, and they were amazed that white people were there. Many of them ran up to see me, surrounding me in great numbers; and, sitting on the ground, they

---

[1] Not the title of a ruler but the name given to the age-set in power at any time, *SRE*, pp. 205–12. Almeida made the same mistake as Lobo, *op. cit.*, p. 138.

looked me over and over again as if they were looking at something monstrous because of the white skin – at all of which I laughed and wondered at their brutishness. They were in doubt, however, as to whether my body was as white as my face and hands, and in order to inform themselves on this point, they uncovered my chest, took off my shoes, and stripped my arms. When they saw the truth of the matter, some expressed wonderment with great intemperance, others showed that the white colour nauseated them. White skin, to their misfortune or mine, became scorned to an extreme degree in that land, which was not very surprising in a land where black alone reigned supreme. And although our colour made such a bad impression upon them, this did not prevent them from asking me for a strip of my handkerchief for them to put around their heads as an adornment, and thus, when by chance I would take one out of my pocket to use, I had to tear it into strips because of the many people who asked for them and I gave them to them to lessen a little the gloomy state of mind caused in me by the people and the place where I was, seeing them very handsome and bizarre with their white strips. And they showed that they would value them more highly if they were red, as they always asked for them whenever they saw clothing of that colour. As they are very importunate, asking for everything they see that pleases them, there were certainly occasions on which we were annoyed. And because one of the three of us Portuguese who were there tried to kill one of them, or at least to give him a good thrashing, because of a certain insult that he did, stemming from his natural brutishness and fierceness, the savage was so abused that he went immediately to seek out his people to come attack us and kill us; for, taking us by surprise they could do us some injury. They came in great numbers in a formed squadron with their javelins[1] and bucklers,[2] making great shouts and threatening noises[3] to strike fear into our hearts and show themselves at their fiercest. And since there were five of us Portuguese and two slaves in the village and since this armed band was coming toward us all, we had to take refuge in our house until we could see to what lengths the fury of the savages would carry them. They climbed a small hill which dominated the

---

[1] *zargunchos*. Almeida describes them as 'a kind of half-length lances that have thin hafts and irons that are sometimes narrow, like those of our lances, sometimes broad like halberds but thin so that they can be thrown vigorously against some and manoeuvred against others', *SRE*, p. 76.

[2] *adargas*, small shields of hide. In the Horn of Africa they were round, with a diameter of something less than a yard, and sometimes had bosses so that they could be used as offensive weapons.

[3] *argazaras*, i.e. *algazarra*, the Moorish war cry.

house and was very close to it. From there with greater noise and shouting, with grimaces and assaults, they expressed the violence of their anger toward us and the harm they intended to do to us.

And although, for the moment and in the place we had, we could suffer little or no harm from them, we were concerned lest they lay siege to us and lest thirst and hunger might force us to leave the house and fall into their hands. It is very true that we had the sea nearby, at a stone's throw from our door, and if the situation were very bad we could get into our boat, although at that particular time we did not have a boat available. In the meantime, while we were discussing various ways of assuring our safety, the festivities, shouting, and threatening noises of the savages were becoming more intense. When they want to do battle, as the time approaches to attack they become all the more feverish in dancing and singing all together with tremendous noise and confusion. With this activity they gradually enter a state of utter fury, and they attack with greater violence and wild abandon. The savages were carrying on in this way, threatening us intermittently with their spears, while we were on the flat roof of our houses observing their ferocity and savagery. And in order to put a damper on the fervour of the fury, we sent for three or four matchlocks that were in the house below,[1] and, with each of them well charged with two balls, we fired all of them at once at the savages, aiming a little high so that the balls would frighten but not wound them. And as the balls travelled furiously through the air and made a loud whistling sound near their heads, along with the thundering noise of the matchlocks, such was their fear that they all suddenly fell to the ground as though dead and remained there for a short time, terrified and very frightened by the whistling of the balls. A short while later some of them raised their heads to see, in the direction from which they had heard the whistling, if by chance it had already passed. And after ascertaining that the whistling had ceased and that there was no longer anything there, they gradually got up, meek and mild and in great fear and trembling, for they still did not consider themselves safe, giving us occasion for great laughter and rejoicing. Their behaviour was especially comical, not only because of their immediate abandonment of the celebration but also because of the rapid change from fierceness and fury to humility and mildness. Little by little they approached our house, without any weapons at all, giving signs that they were coming

---

[1] Le Grand says there were five Portuguese and they had four matchlocks.

with a changed attitude, so that we felt safe and entered into friendly relations with them, which lasted as long as we were there.

After we had made peace and as they were mingling with us in a friendly way, we broached the purpose of our journey, which was to discover a path into Ethiopia. In this I had to speak with their chief or leader, Luba, whom they had two leagues from there in a sort of encampment they had formed. The houses were straw huts, the king's being larger than the others. In this place they had all of their goods and chattels: women, cows, all amounting to the same, cattle and everything else they owned, which was very little. To give audience to those who come to do business with their king, they observe a certain ceremony which is as barbarous as those who invented and use it. The king is in his hut surrounded by as much pomp as such a court and such persons can have, sitting on the ground with the rest of the household around him, his courtiers sitting with their backs to the wall and each of them holding in his hands a long sturdy pole, or a very hard wooden cudgel, depending upon the social standing of the guest they are expecting. If he is a nobleman they have the poles. If he is a common person they have the small cudgels or clubs a *covado* long and with heads the size of two fists. When he has entered the house the poor visitor is immediately attacked and beaten vigorously with the poles, or they have at him with goodly blows so that as long as they are striking him, which is very purposefully and with very frequent blows wherever each one is able to reach, they do not strike the ground until the emissary reaches the door and they even pursue him further. And after he has waited for a while outside the door and the courtiers have returned to their places as peacefully as if nothing had happened, they call the negotiator and receive him with every kindness. The visitor enters, more or less offended in accordance with the number of cudgel-blows he has received but he is now sure of not receiving any more blows and he dispatches his business with the haste that such people and such a reception deserve. They did not do this to me because they say that the Portuguese are sea gods and so they have great respect for them. I certainly inquired and expressed surprise concerning that barbarous custom, and their answer was consistent with the brutality of their lives, for they told me that they did it so that the visitors would enter with humility to speak with the Gallas, the latter considering themselves as the people most worthy of the highest respect of any people in the world, since they consider others, except for the Portuguese, as of no value.[1] And truly all the other savages who were observed and dealt with in the bush and mountains of their lands deserve to be thought of in that way.

Because of the prospect of entrusting myself to them and placing myself in their hands and in company with them for such a long journey through unknown territory, I was constantly observing the fierceness of the people and the brutality in which they live. I was trustful, however, that what I was doing was in the service of God, that He would set things right and that no harm could come to us without permission of His Divine Majesty, in whose protection we trust in all things. I was further fortified by the thought that great things are not done without risks and dangers, that we knew we were exposing ourselves to them, and that, prior to embarking on the expedition, we had envisaged all imaginable eventualities, including death itself. Because we had undertaken the enterprise with all this in mind, I made up my mind to go ahead with the negotiation, especially since, if we must place trust in human matters, there was among these barbarians a certain ceremony and oath which, when taken, is so inviolable among them that there is no case in which they would break it. And I determined that I would have them take this ceremonial oath when we should conclude our negotiations concerning the journey. The oath is as follows: They bring a ewe before them and anointing it all over with much butter, the principal people or, as it were, heads of the families put their hands on the head of the ewe, swear on it and promise what is asked of them. They consider that this ceremony binds them to absolute faithfulness, which they observe without fail; for they say that the ewe represents the mother of each one of those who take the oath and that the butter represents the love that the mother has for her children and that it is thus unlawful to break any oath which has been taken on the head of one's mother, that barbarous and ridiculous representation being accorded the same respect as the real and natural mother of each one of them.

Supported by this consideration, I discussed the matter of the route. After many requests we were unable to conclude the business to our satisfaction; for the barbarians confessed frankly that, although they knew about the lands and people we were asking for and knew the way, though it was a very long journey, it was not possible for them to take me by that route. They explained that, although we could travel

---

[1] Le Grand says that they call the Portuguese gods of the sea.

safely in their country to the boundaries of their lands, about which I was certainly in no doubt, from there forward they were unable to ensure the safety of our persons because of the many tribes of people who inhabited that hinterland between the sea-coast and the land of the Abyssinians. Those tribes were continuously at war with one another and each one was scarcely secure in its own land and thus could not provide security for anyone who took a step outside of it. They count six races of these barbarous Gallas who inhabited those provinces we were to traverse. Nine tribes of pagans and Muslims are known in those lands. Each of these tribes extends over an area which, in its longest dimension follows the coastline, and they form successive belts from the coast inward. The first ones are the Muslims on the coast, people who are not so barbarous because of the dealings and contact they have with the Portuguese who frequent them in the business of trading. These are bounded inland by a tribe of inferior people called *Maracatos*, whom I have already mentioned. After these are those called *Machida*, also Muslim and powerful, whose king descends from the Abyssinian emperors and has since been at war with them for many years. Travelling from those further into the hinterland, one finds six tribes or bands of Gallas, pagan, ferocious and barbarous, who gain their livelihood by raising sheep and cattle and by thievery. The first are called *Bretoma*; the second, *Arniza*; the third, *Aibores*; the fourth *Dadas*; the fifth, *Cajutos*; and the sixth, *Adia*.[1] Beyond these there follow various tribes of Abyssinians more or less civilized according to the lands they inhabit and the degree to which they render obedience to the Abyssinian emperor.

We would have had to deal with these barbarians, passing through their lands and experiencing their barbarity and ferocity if we wanted to discover the way to the lands which were our destination. But it

[1] Le Grand has the variants Bresonas, Aruizas, Arbores, Aibores or Asbores, Dades, Cajases or Caicitas, and Adias. Velasco's letter in Beccari, 1903–27, XII, p. 76, has Bretamos, aroisas, iberes, daoas, cagutus and adias. The Macha are a grouping of Galla tribes now occupying territory east of the Didessa and south of the Blue Nile. Bretoma represents Baraituma; according to the sixteenth century Ethiopian writer on the Galla, Bahrey, this was one of the two original divisions of the race. The name applies loosely to the eastern, agricultural, Galla. Aruiza is Arusi, a Galla grouping now on the upper reaches of the Webi Shabelle. Aibores seems to be Boran, the second great division of the Galla, a name now loosely given to the western, pastoral, tribes and to many of those in southern Ethiopia. The next two names may be so corrupt as to make identification merely tentative. There is a Galla tribe called Dadalute north-west of Hadya; there is an Arusi tribe called Dawadin. I can make no suggestion about Cajutos. Adia is not the name of a Galla tribe but of a Sidama people and of a Muslim state that was formed between Lake Zway and the Omo river. The Macha, Arusi and Hadya are shown on the map in G. W. B. Huntingford, *The Galla of Ethiopia* (London, 1955), opposite p. 98.

is absolutely certain that such a route is impossible, and even if we were fortunate enough to escape with our lives from the first Gallas, we could not reach our destination. After we were finally in Ethiopia in following years, our certainty of the impossibility of that route was amply corroborated by knowledge of the difficulties of these roads, the vastness of the lands, the multitude and variety of the barbarians who inhabit them, so that traversing them was to do something of which human strength and skill were incapable.

With the information that I should not be able to discover a way to Ethiopia by that route, and having made other efforts towards the same end, I had to return to the place where I had left my companion; and I was extremely fortunate to be able to extricate myself so safely from the hands of such people and not to have occasion to suffer from their brutality and ferocity. The ferocity of the land however was not so kind to me, for it burdened me with a very high fever, which oppressed and weakened me very much indeed. There were no doctors or medicines nor was there anyone to whom I could turn for aid other than an Abyssinian Black and three Portuguese who were there. In addition to this, I counted only on a rigid diet or abstinence from food, patience, and trust in God Our Lord. However I did not fail to ask if there were someone in that village who did blood-letting; and I didn't doubt that there were many who would be glad to draw blood especially from Christians, since all the inhabitants were crafty Muslims. However, of barbers there were none, so I found myself in the necessity of learning how to bleed myself when I should have need of it, which later was of use to me. However, on this occasion, they recommended to me a person in the village who, they said, could perform this function. I resolved to put myself in his hands, whatever he might be, and sent for him. The functionary came into the house where I was lying in bed and had with him the following instruments he had brought for the purpose of bleeding me: a half of a brick in his hand, a rusty knife half-eaten away with large gaps in the edge of the blade, and three points of horns, each one half a palm in length. The Muslim was old, crippled, poor and in tatters, apparently blind in one eye. Seeing such an apparition, I asked him what he had come for. He answered that he had come to draw blood from me, and in truth, although the instruments were as I have depicted them and worse, they were sufficient for the purpose. And I certainly supposed that since the knife was so ineffective, he was bringing the brick to hit it with when he wanted to gouge me with it wherever it pleased him; and the horns,

I supposed, were to collect the blood like little blood-letting basins. Resigned to whatever might be the outcome of his great skill and knowledge, I directed him to do what he had come to do. He ordered me to turn on my stomach, and putting in his mouth a small piece of paper that he asked for, uncovering my back he thrust in one of the little horns and sucking vigorously, since it was well sunk into my flesh, on the small end of the horn, as a skilful workman would do, he fixed and fastened it as firmly as if it were a heated cupping-glass and tow, doing the same with the other two horns, so that I remained with those horns as firm and straight in my back as if they had grown there. I was fortunate, however, that others were not there to be shocked at seeing them in me and that I did not have to fear being seen with such fruitage and insignia.

As soon as the cupping-glasses made of horn were performing their function of abstracting blood, my barber began to grind the knife on the brick which he had brought for that purpose, giving it the sharp edge with which the patient supposedly would not be able to feel so much the pain of the knife-thrust. The difficulty in this case was that the gaps and irregularities in the blade were so numerous and so large that he could not eliminate them or close them up, and the knife was still what it was and always would be, a very wretched, rust-eaten saw. He came to me with it, and removing the three small horns from my back, he gave me, in each one of the marks, three blows or drains, which I did not feel because of the great pain they caused me, but heard because of the noise they made when they ripped open or sawed the flesh. He set the horns in place a second time and again sucked to draw the blood, plugging them up afterwards with his tongue and putting in them the small wad of paper he had in his mouth. In this way he drew the blood and applied the horns again a number of times until he was satisfied that he had drawn enough blood, and I was much more satisfied to find myself free from his butchery and free from his hands, in which, to finish the procedure and doctor it all up, he put a little raw suet, and planting it in my back on the wounds that were still pouring out blood, with the palm of his hand he rubbed so hard on the wounds that he not only softened the suet but plugged up the wounds with it, and meanwhile I felt a rough hair-cloth on my back, which was what his rough unskilful hands seemed like, and they could in no way be described as soothing or of any relief whatsoever, even though they were a surgeon's hands; for they hurt me much more than the serious sickness from which I was suffering. This first and only visit was sufficient to rid me entirely of my ailment, whether it was frightened away by such a doctor and such a cure or whether it was not a deadly ailment, which was more likely the case, God's divine providence bringing the remedy where all human remedies were failing, for there was no greater treat on that occasion than some cakes made of flour and rice which could best be eaten only when they were hot.

Relieved of this suffering and with the knowledge that we would not be able to do what we had intended, I set out to return to the Father, my companion, travelling entirely by sea in a few days since I was not in condition to travel on land as I had done when coming. We slept on land, each night, however, as a matter of convenience, with the same bed that we had had before.

On the Saturday before Passion Sunday I again arrived at Ampaza. And as we wished to be as thorough as possible in our efforts to find a new route and thought there was the barest possibility that one still might be found, not by the way I had tried but by another way near Monbaça, my companion left that same week to make new efforts there.[1] He was convinced of the impossibility of such a route by the results of his efforts, and his return was hastened not only by the negative results of his investigations but particularly by the weather which no longer permitted sailing in that direction. Upon his return to the same town where I had remained, we found that there were four of us priests during Holy Week in a church of Christians, with four ships in which there were as many as seventy Christians – Portuguese and people from India. And although the city was a city of Muslims, the fact that so many Christians were there and the devotion of those people encouraged us to celebrate the services of Holy Week with the greatest solemnity of which we were capable; and truly it was the greatest ever seen in that land. There were all the sermons which are customary for those days, confession and communion of all the people there, penitential scourges in the evening with great devotion and fervour, in which a Galician who was present exceeded all the others. He had a good constitution and great strength. Not content with the scourges used by the others, he made some of a bundle of slender cords of hemp and when the signal was given to begin the scourging, he began to scourge himself with so much fervour and weeping that we were obliged to finish earlier than intended. He did

---

[1] Le Grand states that when Lobo reached Faza again his companion had already left for Mombasa.

not stop, however, but continued so vigorously that we went to take the scourges away from him, while he was shouting for us to let him take vengeance upon himself, with so much fervour and piety and so many tears and sobs that certainly showed the unusual inspiration he had. But he had to yield to our entreaties, since we were then to spend the whole night in the church accompanying a holy crucifix which we had erected in the place of the tabernacle since we did not have a sacristy. At dawn on Easter Day we made our procession out of the church with the Holy Eucharist. The procession filled the whole road wherever it went from the time it left the church until it re-entered the church, being well fitted out and all strewn with arches made of palm branches. And because we spent the whole day before Easter in this work, there was time for the report to spread that the Christians were having a festival and for an infinite number of Muslims to gather to see the novelty. And it was a glorious thing for God Our Lord to be worshipped in the midst of his enemies and to pass in triumph in their sight.

In the octave following we prepared for our voyage to India and embarked on Low Sunday. That night, by way of farewell, was one of the most disagreeable and difficult that we had to experience in that locality; for, departing late for the ship which was standing out to sea, we were overtaken by darkness half way to the ship, and losing all sense of the direction in which we should be heading, we had to stop in order to avoid the danger of putting ourselves in a place from which we could not save ourselves. And in addition to this, the ebbing tide made it impossible for us to go any further, leaving us stranded high and dry in the middle of the slime, and with the boat resting on props as we spent the whole night standing without any relief, since the boat had no conveniences whatsoever, not even a place to sit down. The worst part was when dawn came and we thought our troubles were coming to an end. With the arrival of daylight, another more vexing thing happened to us as the boat capsized suddenly and threw us into the mud and slime that the tide had left there, covering us so thoroughly with mud that it very effectively increased our suffering, which, however, came to an end as we boarded the ship and immediately set sail and continued our voyage which ended in 29 days, without any notable or disagreeable occurrences other than the usual ones experienced by those who sail, with seasickness, etc. We came into port at the famous city and fortress of Dio at the end of May.

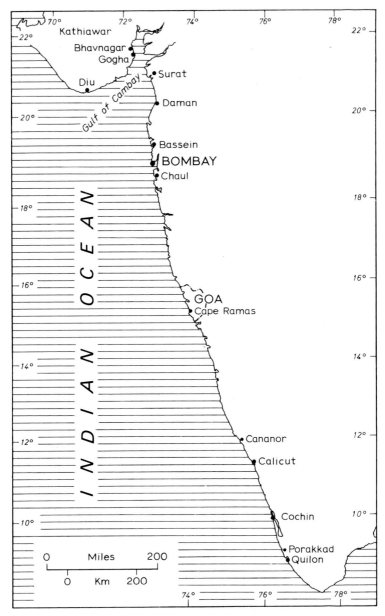

Map I. The west coast of India

CHAPTER 8

[How I departed a second time for Ethiopia in the company of the Patriarch Afonso Mendes]

At this same time the Patriarch of Ethiopia had arrived at Goa. After leaving Portugal he had spent the winter in Mosambique at the time when I was travelling along the coast of Melinde; and, leaving that island in March, he arrived at Goa after a voyage of fifty-four days. And since he was coming there to go to his Church of Ethiopia at the first opportunity, when he learned of our return and of the information that there was no possible way to enter Ethiopia by way of the coast of Melinde, communicating with us through letters, he settled upon entering Ethiopia by way of Dio and Muslim ships which go every year to the Strait of the Red Sea. He wrote that he was relying upon us — those of us who were in the locality of Dio — to make arrangements so that there would be a ship to take both him and those of us who were to be his companions. From May to November we stayed in Dio both because of the winter and to try to see that there would be some ship for our purpose.[1] Even with the captain being a friend of ours and working hard for us on this matter, it was impossible to make any such arrangements. The reason for this was that the merchants who went to the Red Sea were so victimized by the cruelty and robbery of the Turks there that none of them wanted to return for more of the same, but wished rather to recoup their past losses by sailing to other places. With the information that we could not depend upon Muslim merchant shipping to take us into the Red Sea, we left Diu for Damão and Basaim. On the way we entered the Gulf of Cambay where we saw Goga and the memorials that are there to the former deeds of the Portuguese, the islands of the Cows and of the Dead, Castellete, Baroche, Surate, in which port, according to the reports of the people, there were at that time fifteen beautiful Dutch ships.[2] On

---

[1] By winter, *inverno*, is meant the rainy season.

[2] These places are all in or near the Gulf of Cambay. Gogha is in Kathiawar, on the west side of the Gulf. Le Grand reads: 'Goga, where are all the archives of the Portuguese and the memorials relating their great deeds in India'. This would be an odd mistake for Lobo to make. Did Le Grand perhaps confuse Gogha with Goa and add this phrase himself?

that day, which was All Saints' Day, there must have been exceptional toasting aboard those ships, for a gun was fired each time there was a toast. I counted thirty-four of these on the occasion. And as we were passing within sight of them, because we were avoiding their vicinity and because the water at the same time was carrying us more than we thought, we found ourselves at midnight with the whole fleet in the midst of the famous shoals in the sea of Damão.[1] All of the ships struck against them, and the danger was not so little that, if the water had been more rapid and running with greater force, and most certainly if there had been the slightest high wind, we should have been irremediably lost. For the whirlpools in that dangerous gulf were large, and turning into them with the force of the current and wind is the equivalent of the ship's hitting on the rocks. God's mercy spared us this, and the danger ceased to be anything for us to fear. On the following day we entered Damão, a fortress and city of the Portuguese.

Meanwhile, the Patriarch was also coming, sailing from Goa in the Northern Fleet, whose Captain-Major was Dom Felipe Lobo, with the intention of going to Dio to make the voyage to the Red Sea with us, thinking that there was a ship which would take us. Finding our letters, however, and because of other transactions that occurred on the same day on which we[2] saw each other in Basaim, where I had already arrived from Damão, he[3] informed me of his desire for me to return to Dio in that Fleet, which I did, embarking that very night. Setting sail in the morning, we went from there, going along the coast with more than one hundred and fifty ships.[4] Most of them were trading vessels which were going to Cambay, with the Fleet providing protection for them as far as Cambay, which it did. The Patriarch stayed at Basaim awaiting my return, having decided not to go on to Dio but

The Island of Cows was the name given by the Portuguese to Arnala Is. near Bassein, João de Castro, 1971, p. 92 and n. 242. The Island of the Dead (Ilha dos Mortos) is marked on Lavanha's map, reproduced in Barbosa, 1918, opp. p. 108. It is identified by Sir William Foster in his edition of *The Voyage of Thomas Best* (London, 1934) p. 37, n. 4, as the islet of Savai, which is joined to Shial Is. (Jackal Is.) by a reef which dries at low water. Castellete is not mentioned in the modern gazetteers of Gujerat, but it is marked on Lavanha's map, on the map of India and Ceylon in P. Barreto de Resende, 'Livro do Estado da India Oriental' (B.L. MS. Sloane 197), ff. 163 v. and 164 r., and on the map of Fernão Vaz Dourado, reproduced in *The Commentaries of the Great Afonso Dalboquerque* (London, 1875–84), II, opp. p. 1. The first two maps mark it further into the Gulf than Gogha, somewhere near the modern Bhavnagar; the third shows it near the entrance to the Gulf. It is mentioned several times in Best's narrative as Castelleta and *The Travels of the Abbé Carré* (London, 1947, 48) I, 137, refers to 'the Point of the Castellet', which the editors identify as the promontory of Gopnath.

[1] Daman, a Portuguese possession on the coast between Bassein and Surat.
[2] I.e. Lobo and Juan de Velasco.
[3] I.e. the Patriarch. [4] Le Grand says there were fifty ships.

to try to find there a way of getting some ship to take us to the Red Sea. With this purpose in mind, I was to bring our remaining companions and equipment from Dio, which I did. After we had passed Damão and Surate and had arrived at Gandar[1] the merchant ships lined up to enter as far as Cambay making the usual preparation. That labyrinth can be navigated only in the spring tides, which occur in that gulf during the three days before and the three days after the full moon as well as the new moon. In this navigation all ships remove their masts, sailing with hulls only, and all the people on the alert watching for the flood-tide, which comes so furiously that it carries the ships away so rapidly that in six hours it causes them to go thirty leagues without sail or rowing. Even though they always have pilots aboard who are experienced in navigating in that locality, there is nothing that can be done against the fury and rapidity of that water which does what it wishes with the ships. The worst part is that as the sand banks are so numerous there, if a ship hits one of them it is immediately turned over and everything aboard goes to the bottom; nor, with the whirlpools and fury of the water can anything rise to the surface but it all tumbles back to the bottom. There is another danger in addition to this one and that is if the ship happens not to have reached the usual place where there are good facilities for landing and provision for securing the ship and remains in the middle of that place which the tide leaves uncovered. If it happens to rest upright in the mud, it simply waits for the next tide. However, as there are many channels there made by the fury of the water, if by chance the poor ship happens to come to rest in one of these, it immediately turns over and everything aboard is lost. If, however, it reaches the landing place, many people immediately come and throw ropes to the ships to tie them fast, for the tide ebbs just as furiously as it rises and carries the ships back again if they are not tied fast with ropes from land. Concerning these very obvious dangers, although they are now less serious than they were formerly because of the increased frequency of navigation in that gulf, when a ship was to enter that gulf in years gone by, it was rare for a ship that went in to return. They say that anyone who had only one son would not risk his going in there because it was almost certain he would lose him. If he had two sons he could send one, for the danger of navigation in that place was so notorious at that time. I found myself there in this same situation one night, for there was also a full moon, a time which was extremely dangerous in such a place, and I was in great suffering.

[1] Rander, near Surat. The initial G is a mistake.

For, all the ships of the fleet being at anchor, there came at night such a storm that it forced us to set sail among an infinite number of shoals, the fury of the current being such that it carried the ships away with anchors and all. And if by chance they became entangled with another ship the current carried them along pell-mell at the whim of the storm and their good or bad fortune. We were carried along in this manner all night long, in extreme danger, expecting at every moment to hit some sand bank and perish irremediably. But with the morning the storm abated. The ships assembled, assessing the danger they had run and the damage the storm had inflicted on them.

We went to Dio and after a few days' delay returned to Gogha, the Captain-Major having already dispatched a fleet of four ships to go privateering along that coast as far as Sind. A storm overtook those ships and forced them far out to sea, so that they found themselves lacking water because they had only taken what was necessary for each day. They were in such need of water that a few men perished, and all of them would have died if God Our Lord had not come to their rescue; for all they had left was one bottle containing, possibly, two *canadas* of water for all the people aboard. The captain kept this in his possession, and when someone felt himself at the point of giving up the ghost he could come and ask for some refreshment, but he would not receive any unless he first swore he was dying. Then the captain would dip a small cloth in the water and moisten the sufferer's tongue and lips with it, after which he would take it away. A foreigner however saved the day by distilling the seawater in a sort of alembic. The water came out fresh and in sufficient quantity to supply what was needed. His method of distilling was to take a large earthen vessel full of water with a stopper securely plugged in its mouth and set it to boil. A tube ran from this vessel to another vessel which was empty and very tightly closed so that none of the steam which was given off from the boiling water could escape into the air. The water that was on the fire turned into water so fresh and pure that they would have wanted for nothing if the supply had been greater. They were in any case spared the extreme suffering they had been experiencing until then. The quantity was sufficient to fortify everyone so that their lives, by God's will, were saved by this means until they reached land. Although the ship did not carry much firewood and the people needed and used a great quantity of it, there was enough to sustain them until they reached port. I saw our friends the captains in the port of Dio, still showing the ravages of the suffering they had endured.

The Patriarch was waiting in Basaim for me and for the satisfactory completion of the business that he was going to dispatch. As it was necessary for me to be with him soon and the Fleet was to be detained in the mouth of the gulf waiting for the merchant ships that were in Cambay and were to leave with the following moon, the Captain-Major took the entire Fleet, however, and sailed along the coast one day as far as Currate, and at nightfall we were eight leagues above Damão. The Captain-Major took four ships as an escort and, leaving the rest to wait for his return, put me ashore on the beach of Damão where I remained, the Captain-Major returning to his Fleet that same night. As soon as I went to the College I made arrangements to travel by land to Baçaim to relate to the Patriarch the outcome of what I had negotiated, and to accompany him again to Damão; for I had learned from a letter that he had arrived with the intention of going to Dio, according to what had been decided in conformity with the letters he had received from Goa.[1] I made the journey from there by land, as is the custom, in hammocks on the backs of men called *bois*,[2] whose duty it is to load and carry in this way. The chair is restful and very comfortable, for a person travels in a reclining or sitting position with bed made and a writing-desk at his feet since this is the required load. It has very convenient protection against the sun. The *bois* who carry it, who, as I say, are those men, travel at a very regular pace as swiftly as they wish. The hammock is suspended from a long pole of cane about the thickness of a man's clothed arm, which they call bamboo. This bamboo pole has enough of an overhang beyond the hammock so that two men, one behind the other can hold it on their shoulders, and walk without getting in each other's way. In this way there are two behind and two forward who travel six or eight leagues each day with very little pay; for less than seventy *reis* is enough for each of them for one day. In this manner I travelled the twenty leagues or so from Damão to Basaim. The Patriarch arrived there at night on the very day of my arrival. He had three other Fathers with him, and all of us were fellow-members of the Mission.[3] After arriving at Damão we waited

---

[1] The Patriarch had arrived at Bassein on his way to Diu, having been instructed by the Viceroy to go there, whence merchants would take him to Massawa or Suakin. The Patriarch had informed the Viceroy that he intended to go to Daman and from there to Bailul, a village near the Ethiopian coast of the Red Sea, about 26 miles north-west of Assab. The Viceroy considered this to be a new and untried route to Ethiopia. PP. Machado and Pereira, who were killed in Aussa, had landed at Zeila, *SRE*, p. 195.

[2] A word of Dravidian origin meaning a palanquin bearer, *HJ*, 'Boy' b.

[3] They were Bruno Bruni (Bruno de Santa Cruz), an Italian, Francisco Marques, and possibly Juan de Velasco.

there for passage to Dio, which was provided us by António de Souza de Carvalho, Captain-Major of the Gulf of Cambay, who came to fetch us. The voyage to Dio was uneventful. We entered the harbour, and we Fathers went to our College that we have there on the day of the Purification of Mary, the second of February, sixteen hundred and twenty-four.[1]

The information that we had sent to the Patriarch in our letters and that of the Captain of the fortress, António de Moura, that there was no ship in that port bound for the Red Sea, and the Patriarch's desire and determination to go ahead and enter Ethiopia by whatever way possible to him made him seek a means for carrying out his journey. A nobleman from Basaim, Lopo Gomez de Abreu, promised to fit out three ships at his own expense if the Viceroy would give him permission for those ships to engage in privateering in the mouth of the Red Sea on their way back, so that they could in this way help the Patriarch in his predicament, do service to God and to His Majesty and, with the booty, recoup the expenses incurred in fitting out the three ships. The Patriarch offered to obtain the Viceroy's permission, and as he had written to him on the matter, leaving instructions that upon the arrival of the answering letter action should be taken in accordance with the order contained in it, he departed, as I have said, for Dio to wait for it. He went there because it was a more convenient place for ships and because the pilots necessary for that voyage and sea were to be found there. Soon after our arrival, the Patriarch received the Viceroy's reply in which he granted what was requested of him, whereupon we prepared for the voyage and awaited the arrival of the three ships. Since they were warships and carried Portuguese soldiers and no other cargo, they could not safely enter the Red Sea nor could they call at any of the ports controlled by the Turks on those coasts, nor, certainly, could we enter Ethiopia through any of them. Troubled as we were by these considerations, we welcomed the advice sent to us from Ethiopia by Father António Fernandez, Superior of those of the Company who were in those provinces. By order of the Emperor he advised us, for the security of the Patriarch's person, whose presence in those kingdoms was so much desired, not to go to Masuá but rather to disembark at Dagher[2] at the entrance to the Red Sea, near a Muslim petty king

---

[1] A mistake for 1625; Le Grand gives the correct year.
[2] Probably Tajurra, which appears as Tugora, but on the wrong side of Zeila, on the maps of Diogo Homem, A. Cortesão and A. Teixeira da Mota, *Portugaliae Monumenta Cartographica*, 6 vols (Lisboa, 1960), II, pl. 104, 138A. Dr R. J. Hayward informs me that the sound of English *j* does not exist in the local language, Afar, and that the name is pronounced Tagorri.

subject to the Emperor, whom he would have prepared in advance to receive us and give us safe passage through his lands. With the assumption that his port would be the destination of our voyage, we awaited the arrival of the ships. As they were delayed in their preparations and departure and the monsoon season was already very nearly over, we so lacked confidence in his coming that it was necessary for us to look about and consider another way if such there were. There proved to be one, occasioned by the Patriarch's presence; for the Captain of the fortress of Dio, Antonio de Moura, through that courtesy and benevolence he displayed toward the Patriarch and his affairs, considering the difficulties the Patriarch was experiencing and so that the journey and purposes which had brought the Patriarch so far would not be frustrated, offered to prepare a ship at his own expense with no other profit or intention than serving His Majesty and taking the Patriarch to the port where he wished to disembark. To show that his decision was in earnest he selected the ship, with our approval, and ordered work to be begun on preparing the ship for the voyage, with the help of the money he was spending and the Captain's authority, which promised a thorough and speedy preparation of the ship. And since the business was being undertaken with such enthusiasm, we doubtless would have made our journey to the Red Sea by this means if, when we were most dubious about their coming, the three ships did not suddenly appear out to sea in full sail. They were sailing straight to the mouth of the harbour, which they entered on Good Friday at nine o'clock in the morning and entered the port in a few hours to the joy of all. We were of course delighted to have our doubts completely erased concerning the good faith with which Lopo Gomes de Abreu had offered this service. He had been delayed so long because of difficulties and bad weather which occurred at the time of the preparation and departure of the ships.

After they arrived and had attended to a few trifles they needed, we talked eagerly about embarking, for the monsoon was nearly over. The three ships were a *sanguisel*,[1] a man-of-war and a galiot in which sailed the commander and Captain-Major of the others. All three were well supplied with soldiers who had enlisted and embarked on this expedition, partly because of the novelty of the journey and the honour to be derived from it and partly because of the hope for the booty they were to have, which was not inconsiderable. The Patriarch chose the galiot as being the most suitable ship for him and his companions and

[1] A small light ship of war used in Indian waters especially for pursuit, *HJ*, 'Sanguicel'.

some of the servants who accompanied him, dividing the rest, who were not many, between the other two ships. Our baggage, not amounting to much – a few books, church supplies, and other things that the Patriarch was taking with him – was soon loaded aboard.

It was the year sixteen hundred and twenty-five, in which Easter fell on the thirtieth of March. Since we were all extremely anxious to be on our way to the Red Sea, it took only six days after the ships' arrival for everything to be ready for the voyage. In the afternoon of the second of April, the day before we set sail, the Patriarch secretly called together the most important people of the land – the Captain of the fortress, the Vicar Forane,[1] Superiors and important Fathers of the religious orders, officers of the Custom House, as well as other friends, and he secretly said good-bye to all of them. I say secretly because most of the inhabitants of that city were Muslims and Hindus who did much trading in the Red Sea. The Patriarch concealed his identity from them and pretended to be a Father of the Company both in his dress and in the manner in which he was addressed by others. This dissimulation was so that the Turks would not have forewarning of his coming and thus endanger the journey. These fears were certainly well founded. If they knew who he was and the prize they would have in his person, they would lie in wait in the Red Sea ports to have him in their power. The leave-taking was celebrated with many tears. After the Litany of the Virgin Mary was said in the presence of the Holy Eucharist which, taken out of the tabernacle, was displayed on the altar, the Patriarch rose, everyone else remaining on their knees, and made a devout, fervent speech in the form of a colloquy addressed to His Divine Majesty, there present and displayed. He spoke with great spirit and eloquence, expounding the reasons for his journey, his personal desire to do it, offering himself as a sacrifice to his Divine Majesty, for the good of that Church with which he had been entrusted, asking His favour in obtaining a successful outcome for His glory in such pious purposes as he was undertaking, and praying that that journey, exposed to so many dangers, would be brought to a safe conclusion. The presentation or speech was very well received. It was heard in a spirit of great devotion corresponding to the spirit in which the Patriarch delivered it. All present wept copiously; and it was one of the saddest, most devout acts that I have witnessed. Finally, all present embraced

---

[1] *vigario da vara*. 'Vicar of the (pastoral) staff', a synonym for *vigario forâneo*, an ecclesiastical functionary, usually a parish priest, appointed by a bishop to exercise limited jurisdiction in a part of his diocese, usually one remote from his own residence; in canon law equivalent to a rural dean.

the Patriarch one by one and received his blessing. They afterward embraced the rest of us who were accompanying him. During all this time the tears of those who were remaining there continued to flow, necessarily accompanying those of the voyagers. We went together in this way as far as the ships we were to board. The people following us, Christians as well as Muslims and Hindus, were countless because of the novelty of the event, the fact that the most important people in the city were accompanying us and because the number of us who were embarking was the largest that had gone to Ethiopia until that time. There were seven of us who were going – five priests, including the Patriarch who was pretending to be an ordinary Father, but with the title of Superior of the Mission, and two lay brothers. In addition to this, the Patriarch was accompanied by some people whose various skills could be used and were used in the service of that church, as, for example, musicians, of whom there were two music directors, very well versed in music and highly skilled in playing a variety of instruments.[1] At sunset we boarded the ships, and as we were away from shore, all the people left the shore and made their way back to the city in great sadness, as they demonstrated by the tears they shed in this last farewell and which continued until they entered the city and their houses. Meanwhile, we were watching for the land-breeze and the tide in order to set sail, which we did at dawn the following day, the third of April, and, as the monsoon was nearly over, it was weak.

Out on the open sea and heading on course, in a few days we caught sight of the island of Socotorá, where a serious occurrence befell us. The island throws out to sea a long shoal on the eastern side. Having seen the island before noon, we were heading toward it, with the pilots showing very little caution and paying no attention to the shoal since they were unaware that it was in front of us. Night overtook us when we were at a few leagues' distance from the island, but since it was a beautiful, mild, moonlit night we continued our approach to the island, following the same course we had been following until then without any fear of what was awaiting us. It was about midnight and I was staying up, not being able to make up my mind to go below, conversing with the captain at the top of the galiot's stern. He had stayed

[1] The names of the priests have already been given, p. 75, n. 3. The two lay brothers were Manuel Luís and João Martins. There were also a youth who had followed the Patriarch from Portugal, five musicians, three Ethiopians, and two masons who were wanted in order to build churches. These details are given in a letter which the Patriarch wrote from Fremona on 5 July 1625, (Braga MS. 779, doc. XXII), partially published by Beccari, 1903–17, XII, p. 83. Le Grand says there were ten missionaries in all.

up to keep me company, which was what saved all of our lives. Everyone else was sleeping, especially the Muslim sailors, who do not like to stand watch, ordinarily sailing under their lucky star, as they say, which means trusting entirely to luck and having more trust in God's mercy than is justified by their works. They say that God knows what will happen and He will prevent anything evil from happening and will allow anything beneficial to take place. They pay no heed to the good diligence that is required on our part. Following this manner of reasoning, they were all asleep trusting in the mildness of the weather. I left the captain and went down to the shelter of the quarterdeck to go to bed. The captain, meanwhile, went to the bow of the ship, and, being there, he suddenly saw how close we were to the shoals, with the prow of the ship almost upon them. Because of the danger and closeness of the shoal, he immediately shouted orders for them to turn the ship sharply to leeward, for we were about to be wrecked. Thanks be to God, the galiot turned to leeward, responding more swiftly than ever, but already so close or so thrust into the danger that it almost touched its prow on the shoals as it cleared them. As I had just lain down in the opening of the shelter, I ran up at the sound of the shouting and, reaching the side of the ship, I leaned against it and saw how close we were to the danger and how God had miraculously saved us from it. It was dawn on a Saturday at a time when a Mass was being said for us in the College of Dio according to the promise given us by the Father Rector of that House for the whole time that our voyage was to last. And it is to this intercession and the virtue of the Mass that I attribute, and we all attributed, the mercy God showed us in delivering us with His special protection. And it was of no small help that I kept the captain most of the night in conversation until we both became tired, each of us going off to go to bed, and the captain reaching the bow in time to become aware of the danger and be able to get us out of it. For, if we had retired earlier, considering the little watching being done by the sailors, the first blows of the ship against the shoal and our shipwreck at the same time would certainly have been the first notice we would have received of our misfortune.

With the coming of daylight, we had recovered from our fright and were sailing along the island all that day, very close to land, almost touching it at times. We did not discover anything notable there other than high mountains, shelves of land that protruded into the sea, rocky places and steep river banks into which the waves crashed. Nor is there anything of consideration on the land beyond the fact that the people are few, poor, and miserable, almost all of them of the Muslim faith. Some of the natives were Christians many years ago, but now there are scarcely any traces of Christianity, time obliterating everything, the little communication and instructions they had from ministers of the Gospel, and much more importantly, the trade and friendship with the Arab Muslims, located opposite them and a short distance away, who came to conquer and assume authority over the island, which now belongs to a petty king, Xeque or lord of Caxem in Arabia Felix which lies opposite, a friend of the Portuguese for many years and a subject of the king of Portugal. There is, however, on the island the most precious aloe that is known. The best comes only from there because of the great quantity of *erva babosa*[1] growing there and because the very intense heat there and other elements of the climate peculiar to the island are particularly favourable to it. The juice or liquor which comes from this plant when cut is boiled in such a way that the drug or merchandise aloes is produced from it. Also, because of the many fish, large whales in excessive quantity, and especially the dolphins in even greater quantity, they produce much tallow, which is the oil derived from fish by allowing them to rot together. This oil mixed with lime, called *chanambu* in India,[2] is used to daub the ships from the keel as far as the middle, which is called paying the bottom of the ship. The procedure causes the ship to sail better, prevents rotting, it does not collect so much dirt in the water, and lesser quantities of seaweed, barnacles and other troublesome things stuck to the ship than when it does not have this coat of tallow.

We arrived at a principal port of the island after noon. At first the people were surprised at not knowing about such ships on their coast. Some fled to the mountains, which account for the greater part of the land and which, along with what level land there is, is mostly barren. Some ran to the beach, armed and ready for anything; but, seeing that we were friends, they came to visit us. The Seque, subject to the one of Caxem, who is his king, presented us with sheep, water, chickens, fish, and received a greater return in painted cloth from India which we sent them and which they value very highly. We were in port that night and set sail again in the morning for Cape Goardafui, which is a little more than forty leagues from there. Before sighting it, we passed

---

[1] *Aloë socotrina.* A drug made from the thickened juice was in demand in Europe in the early seventeenth century, partly as a purgative.

[2] Usually written chunam in English. Prepared lime, or fine, polished plaster, *HJ*, 'chunam'.

the Two Sisters, two uninhabited islands given this name because of their similarity.[1] They are two rather small peaks or mountains. As soon as we had passed them we sighted the famous Cape Goardafui, celebrated in ancient times under the name Cape of the Aromas,[2] a name which it acquired either because of its proximity to Arabia Felis, the source of spices, which is only fifty leagues away or because spices were produced there at some time, or because all the ships from India entering the Red Sea, very numerous in former times, heading for that Cape and catching sight of it before entering the Red Sea, are laden with drugs and spices.

This point of land is the easternmost point of all of Africa. There is another smaller point before one reaches this one, or a short distance before reaching the large one. The smaller one is only ten leagues before one reaches the larger. It is called Cape Fu,[3] while the larger one is called Cape Goardafu or Goardafui. From this point inward the ocean sea begins to narrow, being pinched on the African side by Cape Goardafui and directly opposite on the Arabian side by the Cape called Fartaqui.[4] They are 40 leagues from each other, and the two of them form the beginning of what is properly called the Sinus Arabicus which runs from there to the entrance to the Red Sea, where it loses its name and takes the name Red Sea, Strait of Moqua, Erythrean Sea, or Red Sea. So the ocean keeps the name Mare Indicum until it reaches these two capes; from these inward the name Sinus Arabicus; and from the narrow entrance inward, the name Red Sea. The length of the Sinus Arabicus from the said Capes to the narrows, is one hundred and fifty leagues. From the point of its beginning, beyond the narrows, the Red Sea keeps narrowing until its end. I shall provide later a full discussion of the length and breadth of the Red Sea.

In this locality we had great difficulty for two nights, whether it was the aftermath of some storm or that the sea was reacting from being compressed between the two lands Arabia and Ethiopia. It seems that they do compress the water since it crashes against both sides. The water was agitated in such a way that it amounted to a greater storm than if we had had a stiff wind, of which we had very little or none, so that we were more greatly affected by the rolling of the ships. They pitched and tossed so much that, no matter what direction the ships faced because of the sea being stirred up, the side of the ship and the

[1] Now called The Brothers.
[2] The Arōmatōn akrōtērion of the Greeks.
[3] Cape Shenagef, or the False Guardafui, in fact about 12 miles from Cape Guardafui itself.   [4] Ras Fartak.

yard were plunged under water, and each time it seemed as if the whole ship was turning over. The troubles ceased very quickly as we were able, because of the little wind, to sail out or into the gulf, whereupon we could see the land of Ethiopia, whose coast we followed from Cape Goardafui inward. Until we reached the narrows at the entrance to the Red Sea nothing noteworthy occurred except that one morning we caught sight of a *gelva*, which is a type of small ship without any nails at all, with its planks sewn together with coir and with sails of matting.[1] This one had apparently come from the port of Zeila. Since we wanted to talk with them and find out what lay before us in that sea and if some Turks were on guard in the ports, as they usually are, we were following them with the intention of speaking with them. However, the Muslims who were aboard the *gelva* either did not recognize our ships or knew they belonged to *Afrangis*,[2] which is the name they call the Portuguese, and made every possible effort to escape, which was the cause of their coming to grief. Their boat was not capable of doing us any harm and we only wanted to catch up with it so that we could have exact information concerning our voyage. If they had provided us with this information, we would have rewarded them, but since the *gelva* was fleeing in a desperate attempt to escape, we followed it with an even greater desire to catch up with it if only to prevent it from informing the Turks about us. Since our ships were faster under sail, we were soon overtaking it. When the Muslims saw this, they immediately headed for shore, running aground there at a poor village called Meth,[3] formerly a good town famous for its commerce, but now a shelter for fishermen from the kingdom of Zeila or Adel.[4] Leaving the stranded boat, they all jumped ashore and hastily began to climb a mountain of sand of which we had an uninterrupted view. The *sanguicel*, being the lightest of our ships, went ahead and, getting a much closer view, fired a musket-shot at those who were fleeing and the musket-ball landed between the feet of one of them. When he saw what it did to the ground, he was afraid that another shot would do worse to his body if he should be hit. He and his companions started to run even faster until they disappeared over the crest of the mountain. Those aboard the *sanguicel* soon reached the *gelva*, which they found laden

[1] Arabic *jalba*.
[2] I.e. Franks, a word applied in the Islamic world to the peoples of western Europe generally.   [3] Mait, on the north coast of Somalia.
[4] The former kingdom of Zeila or Adal had been in the first half of the previous century the most powerful Muslim state of the Horn of Africa. It was now very much weakened and its rulers resided at the oasis of Aussa in Dankali country.

with millet in sacks made from palm, with no other merchandise. As the other ships soon arrived, together they all pillaged the *gelva*, the wretched Muslims soon appearing seated on the top of the mountain with a white flag on a pole, apparently asking for peace. They then sent the small boat to them with two Muslim sailors and an Abyssinian boy who knew the Arabic language. The rest of the ships went well away from land to show them that it was safe for them to come down. Our own people, however, were advised not to go ashore, which was good advice; for the Arabs were never willing to come down the mountain despite all the invitations to do so from our three men, there being ten or twelve of them. They motioned to our men to jump ashore, doubtless so that they could capture them and use them as hostages to recover their *gelva*. Understanding their intent, our men returned to the ships, with the result that the wretched Muslims remained in that sandy wilderness with their boat ruined and pillaged by our people and sent to the bottom of the sea for greater precaution, even though the booty we took was to cost us very dearly after our arrival at Beilur. For the sacks full of millet still had the marks of their owners and there was someone who knew them. Although he examined the sacks very closely, he could not decide nor could he have any way of knowing how they came into our possession, since there had not been enough time for news of what had happened to the *gelva* to have reached them. If they had known of it we would certainly have run the risk of having done to us what the soldiers had done to those on the *gelva*, at least the Patriarch and the Fathers who remained in that land after the ships with the rest of the people had left, as I shall presently relate.

The rest of the day and that night, we were in the same place waiting to see if the Arabs would be willing to converse with us and give us information concerning the remainder of our voyage. But seeing that they did not want to have anything to do with us, on the next day we set sail for the entrance to the Red Sea to pass through the narrows, always hugging the coast of Ethiopia. Because the winds were weak, we took two days to reach the narrows. On the second day in the afternoon we caught sight of the narrows, the pilot recognizing the island that lies there.[1] It was four o'clock in the afternoon when we saw it at a distance of nearly five leagues. We continued our course straight to the island, and we recognized it positively at sunset when we were very close to it, at little more than a league's distance from

---

[1] Perim.

it. The island is called Bab-el-Mandel or Naum.[1] Nature located it in the narrows between these two seas, the Sinus Arabicus on the outside and the Red Sea on the inside, but both of them continuous. The island is up to two leagues in length and half a league in width. Its ground is high, and its location in the narrows creates two entrances to the Red Sea, one of greater depth on the Arabian side, the usual route taken by ships entering that sea, which must be no more than an eighth of a league wide,[2] the other, on the Ethiopian side, approximately three or four leagues wide, but with this difference that while the channel on the Arabian side is clear and deep enough for any ship no matter how large, the Ethiopian side is all full of shoals and rocks, so that no large ship can sail there, and when a small ship enters on that side it must stick close to the island where there is greater depth. Since the usual entrance is by the channel on the Arabian side, the Turks stand guard under protection of the island in some one of its coves, so that no ship will escape them. Escape is impossible, since the channel is so narrow, except at night under the protection of darkness. The Turks force the ships to go to the port of Moca to pay fees or rather ransom; for the whole business is nothing but robbery. At the entrance to this channel on the Arabian mainland is a village called the Village of the Pilots[3] because the ships take on pilots from there to enter this sea and to sail in it because of the danger undergone by those who sail there without this guidance, because of the many shoals with which the Red Sea is infested, especially on the two sides bathing the lands of Arabia and Ethiopia. Since we had especially strong reasons to fear any encounter with the Turks so certain to be in that locality, we decided not to take the usual, more travelled channel, and took the channel on the Ethiopian side, trusting in the lightness of our ships and defended by the dark of night, which better assured our passage. With this assumption, we were entering that famous sea, mentioned so often in the Holy Scriptures and in humane letters, devoutly singing the litanies

[1] Bab al-mandab, 'The Gate of Lamentation', is properly the name of the strait, not the island. Naum was one of the Portuguese names for Perim.

[2] *de largo meo quarto de legoa*. Le Grand says a quarter of a league; probably he overlooked the word *meo*. The actual distance is about a mile and a half; the strait between Perim and the African Coast is about twelve miles wide.

[3] The reference is not to a village on the mainland but to Oyster Island, 12° 40' N., 43° 28' E., an islet about ¼ mile off Cape Bab al Mandab, sometimes called Pilot Is., *Red Sea Pilot* (London, 1883), p. 240. It is connected to the cape by a rocky ledge, *Red Sea and Gulf of Aden Pilot* (London, 1955), p. 130. It is also called Shaikh Malu, and was known to the Portuguese as Ilha de Roboês, J. de Castro, 1971, p. 213, n. 104. Roboês is a Portuguese plural of the Arabic word *rubbān*, meaning a coastal pilot, G. R. Tibbetts, *Arab Navigation in the Indian Ocean before the coming of the Portuguese* (London, 1971), p. 525. Le Grand says Abreu had brought pilots with him.

and thanksgiving because we found ourselves already so close to the end of our voyage and those faraway provinces which we had come from such a distance to find. And since we are entering the passage to the famous Red Sea and are beginning to sail in it, it may be appropriate to give some account of its features, a curiosity which may please many of my readers.

CHAPTER 9

[Description of the Red Sea]

This is that very famous sea crossed dry-shod by the Children of Israel. It is three hundred and eighty leagues long and, at its widest point, is between fifty and sixty leagues wide. Taken in its entirety it has, in the best opinion of those who consider it, the shape of a lizard. The body of the lizard is the entire sea from the narrows up to Sues where it comes to an end and up to which point it keeps getting narrower. The neck or throat is the strait; and the head is all of that part which extends from the strait outward as far as the two Capes, Goardafui and Fartaqui. The full length of this large lizard is thus a matter of five hundred and thirty leagues. Nature divided it, from the strait inward to Sues, into three approximately equal parts. There is the middle part, corresponding to the backbone, free of rocks and shelves and navigable to Sues. It has some small islands, crags, mountains and large rocks, all protruding above the water, scattered everywhere in great profusion. The first of these, a mountain or rock fourteen leagues beyond the strait, is a volcano belching fire day and night.[1] This middle part is navigated safely day or night; for the rocky islands protrude above the water and there is no danger of running into them without seeing them first. The other two parts are very dangerous because they are infested with hidden rocks, shallows and shoals, both on the Arabian side, on the right, and on the Ethiopian side, on the left. Because of so many shoals these two parts can in no way be navigated at night. They can be navigated by day only by experienced pilots which the ships formerly took aboard for this purpose at a poor town where they lived, located in the narrows or entrance to the Red Sea. Nowadays each ship brings its own pilot from India for greater security, since the ships sail to various ports in this sea according to the requirements of their trade,

---

[1] There are a number of islands and islets in the Red Sea of volcanic origin, though none are now active. John Wilson, who sailed in the Red Sea in 1843, recorded that one of the craters on Jabal Tair 'continued to emit smoke till very lately', *The Lands of the Bible visited and described* (London, 1847), I, 33. *The Red Sea and Gulf of Aden Pilot* (London, 1955), p. 107, states that 'sulphurous jets exist at the sumit (*sic*) but for many years no smoke has been seen issuing'. This island is, however, much more than fourteen leagues from Bab al-Mandab. If the distance given by Lobo is approximately correct he was probably referring to one of the group that includes Zuqar and Great Hanish islands.

and since the Turks, having got all of Arabia and the Red Sea under their power, oblige the ships to go and pay duty and sell them merchandise at Moqua, a famous port at this time, twelve leagues beyond the narrows on the Arabian side. To enforce this obligation they keep warships in the narrowest part of this passage to take the entering ships to this port. All the ships from India that do not want to go there, because of the oppressive treatment they receive at the hands of the Turks, try to escape the danger by night, for which purpose they bring pilots to guide them. If they did not bring their pilots with them, they would have to take pilots aboard at the very place where there was the greatest danger of being caught by the Turks. Since my narration has reached the point where we are entering this renowned sea, I shall give a brief account of the famous cities and towns, both of former times and of the present time, which existed or now exist on its shores.

Beginning with the Arabian side, twelve leagues from the narrows is the city of Moca at the water's edge. Formerly of limited reputation and trade, it is now, however, populous and much frequented as a result of the changing times. Since the Turkish assumption of power throughout Arabia, it has become the major city of the territory under Turkish domination, even though it is not the Baxa's place of residence, which is two days' journey inland in the city of Senaar.[1] He, however, has his representative in Moqua. Approximately forty leagues beyond is the island of Camarani,[2] small and uncultivated but provided with all the food produced in Arabia. The island is slightly more than a league's distance from the Arabian shore. It is now bustling with trade. To the misfortune of its inhabitants, one finds here the famous basilisks.[3] Although these reptiles do much harm, biting and killing the unfortunate person they reach — and for this reason they terrify the wretched Arabs who come across them quite often in their houses, where they are very common — there is no indication that they do the damage which the Ancients proclaimed; and if we are to trust in the truth of the time-honoured belief, we must say that it refers to basilisks of some other lands.

Sixty leagues further along is a famous town formerly called Besan,

[1] The Pasha resided at San'a in the interior. Le Grand noted in the margin of his translation: 'If that was so formerly it is no longer so today, as will be seen subsequently in this Relation'. Sennar is in the Sudan, on the Blue Nile.

[2] Kamaran Island.

[3] A fabulous serpent supposed to be able to kill by looking at its victim. Lobo may perhaps have been misled by reports of scorpions.

now without a name. This place is now claimed by two towns, known
to us because of the ships which go to them, one called Odida and the
other called Loia.[1] Forty-two leagues beyond Bezan one sees some
traces or remains of the famous Lider, a very famous city, which now
has only the name of what it formerly was and the ruins of its former
greatness,[2] having suffered, along with many other famous places, from
the cruelty of the Turks who destroyed everything of value when they
occupied the land. A little more than thirty leagues beyond is the port
and city of Juda, which has been made so famous in these times in all
of the East by the great number of ships that go there and the rich
trade the merchants find there, and the superstitious custom of
pilgrimages to Mecca made by those who follow the infamous Koran.
The adherents of the Muslim sect frequent that port because it is the
port of access to the abominable house and sepulchre of the sect's false
prophet and true deceiver. He chose this place, twelve to fifteen leagues
inland, for his final resting place and as the seat of his false religion, in
the city of Meca or Medina. The word 'Medina' has the meaning of
'city', so that one might think that the city of Medina became a city
through autonomasia. And it is for the Muslims what Rome is for the
Christians, which city acquired such fame among the pagans in ancient
times, and which now deserves it among the Christians.[3] Since the ships
which sailed to Juda made excellent business profits, because of the great
wealth of the universal market of people and merchandise carried on
in that city, they became so famous in India that when people wanted
to indicate that something was very costly and valuable they would

[1] Le Grand's text uses the same spellings for these three places, but makes better sense:
'Today all its trade has passed to Odida and to Loia'. The last two are easily identified
as Hudaida and Luhaiya, ports now in North Yemen. Besan is puzzling. It may be meant
for Jizan, which, however, has continued to exist as a place of some importance till the
present. Barros, Asia, dec. II, liv. viii, cap. I, states that it is sixty leagues from Kamaran
to 'Gezão'. It had been a flourishing port before the Ottoman conquest; Varthema found
'forty-five vessels belonging to different countries' in the port, The Travels of Ludovico de
Varthema (London, 1863), p. 55.

[2] Again, Le Grand has the same spelling. The name presents difficulties. Barros, loc. cit.,
says that it is forty-two leagues from 'Gezão' to 'Zidem' which is thirty-six leagues from
'Judá', i.e. Jidda. However, Jizan is much more than seventy-eight leagues from Jidda.
There is no place on this coast with a name like Lider. If the distance from Jidda is taken,
rather than the distance from Jizan, Lider might be Lith, on the coast of the Hijaz. For
obvious reasons the Portuguese had little direct knowledge of the Arabian coast of the Red
Sea.

[3] Muhammad's tomb is at Medina. However, it was commonly assumed in mediaeval
and Renaissance Europe that the object of the Muslim pilgrimage was his tomb and that
it must therefore be in Mecca. Usually only writers like Varthema, who had visited both
places, realised what the facts were. Medina is Arabic madīna, 'city', and Lobo evidently
supposed that it was an alternative name for Mecca, as the city par excellence. Sandoval
makes the same mistake. He may have been misled by Lobo.

call it a ship from Meca or Juda. And any of those ships which came to any of the ports of India were laden with the profits from their trading and with many rich people. The greed of some who knew about their wealth became so intense that they would turn heaven and earth to get one of these ships in their power and plunder it. This happened occasionally when a ship would fall into the hands of the soldiers of our fleet, who, enjoying the rich spoils they found on the ships, enriched themselves in this way and left the Muslim sailors with only the memory of the many hardships they had endured during the voyage of two years. The voyage was made to last two years so that it would be a good and profitable one, not because the distance, though considerable, required all that time, but rather because of the great care and slowness with which they sailed, once inside the Red Sea. This was because of the shoals and the large size of the ships which were in great danger among them. It was also because of the delay necessitated by the delivery of the rich merchandise they carried and the collection of the excessive profits they derived from the sale of the merchandise.

There are approximately fifty leagues of coastline between this city of Juda and the city of Imbo.[1] In all that stretch one does not find a port of any importance, although formerly there were some very important ones. The Turkish domination and tyranny unfortunately ruined everything and it has all been forgotten. There is a distance of about sixty-eight leagues between this city of Imbo and Toro, which was destroyed by Dom Estevão da Gama.[2] Toro boasts some of the wildest, most sterile land that exists along the Arabian shore of this sea. In this whole tract of land there is no place under the authority of any person of note. It is infested, however, with Arab highwaymen whose living is almost exclusively derived from robbing the blind pilgrims who visit the infamous remains and memorials of Mafamede. Near this city of Toro are found some traces of a famous monastery of the friars of Mount Sinai, although the largest one is located at Mount Sinai itself at a distance of slightly more than eighteen leagues from there. It is a very old and constant belief among the natives that this is the place where the Children of Israel came ashore when they came out of the Red Sea. It is opposite the town on the other coast named Corondolo,[3]

[1] Yanbu' al-Bahr. Le Grand has Jambo.

[2] Tur, on the east coast of the Gulf of Suez. The little town was destroyed by D. Estevão da Gama when Governor of Portuguese India in 1541.

[3] The west coast of the Gulf of Suez opposite Tur is a salt marsh. Corondolo probably represents Wadi Gharandal, which is on the east coast, some 85 miles further into the Gulf than Tur. It has often been identified with Elim of Exodus xv 27 and xvi 1. Le Grand reads Rondelo.

where they began their crossing, going into the midst of the water and emerging from it dry-shod. There are three leagues from one shore to the other, and that numerous host travelled the entire distance with the water on either side of them serving as walls and miraculously opening up to them one or two[1] free and spacious highways so that they could tread the ground so hidden to human sight. There are some signs of this prodigious marvel if we are to believe those that are held to be fact by the inhabitants of the land. They are as follows: Despite the fact that the forty leagues of coastline from Toro to Sues are extremely barren and all the mountains are virtually without water as the shores usually are on both sides of this sea, in one place, however, they form a vast plain of abundant waters which descend to it from some mountains at the base of which it spreads out and where one also sees twelve beautiful palm-trees. And closer to Sues, three leagues before reaching the town, one finds many wells, which, the Muslims affirm, were opened by order of Mouzes because of the entreaties and lamentations of the people. These wells, as well as the palm trees, which of course could not be the original ones, but rather new ones planted in their place in commemoration of the event, are considered by the Arabs to bear witness to the truth of this ancient belief.

At the end of this famous sea is a town called Sues, formerly the market-place of all the nations in the world, where drugs from the Orient were sold and where a universal market was continually frequented by people from all nations. Now, however, suffering from the violence of the time, it serves only as a poor haven and small village for a few Arab or Bedouin fishermen, very barren and lacking in water, as it always was. This lack is supplied by the work of camels who bring water from a distance of two leagues[2] – brackish however, but enough to satisfy the needs of those wretched people. Yet the wealth of this town so satisfied the thirst and greed of the merchants who came in search of it that it did not let them feel thirst for the water which they needed so much. It is very true that the industry and power of the princes of Egypt, when their power was greater, in order to ensure the uninterrupted flow of profits from the duties they received from this market, caused them to order a beautiful ditch to be dug from the city of Grand Cairo to the town of Sues, so that the water from the River Nile, which bathes the walls of Cairo, would be drained off by it and

[1] The Braga MS. reads *doze*, 'twelve'. Either this is a copyist's error for *dous*, 'two', or Lobo thought that each of the twelve tribes had its own path.
[2] Le Grand says three leagues.

would fill many cisterns in the city of Sues to supply the needs and comforts of both the native inhabitants and the foreigners who came there. And even today one can find in places some ruins of both the cisterns and the canal among the stretches of sand which occupy the territory between the two cities; but the rest is buried under large heaps of sand and also filled in through the industry and cruelty of the barbarians. Since the city of Grand Cairo is three days' journey by camel from the city of Sues, which is approximately the equivalent of thirty leagues, the ditch was also approximately thirty leagues in length.

Having covered the entire Arabian coast of the Red Sea up to Sues, there being nothing beyond, we must now come down the other coast of the Red Sea, that of Ethiopia, mentioning even more briefly the towns of some importance there. Since there are few of them, the account will similarly be brief. Returning again from Sues toward the entrance to the Red Sea, in the first fifteen leagues we find Corondolo, which, as I have already stated, was the place where those of the Israelites began crossing the water to come out on the other shore. Forty-five leagues beyond Corondolo one discovers a town named Alcocer,[1] the most famous town on this coast because it is the usual port used by pilgrims going to Meca, Africans as well as Egyptians and all the other Near Easterners, when they wish to avoid the inhospitable overland route, which is rough and dangerous because of the sandy plains and deserts there (as one goes around above Sues and traverses the entire part of Arabia Deserta bordering the Red Sea). They embark here at Alcocer because the crossing at this place is very short and consequently they arrive at the shameful destination of their futile pilgrimage in fewer days' journey. There are two things of note in this locality. The first is that a chain of high mountain ranges ends here. These ranges run within sight of the entire Red Sea from its beginning. Their distance from the Red Sea varies. At some places the foothills bathe in the sea and at others they are from half a day's to two days' journey inland. They are all high and craggy, either totally wild or with very little cultivation, although many of them are pleasant and covered with thick groves of trees. Some, however, are so sterile and barren that they give indication enough of the excessive heat which ravages this whole sea, as I shall presently relate. When it is winter from these mountains inland, it is summer on the side which is in sight of the sea along with all its lands and shores. And correspondingly when it is winter on the Red Sea and up to the top of these mountains, it is summer

[1] Al-Qusair.

from the other side of the mountains inland. So that when on one side the fields are under water, the sky is covered with thick heavy-laden clouds and the air breaks out in thunder and lightning, on the other side one finds beautiful sunlight, clear days, much heat and a hot summer. The effects of such contrasting weather in an area as restricted as the tops of these high mountains divided by nature into such contrasting climates I was able to experience in the years thirty-three, four and five (beyond having noted them in many other years as well) at the time when we were being persecuted and hounded by the heretics. It happened that in the place to which we had withdrawn, two days' journey inland from the mountains, it was summer weather, and we could see that from the mountains to the sea were rain, masses of clouds and continual thunderstorms and the sky was continuously dark. And at the very same time not a single cloud could be seen in any other part of the sky and we were enjoying very peaceful weather. In a short time, however, we were taken prisoner by the heretics and handed over to the Turks as captives, which, along with the rest of the story, I shall report further on in my narrative. When they took us to the shore of the Red Sea and we sailed on it as prisoners for forty-five days, as the winter was already over, the sun afflicted us with excessive heat, and at the same time we saw that the half of the mountain top where we had been, which was very close to the shore, along with the land inland from the mountains, was enveloped in a very heavy cover of clouds, with frightful thunder and lightning, and the land was being bathed and cooled in the rain. We certainly yearned for the excess of it being lavished on the land to relieve the fiery heat in which we were roasting and melting in sweat. The rains, however, did not penetrate beyond the mountains, although they did send abundant streams which ran violently down those mountains and rocks until they either reached the sea or became hidden in the dry, burning sand which quickly absorbed them.

Let us return then to the chain of mountains which run for more than three hundred leagues. They end at this place and leave an opening here in the direction of Egypt. The place is called Rifa,[1] providing facilities here for commerce, merchandise and drugs coming in and going out. It links the Red Sea with those Levantine provinces. The

[1] Arabic *rīf*, 'cultivated countryside' and especially the fertile part of the Nile valley. In European sources such as the Zorzi itineraries and Alvares the name Rifa is applied to the stretch of the Nile from Qena to Aswan, where the river is closest to the Red Sea, O. G. S. Crawford, *Ethiopian Itineraries* (Cambridge, 1958), fig. 11; Francisco Alvares, *The Prester John of the Indies* ed. Beckingham and Huntingford (Cambridge, 1961), I, 449–451.

second of the two things deserving consideration here is that the waters of the Nile are so close to those of the sea here that they are separated by a distance of only sixteen leagues, so close to the Red Sea does the Nile trace its course, with which it goes to bathe the foot of the walls of Grand Cairo and empty into the Mediterranean Sea with its famed seven mouths, or with four according to what the modern geographers more accurately write. I take this opportunity to point out how very near the whole of Africa, one of the four parts of the world, smaller in size than Asia and America and larger than our Europe, is to being wholly a beautiful and the largest island surrounded by sea, since it is bathed on all sides by various seas and is united only by a narrow tongue of land with Asia and with the rest of the continent. It is obvious that the power of some great prince could very easily order this tie to be severed, since it is here no more than sixteen leagues and at its greatest distance is no more than thirty-four leagues. If one sea drained into the other straight through Grand Cairo, by which means the Mediterranean would be connected with the Red Sea, the coast all around our Africa would be encircled by water and it would thus be a true island. Even as it is, no one can rightfully deny that it is a peninsula if he takes into account what I am saying. And according to the existing information on this subject in the ancient histories, it is told that there was a Sultan in Egypt who was not unaware of the advantages of this project, and although he was intimidated by the great expense required by such an undertaking, the consideration that he might lose all of Arabia through flooding from the waters of the Mediterranean, which has a higher altitude than Arabia, caused him to refrain from such an enterprise.

Continuing, then, our journey along the African coast of the Red Sea, I say that one hundred and thirty leagues beyond Corondolo[1] is found today the island of Suaquem, famous at the present time because it is the residence of the Baxa, called the Baxa of Abassia, who selected it as being more suited to his interests than Dalec or Maçuá where they first had his residence when they first assumed authority over the Red Sea because there he could share in the profits derived from the trade with Ethiopia and with the kingdom of the Balouos, who use this island as their seaport.[2] I was a prisoner for some time in this town, as I shall

[1] Qusair must be meant here rather than anywhere in the Gulf of Suez.

[2] The Ottomans took possession of Suakin within a few years of their conquest of Egypt in 1517; the exact date is not known. The province of Habesh (Abyssinia) was established in 1555. Massawa was occupied in 1557, Orhonlu, 1974, pp. 2, 37, 43. Dalec is the Dahlak islands. The Balaw (Bellu, Balou) were at this time the dominant people in the region

relate in its place when I tell of what happened to us there. For the moment I shall treat only of its physical aspects. It is small and formed by an almost round shelf of sand, which must be slightly more than four hundred *braças*[1] in circumference, all occupied by fairly substantial houses of stone and lime. The Baxa's houses are not noticeably superior to the rest of the houses on the island except that they are graced by his presence. They have neither walls nor bastions nor artillery of any importance. This little sand shelf is set in a depression which is also round and so formed that it seems as if it had been purposely made with enough depth around the island for ships of any size, being less than a matchlock shot's breadth to the mainland, where the Baxas had made two small strongholds with towers and with their walls where they have a few small pieces of artillery; and these bastions serve as a place of refuge for them, where they can find protection and defend themselves against the violence with which the new Baxas customarily treat their predecessors, trying to get them in their power. Without any more justice or reason than what is suggested to them by their cruelty and especially by the greed that dominates them, they cut off their heads and strip them of everything they have robbed; so that the outgoing Baxas are forced, by a just judgment of God, to pay for the evil they have done by falling victim to the very same cruelties they themselves had committed. They therefore quickly take refuge in these places when they are given occasion to do so by the sudden arrival of the successor who, in order to conduct his business better, usually arrives unexpectedly without sending ahead any other news of himself than that carried by his officers when they attack the Baxa's houses, ordinarily at night. The measures taken by those who await their successor and death sentence, stimulated by their consciences, and by what they themselves had done to their predecessors, are, for the most part, of no avail, for they are all thwarted by the newcomers who are already skilled in this sort of business because of the great gain they derive from it.

From this depression, in which the island makes its appearance, toward the open sea, there is a channel of probably a little more than half a league's length and from ten to fifteen *braças* in width, cut so

immediately north of Ethiopia. They were Muslims and were displaced by the Beni Amer about the end of the century. They have now lost even their tribal identity, O. G. S. Crawford, *The Fung Kingdom of Sennar* (Gloucester, 1951), pp. 109–117.

[1] Usually translated 'fathoms'. Traditionally a *braça* was the distance between the tips of the fingers of an adult man whose arms were outstretched, or about 5 ft 8 inches, Boxer, *Further Selections from The Tragic History of the Sea* (Cambridge, 1968), p. 139, n. 2.

symmetrically that, although it is natural, it seems as though it has been fashioned with a pick-axe. It is all of living rock but so soft that when a ship touches it at times it receives no damage from this but rather does damage to the rock, breaking it in many pieces. The rock thus seems to be more white coral, and as such, soft, than living rock. It is all, however, covered with water, and there are shoals everywhere which extend for many leagues, running along the coast toward the narrows as well as toward the upper end of the Red Sea. The width of this shoal, extending outward all around the shore of the island except for the channel, is half a league, so that the island is defended on all sides; for the only entrance is by the channel, to which the approaches from the sea for more than twenty leagues are so infested and complicated with shoals and shelves of sand that for this reason they are referred to as a trap. The shoals are so numerous that one cannot see how a ship could make its way unless it were by cutting them down. However, when one comes closer, one discovers the channel, which turns and winds more than a moving snake, which causes fear and anxiety in those who come here for the first time. In the interior opposite this island lies a kingdom of Muslims called Balous, great horsemen and valiant soldiers who have shown their valour many times in encounters with the Turks, so that they have forced the Turks to give their king half of the customs fees in exchange for peace. And in order to collect this duty the Balou king has his representatives there on the island. The kingdom is abundantly rich. It has some gold and much silver which, melted into something similar to bricks, is brought by the black merchants who exchange it for cloth. It has an abundance of ivory, hides, slaves, many foodstuffs and meats, especially sheep. The sheep, men and horses, all of which are in great supply, are all the largest I have seen in that part of the world. Both because of the many advantages they derive from this place and because of the warlike nature of the Muslims, the Baxas changed their residence to this island leaving a lieutenant of theirs on the island of Masuá, so that they enjoy the profits from both places. On the mainland around the island at the edge of the water, the Turks have some coolness from gardens and refreshment from various types of fruit, which, though not in great quantity because the land is so barren, are sufficient, such as lemons, prickly pears, sugar canes, citrons, and other things of this kind along with watermelons so large, sweet and red inside that I have never seen any similar to them. And since the land is very sandy and very hot, it boils the moisture in this fruit in such a way that it makes it very sweet, and any juice that runs out of it quickly coagulates and hardens as if it were sugar. This small quantity of refreshment, gardens and greenery, amounting to from eight to ten very small gardens, is the largest such concentration of this whole coast, both inside and outside the entrance to the Red Sea for a distance of more than nine hundred leagues, running from Sues to Melinde. However, there are dates in abundance, especially from Suaquem to Sues, a land inhabited by poor Muslims, mostly fishermen living in small villages in that land, which we can call, along with all the rest below for the nine hundred leagues I have mentioned, an extremely unpleasant untracked desert. And it is above all for the very reason that the heat is so excessive, violent and harmful, especially from the entrance to the Red Sea inward, that no people could live with it.

On the shores of this famous sea grow in great abundance the famous ostriches, so well known and so highly valued for their feathers, especially those that grow under their wings, so fine and soft. There is no food here which is very appropriate for these birds, but they are very easily pleased and seem to digest quite naturally anything they find before them. They can nourish themselves anywhere because they do not spare, as I observed, sticks, stone, paper, or cloth. I did not see them eat red-hot iron, but that too must serve them as meat, which I believe because of the reverence due to antiquity, especially since it is consistent with their antipathy to water, hot as they are and growing in lands which seem to be the very homeland of heat. This must be an extraordinary piece of foresight on the part of nature, because of the lack of water the birds were to experience because of the small quantity of it they find in this land where they grow and where their famous eggs, so familiar in the decoration of church lamps, are laid in the burning sand where their offspring are hatched and reared.[1] The eggs have an extraordinary property for curing eye trouble, for when the shell is ground into a fine powder and put on the eye over a nebula it consumes the nebula in a short time without anything else mixed with it except that, if this is desired, it can be dissolved in rose water or woman's milk to keep it thoroughly liquid. These animals do not fly. They run, however, with such velocity that a swift horse cannot keep up with them. For greater swiftness they spread their wings and, with them opened but without flapping them, they start running. This use of the wings doubtless utilizes the air they take to make their bodies

[1] Le Grand adds: 'As they lay many eggs, they break some of them in order to rear their offspring'.

lighter and, easier to move. It is told of these animals that when they run they throw stones behind them, which they do, certainly not because of any instinct they have for this, as if they did this as a means of defending themselves by inflicting harm on any pursuers, but rather because they have two large toe-like protuberances for feet which, in combination with their large, heavy bodies and the great swiftness with which they run, doubtless exert much force on the ground, and as they go forward they shoot rapidly behind them any stones they happen to step upon, not purposely but in the natural course of their running. Many of these birds visited us at the time when I was detained on those beaches as a prisoner of the Turks. I saw a number of them on that occasion in various places. Many other animals are found in those deserts, of which, since they are the usual ones familiar to us, I shall make no particular mention.

I shall, however, comment upon the properties of a certain wind that is very common in the summer season, I say summer season, even though all the seasons of the year are so hot that they could also be referred to as boiling summer. The wind is called Arcer[1] by the natives and corresponds here to our east wind. There, it is the northeast wind plus either a quarter-point east or a quarter-point north. It appears that it is the same wind mentioned in the Scriptures as *ventus veniens a regione deserta*;[2] for it comes from the deserts of burning Libya and the Thebaid and runs through the very hot deserts in those lands. And as it passes through those places which ordinarily are of loose sand, a material so adapted to soaking up the intense heat of the sun which strikes those lands so terribly, and it is also channelled between high mountains, whose valleys could serve, and it seems that it burns in them, the fire of hell. It keeps collecting all the heat with which the little which the land produces is ravaged, so that when it reaches the shores of the Red Sea it is so excessively hot that in a quarter of an hour or, when it takes a long time, in half an hour, it stifles and kills the poor travellers if they do not come supplied with a large quantity of water, which they carry either on their backs in leather bags or in the same containers on camels, the usual means of transportation in those lands, already thus prepared both for these attacks by the wind and to make up for the lack of water which exists in those same places. And when travellers feel themselves being attacked by the heat, they hurriedly try to cool

[1] Le Grand spells the word Arur and adds that the Arabs call it Uri. In his *Rellação de Maçuá* Lobo writes *orur*. P. da Costa notes that *arur* would be a possible but palaeographically less acceptable reading here. The word is Amh. *ärur, härur* Arabic *ḥurūr*, 'extreme heat'.
[2] Job i. 19, 'a great wind from the wilderness'.

themselves by drinking what water they can and washing themselves with the rest, whereby they avoid the danger which is obvious and irremediable when this relief is not available. Often even this is not sufficient to avoid death, because, being violent and very furious, the wind drives before it such large clouds of sand that it easily moves whole mountains of sand from one place to another; and, catching the poor traveller, whether on foot or on his camel, along with whatever company or baggage train he has with him, it buries him under the sand, stifling him with it, so that even if he had had the foresight to come supplied with water it would be of no avail to him. The flesh of these wretched people, who are victims of such a misfortune in these and many other localities, is mummified; for the heat serves as myrrh, leaving them whole but dried out. I found one of these mummified bodies in a sandy place. No part of the body was lacking, and since I had known him, for he had parted from us a few days earlier, and since he was a Christian, I gave him burial. Having been dead for so short a time and being perfectly intact, he did not smell bad no matter how close I came to him to cover him with sand and stones as I did, placing a cross at the headstone, a sign which, although so sacred, is little known in those lands. This hurricane of the land has two features which serve to keep it from seizing many people suddenly and doing them harm. The first is that since it blows most frequently and violently from June through all of August, travellers, whenever possible, avoid taking journeys during those months, and when they do take them, they are prepared and watch carefully for the wind, for it can be seen long before it arrives because of the clouds of sand that it drives before it. The clouds are very red because of the extreme heat with which they are impregnated, so that travellers cannot fail to see them and move as far away as possible from that fury; for these winds do not cover a very large space of land, so that either they do not come to the place where the travellers are, or if they do come, the travellers make an effort to avoid the greatest fury of the wind, and, if successful in this, escape. A few times this furious wind caught me on land[1] and a few other times on the sea, but the latter were not so dangerous, both because its force was somewhat spent and also, despite the goodly quantity of sand it threw into the ship, the air was cooler because of the nearness of the water. The times when that wind caught us on land were more

---

[1] Le Grand adds: 'I do not think that any European has travelled as much as I have in all these countries; I have often run the risk of dying of thirst or of being buried under the sand'.

dangerous, but we had recourse to the same means and I always carried with me at least some small kid bags provided with water, and when I lay down in the shade of a thicket, the sand being the softest and most pleasant bed, the leather bag was hanging there with water ready for any event, both for this wind and for cooling the extreme heat which is a source of great torment and against which it is useful to have water in one's mouth at all times. The best thing one can say about this fiery wind is that it does not last very long but passes on. Its full strength probably lasts approximately a quarter of an hour, but after this comes another hurricane and it continues in this way all day long, and at times at night, with respites of a few hours more or less, from one to the other. This fury and continuity of winds is found along all the shores of the Red Sea on the Ethiopian side. On the shores of Arabia it is not so prevalent – I mean Arabia Petrea and Arabia Felis – for in all of Arabia Deserta, which ends at the Red Sea and with its uppermost point is continuous with Ethiopia, the forge and furnace of this heat and winds, as it comes out of its sandy plains, continues through those of Arabia Deserta, with the same and even greater effects because it has traversed more lands and deserts, increasing its heat with the heat it finds in the places through which it passes.

[The same description is continued and the reason for the name of the Red Sea is given]

We had broken the thread of the story of our journey which we are now taking back down on the Ethiopian side, the left shore of the Red Sea when one enters it, now once again bound for the narrows. And as we were in its heat, I digressed to tell what I have just related. Resuming the thread of our journey at this place, I say that it was destroyed years ago by Dom Estevão da Gama on the occasion of that incursion he made into the Red Sea with his powerful fleet.[1] There is a distance of sixty leagues between this place and Masua, and in those sixty leagues there is no place of any importance beyond ports and watering-places I visited as a captive when the Turks took me that way to the islands. The island of Masua is flat and one thousand two hundred *brasas* in circumference. It is divided into three parts. The easternmost point is occupied by a small, dilapidated tower, and from there inward continues one of the three parts, in which the inhabitants have many cisterns, most of them broken and in a state of ruin, a very few in good condition and containing water for the most privileged inhabitants. The second or middle part serves as a burial-place for the Turks and Muslims. The Christians and pagans, however, whom they call *cafar*,[2] meaning accursed, infamous, lawless and Godless, unclean, etc., are not permitted to be buried next to the Muslim dead, but are thrown to the birds and wild beasts, which feed on them on another island nearby. The third part, which is to the west, contains the population, which occupies all of it. It is small and composed of dilapidated houses, some of straw, some of stone and clay, and some of stone and lime. The island is provided with food and meat. Water comes to it by sea every day in leather bottles brought in three boats, used only for this purpose, from the mainland, a distance of two leagues going up a bay. The Turks have there on the mainland a very weak fortification of stone and clay, a sort of fortress with some soldiers and artillery guarding some wells which they make in the sand. They take the water from these wells

[1] In 1541. [2] Arabic *kāfir*, 'infidel'.

for the population of the island. Their finding water in this place can be explained by two peculiarities. One is that it is close to the sea and the salt water, strained by sand is made fresh, which we too found to be the case when we dug into the sands on this shore. And although it was fresh at first, in a few hours it kept getting briny until it was of no use. The second peculiarity is that streams of water come down from the mountains and come to this place and go underground in the sand and remain fresh and useful so that, by digging down a little, they find water as we also did in places where there were signs of streams having flowed in winter.

From this island of Masua to the Strait there are almost eighty leagues, in all of which distance is found only one place of importance, which is the island of Dalec, twenty leagues from Masua, where pearl-fishing is done in great quantity, but most of the pearls do not have a good colour, because they have received too much light, some of them being similar to a burnt yellow. Twelve leagues inside the entrance to the Red Sea is the port of Bailur, of which it is necessary to speak in more detail because it is the place through which we entered Ethiopia and because I have much to tell about it as I finish here the brief narration and report which I promised concerning the Red Sea, which is found above. It is necessary, however, to add here a paragraph concerning the reason why this sea is called the Red Sea, both because of what I have observed on this point and because this is the first and main point of general interest concerning it.[1]

I say then that the Red Sea has been the object of much toil on the part of authors who had tired themselves out trying to give the reason for its name, adducing as many causes for it as there were authors who treated the subject. Each one presented as a proven fact his own particular explanation for it. I too shall add what I have observed on this matter during the time when I sailed on it for a period of forty-five days. We were captives of the Turks, the winds were not favourable, and for that reason we were sailing slowly, putting into harbour at times and at other times stopping at certain places where in all this time I noted, in company with the Patriarch of Ethiopia, who also made the same observation, as we were discussing the matter together, that it did not receive the name Red because of the great clouds of clay-dust of this colour which the fury of the wind brings, which dust falling

---

[1] Le Grand adds: 'All the more because, when I was there, I hardly talked about anything else with the Patriarch Afonso Mendes, who is a man of worth and considerable ability'.

on the sea, tints it with its colour, for neither is there any such clay near there nor do the winds, that is the *arur* of which I have already spoken, drive before them this dust but rather sand of the usual colour. And much less does the name come to it from the optical illusions reflected from red clay pits on the water's edge, for there are no such reflections from any clay pits. At the water's edge one finds, on the contrary, bare, black mountains, barren sandy places, level expanses of low undergrowth and rocky places burned by the sun and blasted by the winds. Furthermore the red colour which is supposed to appear on the sea is no more factual than the winds that carry the red dust or the alleged proximity of the red clay pits. The same false reason for the redness of the water is also adduced in the explanation given by an author who saw a vein of red water in the sea and attributed it to whale eggs, which he claims to have seen. He says that he ordered a person to climb to the crow's nest and that that person observed the same thing for as far as he could see.[1] I say that this could not be the basis for the name of the Red Sea, for it is a very rare and transitory phenomenon, certainly not constant enough or of common enough knowledge to account for the name. I saw no such thing during the many days I sailed in the Red Sea, being very much on the alert concerning this very matter. A vein of water and an agent which makes it red, just because someone saw such a thing on some occasion, cannot have given so ancient and permanent a name to an entire sea. Finally, there is the more usual, modern explanation which affirms that the name Red is given to this sea by the large quantity of coral which grows on the bottom and sends to the surface an optical illusion which, while it could not actually tint the water, gives the illusion of dyeing it by communicating to it the appearance of the red colour which the coral has in reality. I say then that if this were the true reason, the phenomenon would have to appear in most of that sea or in so many

---

[1] Le Grand reads: 'A writer, who has been on this sea, holds a rather peculiar opinion. He says that he saw there only red patches, that these patches could be whales' eggs floating on the water, that he drew the attention of one of his companions to the same thing, and that, when they had both examined these patches, they took the same view; as if something that happens so rarely could have given to this sea a name by which it has been known at all times and in all languages.' A passage in the *Breve Noticia* makes the same statement and ascribes it to D. João de Castro, who is alleged to have sent a man up the mast to observe the dimensions of the red patch, adding that whales are very plentiful both within and without the entrance to the Red Sea', Portuguese text, p. 779. Lobo, however, is misrepresenting what J. de Castro said. In his *Roteiro do Mar Roxo* he attributes such red streaks to coral on the sea-bed and says that he sent down divers to procure specimens, *Obras Completas de D. João de Castro*, ed. Armando Cortesão and Luís de Albuquerque, vol. II (Coimbra, 1971), pp. 368–71. It was, of course, known to naturalists that whales are not oviparous, Conrad Gesner, *Historia animalium*, IV (Tiguri, 1558), p. 229. Lobo may be confusing eggs with ambergris, which was believed to be vomited or excreted by whales, p. 58 n. 3.

places, even though each one might cover only a small space, that it could give this name to the entire sea. This is certainly not the case. Even though I sailed this sea along both coasts, Ethiopian and Arabian, not only close to shore but also in mid-channel, I never saw such red spots coming from the coral. Furthermore, the coral is not red when it is under the water. It becomes so only after it has been removed from the water and has been treated with a baking procedure which enlivens its colour, or the heat of the sun does it to the pieces cast up on the shore by the sea, and I saw and noted on the many occasions on which I walked along these shores and found pieces cast up by the sea, some white, others a very pale red, and others finally of a bright red colour which the heat of the sun had brought to perfection.

Everything I have reported above conforms with what I noted in company with the Patriarch of Ethiopia, for we were in the same ship as prisoners of the Turks and we often went ashore walking slowly along the shores. What I observed, as I say, is that the sea called Red did not receive its name because the water is any of these colours, for the water is in every way similar to the water of any sea or river when it is taken in the hand, but rather because it gives the appearance, for which I shall presently give the explanation, of having a very natural red colour. To understand the phenomenon I am describing, the reader must know that this sea gives the appearance of having stretches of various stains or colours which vary with the depth of the water. Anyone who sails on it sees sometimes blue stretches, true of the greater part of this sea, especially when sailing in mid-channel, which comes from the great depth it has there, as is seen in any part of the ocean sea. At other times one sees green places because of the seaweed and stones where there is little depth. Some other stretches are white from the sand or some stone of that colour in places where the water is very shallow. Others, finally, are of a beautiful red which, though an optical illusion, gives the appearance of being its true colour. As we were sailing in a small ship, called *gelva*, capable of sailing in any of these stretches I have mentioned, deep or shallow, it happened that we sailed through these various stretches observing the causes of these differences. At times we were anchored on some of the spots mentioned and could see them at close range and in great abundance. And investigating with greater curiosity the reason for the red appearance of the water, at times I had a *Cafre*[1] whom we had with us as servant, dive to the bottom

---

[1] Arabic *kāfir*, 'infidel', here used in the sense of English Kaffir. 'Under this term the Portuguese included Bantu, Hottentots, and crossbreeds, indiscriminately', Boxer, 1959, p. 293.

and uproot bunches of herbaceous plants which were what caused the
red appearance of the water. I was able to identify this herb as being
the cause more from looking down to the bottom from a vantage point
over the water and seeing the apparent colour. That this, and not
anything else, is the cause is borne out by the fact that there is nothing
else on the bottom which could cause it and by the fact that the same
grass caused the same appearance after it had been snatched from the
bottom and, with nothing else with it, was placed just under the surface
of the water. And, what is more, the part of the water where there
was none of this herb did not have that red colour, and all of the water
where that herb was on the bottom did have it; but this was where
the water was shallow, about a *braça* or a *brasa* and a half in depth.
This herb is the same as that called sargasso in the ocean. There is a
great quantity of it in the place the ships pass through on the return
voyage from India to Portugal when they are approaching the latitude
of Terseira Island, where the ship often cuts through stretches of this
sargasso weed, which floats in the water torn from the bottom by the
motion of the waves. The same thing happens in the Red Sea, where
this herb, almost a bush, corroborating what Scripture says, *germinans
de profundo*,[1] is apparently not the only plant. Some claim that there
are many other plants whose growth is not impeded by the sterilizing
effect of the salt. The claim receives some support from my own
observation of a great abundance of trees called *mangas*,[2] so close to
the water that not only did the tide cover a good proportion of its trunk
but it continually had its roots bathed in salt water up to the middle
of its trunk, so that, when it split or dried up, I many times collected
the beautiful white salt from the foot of the same tree and from the
trunk where it had adhered and was coagulated by the sun and used
it for my poor meal when I was a prisoner of the Turks there. The
evidence is not limited to plants exposed to the rays of the sun: a greater
marvel is that of the palm-trees which grow on the bottom of the sea,
whose fruit are called Maldive coconuts[3] because the greatest quantity
of them are found in the vicinity of the Maldive Islands, whose pulp
is so excellent and so highly valued. Even the shells are held in high
esteem. People make precious vases of them, these coconuts being as
large as a man's head. Two grow together, one stuck almost half-way
into the other. The sea casts them up on the nearest shores. I can report

[1] *campus germinans de profundo nimio*, 'out of the violent stream a green field', *Wisdom of Solomon*, xix, 7.
[2] *Manga* is the mango, but the mangrove, properly *mangue* or *mangle*, is obviously meant here.   [3] See p. 58 n. 4.

in this regard that many are washed ashore all along the coast from Melinde to Brava and Magadacho,[1] where I saw many of them when I walked that shore in the year 1624, as I have related earlier in my account. At that time I also saw many of a type called Melinde beans,[2] the size of a fist and produced by the sea. They must grow in large trees and must have been cast up on the shore where I found them. The pulp is bitter but excellent, dissolved in water, against fevers and any malignant illness which causes one to waste away with fever. Returning, however, to the subject of sargasso which, as I say, is the cause of the apparent colour the Red Sea has and is possibly responsible for the name, and discussing further the nature of this herb, we remembered that Saint Jerome refers to the same sea, in the Hebrew language, as *Sansuf*.[3] As for the word *San*, there is no doubt but that it means *sea*. The word *Suf* is more mysterious, especially because in Ethiopia there is a certain herb or bush of exactly the same name, which, similar in appearance to the stalk of a thistle when it is going to seed, but slenderer and longer, puts forth on the end of the stalk a flower similar to the knob of a thistle, although the colour is more like that of saffron. This flower is much used by the Ethiopians to dye cloth, and they temper it in such a way that it gives a beautiful colour very close to vermilion, which they call Suf.[4] They use its seed to make a spread of the same name, which I know to be very tasty because I have eaten it many times. It is white and is similar in taste to the milk of sweet almonds. This herb, then, is that which grows in the sea and which we call *sargasso*. It is similar to it in every respect, even in having various thorns on the trunk, except that the ones on land are hard and prickly and those in the sea, because of the water, are soft and with stems that do not hurt. Because in those parts they call the herb that grows on land Suf, since the herb that grows in the sea is so similar to the other they must have given it the same name. And hence this word and many other words used by the Abyssinians were taken from the Hebrew language, so that the Hebrew expression São Suf, then, must mean the sea in which that herb grows. Since the herb grows abundantly everywhere in the Red Sea and its colour causes those reflections in the water which give it its apparent colour, this must have

[1] Brava and Mogadishu on the Somali coast.

[2] *favas de Melinde*.

[3] P. da Costa notes that the reading *Sansuf* is inescapable diplomatically, though it is certainly a copyist's error. Le Grand has *Jansuf*. It is Hebrew *yam ṣūph*, 'the Sea of Reeds', translated Red Sea in the Authorised Version of Exodus xv. 4 and 22.

[4] Amh. *suf, carthamus tinctorius*, Lin.

been the reason for the name Red Sea. This is corroborated especially by the colour and true effect of the land herb used as a dye for cloth, the word *Suf* being used in those parts to designate the red colour coming from that herb.

The ships that sail everywhere in this sea are of every type, large ones of any kind and small ones of every sort, for the sea is appropriate to all types because its depth, especially in the channel in the middle, accommodates the largest galleons that plough the sea. The ships that deserve particular mention, however, are those called *gelvas*. They are as large as a Tanquos[1] boat or an Alfama[2] caravel. They have no nails at all. They sew the boards together as if with a needle, binding them together with a very thin cord. And stopping up the seams with a splinter of wood, hammering several additional wooden pegs into them where necessary, and then doing it over with pitch and tar, they make these ships capable of sailing, but not strong enough to resist heavy waves or a violent sea. They are very serviceable, however, in places where there are dangerous shoals; for even if they strike a rock they do not break up easily since the sewing, yielding to the force and impact of the stone, gives way so that the ship does not suffer so much damage. These ships are also light and easily manoeuvrable, but they do not venture to sail in large seas so as not to run the risk of storms. Since the Red Sea does not have many storms it is safer there for sailing in these ships. I, however, suffered from some very severe and very dangerous storms on the Red Sea and in these ships. These are the famous ships in which it is said that everything carried in them as well as the very wood of which they are made – the mast, the sails, the rigging, the victuals on board, and the merchandise – are contributed to them by one or many trees of the same species; so that one of these ships is built and sets sail laden with bread, water, wine, vinegar, sugar, oil, and other goods, all coming from the palm-tree. All of these things could not come from one palm-tree, but from many of the same type. And to clear up the mystery of what I am saying, one must know that, while not suitable for many uses, the wood of the palm-tree is suitable for some; and for the manufacture of the *gelvas* I have been discussing it is quite sufficient. So that when it is cut down it provides boards sawn from the wood for the construction of the ship, wooden pegs for nailing, fine cord for sewing, which, along with the thick rope which

---

[1] Tancos, on the Tagus a little below its confluence with the Zezere.
[2] One of the oldest quarters of Lisbon, between the Cathedral and the river. As in the preceding note the reference is to ferry-boats.

serves for the rigging and even for the cables for an Indian ship – which cables are very good and strong and yield when the ship pitches at anchor, and are thus more secure; they also have the advantage of becoming stronger under the water – all of these types of cord and rope are spun and made from the outer shell of the coconuts. This outer shell, buried on the shore near the water, deteriorates and becomes tow which can be spun so fine and can be worked so perfectly that it is very highly valued. The mast and yards come from a trunk of the same tree planed to the proper size. The sails are woven from the leaves of the palm-tree, from which they also make sacks called *macandas*,[1] in which they carry their merchandise. With the sail put on in this way, the cargo it carries is often completely derived from the palm-tree. This tree, before giving its fruit, which occurs twelve times a year, each month a bunch of coconuts, from twenty to fifty approximately in each bunch, the number of coconuts varying with the fertility and vigour of the tree, first grows a sheath formed like a crescent-shaped scimitar, inside of which comes the bud; and before it opens up they cut off the end of it, and, placing in the opening something they call a *gorgo*,[2] the shape of a medium-sized cooking pot, they distil a white syrup-like juice, which they also draw from the trunk of the tree by making a hole in it, although this means of drawing off the juice is harmful to the tree, violent, and soon destroys it, which is not the case when the juice is obtained from the fruit. This syrup is very sweet and is called *sura*.[3] It is collected twice a day, in the mornings and afternoons. It is good for the health. It cleanses and fattens. When this syrup is boiled, it coagulates into sugar suitable for all uses and highly valued among the people of India. When it is distilled it makes a very strong wine called *nepa*,[4] similar to brandy, which, when soured, becomes very good vinegar. These three things are obtained from it before the fruit comes out. After the fruit has appeared and has almost attained its full growth the substance inside which finally would form the meat of the coconut is a very beautiful water, sweet, fresh but very cold. When the coconut is in this unripened state it is called *lanha*.[5] When many of these are carried on board, the *gelva* can have a supply of good water, and the inner husk of the coconut, inside of which is the water, is so

[1] Swahili *makanda*, bags of plaited fibres, larger at the base than the top, generally used for grain. The form is plural, sing. *kanda*.
[2] Perhaps *gorgoli*, the bowl of a hubble-bubble (narghile), S. R. Dalgado, *Glossário Luso-Asiático* (Coimbra, 1919, 21), I, 439.
[3] 'The fermented sap of several kinds of palm', H.J., 'Sura', a synonym for toddy.
[4] 'Arrack made from the sap of a palm tree', HJ, 'Nipa'.
[5] The fruit of the coconut palm when still green and tender. Dalgado, 1919, I, 510.

tender at that stage that it is eaten like artichoke, has the same effects, and is rather tasty and well-flavoured. After the coconut has reached its full growth it serves as merchandise and is loaded on ships bound for various parts of the world. If the fully matured coconut is broken into pieces and put into a shredder or grater, it is converted into a certain coarse flour which, when cooked, makes some raised cakes of bread in certain tubes in which it is placed. This is called *puto*, with the accent on the last syllable.[1] When these same coconuts are left to dry, they lose all their juice and become withered. When the coconut is in this state, they break the hard inner shell called *chereta*[2] and use it for spoons and also for porringers. The heart of the coconut, when thoroughly dry, is dissolved into an oil, called coconut oil, which has many uses in all of India, both for eating and for their medicines and ointments. It is white, mainly coagulated, and rather sweet smelling. They ship great quantities of it, but much greater quantities, however, of the dried coconut itself, which is called *copra* and is eaten by the natives of India as a great treat. It can thus be seen that from the palm-tree alone a ship can be put in the water, have its sails set and be fully loaded with merchandise with nothing aboard that did not come from the palmtree. These are the ships which in those waters along the coasts of Arabia and Ethiopia are called *gelvas*. They do not venture into the open sea, but sail along the coast close to land, although they do extend themselves and sail many hundreds of leagues.

[1] 'The Singalese also prepare a dish called Putoo, considered a great delicacy, of the Kelingoo flour. To the meal is added a little water, some prawns or small fish, scrapings of cocoa-nut kernels, unripe Jack-fruit (the produce of *Artocarpus integrifolia*), etc.; this mixture is put into an ola (i.e. Palmyra-leaf) basket, placed on the top of a pot of boiling water, covered over...and cooked by the steam.' Berthold Seemann, *Popular History of the Palms and their Allies* (London, 1856), p. 107. By 'Kelingoo' is meant the young Palmyra palm, *Borassus*. 'Puṭṭu...salted dough baked in steam.' F. Kittel, *A Kannaḍa–English Dictionary* (Mangalore, 1894), p. 991.
[2] More often *chireta*, sometimes *chareta*, the hard inner shell of the coconut, Dalgado, 1919, I, 264.

[How we disembarked at the port of Bailur and reached the Kingdom of Dancali]

I return now to the story of my voyage, which I interrupted at the point where we were entering the Red Sea to give an account of its coasts, waters and name, and of the other things I observed there, as I have related. We did not consider ourselves safe on passing through the entrance to this sea because of the Turks who lie in wait there for the ships from India. Through God's mercy we caught sight of the narrows toward evening – excellent timing since we could sail through the narrows under cover of darkness without danger of falling into the hands of the Turks. And this we did, entering the narrows at approximately nine o'clock at night. And as we had a weak wind we were not able to sail far enough during the rest of the night to be far from danger in the morning. However, since we entered by way of the channel on the Ethiopian side and the ships were not large, we stayed as far away from the island as possible, and with the little wind we had, we found ourselves in the morning far enough away so that we could not be seen from the other side of the island as long as the Turks were in the other channel. And as we purposely sailed close to the mainland as long as it was daylight, we began to keep a careful watch for the port of Bailur which was our destination. Since this port was not very well known, even though we had pilots of that sea aboard who had often come to it, they did not have much information concerning that port because it was not frequented by ships from India. All agreed, however, that it was a few leagues beyond the narrows, and, in the opinion of those who spoke with most authority, it was only twelve leagues beyond the narrows.

For this reason we sailed very close to the land so that we could obtain information by meeting some fishing bark or *almadia* or by discovering people on land and sending someone to get information from them. And although we saw some fishing vessels, as soon as they observed our ships with their oars, prows and cotton sails and, through these peculiarities, concluded that the people aboard were different from

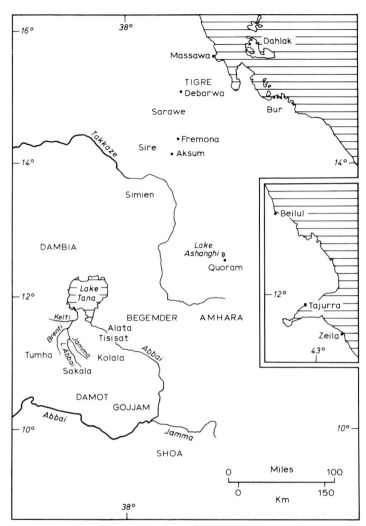

Map 2. Ethiopia

those who usually sail that sea, they would fly for safety as fast as they could, completely distrustful of the signals of peace which we made to them. This was very annoying to us because this search lasted two days, during which time we sent an *almadia* with an Abyssinian boy who knew Arabic to ply the shore and try to obtain information about the place where we were and the port we were seeking. Returning periodically, he could bring us no information until, going around a point or shelf of sand which jutted out into the sea, we found ourselves in a beautiful bay in the middle of which, almost invisible against the background of the shore, were some masts of small ships landed on the beach, which we could barely make out. In order to be surer of the truth of the matter and to cause less fear among the people, we sent the *almadia* and the Abyssinian to obtain information. It was the first of May when the latter set out to observe the land while we remained at sea, waiting all afternoon and all night for definite news, which did not come until the next morning when the *almadia* with the Abyssinian returned to inform us that this was the port of Bailur that we were seeking and that the ships on shore belonged to Arabian Muslims who were there. That night they had completely evacuated their ships on the shore, everyone taking refuge on land. It caused us great joy to learn definitely that we had arrived at the port we were seeking. We were especially glad because of the soldiers on the three ships that were bringing us. These soldiers were impatient and very greedy for the booty they expected in the mouth of the Strait. It seemed to them that with so many delays they were likely to lose all that booty. They were very restive because of the slowness and were already grumbling against the captain and demanding that, since they were not finding the port, they should return. They pretended to be much afraid of the Turkish galleys, but their real fear was that they would be too late to find booty when they went out. With the news that we had reached our destination, all this grumbling quieted down. It became a question, however, of sending someone ashore in the *sanguicel* to talk with the Seque of that land inquiring if there were a message from the Emperor of Ethiopia concerning us or news of our coming and also noting his behaviour and disposition for the purpose of assessing what confidence we could have in placing ourselves in his power if we were to remain there. The Patriarch and other Fathers chose me for this task. Since there was no time for delay, I got into the *sanguicel* immediately with a few Portuguese from the flagship along with others already aboard the *sanguicel*. Starting to row, we headed for shore, while the two ships remained out to sea. By this time there were many people on the shore, and one of the xeques, on horseback, was waiting to see what we had decided to do, especially the *sanguicel* which was coming toward them. And because it was then the time to discuss peace, before reaching land, I ordered the rowing to stop and again sent the Abyssinian to the Xeque with a message that we had come there in friendship by order of the Emperor and that they must already have news of this in a letter from the Emperor, and since we had to pass through that land to his court we wanted to disembark but that, in order to discuss first the means by which security would be given for the safety of the person or persons leaving the protection of his own group, that is, either they would give security to me if I were to go ashore or they would take security for one of their number if he were to come to our ship. While the boy went on his errand, so that they would not be startled by the unfamiliar clerical garb when I went to them or they came to me, it seemed appropriate for me to dress as a *sodagar* which means respected merchant,[1] for which we had brought appropriate clothing from India. I wore a tunic of black gingham[2] down to the middle of my legs, slit Moorish breeches just down to the ankle, slippers on my feet, a robe with wide sleeves, made of fine cloth[3] of silk and white and blue linen, and a small Moorish cap with a turban wound around many times. In this garb I stood at the opening of the rain or sun canopy with all the dignity and gravity I could muster, for those people are much swayed by outward appearances. And to make all the greater impression, all the Portuguese were standing before me on both sides as if they were accompanying me with great respect.

Meanwhile, after they had received my message and had discussed the matter among themselves, the Muslims decided that the Xeque would send as hostages four captains of *gelvas* who were in port, asking me send mine also so that the Xeque could come to see me. When they had arrived and had boarded the ship and saw how it was fitted out, the order of the soldiers, the guns which were at the bow and along the head-rails, the elegance with which everyone was dressed, the smiling countenances and peaceful manner with which they were received, and my dress and appearance and the retinue I had with me – all

---

[1] Persian *saudāgar*, 'merchant'.

[2] *gingão*. A fabric made from cotton that was dyed before being woven and was sometimes mixed with another material, *HJ*, 'Gingham'.

[3] *pecutilho*, a finer version of the coarse cloth called *picote*, itself similar to the *burel* often used for friars' habits.

these things they noted, and they appeared not to be displeased by them. They came toward me, making their salaams, kissing both hands, bowing their heads and saying aloud, 'selamale', which means 'peace be with you'.[1] I received them with the same courtesy, standing in the entrance to the shelter, where they gave me the message from the Xeque which said he trusted that we came with no other intent but a peaceful one and since we wanted peace it was pleasing to them also. And to give us complete satisfaction he was sending me those four captains as hostages and he asked that I send him mine so that we could talk. I answered that, since I was coming in peace and I was sure of his peaceful intention, I wanted only to give him satisfaction concerning mine and I thus sent him a Portuguese as a hostage and sent his four captains back to him so that he could see the spirit of good faith in which we were coming. The captains were very appreciative of the courtesy and kindliness with which I treated them, especially since they appeared to be important people, dressed as they were in *cabaias*[2] and turbans. They all went back to the shore, and the Xeque was so obliged by my confidence and courtesy that he refused to permit my Portuguese to remain ashore, but bringing him with him, along with the captains again and the second chief, they all came aboard my *almadia* with no weapons whatever. Our weapons, however, were secretly ready for any event. After they had arrived on board, I received them in the same way and with the same display as I had done for the first visitors. Having them enter the shelter after the first greetings, I invited them, in the customary fashion, to have some wine, which they drank with no apparent concern that this is prohibited by their religion, and some sweetmeats, which they liked very much and to which they were not very much accustomed. After the refreshments, I asked about the king, who, I learned, was a few days' journey from there, that he had received a message from the Emperor concerning our coming and was thus expecting us, and that one of the xeques, named Furt, who was present, had arrived a few days earlier from the court of this king, who was his king, where he had been present when the message arrived, which the Emperor had sent concerning our coming, but he was unwilling to reveal to me that a Portuguese and a Muslim captain were there and that they were coming to accompany us. With the news he gave me and because many of the things he said coincided with the letter and words used in it by the Emperor when he sent word to us

---

[1] Arabic *Salām 'alaikum*, the normal greeting among Muslims.
[2] See p. 51 n. 1.

to come via that place, I considered our immediate business concluded. Since the people in the two ships had been waiting out to sea since morning to learn of the outcome of this negotiation and so that they would understand how well everything was settled to everyone's satisfaction, I ordered the flags flown and some small artillery fired, that the ship carried. At this signal, the two other ships, which were larger and more heavily armed, did the same. I explained to the Muslims the significance of all this as an expression of our joy and how I was celebrating his friendship and his king's health and my companions were doing the same. The Muslims, however, were terrified by the salute, although it did not cause them to be distrustful. As the hour was late they all left, offering us the hospitality of their land and telling us that we could disembark if we wished, since their king had sent word and they promised in his name that we were as safe in that land as we would be in our own. After they had left, I stopped playing the role of a *sodagar*, and the Portuguese, in a spirirt of great hilarity, abandoned their role of respectful courtesy. Since it was almost night, I did not go to the other ships because I also was to disembark in the morning. I sent information to the Patriarch, however, concerning what had happened with the Muslims and advised them to come closer to shore so that we could try to land, which they did.

What with our joy at the prospect of entering [Ethiopia] and the fact that we had been talking with the soldiers all through the voyage about the lands to which we were going, the Portuguese who were going there, the great opportunity which attended our entrance there, and the service of God in which we hoped to be employed, some of the soldiers were moved to accompany us, moved partly by Christian piety and partly because it seemed to them that they would not lose anything on the journey in temporal interests by serving that prince since he was showing so much benevolence. Many of them were preparing to accompany us, but the captain forbade it because of his plans for privateering and trying his hand with the Muslims, where he would feel the lack of the soldiers if he let them go. And although he wanted to prevent all of them from leaving, as he did, one, however, more zealous than the rest, succeeded in obtaining permission and went ashore with me the next day when we landed the ships and unloaded what little we had brought, all of which came down to priests' vestments, our little books, the Patriarch's good library, and some small devotional items belonging to each of us.

On this occasion we were to have some unpleasantness, which could have been very serious, because of the *gelva* taken by the soldiers in the port of Meth. As we had kept a few sacks of millet, all with the marks that their owners had put on them for identification, as well as a few other items, all of which obviously did not belong to Afrangis, which is what they call the Portuguese, it happened that as they were being brought ashore to be sold, the Muslims noticed that the goods were the property of others and that they belonged to people who were not so friendly and communicative that they would have given those goods to our men, so that they became suspicious concerning what had happened. It came to our attention that the Muslims were murmuring about this. We were very much disturbed by this, we priests more than the soldiers who were leaving, because of the difficulties it could cause for our journey and the danger to our persons since we were remaining in their hands. We discussed ways of correcting the situation. As for what little had already been sold, that would have to go at its or our risk since there was no longer anything that could be done about it. All we could do with respect to that was to have excuses ready to give in case they should be necessary. As for the rest which still stayed on board, we saw to it that it did not go ashore, so that the murmuring stopped, especially with the departure of the three ships, which at the end of three days set sail for the mouth of the Strait to wait for the large merchant ships.

Of those three ships I shall only say that they had it in their power to make a great deal of profit but that they lost everything because of their greed. Unwilling to share the expected booty, which was more than certain, with one another, they separated. And although merchant ships carry very little artillery, they do have many soldiers, who are the only passengers they carry and who defend the ships with matchlocks, lances, arrows, and stones and are effective especially when our ships are inferior to theirs because of their smaller size and lower sides. Separated as they were, then, so that each one could enjoy whatever fortune was delivered into its hands, they spread out outside of the entrance to the Strait. They were thus very sparse when they should have been close together in a place so narrow that none of the merchant ships coming there could escape through the opening or could prevail against the strength that together they would lend one another. Divided, they were weak and scattered so that singly they were unable to take by force the merchant ships that each one of them met; and through excessive greed and covetousness, they thus lost what they could have gained if they had joined together and had moderated their greed. The booty they obtained was very inconsiderable so that they returned to India, ill content with the journey and even less content with the profit they derived from it, after leaving us in the port of Bailur.

It is the port of a small, barren, poorly populated kingdom called Dancali. It is ruled by a Muslim, the entire population being of the same faith. This ruler recognizes a certain vassalage to the Emperor of Ethiopia, either for reasons of self-preservation or because of a historic feudal relationship. He was always loyal and obedient to what the Emperor ordered him to do. When the Emperor saw the risk the Patriarch was running by attempting to enter his lands via Masua and the hands of the Turks, he wrote to India that the entrance should be made this way. He had first notified the king that we were to enter through his territory and at the time of the monsoon he sent on the same mission a Portuguese named Paulo Nogeira,[1] the grandson of another Nogeira, one of the Portuguese who went to Ethiopia with Dom Christovão da Gama, along with a Muslim xeque of a land near this kingdom of Dancali, named Xumo[2] Salamai whose land was called Sanafe,[3] the furthest outpost of the empire of Ethiopia in this direction. These ambassadors reached the king a few weeks before our arrival at Bailur, where the king detained them until he had news of our coming. But we shall leave them until we go and find them at the same place, and I shall relate in the meantime what happened after we went ashore and after the departure of the ships.

On the following day we walked from the shore to the town, which was half a league in distance, some camels coming to get our belongings. However, as is the custom, to say nothing of the greed which is so much a part of the nature and faith of these people, they refused to leave there without our giving them our gifts. Since I was the one entrusted with this responsibility and the one whom they had visited first and with whom they had dealt, they were expecting this courtesy from me. For this purpose, I had a tent that we carried with us set up and I installed myself in it with some cloth from India. Cloth from India is a very popular item of merchandise in those lands. Because of its popularity we had come with a good supply of it for these

[1] Properly Nogueira. He had reached Ethiopia in the previous year by way of Massawa. The Emperor sent him with a mule and a horse as presents to the Dankali ruler. P. da Costa derives this information from Braga Public Library, MS. 779, doc. XXII, f. 7.

[2] Amh. *shum*, a district chief.

[3] Senafe, in Tigre, about 30 miles north of Adigrat. It was by no means the part of Ethiopia nearest to Bailul.

occasions, which are numerous, and also for us to use as money with which to buy what we needed. I had a few bales opened, from which I took some pieces of painted cotton cloth and some pieces of cloth called rough-weave, like sack-cloth, the size of two sheets. I divided these among the xeques and the captains of the *gelvas*. I estimate that each one of them received at the most five *cruzados'* worth of this cloth.[1] I also gave some to other less important people; for many gathered round to watch the distribution. All this was necessary for newcomers who wanted to have friends in a land which produced so few friendly people. We withdrew to the town, where we stayed for thirteen days, which should have been a shorter time since there was nothing for us to do there. It was a small town of no more than fifty inhabitants, straw houses, not much in the way of provisions beyond a few goats and kids which the Muslims sold us since all the people in that kingdom are poor, rough and usually very wretched. Our shelter was under a shed open on all sides. Our beds were the ground or mats, and at most our bales – a practice which we continued for our entire journey so that we soon became used to it, and it stood us in good stead for later experiences. Even here, we had some delicacies to eat because we had some things from the ship's provisions: rice, dates and biscuit. On land we found some flour, a few goats and kids which did not cost us much and whose only drawback was that there were too few of them. Since we did not know how much trust we could place in the friendliness of our hosts, we stood watch by turns all through the night, not because we would be able to defend ourselves against them if they intended to harm us, since we did not know our way by land, the land being so strange to us, and there was no recourse by sea, but rather so that we would not be taken by surprise – which we considered an advantage well worth the effort for the whole journey, during which we kept up this practice of standing watch. During the thirteen days we stayed there, with nothing remarkable happening to us, we hired camels for our belongings and bought a few donkeys of which we could avail ourselves when greatly fatigued and which would, in the meantime, carry the bags containing the breviaries and each one's little books. And because we did not find enough donkeys for each of us to have one, we bought one for every two Fathers. The owners loaded and unloaded them, took them to pasture and brought them back, since each of us had no better or worse servants than himself.

In this way, we set out in the afternoon of Ascension Day, when

---

[1] 1 *cruzado* = 400 *reis*. It was a gold coin weighing 3.56 grams.

we travelled a little more than a league so that our day's journeys from the next day forward would follow a regular routine. The camel drivers, in addition to the price of their five large pieces of rough-weave each, for the hiring of each camel, which was a gold mine for them, forced us, all through the journey, to give them boiled rice to eat. This was a great encumbrance, not only because of the effort it cost us when we arrived, tired at the end of a day's journey and had to cook for the Muslims, but also because we were wasting much of our provisions on them, provisions which we were to miss sorely at a later time. However, in the circumstances in which we found ourselves, it was advisable for us to submit to almost anything. The first malicious thing perpetrated on us by the Muslims – and there were many such things, as one might expect from camel drivers who were relatives, followers, and of the race and condition of Mafamede – was that, although the king of Dancali was very close to where we were and we could have reached his court in two or three days by travelling inland on a good pleasant road with water and food available, they purposely led us on a detour always at the edge of the sea, lacking water, through sandy places and untrodden, unpleasant deserts for the purpose of keeping us from seeing their more desirable lands which they feared we might come to conquer; for they were certainly not without fears in this respect where there was so little reason for them to have them. Who is there, however, who does not believe that his own uncultivated field full of brambles and briars is in all ways the best ground in the world, especially when he hasn't seen others? The Muslims were also motivated by something else in taking us on this detour, and this was that they had received payment for the hiring of the camels much larger than what was normally paid in that land, although we considered it cheap, and gave us so much work in order to deserve the pay. Needless to say, if we had known this, we would not only have excused them but would have paid them even more. We travelled on foot behind and at the pace of the camels, with our walking sticks in our hands, dressed now in our Jesuit garb. The Muslims did not show any surprise at the difference between the present garb and that in which they first saw me. They believed that both belonged to us and were appropriate to our functions. The day's journeys were not very long but from six to eight leagues. The heat made them seem longer, as well as our fatigue because we were unused to it. We never met any people, nor did we want to. We found some water, but so little that sometimes two days passed without our finding it more than once. It was often brackish, dirty and foul-smelling because of being stagnant, and with filth of dead animals in it. At other times, because some cattle and other animals had got into it to drink, it was so full of dung, dirt and urine from these animals that we had to cover our eyes and noses and take it out quickly so that our natural instinct would not revolt against it so much. Necessity, however, made it seem fresh and sweet to us. The worst part was that it was necessary for us to carry it in leather bottles on the camels and in small leather bags hanging from our necks, the latter to give relief against heat and fatigue, and the former for us to have at the end of the day's journey for cooking a little rice to eat, sometimes with little else and at other times with nothing to go with it. What this land lacked in people it had in superabundance in ferocious animals: lions, tigers, leopards, and many other fierce animals of various types, of which we were continually finding traces and fresh tracks. We did not sleep at night with any feeling of security, but the watch we always kept protected us from the dangers. We did not meet with any highwaymen, for we already had them with us as part of our entourage. One night, however, gave us a great fright. At nightfall we had seen a *gelva* which, within sight of us, was sailing close to the shore. Later, a man suddenly was coming out of the brushwood and came toward us with a goat, asking if we wanted to buy it and asking to be allowed to take shelter with us. We were persuaded that he was a spy. He thus forced us to keep watch more carefully all night long, as we doubled the watches and kept the man continually under surveillance so he would not flee. And as a few young Portuguese laymen participated in this guard duty and since we, although in religious orders, did not consider ourselves exempt from justly defending ourselves, as soon as we were stopping at the place where we were to spend the night, we busied ourselves forming a circle of the camel loads which we manned at various stations with the muskets we carried with us and a few matchlocks, the people sleeping in the middle of these barricades, and the sentinels at certain posts guarding them on the outside. They did not fail to give one another signals periodically which encouraged them to be alert. This was very necessary because of our lack of sleep and the need our bodies felt for rest and sleep. Someone would shout periodically 'Vegia, vegia',[1] to which the others around the circle would reply. The camel drivers made a great joke of this, repeating together 'bugia, bugia',[2] thinking that

[1] 'Keep watch, keep watch.'
[2] 'Act like a monkey, act like a monkey!'

they were saying the same thing according to their understanding of it. We spent the night in these activities until in the morning we were disabused of our error when we saw the innocence and sincerity of the man who had come to sell us his goat without malice. We kept the goat, paid for it and continued our journey.

When we left the town, one of the xeques, named Furt, wanted to accompany us on horseback in order, so he said, to show us the way and to do us honour, but there can be no doubt that his greedy nature told him that this was a good opportunity and he wanted to profit by accompanying us. And since the whole affair was based on his self-interest and he saw that I was the one who made disbursements, gave presents, and was most responsible for managing things, he immediately fastened himself upon me and offered to let me ride his horse from time to time, which I was glad to do. I also rode at times with both of us on the horse. At times I would try to give my turn to some one of the members of the company because they were tired, but Furt, our guide, would not consent to it, saying that I was thin and weighed little. From this I saw that sometimes it is useful for a man to be a skinny wretch, since my not weighing so much was of use to me in this instance. The horse was such that it could not carry a heavy load but needed some relief to be able to keep on its feet. One day, however, it ran the risk of paying with its life for the kindness it showed me and we ran the risk of paying for it many times over. Furt would have been very glad because he would get a better horse and would stand to gain the price of two or three horses of that quality. This is what happened: We arrived at a place where there were wells of water, the only such place in that locality. Since all kinds of wild animals and deer came there for water, it seemed to me that we could kill a deer which would provide us with a good feast. For greater security, four of the members of the Company went out with four good matchlocks to wait for their quarry at the wells, and although they stayed there for a long time, they did not have occasion to use their weapons. Because it was late, they [some people from the caravan] went to bring back their companions, who suddenly heard a noise at the edge of the road in the undergrowth. Since it was an uninhabited place, and the rest of the caravan was far away, they thought that it must be some animal from the wild, uncultivated, bushy area there, not believing that any camel or any other of our animals would stray so far. And thus all of them were ready to fire their matchlocks point blank at whatever might come out, persuaded as they were that it was some wild animal and one of considerable size from what they could see of its shape, which they were beginning to make out in the shadows and undergrowth. When they were already taking aim at it, the poor horse put forth his head from the foliage just in time to be recognized as Furt's horse. If he had delayed approximately the time to say Ave Maria, he would have felt in himself the pain of eight shots from the four matchlocks. The wretched animal was so close to their muzzles that it was nearly impossible for him to escape or avoid being hit by all of them. If this had happened, Xeque Furt would have been without a mount for the journey, I would have been without any respite for my suffering, the Xeque would be very much at odds with us, and we would have been condemned to make amends by giving them great quantities of goods which is the word they use in referring to property. If we paid all this, it would be at great risk since we were in a part of the world where there was no recourse or justice beyond that dictated to the judges by greed. The danger having passed and the misfortune avoided, which for anyone in our situation could not help but be great if it were to occur, we continued our journey, and we shortly found ourselves visited by the king's brother, who, to do us courtesy, came to receive and accompany us with as many as fifty guards armed with *adargas* and *zargunchos*. Although this was ostensibly to do us honour, the true reason was that he wanted to obtain his gift on the way, making a profit from the visit; for Xeque Furt who captained the caravan and took command of all opportunities for gain, informed us that it was proper to give a present to the Infante and wanted to see what we were giving him and said it was to his liking, which was very little to our liking because he helped himself handsomely. He was taking his godfather's bread for his godson.[1] And since we were new to the land, and therefore new to its customs, we accepted as truth what he said was necessary. Although we did not believe it, we endured it since we could not do otherwise. The gift consisted of some pieces of rough-weave, painted cloth from India, trinkets from China, namely large and small items of china-ware, serving trays, a little box and a writing set. He liked all of it. He accepted anything that had a relation to clothing and rejected anything made of wood, asking that the latter be exchanged for clothing. We made the exchanges, but he came back afterward in full confidence to ask us to give him the items he had rejected. We acceded to his request to make him the more content, after the manner

---

[1] *Fazia do pão de seu compadre pera seu afilhado*, a proverbial saying meaning that he was helping himself.

of a person setting out to test the temper of new masters. We had to look upon the Muslims as masters in that land where we were travelling as servants or captives. The black Infante being satisfied with the gift, and somewhat less satisfied with a salute of ten or twelve muskets given to him by a soldier who had disembarked with us and served as chief of what little artillery we had, which, however, was considerable for that land, according to his profession, we continued our journey, which I could not do without great difficulty. Since the chief of artillery was not very skilful at firing muskets, the forks of trees serving him as musket-rests or supports, on one of which he tried to make the musket more secure and did it with such impetuosity that when it fired it jumped back with so much force that, because I was closer to it, I had to move aside quickly to avoid being hit on the head. But I could not get my feet out of the way, so that, as it reached one of my legs it ripped my shin from top to bottom, tearing the flesh with the end of the musket-barrel. And since it met with no resistance whatsoever, because most of us were by that time without boots, and I was one of the bootless ones, the blow met no obstacle to counter the force with which the musket-barrel came to me and left me in very wretched condition. Unfortunately there was no rag to bind the wound so that a medicament could better be applied to it. As it was necessary to keep travelling, a piece of the gingham cassock I was wearing served as a bandage. I was fortunate to have this to use for this purpose, for I had few pieces of it left, the rest of them having been caught and left on the thorns and sharp protuberances all along our route. For the rest of the journey, my good friend Xeque Furt fortunately came to my rescue with his horse, on which I continued slowly, for it was only to this that the Muslim's friendship extended. It was no longer a matter of relief but one of absolute necessity.

CHAPTER 12

[What happened with the king of Dancali]

The morning before we arrived where the petty king was, some of his servants appeared with five mules and a message brought by a Muslim authorized by his king, in which he welcomed us and sent us other greetings and said that those five mules were to carry five of the most important Fathers, which included all of us who were there since the other two were lay brothers. After we had given our reply and accepted the gift, all of which was given for the purpose of creating more reasons for his deserving the gift he was expecting and wages for the messengers, because all of them were out for profit, we mounted the mules and travelled a distance of two leagues, still through uncultivated, scrubby terrain where all the ground appeared to be moving because it was covered with locusts, so thick that nothing else could be seen, a very common plague in that land. They did not fly because they were not yet fully grown, and those of the preceding year had laid their eggs there, covering the ground with so bad a type of seed from which soon came clouds of that plague which destroy whole provinces, as I shall later relate. For the last half a league we followed a river upward to where the king had his court. The river was wide and ran in the winter between the mountains which surrounded it. When we were there it had only an abundance of white pebbles.[1] By digging anywhere, however, one found water, as we later experienced. The king had his palaces at the foot of a small hill among several thorn bushes and wild trees. They consisted of four or five small shelters and fifteen or twenty thatched huts, two or three of which were the king's and the others belonged to his mother, brothers and some of his more honoured servants. The pomp and decoration of the houses were consistent with the material of which they were made. The houses were, however, wretchedly and barbarously scattered about.[2]

After dismounting the mules at a musket-shot's distance from the royal residence under some jujube and other trees with which the

[1] Le Grand says reeds and rushes.
[2] Le Grand says the huts were placed among bushes and some wild *Natega* trees, which gave a little shade. *Natega* is an error for *náfega* or *anáfega*, Jujube.

123

riverbed and its banks were well covered and shaded, we went to visit the king who received us in a thatched hut or little round house, of which the walls were of sticks and clay and the roof of straw. Fifty people could fit in it seated on the ground. In one part was the royal throne, a platform made of stone and earth covered with a carpet and two velvet cushions. In another part was his horse with all the harness and items appropriate to a stable, since it is the custom of these people to have their horses or mule right in their homes and in their sight. This is true of the king as well as his subjects. After we had entered the royal hall, which was as I have described, we sat down on the ground with our legs crossed awaiting the coming of His Highness who was not very long in coming after the prior entrance of the ordinary pages and messengers, one with a gourd of mead,[1] another with the china to drink from, another with the tobacco pipe which was a coconut shell full of water in the mouth of which was the bowl of the pipe with fire and tobacco and a silver tube through which one smoked, filtering the smoke through the water so that it would be more refined and mild.[2] There followed some more honoured servants. After them came the king, well dressed in silken *cabaias*, a turban on his head, with some jewels for adornment, in particular two amulets of finely wrought gold which came down over his temples. He had a small lance in his hand by way of a sceptre. A small velvet-covered chair was in front for him to sit on. Behind him came his officers, such as his major-domo, comptroller, captain, etc. We rose to pay our respects to him, and, when they were seated, we went up to kiss his hand, grasping it and kissing our own and he his, whereupon we returned to our places. Everyone was silent, as is the custom, for about eight minutes, during which time the king, we ourselves and the others present were observing all that could be seen of persons, clothing, etc. The period of silence was ended by the king, who gave the signal to talk by saying to the interpreter that we were welcome, that he had been expecting us for days because of the information he had received from the Emperor, his father (a term and name they use to show love and good will with a suggestion of filial devotion to persons to whom they profess obedience), to the effect that we had crossed the sea and other things of this sort, and, in conclusion, that we should be as unworried and free of fear as if we were in our own homelands since his lands belonged to the Emperor, who loved us so much and recommended us so highly. We responded in the same tenor, replying satisfactorily to everything he had said and

---

[1] The Ethiopian *ṭej*.   [2] The narghile, hookah, or hubble-bubble.

showing gratefulness for the good will and kindliness he offered us. With little more than what I have related, that day's visit came to an end. The servants who had taken the mules came after us asking for their wages, customary for such service. It is necessary to pay them for this. They do not have the patience to delay for long any possible occasions for personal gain. They soon advised us to prepare the present for the king, which gave us an excellent means of determining the extent of his greed. Furt told us that on the occasion of the first meetings it was necessary to bring some small present, keeping the major part of what we had for the large present, informing us in this way that we had to give both a large present and a small one. The small present we brought consisted of two pieces of fine Indian cotton, a few porcelain objects and trinkets from China with other trifles of this kind. The king refused to accept them because they were not enough, an example of the courtesy they display on such occasions. We tried to do better with the large one, making it to Furt's liking. Furt wanted to see everything in order to augment the gift to what seemed appropriate to him. It consisted of a small carpet,[1] pieces of a thin, cotton cloth from India[2] and other fine materials from India, pieces of cloth from China, not of silk, all of which came to twenty pieces in all, and was probably worth almost a hundred *cruzados*. After he had counted it all up, the wicked old man went off to prepare for our entrance or to advise the king to accept nothing in order to shock us into giving more. Since I was the most experienced in this sort of thing, I was the one to present the gift along with a few of our party who carried it. Arriving at the same room as before and finding the king there who was already expecting me, I proffered my usual polite remarks and then, ordering the pieces to be uncovered, presented them to him on behalf of all of us. I explained how limited our means were because of our condition as members of a religious order and the vows of poverty we had taken. I told him that, nevertheless, he was due all the courtesy required by his royal position and that in order to show him all the courtesy in our power, I was bringing him, in the name of all of us, those tokens of our good will. I said that, although they were not commensurate with his greatness (it is certainly true that I thought I was greatly exaggerating as far as he was concerned), it was all that was within our power in a land so foreign to us. They were destined for him, however, if he would look upon them with benevolence as a kindness to us. To all this, as I was making a thousand

[1] *alcatifa.*   [2] *bofetas.*

compliments and expressions of humility, the king kept silent, showing displeasure as he turned his head this way and that in the manner of one who was insulted by what was being brought to him. He replied to me that, although he appreciated our intentions, he was not accepting their concrete results in that present since it was not commensurate with his person or with what he expected from us, and he motioned with his hand for it to be taken from his presence just as I had brought it. Although I tried to persist in excuses, he did not change countenance, whereupon I also became angry and, now with greater daring caused by the meanness, greed and rudeness of the petty king, I told the servants to carry the present away with the intention of subtracting some from it, as I did, because I knew that he would ask for it again. Those present were not pleased on seeing my resolve, and, so as not to spoil the gift-giving ceremony completely, Furt came after me excusing the king and blaming us for bringing him so little; whereupon we turned on him, telling him that all of it was brought by his order and nothing was lacking from what he had ordered to be given and that, in any case, we did not have any other things, any greater in quantity or quality, so that, since the king did not want the gift, we would use it for expenses on our travels. Meanwhile, I had already removed three of the twenty pieces we had presented. However, since all of this was nothing more than a series of tricks dictated by greed on the part of all of them, Furt insisted that we increase the gift with something else, and no matter how much he insisted, he had no success with us because we were perfectly aware that if we were to increase the gift, it would have the same result and reception as the first one. Seeing this, the wicked old man ordered the present to be brought there again. He counted the pieces and finding three fewer than before, asked that they be restored. After some arguing back and forth concerning the restitution, we finally did it, and on the next day we went to give the same gift, but now certain that it would be accepted, as indeed it was, but with the same attitude as before. To the mother and brothers and principal courtiers we gave our less substantial gifts, which were, however, better received. We even gave gifts to the king's musicians, who one morning appeared to us with their musical instruments which were similar to contrabasses.[1] They sang so insipidly and out of tune that they provided more annoyance than amusement. At the end of two hours or more they asked for the reward for their efforts, which we would have been more willing to give them before hearing them,

---

[1] *rabequões.*

since we would not have suffered to such an extent, rather than as a reward for their playing. Their request and hope were for the moment frustrated and, although they wanted to force us legally to pay them, the privileges of foreigners ignorant of such customs, to say nothing of our not having invited them to perform, excused us from any obligation to pay. We did, however, give them something when they acknowledged it as a kindness on our part and not as a legal debt as they had wanted it.

As I have already said, the Patriarch had with him some young Canarese bondsmen from the church band, who were good musicians and played very well on various instruments, which we carried with us and which, since they were readily available, they took out from time to time and played to distract us from hunger and the fatigue of travelling. The king learned of this and requested to see them and how they were played. I took them to him with the musicians who very skilfully played some pieces for harp, viols and small fiddle.[1] The king and the others present were much pleased, particularly with the small fiddle since the fiddler played very well and performed several well-known pieces which he often played. One of the pieces imitated the braying of a donkey so realistically that they recognized it immediately with great applause without anyone telling them what it was supposed to be since it was so familiar and continual a thing in their daily lives.

In these activities we spent the days, not forgetting to seek permission to depart, foreseeing the impediments we were to meet, and more importantly so that we could travel to other areas seeking food which we could not obtain there. We were suffering a great lack of food there, both because there was no meat to buy in that land and because the king had proclaimed that no one should sell us any so that whatever we obtained would have to come through him and he would receive the greater gain and profits. The Muslims also wanted to profit and would have brought something to sell us were it not for the king's proclamation. Since they found themselves frustrated in this, one of them, with whom I was on friendly terms, came forward and informed me of the wicked plan, but with earnest entreaties that I should not reveal his identity because his life would be in danger. Since our lives were in no less danger, for lack of the necessities of life, for we had barely a little rice once a day, which was almost gone, I decided to have it out with the king and went one evening to visit him. Since

---

[1] *rabequinha.*

we were already acquainted, as I was the person with whom he dealt and through whom our group dealt with him, after a few polite remarks, I formally told him the following: Hear me, King. We came into your land by order of the Emperor, whom you call 'Father' because of your love and reverence for him. You received us with good words and promises of better actions. We were delighted to find, so far from our native lands, in a place where we were not known, someone who treated us with love and courtesy. We fully expected a happy outcome to our passage according to the offers that you made to us; and although until now we have found in your people and in your lands good friendship as far as the safety of our persons is concerned, we are now finding that you are treating us very differently from what you promised. For, while we thought we were in a land of friends, we find that we are in one of enemies who intend to take our lives. I ask you if this is right and if we have reason to complain to God and men of this falseness. I finished speaking and waited his reply which was, after a show of surprise, that he did not understand what I meant, that he did not know there was such treachery in his land and that if I had knowledge of anything that was being done against us, I should declare it to him so that he could remedy it immediately, and, concerning death, that he had us on his head (an expression they use to signify that they would die before allowing any harm to befall anyone under their protection) and there was therefore nothing to fear. I again insisted that lives are taken not only by the sword but also by hunger when it is extreme and irremediable as was our situation and that we owed our plight to no other than the king himself since he had ordered the proclamation that no one should sell us food, which was a clear intent to kill us, since there was no place for us to find food, that if this were his intention, our throats were there, for it were better to finish us with one blow than with many because in this way he was giving us a death both long-lasting and cruel. I rose to my feet at this point and offered my throat to him. The king was taken aback, partly because of the unusualness of the offer, partly by the resoluteness of it, partly because the blame for all this was shown to be his, and partly motivated by his conscience on seeing that he had been found out by those whom he was offending, and, after fuming a little, justifying himself and denying the proclamation, he insisted that I was to inform him who had told this to me. I told him that, even if it were to cost me my life, I would not tell this to him, and, as for the truth of what I was saying, the proof was that none of his subjects came to sell us anything, although they had done so at first. Finally, after long discussion, from which the king realized that he could not find out who had given us the information, he dismissed me with kind words.

As a result of this interview with the king, we received better treatment. People came to sell us a few goats, two or three for the price of one *pataqua*, and some millet, coarser than our fine millet and smaller than Indian corn, which, with the goat meat, made a meal for each of us.[1] At times we ate it toasted over a fire. We were well provided only with water, for there was good water to be had nearby by making holes in the dry river bed. At a depth of two spans we discovered good water, which we drank at any time of the day. Because the sun and heat were so intense, being trapped in that valley between two mountains and cut off from any breeze, and what did come was a burning flame, the water served to quench it and always moistened it more than it cooled because the water was very hot. However, when it comes to thirst, there is no bad water, but any water seems good and refreshing. We tried to go and look for it before sunrise, taking two small donkeys on which we loaded the water-skins and smaller leather bags. Every day two of us would take our turn, including the Patriarch when it was his turn to go. To add to our difficulties, the Muslims would come to the same place at the same time, seeking water and bringing their donkeys to give them water, and would play a thousand knavish tricks on us which we allowed to pass in order to bide time. One day, however, when one, who had been bolder and more insulting on other occasions, became more insulting than usual, it cost him dearly, serving as a punishment and warning both for him and for the others. What happened was that one morning, as the Patriarch with two other Fathers and two servants in his service were going for water with their small donkeys, the Muslim arrived, whom we had been watching for with the full intention of teaching him a lesson, if the occasion should arise, because of the roguish tricks he played on us. His courtesy was such that not only did he not permit us to take any more water as soon as he arrived, even though we were there first, but he expected and insisted that we draw water from the hole for his donkeys to drink, the quantity of available water being so small that there was never more than a cupful at a time, which, when

---

[1] Le Grand's text mentions three goats and some honey, but says nothing about millet. As on p. 56 there seems to have been either mistranslation or confusion between *mil* and *miel* by a copyist or the printer.

drawn out, came up again in the same quantity. We refused to satisfy his demand despite all his insistence. Extremely angry, he drew the water himself, heaping abusive language and dire threats upon us. Finally, as soon as he had all he wanted for himself and his donkeys, he gave a kick in the sand and covered the source of water so effectively that we had to work long and hard to open it up again. However, the deed was not left unpunished; for three young men who were there, lay servants of the Patriarch, one of whom was a bold Armenian, threw themselves upon the Muslim with a will, and with punches and kicks, since there were no other weapons, brought him to the ground, thoroughly pummelled; for all three tried to outdo one another and their time was not wasted. And continuing what they had begun, while one was kicking his body, since he was on the ground beneath them, the Armenian held him so tightly by the throat that the Muslim gave an indication of the dire straits in which he found himself with a good proportion of his tongue protruding from his mouth, while the third youth continued to punch his body incessantly with his bare fists anywhere he could find an open spot from head to foot. And if the Fathers had not intervened by pulling the youths away, although they were not unhappy about the outcome, the youths were all so furious that the Muslim would soon have ended his days on earth, which would have been a great misfortune. He finally got up from the ground, not so self-satisfied and arrogant as at the beginning of the altercation, and, seeing that he had no advantage there, went to plead his case against us before the king, who did not give him an answer for the moment, but entrusted the verification of the case to his major-domo. It happened that we were all there that same afternoon on a certain matter. After it was finished, with many people present, the Muslim again made his charge against us. It fell to me to answer him, which I did by saying that what he said was true, but that he was more at fault than we because of what he had done to us prior to our actions, and that, being Portuguese, we were not accustomed to enduring such things. And after I answered the Muslim's arguments point by point, it turned out that the judge's final pronouncement was that we in truth had transgressed, for even if that man had behaved outrageously, we should have sought his punishment by legal means and not have taken justice into our own hands, but that, since we were foreigners and were not acquainted with the customs of the land, we had erred through ignorance and thus did not deserve punishment. The Muslim thus received nothing for his pains and was thenceforth so meek and mild that when he met us at the spring, he was the last one to provide himself with water as long as we were there, so that we considered it necessary to use occasionally the sort of treatment experienced by that Muslim so that we could live more peacefully, as we experienced in this instance and also on a later occasion.

[How we left Dancali for the Emperor's court]

Our departure was delayed for a long time, and in that hot furnace of stones we were wasting away for lack of the necessities of life. We kept pressing for permission and for the order for camels to make our journey, but the king was unwilling, intending to milk us dry, continually demanding what pleased him, even copper cauldrons. And as all these petty kings have a favourite for reasons of state, through whom they govern, I negotiated with this person one night in the greatest secrecy. He agreed to bring about our departure if I would give him a certain quantity of cloth. And as it seems likely that this was all he was waiting for, in two days the message came that we could set out on our journey at nightfall if, at the place agreed upon, the said favourite were to receive the payment for his diligence. From that time forward, he was to be our agent for the journey which was soon arranged, camels being brought and our goods loaded on them. We were accompanied by the Portuguese who had come to find us and the Muslim brother-in-law of this same king, also ambassador, along with still others, all of whom were in hopes of some sort of gain. We left that place where we had been for twenty-seven days in the comfortable circumstances which I have described. However, the king wanted to justify himself as we were leaving, ordering us to be called to his presence and asking us to say everywhere that he had done us great kindnesses, especially in our report to the Emperor. We promised him that we would do this, with the truthfulness permitted by the time and place. He begged our pardon, and he gave us a few flint-stones, for they have unusual ones there, and a cow. He sent for his own horse, which, saddled and accoutred just as he himself rode it, he ordered the Patriarch to mount, being the most important of us all, with his own servants accompanying him. This was an extraordinary honour and one which is given only when they want to honour someone very much, and as such we were grateful to him, although we soon paid for it; for when we arrived at the house, all the Muslims in our retinue demanded their customary reward, and it was necessary to give it to them because this was the way of doing honour and providing payment

Plate III. Lake Assal in Dankali country

which was in use. On the next day, we made our first day's journey,[1] and all those that followed were in the same order as the first, with our small donkeys, by twos, each carrying two of us, one of them following behind, however, carrying arms, clothing, and provisions, and with worse people accompanying us than on the first journey. The way was rugged, almost as wild as the one we had traversed before, without any possibility of buying the necessities of life. We had to get along with some millet[2] we carried with us and some slices of cow's meat dried in the sun, the thickness of a finger, but even so they were very little to eat. In places we considered it necessary, because of their being infested with snakes, to keep beating the ground and making a great noise to frighten them away. And when we went through such territory in the daytime, it was not so bad because we killed some that came between our feet, but at night the danger was greater and it was difficult to avoid them except by the threshing made by all of us together and the clamour that we intentionally set up, leaving the principal care for our safety in the hands of God Our Lord, in whose service we were taking those steps. And it was a necessary thing to travel thus at night so that we could arrive where there was water, in which those lands are singularly lacking. For this reason, there are special places which one must reach at the end of a day's journey, where there is water to be drawn from holes made in the sand or in places where rivers or brooks flow in winter, which is usually very bad. It happened that we travelled two or three days along a dry river bed between mountains and very high cliffs, and since the land is so rugged, this road made by the water is of great service to travellers. And at places in this locality we found much good water, which was as cool and running as was the opposite which we found elsewhere. It soon however was hidden underground, coming out again at a point six or eight leagues beyond with an abundant, perennial flow as if it had been continued to that point free and above ground. On these occasions, since they were not many, we satiated our thirst and made merry for a few days.

The Muslims were loath to lose their well-deserved reputation for malice, of which until then we did not have reason to complain. And although the first group had not given evidence of it, this second group did so with a vengeance, making up for the lack of it in the first. For they did everything they could to cause us trouble, especially an old

[1] Le Grand, and the Patriarch's letter already cited, state that they left on June 5.
[2] Here again Le Grand says honey for millet. Compare p. 56 n. 1 and p. 129 n. 1.

Muslim who was the head camel driver and one well versed in wickedness and an inveterate practitioner of it, all the more so as he tried to show himself and pass himself off as a pious person. For he never lost an opportunity to pray and salaam three or more times a day, going ahead and stopping at the edge of the path and at a higher place where he would be better seen by those of us who passed. There he gave the appearance of being extremely pious, rapturous, and reverent according to the teachings of his Koran, provided that it all be in public and nothing in secret. This man, then, with all his devotion, had more of it for all of our things, for he thought only of where he could find them least guarded; and since he kept such a constant watch, none escaped him. With this concern of his and in many other things he did to us, he caused us much trouble, so that we wanted to make him understand, on a safe occasion, how obliged we were to him for his good will; and we were looking forward to the time when we would find ourselves with our own people. However, his many efforts to play the usual tricks on us brought us that pleasure much sooner than we had anticipated; for one morning as we were finishing taking down our tent and, putting the ropes to one side, no sooner were we folding it than he took the ropes so stealthily that the theft was not detected until we found them missing when we wanted to put them inside the folded tent; and no matter how much we looked around for them, we were unable to find them. The evil old man was off to one side with his camel drivers, who were ridiculing our efforts, certain that we would not find the stolen ropes and enjoying the trick he had played, for he had acquired by that theft some harness for the camels at little cost to himself. By chance, however, because the tip of one of them was protruding, the Patriarch found the rest of the ropes under the saddle covers of one of the camels, where the old man had hidden them, and, as he was trying to pull them out and retrieve them, the thief came at him and prevented him from doing it, boldly laying hands on the prelate and offering him much resistance with such outcry and tumult that one would have thought that it was he who had been wronged and not we. His camel drivers rushed to his aid in great numbers, apparently very much involved and his accomplices in the whole affair. We also ran forward to help the Patriarch. The Muslim was so obsessed with greed, because he was losing what he had stolen, that he would not loosen his hold on either the ropes or the Patriarch. And as the rest of them were beginning to go too far, it was necessary to attack them with weapons, for the camel drivers were doing the same. They took their *zargunchos* and *adargas* and formed a group of twenty or more. We were not much smaller in number but were at a disadvantage in that we did not have people who were familiar with the territory and we did not have sufficient protection, so that they had the advantage over us in everything except weapons, since ours, although few in number, were matchlocks. It is true enough that none of them were loaded, but five or six of our people took them, unloaded as they were, and took aim with the same show of confidence as they would have done if each one had been loaded with two musket-balls. This attack was sufficient to cause the Muslims to restrain themselves, standing there with their weapons in their hands waiting to see what would happen. The old man, however, kept on with his dispute, which one of the Portuguese in our company wanted to terminate – he was the soldier who agreed to accompany us – and came forward quickly thinking it was high time to act, and drawing a scimitar,[1] forced the Muslim's head to one side with his left hand, and, given the position in which he put him, his anger and his actions, in addition to the desire that he had, he would have cut off his head with one blow if, just as he was striking the blow, a Father had not rushed forward to ward off the blow, which in fact would have accomplished its mission, but which would have brought great harm to us because of our situation and the land in which we found ourselves. This sufficed, however, to put an end to the dispute, the Muslim giving up the ropes that he was in a fair way to have bought at a higher price than he had contemplated. He was so insulted, however, that he decided to take vengeance by leaving us there, unloading the camels, and starting his journey back with them. But the Portuguese and two of the more intelligent Muslims went to him and, although they had great difficulty in calming him and persuading him to continue the trip with us, he did so for two reasons. One was the hope that he would be given goods in reparation for the wrong done him. The other was his expectation of having his revenge for it later, which, as it turned out, he did attempt. In both things, however, he was unsuccessful, the first because, even though he wanted all the property brought by the Portuguese soldier who tried to kill him, it appeared that he was so unfortunate that nothing could come to him since the said soldier did not have anything; as for the second one, God saved us from it as we shall see further on. However, we gave him some trifling thing from our poor belongings, which put an end to the matter for the time being. And although, on

---

[1] *alfange*, Arabic *khanjar*, a curved dagger.

the occasion of the mutiny, he was also complaining about me, I know not whether with or without good reason, it turned out that good war makes good peace, for from then on, he ordinarily loaned me one of his mules, going on foot and leading me on it, which he did for no one else, in return for some expression of good will or better deed, if he received it in the mutiny. From this and from the other which I related earlier, we came to the conclusion that with these Muslims it is not appropriate to be pleased with anything as far as they are concerned and that it is better to give them two blows on the neck rather than one. For, when their behaviour is intolerable and they receive kindly treatment in return, being accustomed to test the temper of those who employ them as guides and seeing them behave with courtesy and humility, qualities unknown to them, they conceive a very low opinion of those who possess those qualities and mercilessly trample them underfoot. If, however, they are treated severely, they react with mildness and moderation. We acted accordingly from that time forward and were much pleased with the results, regretting that we had not known earlier of the cure for the insolence of these wretched barbarians, who were otherwise, however, the very essence and personification of evil.

After these mischances, we continued our long, rugged, and very disagreeable journey, and after a few days we found ourselves in a narrow pass between two mountain ranges which continue from a great distance and form a gateway there, through which they open upon some spacious but barren and dreadful plains, as I shall presently explain. Through this gulf must necessarily pass all those who want to go on to the kingdoms of Abyssinia, leaving the land of Dancali and others of the same sort. However, since the road beyond this gateway is so rugged and difficult and lacking in everything a person needs to sustain and refresh himself, divine Providence provided for the comfort of travellers by creating at this place a delightful grove of trees and an abundance of cool, running water. And although the place is so hemmed in and is a true valley, there is always a breeze there because all the moving air there is channelled into that place and goes out to the open spaces of those plains. This place allows travellers to gather strength for the difficulties which await them, and since we were about to enter upon them, we stopped here for two days, recovering from our journey and resting from the labour of it, a custom observed by all who pass through this place. We arrived here one day in the afternoon and, staying another whole day, on the following day after four o'clock in the afternoon, we set out with our caravan and began to enter those barren, uninhabitable plains. They are all one big salt mine. They serve and have always served as salterns for all the kingdoms of Ethiopia because they have no others. They extend for many leagues in all directions, and as the sun is excessively hot, its rays beat down in such a way that they convert into steam all the water that comes down to those plains from the many high mountain ranges which form the outer limits of the kingdoms of that empire. These ranges, though covering a large area of many leagues, encircle the plains in such a way that they may be said to form a crown for that large plain. The large patches of steam are so continual, thick, and heavy that when we saw them from a distance, they appeared to be large lakes. Indeed there are many large ones on the northern side with islands in the middle, which are nothing more than a continuation of the ground. Grottoes which appear in many places on the plain reveal a great abundance of a horrible black water which can be seen at a depth of a few spans, sometimes in something like wells and at other times in sorts of open quarries, all of living rock, but as black as iron slag. In other places we came upon bodies of this black water flowing like rivers, which, it seems, were carrying their current via natural aqueducts or subterranean passages. This water changes into salt, which this same land also forms in salt-beds, as if of stone, where the people who live closest to these salterns come to cut it. They then take it to their market-places, where other merchants come to buy it; and they use it in trade, as it serves them as money in all the kingdoms of this empire, as I shall presently relate.

Since the heat is so excessive and the land so dry and barren, one travels only at night and a small part of the afternoon and morning, travelling continuously during those hours so as to pass through the territory more quickly and so that the sun would not lay hold of the poor travellers in such a place, because they would soon lose their lives from the fiery heat. But those who travel in that area at night are also in danger, but of another sort, because it seems that demons have their abode there because it is a place so similar to the place where they are tormented. They give frequent evidence of their presence in that locality by the tricks and pranks they perpetrate on the poor travellers. For, even though there is no population or living thing, at least human, for a great many leagues in all directions from that place, one hears great tumults and uproar, as of people, and, as if they were idling their time away, they make loud mocking noises and laughter at those who are travelling, calling them by their names, and telling them some things they have done elsewhere, with the result that the poor travellers do not dare to continue unless they are banded together in large groups so that their fear will be lessened by the nearness of their companions. The worst part is that from time to time they capture from among the unfortunate travellers that one singled out by fate, who disappears for ever without anyone seeing who carries him off or keeps him prisoner. The others dare not try to rescue him from the hands of those who have seized him, each person trying to seek shelter when he hears the shrieks of the unfortunate captive and former companion. This misfortune happened to a servant of the Muslim who was travelling with us here when he came to look for us and passed this way. He was snatched from among them, and no one knew who had done it.[1] For this reason, when people have to pass here, it is always in great terror, each person thinking that he will not finish out the day's journey.

In spite of this, since these may be considered gold mines for those kingdoms, although they are not lacking in many of the most precious metals esteemed by man, deriving money and merchandise from them, for the salt serves them for both things, they come to cut it and carry it all away at great personal risk, entering this plain at sunset and cutting at night as great a quantity as each one is able. Before the sun becomes unbearably hot, they all leave, hurrying to the mountain range for shelter, laden, themselves and their animals – camels, oxen, mules and donkeys – for their trading. The worst of it is that these poor people have not only these enemies to fear, but also thirst that kills them, heat that fries them even at night, and some barbarians called Gallas who come to lie in wait for them in their path, robbing and killing them, as I shall presently relate. And although there are so many hazards and enemies, these poor people risk all of them because they have no other way to gain their livelihood.

We entered this land, then, with the knowledge of what was to be found there, one afternoon, as I have said, determined to travel all night and to pass through as quickly as possible. When night closed in, we were well into it and, warned of the great distance we had to traverse, we resolved to continue at the pace set by the camels, which did not move lazily. The ground caused us much difficulty when it was soft and spongy, for very often we were bogged down to our knees in what

---

[1] Le Grand adds: 'This poor man did not think that his servant who had gone aside could have been killed by the Gallas who are always on the roads to these salterns.'

appeared to be powder or dust; but it was necessary to keep pressing forward so as not to fall behind the group. For anyone who stayed behind could quickly prepare himself for death, which he would meet in a few hours as soon as the sun came up. There are no roads to follow there, for the land does not permit them. The camel drivers travel by the stars, following a certain course and using as landmarks some piles of salty earth which they already know about. It was about midnight, and all of us very tired and weary, when the whole caravan stopped; for the Muslims, who were travelling ahead of us, had stopped and were consulting with one another in secret. The Portuguese Paulo Nogeira, who had come to receive us, was of the opinion that this was evil-doing and treachery on the part of the Muslims and that they intended to avenge what had happened previously by robbing us in that desert and leaving us there to perish. Whether because he heard something of what they were saying or whether the repugnant nature of the place where we were travelling and the malice of the camel drivers permitted one to believe anything of them, slipping his arm through the rings on the inside of his *adarga* and grasping his scimitar, he came up to us asking us to move to one side and to form one group, because the Muslims intended to attack us. The sudden fear we experienced was not inconsiderable, what with the reasons for it that there were and which convinced him, and which, added to our sufferings from the journey and the fatigue it had caused us, put us in a state of confusion. We followed his advice, however, and went off to one side waiting for the outcome; but we were soon relieved of this anxiety as we continued our journey, the Muslims explaining their consultation and delay by telling us they had lost their way and were taking counsel as to which way they should go. Whether this was the reason or whether they thought that the occasion did not offer them a good advantage, they did not fail to cause us to be much more watchful in such company.

Three times we rested briefly from our labour, but we felt even more fatigued while resting. As the sun was rising we realized that we were already leaving that bad land, but we were going into another which was no better, for we found ourselves in a land composed of a black stone like iron slag, which was so hard and rough that it soon wore out our shoes; and, since we did not have any others with us we used some sandals, which wore out in a very short time and, in my case, made sores on my feet. I and a few others then wrapped cloths around our bare feet in order to be able better to endure the pain of walking.

However, if shoes and sandals could not withstand the roughness of the stones, the cloths over bare feet could not very well do so, so we experienced what those stones could do to our bare feet.

After leaving the land I have been describing and entering the one I have just mentioned, in addition to the difficulty of travelling, we soon experienced a sudden fear. With the knowledge that that whole region was where the Galas come to attack the poor travellers and, paying very little heed because of our extreme lassitude, we suddenly saw a large group of people who were making their way from the lower part of a small valley up to the top of a hill. As soon as they saw us, they separated but were still coming toward us. Because of their distance from us, the danger, increased by our fear and our being so suddenly startled, we did not discern what sort of people they were, all of us being in agreement that they were Galas, either sent for by the camel-drivers, whom, however, we soon observed to be as fearful as we, or having met us by chance in one of their customary searches for travellers to attack. We therefore resolved to defend ourselves; and, because it seemed to us that if there were no more than those visible, we had enough people to cope with them, in order to trick them into thinking we were stronger than we were, we made a show of striding very boldly toward them, leaving our loads and camel drivers behind. The latter were determined to cut the camels' girths at the height of the fray and, leaving the supplies to divert the highwaymen, to make their escape with their camels. This being the resolve of the camel drivers, and there being one of us who, confessing his sins, was preparing himself for whatever calamity might happen, the rest of us set out to meet the barbarians, provided with our firearms. And because we distrusted the Muslim captain who had come to receive us and suspected that he would not be trustworthy in a dangerous situation and would turn against us, as these people are wont to do, one of us along with the Portuguese decided to begin with this man, whether trustworthy or not, walking on either side of him in order to make sure of him, as he gave us all the more reason for suspicion since he was insisting that he be given a matchlock, which we promised him when it was necessary, meaning that it would be given to him in the chest with a good charge and two balls, and the one who was to do him this service was carrying one with two shots all ready to be fired. Both groups were approaching each other with equal fear, because we thought they were Galas and they thought that we were. We soon discovered the truth, however, seeing that they were a poor caravan of wretched people who were carrying provisions to sell and, having seen us from afar, had believed us to be Gala highwaymen and had dispersed for this reason in many directions so that some could escape. There was disbelief in both our groups, even when we were already mingling, each one greeting and congratulating the others upon finding themselves free from the sudden fear.

At this time it was about nine o'clock in the morning when we reached a certain place where the road divides into two. One went to the left on level ground, which was at the edge of the salt plain which came up to that point. The camels had to take that road to avoid the other road which, although it was shorter and both led to a well of fresh water, the only one we had found, ran, however, along the slope of some mountain ranges and went through valleys, and thus was rough, craggy and scorching hot and could be travelled only on foot. Almost all of us Christians took this second route, taking one Muslim with us as a guide, the rest going with the camels by the level route. We had been travelling since four o'clock of the previous afternoon without eating, sleeping or drinking anything, of which we were in great need; and as we were travelling thus until eleven o'clock in the morning, burning up with heat, it happened that the guide, with three or four of our people, took a short-cut without warning the person following them, who, turning to the left, led us into a thicket, valleys and a rocky place to come out at the edge of the same salt land, at the sight of which we were astonished and frightened, both because we found ourselves without road or guide, realizing there that we had lost him, and because of the sun and thirst that were consuming us so much that some of the Patriarch's church musicians and servants were already stretched out along the road, having given themselves up for dead, unable to take another step forward. And they would have perished indeed if help had not come to them quickly, as I shall relate. Two grieved me particularly, one of whom, turning to me, since I was walking ahead of him, in extreme suffering begged me for a drop of water, though I myself was unable to utter a word because I was so parched. And since I was in the same state and in equal need and lack of water, not giving him any because I didn't have any, he fell to the ground and stayed there. And as I kept on walking ahead, another was already overcome by the same misfortune, stretched out in the shade of some bushes and making me the same entreaty. He received the same reply, so that both of them stayed behind, while I kept going with equal agony and full of compassion for such misfortune. Reaching then the edge of that barren land where we had the disappointment of not being able to continue, it was an opportune time for the Patriarch with some companions, also Fathers of the Company, as well as three or four of the laymen accompanying him, to insist that one of the Muslims in the same company give them a very small cup of water from some he was carrying in two small leather bottles prepared earlier for the journey, as by one who knew what was most necessary for it. And as the leather bottles were loaded on a donkey, some holding it back, others insisting on it, all finally, suffering terribly, were begging very civilly for something they could have claimed by any means, however rigorous. Nothing, however, moved the Muslim, who preferred to hunt for the road again, having no pity on the suffering and affliction of the companions. What finally did move him was greed, not the feelings of an ordinary, rational human being, as he demanded in exchange for the water a fine, long turban, many yards[1] in length, which one of those present had wrapped around his head. When this was given to him, he drew from one of the leather bottles a half cup of water, which, as it was for the Patriarch, as the person most important and most in need, and the other who had given the turban, it was necessary to satisfy the Muslim's greed with the half-cup of water for both of them so as not to risk giving a full cup to both. And thus, scarcely had the afflicted prelate raised the cup to his lips when the Muslim took it away and gave it to the one with the turban, while the rest were perishing from thirst; and, although they kept asking for a little water, the Muslim remained unsoftened by such just entreaties. However, seeing one of us who was wearing white breeches, which, although of no better quality than ordinary drawers, were nonetheless better than his, because he didn't use any, for greater elegance, he asked for them in exchange for another half cup of water. And when we tried to oblige the owner of the breeches to do without them and accept being bare while the Muslim wore his breeches, the owner of them was resisting the proposal and arguing that he would be in too sorry a plight, not having any others with which to replace them. We were doing all we could to overcome his selfishness and supply our dire need for water, but the Muslim was unwilling to wait for a reply and was starting off with his donkey and water, taking with him our only hope for life. Since we were sure to die without him, we resolved to follow him and at the foot of the first tree take the water away from him by any means necessary, by the right given us by our condition and

---

[1] *vara*, 1·096 m.

the dire straits in which we found ourselves, and sustain our lives, as that small quantity of water gave promise of doing. Sensing our resolve, the Muslim hurriedly urged on his donkey, turning back to look for the lost road. We followed him and kept him in our midst, since he had in his possession that wretchedly small means of saving our lives. But lo and behold, there suddenly came out of the bushes a Muslim at a distance of fifteen or twenty paces, and waving us on with his hand, and raising it to his mouth as if drinking, pointed to the bushes out of which he had come, indicating that there was water there. We observed the messenger for a long time. If what he was saying were true, we could consider him an angel of God like the one who came to the child Ismael when he was in similar but no more perilous circumstances. We thought it very strange, however, that there were people in such a deserted place and that they would be so unbelievably charitable to foreigners. We were very distrustful of him, although necessity made us inclined to consider as true what we desired so much. Unfortunately we were in such a state because of our thirst, that even at so short a distance we were unable to recognize one of our guides who had been with us for many days, whom we certainly should have recognized had we not been half blind from the heat and thirst. And believing that he was some highwayman luring us into the bushes where he had other companions lying in ambush, who intended, once we were in there, to rob us, since the place was so well suited for this, we resolved nonetheless to take the risk because we had very little to lose now, no matter what happened, since it was impossible for us to be in any more dreadful circumstance than we were already in. Thus, one of those who were coming there took a carbine[1] and taking one of the Patriarch's servants with him, with an admonition to his companions not to let the Muslim with the donkey get away, followed the Muslim who had come out of the bushes, who immediately plunged back into them, shouting to the two following him to stay a little behind looking behind him to make sure that thieves did not attack from behind, while our man with the matchlock followed the one calling them, looking carefully about in all directions and with his matchlock in his hands ready to cope with any attack, and telling his companion that, if he should see him fall, he should turn back and inform the others of what had happened and that for that reason he should follow at a distance in order to have time to take shelter. The one in the lead had decided that, in case of any ambush, he would face the assailants with his

---

[1] *escopeta*, shorter than a musket.

matchlock and thus make his retreat as best he could, since there was now no choice but to take the risk or die. In this manner, they went through the bushes following the Muslim, who from time to time turned his head and made the same gestures, in which the two bold ones no longer had any faith, seeing more clearly the ease with which they could be robbed because of the nature of the place. It is certainly true that the attack would be dearly paid for by someone or by several. Travelling then for some time through the thick brush, they suddenly came out into a field where they saw, already resting, the companions who, with the guide, had become separated from us when we first became lost, and had refreshed themselves with the water that there was there in a well. And because they did not see us, they had sent the Muslim guide, since he was familiar with the territory, to go and look for us; and it was he, because we did not recognize him, whom we were determined to punish in the way I have described for the good turn he wanted to do for us; but the state we were in excused our error and intention. With the relief afforded by the water and reunion with the companions, the two men refreshed themselves and immediately sent word to those who were following the Muslim with the water, sending them some for immediate relief and giving them news of the happy outcome of their adventure. And because two or three of our companions had stayed behind, having already totally succumbed to their affliction, we sent people with water, so that, if they found them alive, they could restore them, which they did, all finally reaching the place, able to endure the difficulty they suffered because of their expectation of the relief they were to receive from the water so close at hand. The first of the arrivals, a dog belonging to the Portuguese who had come to meet us, arrived so spent and dry from thirst that, coming up to the water and unable to avail itself of it, it dropped dead. The same thing almost happened to a young man who before drinking fell unconscious to the ground and doubtless would have died if a little water had not been brought to him. The danger, however, was that he could move neither his tongue nor his throat because of the dryness, and, turned over on his back, he gave indications with his eyes of what he was feeling. There was also great danger if he were inadvertently given too much water; and to avoid either extreme, the water was put into his mouth drop by drop until his throat was moistened, whereupon, recovering his breath, he returned to consciousness, and became refreshed or, one might say, returned from the dead.

It was about one o'clock in the afternoon when we were concerned with these troubles, and our hunger was not the least of them after our thirst had been quenched; for we had been travelling for twenty-one hours without eating, sleeping or resting. Since the caravan and some more companions accompanying it had not caught up to us, we were obliged to stay there waiting for them in the shade of some briers which grew in that place. They all arrived after three o'clock, and shared with us a little millet[1] cooked in water that had remained in a kettle from the day before and was left over from what they had eaten on the way. In addition to this, our larder consisted of I know not how many slices of beef dried in the sun, which had neither time nor need to be cooked, seeming to us more delicious to eat raw.

[1] Le Grand again says honey, not millet.

CHAPTER 14

[How God delivered us from the Gallas]

After this small refection, whose quality I have described, we had to set out again immediately because of the infestation of that region with the Gala brigands, who, knowing that place to be a necessary stopping place for travellers, there being no other water there with which to restore themselves, come there to attack from time to time; and we did not want to experience so unlucky a fate, especially since we knew of spies being nearby. In addition to this, it was necessary to leave immediately so we could reach the passage of a plain where these barbarians are frequently found and a few days before had attacked a caravan, as I shall relate further on; and it was necessary to continue all night at a good pace in order to be out of that plain and its danger by dawn. We therefore hurried our journey. And although we kept constantly alert, we found nothing remarkable all the way. The sun was rising as we came to the entrance to the plain. We were truly very tired, for we had been travelling for two nights and almost two days with the difficulties I have just described. And so, partly from our past sufferings, partly from fear and news of what had happened a few days before to other travellers, we entered that plain with no great feelings of happy anticipation or expectations of great good fortune. We put our trust however in God. The camel drivers kept close to their camels ready to cut their girths and flee with them if they could, with all the more certainty of having to meet the bandits since we suspected that they had sent word to them to come and rob us, partly as vengeance for what I have related earlier, and partly to share safely in the spoils; for, as they were inhabitants of lands dependent upon the Emperor, they did not want to rob us with the danger of being discovered, but wished rather to do their dirty work as secretly as possible, covering their wickedness with the smoke-screen of the highwaymen.

After a few steps into the plain, we kept discovering and seeing fresh signs of the barbarians' attack and their cruelty, for the field was strewn with dead bodies and bones of men and animals with some of the things they were carrying and which the barbarians could not carry away. The sight filled us with pity and horror, assuring us of the obvious danger we were in, all the more so because we saw fresh footprints from that very night, which we knew were made by these barbarians because of the shoes they wear. They had apparently come to wait for us at night, in accordance with the notice they had received and the usual practice of travellers to pass through that area at that time, and, seeing that we had not arrived, had turned back, as it appears. The haste with which the Muslims had forced us to travel must have been for the purpose of placing us in danger at the time agreed upon; but God, whose Providence governs all things, arranged things in such a way that it was not possible for us to expose ourselves to that danger at the time we considered safest, the fact being that at that time our doom would have been certain; and when we found that our passage through that field was now in daylight and, as we thought, more risky, it was, in reality, much safer. We hurried our steps, however, and between nine and ten o'clock, we left the plain, quickly entering and taking shelter in the craggy terrain of some mountain ranges, a place less frequented by those barbarians. At a short distance we came upon a fresh stream with many trees, in the shade of which we partially recovered from our fatigue from the journey, resting and cooking a little millet, all of which we did very quickly because we did not consider ourselves safe there; and we were right, supposing that after our departure the barbarians were to come after us and pursue us even beyond this place, more desirous of finding us than we were to avoid seeing them. We travelled, accordingly, the rest of the afternoon along the slope of a mountain and before sunset we saw passing by one of the caravans that go out to cut and bring back salt, composed of many people and animals. Our Muslim camel-drivers spoke with them and received from them some bread cakes which they call *burguta*.[1] They make them of dough composed of wheat or barley flour with cold water kneaded on a piece of leather they use instead of a mattress, called *nete*.[2] They take a piece of dough the size of two fists together and, after heating a good-sized pebble, they put it inside the dough, and, making a cake of it all, they cover it with embers, from which, very poorly cooked, it is taken and eaten. A Muslim friend gave me one of them as a special treat and delicacy. Since there was not enough for everyone, three of us ate it, as secretly as we could, lying on the ground on the pebbles of the river where we were, which had more pebbles

[1] Amh. *brĕkueta*; Le Grand has *Gurguta*.
[2] Arabic *naṭ'*, a round leather mat. A. d'Abbadie, *Dictionnaire de la langue amariñña*, (Paris, 1881), p. 422. gives *nät*, 'petit cuir employé comme couchette'; I am indebted to Dr Richard Pankhurst for this reference.

than water, our usual bed. Unfortunately, after we had finished our plenteous banquet, they made us a present of some more of the same cakes, and when someone who had counted them said there were twenty and our people found only nineteen, they realized, because one was missing, that I had taken one, so that I was found out. But as there were so many, my companions overlooked my not having invited them to share in the delicacy to which I had treated myself, for the necessitous state in which we found ourselves did not allow such opportunities to be passed over. With the present, such as it was, we renewed ourselves and it was a feast-day for us as we ate those delicacies which, though bread, might be compared to green fruit. We paid for it, however, before long and much more later on, as I shall explain; for, as we were weak and heedless of our stomachs and the bread was almost raw barley dough made with cold water and nevertheless unleavened, it gave us such a stomach ache that the illness it caused us was of little help to us in our journey. It soon passed, however, because the quantity we had eaten was not great. We stayed there that night and the next day until ten o'clock, because the Muslims spent that much time in discussions among themselves; and we learned of the tricks and wickedness they were hatching when they finally revealed their plans. The situation was as follows:

The captain or head of the caravan came to address himself to us – that pious Muslim of whom I have already spoken, so aged in years and Muhammadan law, in which he showed himself extremely punctilious, as well as in hatred and malice toward Christians, in addition to being, by his own nature and race of those who inhabit that land, as great a brigand as the Galas whom we feared. The burden of what he told us was that he had lost his way and that if he was not completely lost, at least the road we were taking was extremely difficult for the camels so that we had to go back to the plain frequented by the Galas, where we had found the dead bodies, and from there we would take another easier, better way. By these words he really meant that, having escaped the hands of the barbarians, we should now return to put ourselves in them; for, as they came frequently to rob people in that place, he would see to it that we did not escape them a second time. We were warned of this by the Muslim captain, who had come to meet us and by the Portuguese, his companion, who advised that we leave immediately because of the risk we still ran there, to say nothing of the risk we would run if we were to turn back. Having heard this and clearly recognizing the soundness of their advice, we tried many times to persuade the

Muslim that we should continue and not turn back. Nothing, however, could persuade him, nor could he do anything to make us turn back. Seeing that neither side would yield to the other, we resolved to leave all of our belongings in their hands and, with some guides who were willing to accompany us, to go ahead without the Muslims, trusting that Divine Providence would favour our cause and help us in our suffering and destitution. Firm in our determination, we immediately put it into effect, with our walking staves in our hands, as we had done up till then, protesting to him that we understood him and the harm he intended to do us, that anything that befell us was on his head, that we were also casting on his head all of our belongings, and that the Emperor would hold him accountable for everything. These terms were used among those people on similar occasions.

With this, the Muslim realized that he was thwarted, and, whether because he realized that we had seen through his plan or because he saw us so determined, being unable to accomplish what he had intended, asked us to wait for him because he wanted to go with us, which he did. We travelled all that day until we reached the narrowest part of a stream which, between extremely high mountains, came plunging over rocks, making sorts of waterfalls. And, although the water was good and the place cool, the terrain was so difficult for the heavy-laden camels that we spent a day and a half there repairing the most difficult parts of the path, levelling it with stones so that the camels could climb it; and, even so, in places they went on their knees. After we had passed this difficulty, which was no small one, we had to continue all afternoon and all night because we entered another plain as dangerous as the last one, which we travelled across during the greater part of the night without resting until shortly before dawn when we stopped at a fresh stream, which we did not very much enjoy because it was at night and we were so weary that we thought it better to use our resting time for a meal which was prepared at that time from our cooked millet. By the time it was prepared, the day was so bright that we had to continue the journey until we could reach a place where we would no longer have to fear the Galas.

We finally reached the foot of some high mountain ranges called Duan, which extend for many leagues and divide the kingdoms of the Abyssinians from those we had traversed, populated by the Galas and Muslims.[1] This place serves as a place for rest and recuperation for the

[1] Probably the range of mountains called Dogua on the GSGS map ND 37, and Doga on Section 7 of the maps in L. M. Nesbitt, *Desert and Forest* (London, 1934). The range extends roughly north and south to the west of Lake Assale.

salt caravans that come here to take their repose, the wives and children coming down from above to help them carry the salt merchandise, bring them some refreshment, as they did for a salt caravan that arrived at the same time we did. It was the same caravan we had met earlier and from which we had received the gift of the cakes of bread. Since there were plenty of these cakes here, I wanted to buy some with some blue glass beads suitable for these poor people. For each string, of about thirty beads, they gave me one cake, so that I collected some ten or twelve. And since I saw I already had a sufficient supply to divide among my companions, I raised the price of my merchandise, asking them give me two cakes for each string of beads. Although there was haggling on both sides, for necessity had made us used to all this, they finally gave the two; but they made ours small because of the speed with which they kneaded and cooked them. Since I saw that I already had more than enough to satisfy our hunger, I hazarded another trader's trick, saying that they had to make them larger, but I lost because they succeeded in deceiving me very neatly. They made the cakes large enough to satisfy me; however, they used not a bit more dough, but rather less. They increased the size of the cakes by putting so large a stone inside each one of them that I expressed my satisfaction with the bargain and gathered up many of those stones masquerading as bread, which had only a thin shell of dough on the outside. After the transaction was completed and the stones gathered up, we discovered the trick. The great quantity of them, however, made up for the little dough they contained. We divided them up, four or five to a person, and thus satisfied our hunger, but much to our cost; for the illness we had experienced earlier repeated itself with such force that it put many of us in a state of extreme weakness.

We tarried in that place for the rest of the day, invited by its freshness, the best we had seen anywhere. The variety and beauty of the trees were beyond compare, extending along that river for many leagues. The water was beautiful, fresh and crystal clear. There was a great diversity of birds and wild animals, among which the multitude of monkeys gave us much amusement and recreation; for the trees were covered with them and were so numerous and dense that they could safely and freely move about in them and travel a great distance from there without having to come down to the ground, passing from one tree to the other as they continue their travels. And since they are accustomed to many people being with them in that place, they were not shy with us, but rather ran up to where we were to have a look at us as if they were amazed at the novelty and colour of the strangers. There were so many of them that they covered the trees, and they were so confident of their safety and so tame that no matter how much they were threatened with a stick or stone they did not flee. Seeing this, one of our number wanted to get a clear shot at them and, to deceive them first with a walking staff, pretending it was a matchlock, he aimed it at them and, acting as if he were firing it, made the sound of a carbine shot with his mouth, to which they paid as little attention as if they knew how little harm they could receive in that manner. And then, seeing or thinking he saw that he had them thoroughly mystified, he picked up the real carbine which he had close by and invited the rest of the companions to watch some fall to the ground. But the monkeys, as if fully aware of the trick, were just as circumspect in fleeing from this second experiment as they had been secure and confident on the occasion of the trial run; for, setting up a great chattering all at once, as if warning one another of the danger they were incurring there, and as if they knew that the first shots were imaginary and that this one was to be real, they all disappeared, throwing themselves from tree to tree as safely and lightly as if they were flying, thereby rendering useless all the assiduous preparation with which their would-be assailant had hoped to deceive them. Those who were watching them were astonished at the uncanny power of their natural instinct which so unerringly enabled these animals to recognize and escape their danger.

It was about three o'clock in the afternoon when we continued our journey up the river, always in the shade and in the coolness of beautiful trees, which deserved to be better cultivated elsewhere, and to be enjoyed by more civilized and less barbarous people than were those who scorned them, taking no notice of this natural beauty so deserving of admiration. The day's journey was a short one because we had to come to a halt before sunset since our guides insisted upon it, the camel drivers demanding, moreover, that we stay there two days while they went to their country near there for a certain festival,[1] if it was not to urge the Galas to catch us suddenly unawares when we least expected them. We were fortunate that they left us the camels with two or three of the camel drivers. We were still very much concerned both about their departure and about the place where we were, which was quite vulnerable to attack from the undergrowth, and there was no safer place

---

[1] Le Grand reads: 'The camel drivers made off to go to a feast of St Michael, celebrated in Ethiopia on 16 June'. The Feast of St Michael is celebrated on the 12th of each month of the Ethiopian calendar, E. Ullendorff, *The Ethiopians* (London, 1960), p. 106. The drivers were Muslims anyway.

nearby. We adapted ourselves to the circumstances as best we could, however, by keeping a very careful watch and preparing ourselves for any eventuality. I had the first night-time watch, and as we were uneasy, there toward the middle of the bushes, I thought there were people silently coming toward us. And by the moonlight filtering through the trees at that place, I could make out two people walking toward us as fast as they could; and, since the place and all the circumstances at that time were extremely suspect, it was necessary to prepare a defence and I awakened all the others. Those approaching were hurrying into an extremely perilous situation, because, not hearing our enquiry as to who they were, they continued toward us confidently because they were friends. One of those watching them, put his matchlock to his face to be sure at least of those who were appearing and to cause any others who might be following them to be frightened off. Luckily they were close enough so that we could recognize one of them as a young man of our group whom we had sent two days before to the Fathers to give news of our coming and who was returning with another young man, letters, and a gift sent to us by a Father, who was about four leagues from there and was coming to receive us. The gift was a cake of wheat flour about half an *alquier*[1] in size and as many as three dozen tarts.[2] It all seemed to us the very best treat and present we could possibly receive. And since we knew the Father was so close, we loaded our camels that very night, with considerable effort, and travelled the rest of the night along the same river; and on the next day toward seven o'clock we arrived at the foot of the Duan mountain range, where we were at last completely safe and in hopes of soon seeing our people who were on the top of the mountain awaiting word of our arrival to come down, which they did, finding us with our tent already pitched, our things unloaded, and our camel drivers having taken shelter, not daring to wait for our people to demand that they account for what they had done to us, as indeed we intended to have done even though their ill-will, the cause of all of this, forestalled it, as they fled that encounter.

Coming to receive us, with Father Manoel Baradas,[3] were a nephew of the Emperor, lord of many lands near there, other noblemen and

---

[1] 1 *alqueire* 13 litres.

[2] *farteis*, plural of *fartem*, sweet paste enclosed in a farinaceous covering, A. de Moraes Silva, *Diccionário da Lingua Portugueza* (Lisboa, 1889, 91).

[3] Barradas was the author of the three historico-geographical tractates published by Beccari, vol. IV (Rome, 1906). He was born in 1572 and came to Ethiopia in 1624. He died at Cochin in 1646.

vassals, and many of the Portuguese that there are in Ethiopia, bringing us mules and necessary provisions, of which we were in much need. And as all were Catholics and were naturally pious and compassionate, when they saw us in such poor condition, without shoes and with our feet pitifully lacerated, our clothes in tatters and generally in the poorest and most wretched state imaginable, understanding that we were suffering all that because we were coming to accompany them in that exile, they could not hold back their tears of happiness and compassion. They expressed in words the value they placed on everything we had done and their sorrow for our past tribulations, which we had certainly forgotten at the sight of such companions, with whom already more independent and strengthened with the mules they had brought us and with the pleasures afforded by the land, accompanied by friendly and benevolent people, relieved of the wickedness of the camel drivers and in lands of good cool air and familiar people, well populated and fertile, in five days, on the twenty-first of June we arrived at our original and ancient residence of Fremona, the dwelling place of the blessed Patriarch Dom André de Oviedo when he was alive, his grave being in the humble church we had there.[1] It served also as the dwelling and burial place for the others who had accompanied him, and for those who up to that time had stayed on in Ethiopia, a large number of Portuguese and native Abyssinian Catholics also living there. They all received us with applause, many tears, and great devotion. And since we have entered these great kingdoms and empire of Abyssinia, I shall give a concise account of all of it, its faith, the races of people in it, the customs and polity observed there.

[1] Fremona is a hill about four miles from Adwa; it became the Jesuit stronghold in Ethiopia. It is named after Frumentius, the apostle of Ethiopia, consecrated first Bishop of Aksum by Athanasius. Andre de Oviedo, a Spaniard from Illescas, was Coadjutor to the Patriarch João Nunes Barreto. In 1557 Oviedo went to Ethiopia, leaving the Patriarch in Goa, where he died in 1562. Oviedo then became Patriarch and remained in Ethiopia till his death at Fremona in 1580. Lobo's companion, Afonso Mendes, was the next Patriarch to be appointed.

CHAPTER 15

[Of the Abyssinian Empire, its origins and progress, of the emperors it has had, the religion it has professed; and when the Catholic faith came to these kingdoms, by whom it was brought, the time it persevered and when it was lost, with many other curious things pertaining to the subject matter of which I treat]

In their annals, the Abyssinians ascribe extremely ancient and magnificent origins to their empire and princes, so much so that they can and do enumerate the princes who have governed them up to the present time, beginning with Adam and continuing up to Faciladas,[1] who is now reigning, and continuing this genealogical series from father to son, all of royal blood, without interruption[2] – a thing which, if true, cannot be said for any other empire in the world. And as for the belief we should place in the historical truth of their ancient genealogy, it is that which is deserved by the human histories authenticated in books and undoubted tradition in those regions, in which books and tradition the history and origins which I shall report are as thoroughly verified and as little doubted by the Ethiopians as the Roman histories are by us; and the history of this empire deserves equal credence, since it is scrupulously and clearly reported in their annals. And we can with equal reason doubt that the power of Rome began with Romulus and his brother as doubt that the power and princes of this empire had their

---

[1] Fasiladas, the Ethiopic form of Basilides, was the son of Susenyos, and succeeded him upon his abdication after the failure of his Catholic policy. Fasiladas reigned 1632–67 and was responsible for the expulsion of the Jesuits.

[2] Such a list is given in the *Kĕbrä Nägäst*, 'The Glory of the Kings,', a work of the early fourteenth century, of fundamental importance for the theory of the Ethiopian monarchy. Slightly different lists appear in various MSS; one of these is given in E. A. W. Budge, *A History of Ethiopia*, 2 vols (London, 1928), I, pp. 187–9, 204–12.

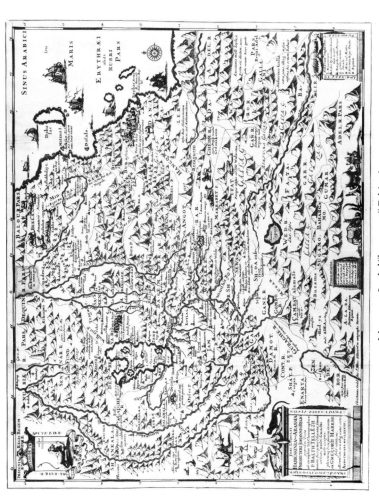

Map 3.   Ludolf's map of Ethiopia
(from *A new History of Ethiopia*, London, 1684)

origins in Cam, son of Nohe.[1] This is the empire commonly called the empire of Prester John of the Indies, erroneously so, however, since the truth is that the ancient and true Prester John and his domain have been lost to human memory. And with the persistence of rumours of Prester John in the eastern parts and the signs of his being a Christian prince, the Portuguese who very much wanted to discover the said Empire and were unable to gain knowledge of it, finding the Ethiopian princes with so many signs of Christianity, and also comparing them with [what they had heard of] the ancient Prester John from the time of the schisms of the Roman Church and Catholic faith in which they lived, they came to believe that this was the ancient Prester John of the Indies; and this same report, brought and communicated by the Portuguese, was then published throughout the world.[2] The Emperor's correct name is Emperor of the Abyssinian Empire or Abyssinia, for he is better known by this name.

The Abyssinian annals affirm that Ham, son of Noah, is the progenitor and root of the family tree of these princes, numbering up to the present time one hundred and seventy-two, among whom there governed a few women of recognized distinction. Two of these women are named in the Holy Scriptures, one, the Queen Sabaa, mentioned in the Gospel, whom the Abyssinians call Nicaula or Macheda and in the book they have of the Gospels in their language, Negista Azeb, which means the same as Regina Austri, as the Sacred Text names her.[3] And the place where she formerly had her court still exists today, with monuments of remarkable magnificence, as well as the town where they say she was born and which still today preserves her name, the land being called Saba by the Abyssinians, all of which I saw and

---

[1] Ham, son of Noah. There is an Ethiopian tradition that the country takes its name from Aethiopis, son of Kush, son of Ham, Budge, 1928, I, pp. 143, 190.

[2] The earliest reference to Prester John that has been traced, in the chronicle of Otto of Freising, locates his realm 'in the Far East, beyond Persia and Armenia'. From the second quarter of the fourteenth century, however, cartographers and travellers began to place it on the upper Nile. This change of venue is now usually ascribed to information obtained from an Ethiopian embassy sent to Europe in 1306, and which spent some time in Genoa. Portuguese writers of the sixteenth and seventeenth centuries normally call the Emperor of Ethiopia Prester John, *Preste João*. C. F. Beckingham, *The Achievements of Prester John* (London, 1966), p. 4; R. A. Skelton, 'An Ethiopian Embassy to Western Europe in 1306' in O. G. S. Crawford, *Ethiopian Itineraries* (Cambridge, 1958), pp. 212–15; C. F. Beckingham, 'The Quest for Prester John', *Bulletin of the John Rylands University Library of Manchester*, LXII, 2 (Spring 1980), pp. 290–310; E. Ullendorff and C. F. Beckingham, *The Hebrew Letters of Prester John* (Oxford, 1982), pp. 5–11.

[3] In the *Kĕbrä Nägäst* the Queen of Sheba is named Makeda. She is called Nikaulis, Queen of Egypt and Ethiopia, by Josephus, who does not mention Sheba, *Antiquities*, VIII, 158. On this name, which does not seem to occur in Ethiopic sources, L. H. Silberman, 'The Queen of Sheba in Judaic Tradition', in J. B. Pritchard, ed., *Solomon and Sheba* (London, 1974), p. 67. Negesta Azeb is Ethiopic for the Queen of the South.

traversed on several occasions.[1] Through this famous queen, the same Abyssinians claim that the princes of this empire descend from the tribe of Judah, for they affirm that from the journey she made to Jerusalem, as attested in the Holy Scriptures, she had a son of Solomon named Minilech, from whom, now with increased nobility, the Abyssinian princes continued; and up to the present time, the Ethiopians have not allowed and will not allow any other to hold the sceptre of these kingdoms unless it be the descendants of Minilech, so great is their esteem for this race and relationship.[2] Candace was the second of the famous women who governed that empire, all the more famous because we are informed about her in Chapter 10 of the Acts of the Apostles.[3] The Abyssinians called her, among other names, Judith,[4] which she richly deserved because she was, as I shall explain, the means by which the Catholic faith came into that empire, since she attained that greatest happiness of being Christian, a state unattained by her predecessors; for they had been living until that time throughout most of the centuries since the Flood in that blindness and ignorance of the true God, by which almost the whole world was oppressed, as they gave to false idols the adoration they owed Him. Beginning with the Queen of Sheba, they had followed the law and ceremonies of the Jews, but soon after the days of the famous queen and her son they abandoned this, which was then the true road to salvation, and returned to the errors of idolatry, preserving some Judaic ceremonies, but being essentially heathen with Jewish ceremonies, as they can be called today since they still preserve them.[5]

[1] The reference is to the surroundings of Aksum. Historically Saba was the name of a state in south-west Arabia.

[2] The story of Solomon's relations with the Queen of Sheba, as recorded in the *Kĕbrä Nägäst*, will be found in Budge, 1928, I, 194–200. It was of great importance in Ethiopian tradition. The constitution of 1931 and 1955 stipulated that the imperial dignity was perpetually attached to the line descended from them. Before the revolution pictures, usually containing forty-four panels, representing the incidents of the Queen's visit to Jerusalem, used to be sold in the streets of Addis Ababa. One of these purchased in 1964, is on display at the house of the Royal Asiatic Society in London. Another, and some panels from a third, are well reproduced in Pritchard, 1974, between pp. 104 and 105. The son was called Menelik, who is often regarded as the first Emperor.

[3] In fact, Acts viii. 26–40.

[4] In the Ethiopic texts Candace is called Hendake. Judith (Guedit) was, on the contrary, one of the names given in Ethiopian tradition to a mysterious, perhaps wholly legendary, queen who persecuted Christianity in the ninth century. The same confusion occurs in Ramusio's version of the narrative of Alvares, though not in the Portuguese text, F. Alvares, 1961, I, 148.

[5] 'Ethiopian tradition as embodied in the *Kĕbrä Nägäst* has come to identify 'Candace queen of the Ethiopians'...with the Queen of the South and has fused the two queens, belonging to such different periods, into one person', E. Ullendorff, 'The Queen of Sheba in Ethiopian Tradition', in Pritchard, 1974, p. 107.

The light of the Gospel, however, having come into the world, also reached and illuminated the Abyssinian peoples who were living in the dark shadows of paganism, typified by the inhabitants there. It was the famous religious eunuch made illustrious in the Holy Scriptures, whom the Abyssinians and some Hebrew authors called Inda,[1] who, after his conversion, brought to his mistress and to all the inhabitants of Ethiopia the first good tidings of the law of grace, which they received with such sincerity that all those kingdoms then subject to the Abyssinian ruler rendered obedience and made themselves subject to the law of the Gospel. And they gave proof of the truth and fervour with which they received it by the great numbers who consecrated themselves to God and have continued the practice up to the present time; although now, because of the wickedness of the times, it is much debased; for the hermitages are populated with an infinite number of anchorites whose lives, habit and penances still persevere to some extent. The people who dedicated themselves to the church and consecrated themselves to God in monasteries were countless. The houses of prayer, churches, brotherhoods, and monasteries that were founded exceed any number one could imagine. The liberality with which the highest princes and lords endowed them with lands, revenues, pieces of gold and silver, silks and many other things of all kinds makes it appear that this was extreme prodigality on their part, if one looks at it in a very human and practical way. The piety of the people, both natural and Christian, in all works of virtue, is very great, inclined as they are to charity, fasting, doing penances, frequenting the churches, the sacraments of Confession and Communion, Mass, and sermons. And although that Church is presently ruined to the extent we saw in its spiritual edifice, it still preserves so much of all these good customs and works that, as far as that part is concerned, it does not have to envy any other kingdom where purity of faith is of greater perfection and excellence. It is very true that, because it is lacking the principle of grace and true union with its Head, Christ Jesus, since they are separated from His Vicar, the Roman Pope, by an ancient and obstinate schism, in addition to the infinite number of heresies to which they cling, these good works I have reported do not have the value they deserve nor the perfection and grace which is given them by the pure, Catholic

---

[1] This name has not been traced. Professor Ullendorff suggests that it may possibly have arisen from confusion with the first part of the Ethiopic equivalent of Candace, Hendake. It is also conceivable that a word meaning 'Indian' has been mistaken for a personal name. In the *Yosippon*, a mediaeval pseudo-historical work which was translated into Ethiopic, Candace is described as Queen of India.

faith, by the true religion. For eight hundred years they had lived in union with the Catholic, Apostolic, Roman faith;[1] but with the schism of the Eastern Church they followed the one closest to them, that of Alexandria, head of this disunion and schism, in which they persevered until the year 1625, when the Patriarch entered Ethiopia and was received by Emperor Seltan Segued and all his lords, who unanimously rendered obedience to the Roman faith and persevered in it, with great spiritual benefits and glory of God Our Lord until the death of the said emperor, at all of which I was present and shall shortly relate in detail and tell briefly what happened.

As far as the temporal side of this empire is concerned, there is no doubt that it was one of the great empires of the world because of the kingdoms and provinces it occupied; for its length and breadth covered a large part of Africa, including vast regions within its borders. It is located in the very easternmost part of Africa, with its boundaries in that direction being the Red Sea, which bathed the beaches of its eastern coast, and the Indian Ocean, which bathed those of its southern coast.[2] To the west, its boundary extended and was adjacent to the large and wellknown kingdoms of Congo, whose princes could not be admitted to the crown and sceptre of that kingdom without receiving the investiture of the Abyssinian Emperor, as it appears from what the serious historian João de Barros writes in his *Crónica*, Decad. [blank], Book [blank], Chapter [blank], to which I refer the curious reader.[3] The lands within these borders in ancient times numbered thirty-four kingdoms and eighteen provinces. In much more recent years they were reduced to a few more than forty. Now, however, the number is smaller and, of what it possesses, the part remaining peacefully in its power covers an area somewhat larger than the whole of Spain and consists of five kingdoms and six provinces. From another part of its possessions, it receives tribute or some other acknowledgment of submission, not very willingly and under considerable constraint. Of the provinces and kingdoms obedient to the Empire, I know that Tigré is as long and wide as Portugal; Begamedir, if not larger, certainly is

[1] The Ethiopian Church followed the Monophysite doctrine of the Church of Alexandria, condemned at the Council of Chalcedon in 451. Le Grand omits the reference to 800 years and says only: 'Since they have been infected with the heresy of Eutyches'.

[2] There is no evidence that the Ethiopian Emperors ever exercised effective authority anywhere on the African coast south of the Gulf of Aden.

[3] The reference is to dec. I, liv. iii, cap. 4, but Barros is not speaking of the Congo but of Benin. It was alleged that the election of the kings of Benin had to be confirmed by a mysterious potentate called Ogané, whom the Portuguese took to be Prester John and hence identified with the Emperor of Ethiopia.

no smaller; Goiama almost as large; Amara and Damote a little smaller.[1] I mention this so that it will not appear that these are kingdoms only in name.

The peoples who populate them are of different types; first, as to religious beliefs, there are Muslims, pagans, Jews and schismatic Christians, the latter comprising the largest number. The variety of peoples is great, some completely barbarian and uncouth, others more polite and civilized.[2] The Amharas are the best people, the most courteous and the most pleasant to deal with; the Tigrés or Abyssinians next, followed by the Damotes, Gafates, and Agaos.[3] After these, the kingdoms and their populations differ in name and customs.[4] The most numerous of the peoples are the Galas, all of whom are pagan. They are a barbarous and exceedingly ferocious people, foreigners to the land, having appeared there, for its destruction, in approximately 542. They came from the interior of Africa in countless numbers, destroying kingdoms and provinces through which they passed, leaving them deserted, for they put to the sword every living thing they found; those who were lucky fled or were vigilant enough to avoid sudden capture. They did not settle in any of the provinces they occupied, but used them only for grazing their cattle, from which they gain their livelihood in the manner of African Bedouin herdsmen. They are great horsemen. Every eight years, they choose a king. They neither sow nor cultivate the land. They subsist on meat and milk. They adore no idols, but have superstitious practices, acknowledging that there is a superior being above, which they call Oac,[5] meaning either Heaven or God, so confused is the idea they have of their creator or so dimmed is the light of reason in them because of their barbarous state. Their entrance into Ethiopia was prophesied a few years before their arrival by the first Catholic Patriarch, who entered those provinces with Dom

[1] Tigre, Begemder, Gojjam, Amhara, and Damot.

[2] Le Grand adds: 'This diversity of Peoples and Religion is the reason why this Kingdom is not equally well-ordered and why there are many different Laws and customs'.

[3] Damot was originally a region to the south of the Blue Nile (Abbay). The inhabitants, linguistically Semitic, were driven across the river by the Galla incursions of the sixteenth century, but the original location is shown on Almeida's map of Ethiopia, reproduced in SRE, opp. p. xcvii. The same map shows the Gafats occupying territory north of Damot ('Damut') and south of the Blue Nile. Like the people of Damot they were displaced by the Gallas; they moved north of the river to a district adjoining Wambarma. They spoke a distinctive Semitic language. In 1947, with some difficulty, W. Leslau found four persons still able to speak it, Ullendorff, 1960, p. 131. The Agaw are the most important substrate population of the northern and central plateau of Ethiopia. They speak Cushitic languages but are often bilingual in a Semitic language as well.

[4] Le Grand: 'One can say that the others are wholly barbarous'.

[5] Waka, the Creator, Supreme Being and sky god of the Galla. Le Grand calls this being Oul.

Christovão da Gama, named Dom João Bermudes,[1] who, because he was not received by the Emperor Claudio, as the Abyssinians had promised, but rather persecuted, mistreated and exiled by him, received an illumination from Heaven informing him of the punishment that was to come to those kingdoms because of their faithlessness and obstinacy; and so he told them that he saw all of Ethiopia being filled with some black ants. By the multitude of these creatures he meant the great number that were to come; and by the colour, the very dark colour of these barbarians who possess and destroy the greater and best part of this empire, which Muslims and pagans kept diminishing on all sides, the latter in the south and west, the former in the north towards Egypt, the Turks to the east on the Red Sea, leaving the little that the Emperor still has today of the vast areas he once had, surrounded on all sides in the midst of so much paganism like the seed of the Gospel that they still preserve, although mingled with an infinite tangle of weeds of Jewish and Muhammadan errors and countless heresies, amid thorns that smother it so much. As it appears, the devil added to this abandoned Christianity and ensnared the poor Abyssinians with all the errors he had sown throughout the world from the beginning of the Church until the present time.

Concerning their customs and civilization, there are many extremely unusual things. The houses they live in are made not of limestone but of straw, like thatched cottages, and are round, from the largest to the smallest. If the house is round it is called *bethnugus*; if long, *sacala*.[2] The villages are composed of these and of a few of stone and clay. There are no cities, only villages. The largest are the encampments where the Emperor is, with the viceroys and governors, which are in the summer mainly camping tents because they are continually in the field attacking and making war on their enemies, either domestic vassals in rebellion or foreigners living on the boundaries of the empire; so that it can be said that they live most of the year in the field making war, and the

---

[1] A member of the embassy of Dom Rodrigo de Lima, which was in Ethiopia from 1520 to 1526. When the embassy left the country he stayed behind and was later sent to Europe to solicit help against the invaders under Ahmad Grañ. In Lisbon Bermudes claimed that the head of the Ethiopian Church had consecrated him as his successor, that the Emperor had sent him to convey Ethiopia's submission to Rome, and that the Pope had consecrated him Patriarch of Alexandria. These claims were probably untrue; certainly, the head of the Ethiopian Church had no power to appoint his own successor. Claudius (Galawdewos), whose throne name was Asnaf Sagad, reigned 1540–59; he was dismissive of the pretensions of Bermudes.

[2] Eth. *betä nĕgus*, literally 'king's house', a term applied to a round house of some size. Eth. *säqäla*, originally 'tent' or 'tabernacle', but used in Amharic to mean a large rectangular house.

same thing happens every year. They are not lacking in enemies; for, as they are all enemies of God – Muslims, pagans, Jews,[1] and heretics – , even though most of them are vassals, since they do not observe due vassalage and acknowledgment to God, it is not much for them to exempt themselves from observing their obligations to men, even though it be to their princes. Each of the lands or villages has its head who governs it directly, called *qadare*.[2] Above this person there is one called *educ*,[3] who is deputy of the lord of the land, over whom there is one who governs and commands the *educ* and everyone else in that province or kingdom, called *afamacon*, meaning *mouth of the prince*,[4] because he collects the revenues for him and is a sort of steward or exterior overseer. Then follows the Viceroy; after him or over him is one in the court called *relatinafata*, which corresponds to *lord steward of the household*,[5] and it is he who has the authority to act for the Emperor, the Emperor being present. Over the *Relatinafata* there is one called *Ras*,[6] meaning *head*, over whom is the Emperor. They all live in this subordination, each one of these princes and lords having his household and exterior officers such as stewards, deputies, overseers, yeomen of the larder. And since we have given details of the peoples who populate these kingdoms and the variety of them, let us say something of the climate of the land and of the things it produces, along with all the other unusual and curious things that exist in that land, which, because they are new, though strange, will be well received.

All types of food produced in our lands are grown in theirs in lesser quantity because the people are not very laborious, although some kinds of seeds yield greater quantity. The lands are vigorous, not

[1] By Jews are meant the Falashas, a people living to the north of Lake Tana. They are 'Ethiopians of Agaw stock practising a peculiar kind of Judaism...all the evidence points to the conclusion that the Falashas are descendants of those elements in the Aksumite Kingdom who resisted conversion to Christianity', Ullendorff, 1960, pp. 110, 111.
[2] Le Grand has *Gadare*. There is no obvious explanation for this word. Prof. Ullendorff suggests that it is either connected with Arabic *qādir*, 'someone having power', or a related word, or else might be a metathesis for *gäräd*, a term sometimes used for a governor in the southern provinces of Ethiopia, such as Bali and Ganz.
[3] Amh. *ĕdug (ras)*, lieutenant of a Ras, Guidi, *Vocabolario amarico-italiano* (Roma, 1901), col. 688.
[4] *Äfä mäkuannĕn*, 'the mouth of the governor'.
[5] Le Grand has *Relatina Fala*. P. da Costa sees in this a distortion of *Blattengeta*. Dr Lockhart refers to Paez, liv. I cap. iv, and notes that the high rank strongly suggests that the Talallaq Blattengeta, 'Master of the great attendants', is meant, rather than the Ṭĕqaqĕn Blattengeta, 'Master of the lesser attendants'. Both offices were of recent origin.
[6] Originally meaning 'head'. Almeida describes him as 'head of all the great men of the empire. He is the chief counsellor and minister both in peace and war, though he applies himself more to the latter', *SRE*, p. 74. In modern times his office lapsed but the word was used more widely as a high-ranking title.

lacking leaves on the trees, green grass and daisies in the fields all year long, which come up in new growth twice a year, once with the winter rain, which is in the months when our lands experience the heat of summer, i.e., in July, August and September, and again with watering in the summer from which the land is fertile, thus compensating with the many new growths for the little that each one gives. The land does not produce any more fruit than it does because of lack of cultivation rather than an inability to produce them; for the fact that it has some varieties of fruit is a clear indication that it could produce the others if they were to be planted, in addition to the fact that when we planted those we brought from India, they all thrived extremely well there. However, they have grapes, but all black, some peaches, and bitter pomegranates, many sugar canes, not many *brigasotes* figs,[1] bananas in greater abundance. The best thing of all is that they gather these fruits in Lent in order to alleviate the suffering from fasting, which is great, as I shall explain later.

The climate is mild, lacking excesses of both heat and cold, and although the latter is not anything to be wondered at, one could be more doubtful about lack of excessive heat in view of the commonly held belief of the Ancients, who depict that land as being uninhabitable because of its location and the torrid zone which encircles and covers it, their opinion being confirmed by the black, burnt colour of the people, caused, as they thought, by the continual heat of the sun burning and toasting them. In answer to this, I say that in my experience of many years living there and traversing most of the kingdoms and provinces of that empire, one can more accurately say that they live in a perpetual springtime, as far as the temperature of the air and its effects are concerned, even in the warmest time at the beginning of the summer, rather than in the stifling heat with which it has been defamed. Distinction must be made between western Ethiopia, including the interior of the Cape of Good Hope, the kingdoms of Congo, Sofala, Monomotapa, where the heat is indeed excessive, and eastern Ethiopia, which is the part in which lies this Abyssinian empire extending as far as the Red Sea.[2] It is in the latter that is found the temperate climate I have mentioned. And although

---

[1] P. da Costa suggests that this word is an error for *borjaçotes* (also *berjaçotes*, *borcejotes*), a kind of fig with purple flesh, Le Grand also mentions almonds.

[2] Almost the whole interior of sub-Saharan Africa was considered part of Ethiopia, and it was often assumed that the Emperor was known, if not acknowledged, nearly anywhere in the continent. Monomotapa was thought to be a powerful kingdom on the upper Zambesi. It owed its name to the Mokalanga tribal confederacy.

the people are more or less black in colour, they are not so much so or so ugly and of such ill-favoured features as those who inhabit the hot lands. The Abyssinians, rather, are of good temper, understanding, inclination of mind, intelligent and good in conversation, penetrating in their judgement of things, and quick to understand them. And as for the black colour of some of them, although the heat of the sun may contribute somewhat to it, this is not the cause but rather the mixture of inherited qualities with such and such a clime. We have an example of this in the whites who have children in this land, who are born as white as their parents. I have seen, by way of contrast, negroes who were children of other thoroughly black negroes and were in a region where no European had ever been and who, however, were born as white and red-headed as any fine German and even had white eyelashes, but saw very little. And on the contrary, those who were born in our lands of black parents were children of a very pure black hue, which corroborates what I have said.

The animals that grow in this empire are extremely abundant as this part of Africa is so rich in them; for in addition to the known wild carnivorous and herbivorous animals there are many other strange ones unknown to us, lions of various types, and magnificent ones. A young man, my servant, killed one of them, with such bravery and success, that I cannot fail to report the incident because of its being so unusual, its importance being no less so; for the lion made extensive and continuous attacks on a church property where I was, killing each night many oxen and cows in the cattle pens, so that the people were continually frightened and were lamenting about it to me. The youth resolved to go after the common enemy, though at great personal risk and with excessive bravery or rashness. Taking two short spears, he went out one Wednesday in search of the lion. But, scouring various pasture grounds, he found not a trace or any news of it. He stopped in a field surrounded by a thicket and was in the process of asking a boy, who was there frightening the birds away from a piece of ground with a stick, if had seen it; and, as he was saying No, the lion suddenly appeared, entering the field and coming toward the bold hunter. It was coming slowly however, because it had just dispatched a cow so that it was moving rather sluggishly. The youth set out boldly toward it while the lion, exhibiting as much confidence as he, kept coming to meet him. When the bold youth came within range of a spear's throw, he threw one of the spears so surely and luckily that he put it between the shoulder-blade and the neck. Feeling himself thus wounded, the lion gave a roar and a jump, so heedless that he fell into a ditch that had been made there for him. The youth rushed on him with the same courage and attacked him, now with even greater confidence because he was sure of victory. He finished killing him, with the other spear he still had in his hand, as safely as if it were a little cub. It was so small that, having skinned it, he brought me the skin with the head joined to it, which was as bulky as a huge loading basket. The mane was extremely beautiful, the teeth very large and red, being those of a veteran. I asked that the skin be stretched out and measured in my presence, and they found that, from the head to the end of the tail, it measured sixteen spans of a man who was measuring it. The reader can picture the size this represents and the bravery of the bold youth, whom I congratulated most heartily after scolding him for his rashness. His courage and the happy outcome, however, are certainly worthy of admiration. Worthy of even greater admiration, however, was another encounter occurring a few days thereafter and involving another man, this one married, who was on another property of the Church. Because another lion killed one of his cows one evening, he went out in search of him to take vengeance, taking as his only weapon a dagger in his belt. He was, however, half out of his mind with the loss of the cow, which for a poor man was a substantial loss, especially because cattle are the major form of wealth for these people. After a few steps, he found the lion going down a hill. He went around to the other side of the hill in order to take him unawares and went toward him from one side on a level with him. The lion went toward him, and coming close to him made his leap to tear him apart. But watching him closely, the daring man, with much presence of mind and assurance, at the moment of impact nimbly removed his body from the path of the lion letting him fall next to him. He immediately threw himself upon the lion holding him by the head and neck with his left hand as tightly as he could; and, quickly drawing the dagger, he began to strike with it with such furiously repeated blows that the lion soon fell dead at his feet with the man over him. It is very true that, while the man was striking him, the lion caught his arm in his jaws from the inside of the elbow downward and, with his teeth, broke and mangled all the bones, so that the man was crippled because of it and still remains so today. The lion was dead and Aile Ieotos, for this was the man's name, meaning illustrious fortress of Jesus,[1] had proved his valour. The two events must cause respect for the courage of the

---

[1] Presumably Haile Iyasus, 'the Power of Jesus'.

Abyssinians, with no lack of respect for the Ethiopian lions, for even if their great ferocity had not been demonstrated by these experiences, their being African, and as such famed and feared, would be sufficient in itself.

Elephants are countless. One time among others, I came across three hundred of them grazing in a field in three herds. This was when we were being chased by the heretics as we were making our way through the woods, where we lay in hiding by day and travelled at night. Since we had a longer distance to travel that night, we set out at four in the afternoon and, on going down a hill, we saw the valley with three hundred elephants coming across the road where we necessarily had to pass. It was impossible for us to stop and even more so for us to turn back, but by going ahead we were running the danger of experiencing the wrath of these wild beasts who are particularly fierce when they go in herds with their young and females. As the least of the evils, we chose to go ahead, imploring God's mercy, which fortunately interrupted the wild beasts in their course as they either turned back or went another way, so that we were able to continue our journey in safety. However, we were not completely out of this danger when we encountered another equally great. Since the people who were leading us are extremely superstitious, being uncivilized and schismatical, as soon as they hear a certain bird singing on their left, they will not take another step forward until they hear it on their right. Unfortunately for us, a bird sang on the wrong side as we were hurrying to be sure to be out of such great danger and they ordered us to stop, dismount and sit down. When I learned the reason for this, it was necessary for me to counteract the spell. After a short space of time, therefore, I came to them in rapture saying that the bird had sung on the right. At this news, they happily continued the journey, as, with that bit of foolishness, I had overcome the blindness of their vain superstition. On another occasion, with greater danger, as we were travelling to Masuá, now as prisoners of the Turks, in another uninhabited place we saw five elephants next to a large rock, one of huge size, the four others smaller. Because they were within a stone's throw of us, we came closer to them to have a better look at them, and a youth foolishly shouted at them, at which they became so enraged that, after the small ones had first made certain turns around the large one, which, with its trunk raised high looking like a large tree trunk or beam, was giving dreadful trumpetings, provoked by anger, they rushed so boldly and furiously at us that they would quickly be upon us and most of us would surely not escape being torn to pieces by them. But God willed that, as they reached the steep bank of a certain dry river bed, they could go no further because the jump was too far down,[1] so that they turned and we began to run faster, watchful not to awaken any more sleeping dogs or to go near any similar wild animals on whose size I shall comment in the following remarks.

One morning I was in a wilderness which I spent the whole day crossing. Having many trees and plenty of water, it is a place well suited to and much frequented by these animals because of the branches and boughs on which they subsist and the roots of large trees which they uproot, eating the tenderest ones as a great treat. The water in pools or streams serves them for bathing as they put themselves into it and into the mud, like swine. I am reminded, by the way, to undeceive those who believe the tales of antiquity that elephants do not have joints, never lie down, but sleep leaning against trees, etc.; for they do lie down and sleep on the ground, kneeling down like any other supple animal. One of these had just refreshed himself in a mud-hole and, going to a nearby tree, had cleaned himself on it as they are wont to do, and I found this mark very recently made, for he did it almost in my sight. Out of curiosity, I wanted to measure how high it was. Although I was riding a good-sized mule and stood up on the stirrups, I was unable, with my arm and hand extended, to reach the mark he had left, falling more than two spans short of reaching it. Such is the scale and size of the wild animals in those parts. Among the wild animals there are also the famous rhinoceroses, whom alone the elephants fear. The famous unicorn, as celebrated in story as it has been unknown until now, has been seen in a heavily wooded province of these kingdoms called Agau at such close range that it could be seen and identified and its features could be noted. It is a beautiful horse of a chestnut colour with black mane and tail. Those of Tuncua[2] have a short tail; those of Ninina, a district of this province,[3] have long tails and manes which go down to the ground.[4] There are many other animals of various

---

[1] Elephants are unable to jump and can be stopped by a ditch too deep for them to step into or out of, and too wide for them to step across.

[2] Tumha, about five miles NW of Danghela. Le Grand reads Tuaçua.

[3] More commonly Nanina. The name does not appear on modern maps but it is marked on Almeida's and Ludolf's. Almeida, *Historia de Ethiopia a alta*, in Beccari, 1905–17, V, 469, says that the Emperor Sartsa Dengel gave the Portuguese lands in this district bordering on Agau territory, 'four or five leagues from the source of the Nile'. The Portuguese won victories over the Agaus and gained more lands, but because of the jealousy of the Ethiopians they were removed to Dambya. Paez, liv. IV cap. 7, says there were many Portuguese there. They were the descendants of the survivors of D. Cristovão's expedition.

[4] Mr I. R. Bishop of the British Museum (Natural History) informs me that there is no animal which has all the features ascribed by Lobo to the unicorn. The animal most

types which follow them. Similarly, deer, goats, gazelles, and other animals of this sort follow the elephant for the purpose of defending themselves, under his protection, against the other carnivorous animals; for the elephant lives only on grass and branches and boughs and provides safety for these poor ones through his protection and generosity.

The number of domestic animals is almost unlimited: mules, asses and horses, the latter very beautiful and excellent; oxen and cows. Since cows are their principal form of wealth, there are an extremely large number of them. Some succeed in having many thousands of them. They have a delightful custom, which they never fail to observe among themselves, that whenever one gains ownership of a thousand cows, he gives a great banquet, inviting relatives and friends, and taking milk from all the cows, for only cows are counted in the thousand, they take a bath in it, which I appropriately used to call 'a fly or huge fly in the milk' when they were in it. This custom is so prevalent that when people ask how many thousand cows a certain person has, they answer that he has already bathed two or some other number of times, which means that he owns that many thousand cows. They use them only for milk and breeding. Every three years there is a general 'burning' in all the the kingdoms of the empire, which means that the Emperor takes one óf every ten cows and the one that he takes has a mark branded on her buttock with a branding iron. For that reason they call it *tucus*, meaning 'burn'.[1] The Emperor collects many thousands of cows in this way. It is one among many tributes the people must pay to him. They use the oxen for ploughing and as beasts of burden, as if they were mules. They are very large and beautiful, usually without horns, but some with horns so flexible that they seem to be disjointed arms hanging from their heads. They raise a certain strain of ox called *gueches*, as large as a pair of ours, used only for slaughter.[2] They feed them from the time they are small with the milk of two or three cows so that they fatten and grow as I have said. Their horns

likely to have been intended is the oryx. 'It seems quite possible that the legendary Unicorn was based on this elegant Arabian antelope; certainly some of the early European visitors to the region, such as Varthema, in 1503, described the Oryx they saw as such', D. L. Harrison, *The Mammals of Arabia* (London, 1964–72), II, 348. Dr Harrison tells me that an oryx seen from the side might easily appear to have only one horn, and some animals may have lost or badly damaged one. For a photograph of an Ethiopian oryx which has only one horn, see W. George, 'The bestiary: a handbook of the local fauna', *Archives of Natural History*, 10 (1981), 189. Dr George remarks that 'frequently, antelopes have broken or misshapen horns because their horns are soft at birth and unicorns, or one-horned oryx, are not unknown'.

[1] Amh. *tukus*, 'burnt in'.   [2] Amh. *gosh*, 'buffalo'.

are remarkable because each one carries as much as fifteen *canadas*, and the Abyssinians use them as flagons in which to carry wine when they travel. Four of them, full, make a perfect load for one ox. It appears that these are the fat oxen spoken of in Scripture, so celebrated among the Jews. The cheapness of this cattle is remarkable, for not one of them sells for more than two *patacas*, and one can usually be bought for one *pataca*, though I was in a part of the empire where I bought them much more cheaply. Sheep and goats can be bought at the rate of about six, and small billy goats at the rate of nine for one piece of sackcloth the size of a bedsheet, which would be worth approximately one *pataca*.

The number and variety of birds, both wild and tame, are endless. Of the wild birds there are many kinds unknown to us. One remarkable one is a certain bird quite similar to a turkey, called *abagun*, a pompous abbot that has, instead of a crest or comb, a short but wide horn with a blunt, wide end.[1] Others, called *seitan fares*[2] meaning 'devil's horse' resemble a man bedecked with strange feathers on his head. They walk about with great stateliness and run very swiftly; but when they see that they cannot flee by running, they use their wings. They are the size of a swan.[3] There are some little birds that we call cardinals because their feathers are of purest scarlet. Their hat, however, looked like very fine black velvet, and was well shaped so as to resemble a cardinal's hat very prettily.[4] Others, like nightingales, being so small and having a fine white feather on their tails, two spans long, appear, when they fly, to have tails of paper.[5] There are partridges of three types.[6] The largest are like beautiful capons. There are turtle-doves of four or five varieties and as many types of pigeons. A small bird called the honey-bird because of its singularly admirable instinct, deserves particular mention, although it is small and otherwise insignificant.[7] It is somewhat like

---

[1] Usually Abba Gumba, the ground hornbill, *Bucorvus leadbeateri*. The illustration in Bruce, VIII, 1813, pl. 34, shows the 'pompous abbot'. Le Grand says it is found nowhere else except in Peru.

[2] Le Grand has Feitan Favez.

[3] Amh. *säytan färäs*, with the meaning given. Possibly the secretary bird, *Sagittarius serpentarius*.

[4] Bishop birds, *Euplectes*, of which there are several species. Le Grand says it is the belly which is like black velvet.

[5] The Paradise flycatcher, *Terpsiphone viridis* or *Tchitrea viridis*, in the white phase of the male.

[6] There are numerous species of partridges, francolins and guinea-fowl which may be intended.

[7] The Black-throated or Great Honeyguide, *Indicator indicator*. These birds are all described, and most of them are illustrated, in C. W. Mackworth-Praed and C. H. B. Grant, *Birds of eastern and north eastern Africa*, 2nd edition (London, 1957, 60). I am indebted to Mrs E. Warr, formerly of the British Museum (Natural History) for help with these identifications.

a nightingale; and, as it loves honey, nature has taught it to know when the honey is matured in the beehives, whether in those kept by the villagers at their homes or in those built by the wild mountain bees in the woods, or in the holes of trees or in holes they make especially in the roads, hollowing underground a place the size of a large water-pitcher, which they clean out, smooth and embellish, filling it with combs of honey as good as domestic honey, but blacker. This must be the kind of honey spoken of in Scripture, eaten by St John the Baptist. The time when the people go out to collect it is at the end of October and the beginning and middle of November. They assemble a group of people for this and, going into the woods, disperse with their containers looking for these little birds, which they call *marof*; 'Bird' is signified by *of*, and 'honey' by the sound *mar*.[1] And as this careful discoverer searches no less diligently knowing that people are following him, he keeps searching and singing very gaily, placing himself where he can be seen and heard, giving evidence of his presence until they discern and take heed of him, and flying in search of the honey, he leads behind him the investigators or collectors of the poor little bees' work, flying from tree to tree, arriving at the honey place to burst into song with a thousand trills, pointing out to them as well as he can that they have at that place what they are looking for. Then the diligent people do not rest until they find it, and pulling it out, gather it in their containers, leaving his reward to the discoverer, with which he is content, eating his well deserved share. Every year, the Abyssinians collect a great quantity of this honey afforded by the wooded areas, although the best and most abundant, undoubtedly extremely abundant, is the domestic kind, so that, by reason of this liquor and the butter, which is very abundant in this land because of the cows bred there, it can be said that this is a land where honey and butter flow.

[1] Amh. *mar*, 'honey', and *wof*, 'bird'. Le Grand has the inferior reading *moroc*.

[Of the customs, religion and civilization of the Abyssinians]

In their cooking there are few dressed dishes, and on the tables even of the greatest princes and of the Emperor himself the vanity of silver is unknown to them. They use plates of black earthenware, a favourite colour of most of them, seemingly because it is native to them, except when it comes to clothing. The more ancient this slab of earthenware the more highly it is valued. On it they bring in their food prepared in their own way and of which they are very fond. We or other Europeans find it very little to our taste because they consider that the more highly seasoned it is with salt, pepper and butter the better it is. Bread is made on the same day it is eaten. It is made in cakes called *apa*[1] as large as the wide brims of a cleric's hat of the very largest kind and as thin as those same brims. These *apas* serve them as tablecloths, napkins, and bread on tables which are round trays, well turned and some of them able to seat twelve or fifteen people around, which is remarkable because each of these tables is made from a single piece of timber.[2] They invariably wash their hands before eating but do not dry them. Those of greater nobility are not to touch the food, but each of them has his page, who could properly be called 'gentleman of the mouth', who puts a mouthful of food in it, the greater quantity at a time the better, since it is also an expression of courtesy to eat greedily, with both sides of one's mouth stuffed with food and lustily chewing at what is proffered, because only the poor eat with food on one side of their mouths because of their poverty, and only thieves eat quietly so as not to be heard. But a rich man or a nobleman, who is not a thief, will eat with both sides of his mouth full and very audibly. Their best dish is one of raw cow's meat, as raw as when its dam gave birth to it, with no more warming than its own natural warmth, for it is best eaten immediately after the cow has been killed. The leg, being

---

[1] Anglo-Indian *hopper*, from Tamil *appam*, any round, flat cake, made in Ethiopia from *tef*, the grain *Eragrostis tef*, Zucc.

[2] They are of the height of a table, are portable, often shaped like an hour-glass, round at the top, and are now often made of wicker-work.

the best portion, is brought immediately to the table, still palpitating. It is cut into pieces, seasoned with salt and pepper with the gall of the same cow poured over it as if it were the best oil and vinegar dressing available. The gourmets among them dip the pieces of meat into a kind of mustard called *manta*,[1] which is made of the finest marrow of the tripe, taken warm from the same cow, although they add to it over the fire a mixture of butter, pepper, onion, and salt. On one occasion I was brought a saucer of this mustard as a great delicacy, and if I had not already known about it, I should have used it along with the others, but I put it to one side and someone did not fail to empty it immediately. The best part was when the mistress of the house, thinking that I liked it, brought me a second helping, but having avoided the first one successfully, I informed her that having such a treat once was really too much and if it was considered a delicacy it was not suitable for a religious, because it would be too much of an indulgence.

After they are finished at table as far as eating is concerned, in which they do not spend much time, their drinking starts, for which any time they spend seems short to them, for in this occupation they spend their days and most of their nights; and when they are able to do this many times, life has no happier occupation for them. These are their games, recreation, visits, conversations, and relaxation. They place themselves in a circle around the house sitting on the ground. They bring into the middle of the circle one or two large pitchers full, immediately replaced by others as soon as they are empty. Each one has its pourer who pours the wine and a page who serves it. However the pourer and the server taste the wine before it is served, each drinking first from glass or porcelain goblets. Afterwards they go about presenting the wine, starting with the most distinguished guests; but they must fill the glass two or three times in succession for each person. The guests drink in this way until others carry them off to bed, and when this event occurs, the guest is considered fortunate and the master of the house considered generous since he has provided so much wine that he has succeeded in making his guests drunk. This drink is of two kinds, one called *sava*, which is like Flemish beer and is made from grain,[2] or one called *saie*

---

[1] 'A dish prepared of the tripe and liver cut into small pieces. The contents of the gall-bladder are then squeezed over it, as also a part of the half-digested green matter found in the intestines of the animal', Mansfield Parkyns, *Life in Abyssinia*, (London, 1853), I, 376–7. Amh. *manṭa*, 'intestine'.

[2] Amharic *ṭälla*, made from barley fermented by the leaves of the *gesho* tree, *rhamnus pauciflorus*. Lobo's spelling represents the Tigrinya form of the word.

which intoxicates like wine, which is the meaning of the word *saie*.[1]
It is made of honey in a certain amount of water, more or less water
according to how strong they want it; a little germinated barley is put
into it and an equal amount of the bark of a certain root of a bush
called *sardo* which corresponds in its effects to our mastic.[2] The liquor
ferments for three or four days, and, becoming quiet, takes a couple
of days to become composed, then they drink it. The drink is neither
sweet nor unpleasant. At least as far as the health is concerned it is
excellent. Their stomachs could not digest what they eat of raw meat
and other things if this great quantity of wine did not help them with
its honey, which is excellent for digestion. When they finish drinking
wine, even though they are there to converse, the gathering is over,
for it lasts only while wine is being drunk. Grape wine does not taste
bad to them; however the lack of grapes and the great abundance of
honey has taught them to take advantage of the latter, as being easier,
and not to pay much heed to the former.

The ordinary people do not spend much on dress. They are satisfied
with pieces of cloth like large sheets, of which they also make breeches.
The nobility dresses more expensively, the more so as they go closer
to the court, where they wear many Turkish brocades, velvets, and
every other kind of silk, which, since they must be of different colours
to satisfy them and ample in the Turkish fashion of *cabaias*, breeches
down to their feet, clothes called *camizas*[3] of any kind of silk or other
material and of any colour that best suits them, they are very pleasing
to behold, mainly, however, because the Abyssinians like to wear on
their persons the very best things they possess, making for the
embellishment of their persons many objects of gold and silver, in
which metals their land is extremely abundant, particularly in gold.
They ordinarily wear their hair long and made into various arrangements which serve them as embellishment and in lieu of hats. The old
and more distinguished men wear wide red caps with a definitely round
crown. Some also use turbans in the Turkish fashion. The dress of the
distinguished women is stately, because their dresses are like the
religious habit of Bernardine monks, their heads, necks and ears well
decorated with jewels, their hair in a thousand different arrangements

---

[1] *Saiia* occurs as a variant spelling, or more probably a copyist's mistake, for *saua*, but
what Lobo describes here is the well-known *ṭej*.

[2] Amharic *ṣäddo*, the tree *Rhamnus saddo*.

[3] The Portuguese word means a shirt, but it is here used for Amh. *qämis*. 'Men of
distinction wear a silk tunic (*kamis*), magnificently embroidered and coloured according
to their rank.' Ullendorff, 1960, p. 177.

and with a graceful manner of being woven with ribbons. A life of retirement and protection from the outside world was not made for them, and so they go out and make visits as much and more than their husbands. A thousand difficulties arise from this, and the husbands do nothing about them, indeed are unable to do anything about them, especially if they are married to some called *oisoros*, which means that they are of royal blood or princesses.[1] Their houses do not make much use of tapestries. When they are used extensively they are sheets of printed calico used as a covering for their beds. They do not use nor do they possess any furniture such as chairs, chests, etc. They could not take them with them on the journeys they make. They live and travel with very few impedimenta, most of their expense going for entertainment, especially for wine.

There are no inns anywhere in the empire, but a person can always find shelter in villages no matter where he goes, without taking any money with him; for, in addition to its being very heavy as I shall presently explain, it is unnecessary for him to carry any, because wherever one arrives after three o'clock in the afternoon there is an obligation for them to give him a house, a cot on which to sleep, and food to eat appropriate to the person's station in life, and he may be given a live cow for his servants' supper in addition to bread, wine and also cooked food. The person assigned to him, or who nominates himself, to provide supper for him – the one who acts as steward is always the head of the village – is accountable to the head of the village, and if anything is lacking, he is under an obligation to pay doubly. And whenever it is ascertained that a person designated to do so has not given that food, that person receives severe punishment on the following day. For this supper the entire village contributes, each one providing what he is asked to give. Since this is such a common usage in this land, it is wonderful to see the assurance with which a stranger goes into a home and acts as if it were his own and as if the people in it were old friends or relatives. The custom is certainly very convenient for poor people, but much more so, with its difficulties, for vagrants who are no more lacking in this land than in any other.

I was saying that there is no money in these kingdoms except in some located further in the interior, where small pieces of iron are used as the usual coinage. In most of them and in the principal ones they use what can be properly called barter, for pieces of cloth like sheets, cakes of salt a span long and three fingers wide on each of its four sides,

---

[1] Amh. *wäyzäro*, a lady of rank.

pepper, foodstuffs, gold by weight, oxen, cows, tobacco, goats, chickens, serve them for buying and selling. Salt especially is the commonest money. It also serves them as merchandise which they carry from region to region, and the further they go into the interior the more value it has. At first it takes more than a hundred of these cakes of salt, called *amole*,[1] to equal the value of one *pataca*. As one proceeds further inland the number drops to eighty, then sixty, forty, twenty-five, fifteen, and twelve at the court; and one comes to a kingdom where three of these cakes are worth one *pataca* of gold, which they call *Derime*.[2] And in this last kingdom, salt is of such high value that each person carries a piece of one of these cakes, small or large, in a small pouch hanging from his waist. When relatives and friends meet each other on the roads, their first 'God save you' is for each one to take out his piece of salt and give it to the other so that he may lick it. After this ceremony has been performed by both of them, each one takes back his cake of salt and makes whatever enquiries of the other he wishes, using the civilities which come afterward.

Many other customs, of the kind called civic, are in force and thoroughly accepted, and, for us, are very barbarous. In their lawsuits, they use legal procedures, but it is all done verbally, the judge being anyone the plaintiff and accused wish to select or whom the lord of the land appoints. There is provision for appeal to the viceroy and also to the king, if they so wish. A man's life, death and property are often dispatched in half an hour, unless more time is needed to examine witnesses. The judge sits on the ground and an effort is made to have it in some field where people can assemble. They all hear the plaintiff and the defendant, who stand, each supported by as many procurators as he wishes, and they all speak in turn. After the plaintiff has presented the accusation, the defendant answering, the plaintiff replying to the answer, and so on, each one thus speaking, two, three, or four times, the judge orders them to be silent, and those who are present, i.e. the most important ones, first giving their judgment, the judge, who has the sole deciding voice, then gives the sentence. If the defendant does not wish to appeal, justice is done on the spot. The culprit is arrested and handed over to the judge; and, if he is to die, he is delivered to his opponents who kill him in any way they wish, joined by the relatives of the dead man, and all of them take part in striking the poor condemned man.

[1] Amh. *ämole*, a piece of rock-salt, often shaped like a whetstone, 10–12 inches long and 1½–2½ inches across at the widest part.   [2] From Arabic *dirham*.

Adultery is punished in a gallant fashion; for an adulteress is condemned to loss of all her property, to leave her husband's house poorly dressed never to return again if the husband so desires, each of them being able to marry another, and with a large needle in her hand with which to earn her living by certain handiwork they perform with it. At times, also, they shave either her whole head if the husband wishes or parts of it, leaving some tufts of hair which give her a very ugly appearance. The woman with whom the husband was unfaithful to his wife is accused by the latter, and both she and he pay her for the wrong perpetrated against the wife by their observing the faithfulness owed to the state of matrimony. She is condemned to the loss of much property and they also cut her hair as if she were an adulteress. They condemn the disloyal husband to loss of property, which is kept by the wife, and the deposit in custody, if she wishes, of the greater part of what he owns. As far as the adulterer is concerned, however, if the husband can prove he has committed the offence, in the first place it is not a matter of the death penalty. He is, however, given a strange sentence; for they impose on him a penalty called *sircoarba*,[1] meaning 'forty of each thing' whereby he is under an obligation to pay forty oxen, forty cows, and the same number of horses, sheep, chickens, pieces of cloth, garments, etc., even needles, and in reparation he must give all he has and what he begs from friends and relatives. If he does not discharge his obligation or receive pardon from the offended party, he remains a prisoner and is under the control of the plaintiff after his release upon swearing to keep earning and paying or requesting pardon, which they do, bringing wine in several large pitchers and a cow; and with this, after all have eaten, he asks for pardon on this and many other occasions until he is completely pardoned, which is never done on the first such occasion but only after several. And it certainly is true that an offended husband is amply repaid for any loose behaviour on the part of his wife with another man, but one cannot believe that they can be glad for it to occur. It is, however, an advantageous thing to have happen in view of the gain that accrues to him, and the opportunity he has to remain free of obligation to such a woman if he chanced to be tired of her and wanted, as permitted by their barbarous laws and aberrations, to marry another woman. It is their good fortune or curse that after their divorce, so contrary to the holy laws of the Gospel, and after both he and she have remarried anyone

---

[1] Amh. *serqo ärba*, literally 'he who has stolen – forty', i.e., the penalty for a thief is forty times.

they have chosen, if they afterwards become reconciled, they can abandon their second marriages and return to the first one without there being in this any difficulty either from the second contracting parties or from their having been with them for however long they desired. It seems that it is all among friends or that they are very obliging indeed. This is an example of how ruined this very ancient Christianity has become, how changed from its original zeal and from the beauty and purity of the faith it professed, as I shall further demonstrate in my description of the state in which it finds itself. In the matter of holy matrimony, their behaviour is so erroneous that a man and woman will not join in marriage without giving each other security in order to consent to divorce no matter how unwilling or opposed one of them might be, the other wishing divorce, so that the one wishing divorce can force the other by means of the security to yield and give him permission to marry anyone he wishes.

The barbarity in Abyssinian polity and customs which I have described up to this point as far as their temporal life is concerned is found to an even greater extent in their spiritual life and Christian polity, all of which came into being because they were so far from the Roman Church and because of the location of their lands in the most distant and easternmost corner in all of Africa, which was aided by the fact that these kingdoms were surrounded on all sides by countless pagans, who like thorns spoiled the seed of the Gospel which was planted in the field of that Church. For these reasons it happened that, by losing communication with the Christian polity that is received in the Roman Church and is found among true Catholics, they remained an uncultivated wilderness, an untilled field, a land of thorns and thistles, for such were the errors, heresies, and abuses that, with the passage of time, kept penetrating these poor people as they followed the schism of the Eastern Church and drank, as from a spring, the poison of the heretical doctrine with which it was infected. And in this way they gave access to that damnation and permitted the devil to sow among them the weeds of all the errors that the enemy sowed and re-sowed in the field of the beautiful fertile church in all the centuries of the world, so that it seems that this enemy of human kind has summed them all up in this one part of the world, not omitting the speculations with which he has troubled so many minds or the practice of evil customs, with which he has facilitated their damnation. The fact that in all directions the roads and gates were closed to them by which they could have recourse to the Roman Church and receive, as from a chief, the influence of sound doctrine was the cause of their coming to the ruinous state they have reached. Considering the state in which the Abyssinians live and have lived in matters of faith, we can say that it is a miscellany of all possible confusion with the truth so as to better ensure their condemnation, because, with the name of Christians which, in truth, they retain, but not that of Catholics because of the schism they follow, they have some customs of piety and Christianity in their belief in the principal mysteries of our faith, their devotion to the Passion of Christ Our Lord, which they hear about day and night, always ready to shed rivers of tears over it, their sincere devotion to the Virgin Our Lady, the Cross, the Angels and Saints, observing their days and Sundays without fail. They celebrate the glorious Assumption of the Virgin Our Lady one day each month, being convinced that they alone know and venerate the excellence and greatness of the sovereign empress of glory. There is a people or tribe among them that will not swear on the name of Our Lady even if it were to cost them their belongings and their lives. I say tribe or people because they are divided into particular lands and names like the Hebrews in their tribes. They also celebrate the angels and apostles each week with a feast. They are assiduous in their attendance at church, Mass and preaching and are always prompt and eager to hear it, and much more so for communion; not so much so, however, for confession, although they do also confess.

Their giving alms to the poor is more through natural inclination than through piety, whereby they bring about the existence of many vagrants, who know they have, by this means, a sure dinner and supper. The bad thing about it is that they ask for alms as something due them, and this applies to whatever they desire, such as any clothing, any supper or dinner; and they even ask for the food one is raising to his mouth: 'Give me that food you are raising to your mouth, that plateful of food you have in front of you; I feel like having some soft bread, a chicken leg; I want some *brindo*, meaning raw cow meat,'[1] etc. And they are usually successful in getting what they ask for. Often, if you do not give them what they have asked for, they do not accept what you do give them, if it is something different or not as much as they ask for. One of them once begged me for alms. I had a loaf of bread brought and given to him. When he saw it, he said he did not want it, but was asking for nothing but a cake of salt. I answered that I didn't have any. 'Well, I certainly do not want bread,' he replied. I took leave of him

---

[1] Amh. *berundo*, raw meat.

as politely as I could, but he came back after a few steps and said that since I was not giving him salt, he wanted the bread, to which I replied that, since he had refused what I had offered him, I was going to teach him to be polite, humble and grateful, as befits a poor man, and that he would get neither the one thing nor the other. He insisted that I give him the bread anyway, but I persevered in not giving it to him, whereupon he left on that occasion with nothing to eat; which taught him that from that time forward he should accept what people gave him. On this subject I often used to say that the poor in Ethiopia are objects of indulgence more than charity, because the latter is found only in our lands.

They have a great fear of excommunication, since their monks and clergy are very free with it. Giving of oaths by St George is much revered and feared among them. They worship images, principally painted ones, for not all of them have equal devotion for solid statues. In their fasting, they still observe the custom of the early Church, eating only once a day and, during Lent after sunset and on every Wednesday and Friday at three in the afternoon, which time they tell by means of a fine clock, i.e. the shadow of the human body measured by the same person who casts it. When they find that the shadow measures seven feet, they consider it to be three o'clock in the afternoon. And in this fasting time it is forbidden to eat meat no matter how much indisposition and illness a person may have. The same is true of dairy products, and as the land is very much lacking in fish, the suffering is great on these days when they must get along with vegetables and much wine and beer. The greatest trouble is that the fasting is more by natural inclination than for ecclesiastical reasons, for they abstain even from water; and in Lent they say Mass late in the afternoon because they think they are breaking their fast with the sacramental elements of the bread and wine they consecrate. It is very true that for them to consider themselves obliged to fast, they must have a marriageable daughter or one with a child; but since they marry young, the daughters much younger than the sons, the daughters marrying at nine or ten years of age or as soon thereafter as they have the opportunity to marry, the obligation is soon upon them.

The monks and clergy are innumerable and I believe that one third of the people of Ethiopia devote themselves to God, serving in the churches, which are so numerous that one can nowhere give a shout without it being heard at least at one church or monastery and very often at many of both. In these churches, I say, they recite their breviary, reading the Psalter of David, for they have all of it and not very much corrupted, as well as the rest of the Scripture except for the books of the Maccabees, although they acknowledge them, but have lost them.[1] The monasteries always have one church for the men and another for the women. This restriction, however, is found only here and not in places where it would be more fitting. In the men's church they sing in choruses, always standing because they do not have the custom of kneeling, and in order to be more comfortable they have various crutches curved in different ways and shapes in accordance with the position of the body they find most comfortable as they lean on them. The ecclesiastical musical instruments are some small drums, which the most important monk or priest has hanging from his neck and which he beats with his hands, and some tambourines, which are entrusted only to similar persons. All present are standing and have staffs in their hands with which they beat time, putting their whole bodies into it as they also set up a great stamping with one foot on the floor. They begin in this way and they keep getting more and more animated or inflamed with fervour in their music in such a way that, no longer able to suffer pauses or keeping time, they burst forth with all the instruments in total confusion, all trying to outdo one another in playing the instruments, clapping their hands, shouting at the top of their voices, leaping and dancing, finally with such tumult that it is more of an enormous cacophony than church music. They say that they do this because of the instruction in the psalm which says: 'Omnes gentes plaudite manibus, jubilate Deo,' etc.[2] Having, then, all these things I have mentioned, though with the flaws I shall presently point out, they have such an opinion of themselves and think so highly of themselves because of them that they believe they are the only true Catholics and are unwilling to commune with those of the Roman Church as if the latter were heretics, holding them in the same repute as Muslims, and being very much surprised when they heard us speak in our sermons of Our Lady the Virgin, saying that we were not totally barbarous since we acknowledged her.

[1] The Books of Maccabees as contained in the Apocrypha were not translated into Ethiopic with the other books of the Bible; manuscripts of them which do exist were translated much later from the Vulgate. There is an Ethiopic Book of Maccabees, however, which is completely different and recounts a late legend, J. Horowitz, 'Das äthiopische Maccabäerbuch', *Zeitschrift für Assyriologie*, XIX, Heft 3/4 (1906), 194–233, which gives the text and a German translation; Guidi, *Storia della letteratura etiopica* (Roma, 1932), p. 15.

[2] Psalm xlvii. 1.

In spite of everything I have related and the great piety of which they give clear evidence, I say that these are only vestiges of the piety they had in the earliest time of their Christianity and of how well founded that Church was from its beginnings. Now, however, it is no more than a shadow of what it was and a very faint, disfigured sketch; for, with all these appearances of Christianity, they lack the true essence of it, which is being Catholic. They live as schismatics with mortal hatred for the Roman Church and its sons and followers. They were penetrated by the existing heresies against the Holy Ghost, against the person of the Son, against the two natures which we acknowledge in Christ Our Lord, against several mysteries of the faith, against Purgatory, the creation of souls, all of which they deny impiously, but in much ignorance because of their being deprived of knowledge which they do not acquire.[1] They repeat baptism every year.[2] They also are circumcised and keep the Sabbath, observing a thousand ceremonies of Jewish Law. That of foods forbidden in the law and that of the purification of women do not escape them, and even more prevalent is that of marrying the wife of one's brother, one's sister-in-law.[3] Finally, they did not baptize babies, as is necessary, saying the words in proper form; for, although they knew them and acknowledged them in the Gospel, they found it preferable for each one to invent his own form, even though it might be very nonsensical. They were happy with it, however, because it was new. In this I see proof that none of them were Christian since they had not come into the faith and Gospel through the gate of Holy Baptism. However, they had very holy names. Some were names of the Saints of the Roman Church. Most were invented and customary in their land. There was, however, abuse in applying them to themselves, although their intention was good. I shall write some of them here, supplying the meaning for each one: *Zama la Cota*, life of truth; *Zasilasse*, of the Trinity; *Sebat Laab*, glory of the Father; *Guebrama Nifez Kedus*, slave of the Holy Ghost; *Onguelavi*, Evangelist; *Cela Mariam*, plant of Mary; *Alfa Christos*,

---

[1] Being in communion with the Coptic Patriarchate of Alexandria the Ethiopian Church is Monophysite, that is, it teaches that Christ had one nature only, His human nature being absorbed in His divine nature. 'The belief in Purgatory is unknown, although prayers for the dead are in frequent use', Budge, 1928, I, 157. 'Souls they think are transmitted into children from their begetters with the body', *Ibid*.

[2] The annual festival of Temkat, i.e. *ṭāmqätä Krĕstos*, the baptism of Christ, held at Epiphany, was understood by the Jesuits to be an annual rebaptism, which they strongly condemned.

[3] On these and other Judaising practices of the Ethiopian Church, which shocked the Jesuits, see E. Ullendorff, 'Hebraic-Jewish Elements in Abyssinian (Monophysite) Christianity', *Journal of Semitic Studies*, I no. 3 (July 1956), 216–256.

mouth of Christ; *Amde Jesus*, pillar of Jesus; *Asca Gorgis*, bone of Saint George; *Sena Gabriel*, story of Gabriel.[1]

---

[1] These are Ethiopic (Ge'ez) and the meanings given are mostly correct. *Za-malakot*, 'Of divinity' or 'Of divine nature'; *Za-Selasse*, 'Of the Trinity'; *Sebat la-Ab*, 'Glory to the Father'; *Gabra Manfas Qeddus*, 'The Servant of the Holy Ghost'; *Wangelawi*, 'Evangelist'; *Se'ela Maryam*, 'The Icon of Mary'; *Afa Krestos*, 'The Mouth of Christ'; *'Amda Iyasus*, 'The Pillar of Jesus'; *'Asma* (or *'Atsma*) *Giyorgis*, 'The Bone of (St) George'; *Zena Gabri'el*, 'The Story of Gabriel'. Instead of *Cela Mariam*, Le Grand has *Tecla Maria*, 'The Plant of Mary'.

[Of the Residence at Fremona and of some missions that I undertook]

Into this land, with the nature of the people being so different from that of the people in the land in which we were reared, the same being true of the climate and customs, as well as its faith and ceremonies, into this land, I say, we went to instruct them, exposed to whatever this cause should bring upon us, adapting ourselves to the life of these people and regions to the same extent as a person who was to live his whole life among them as among relatives and brothers; for we took them as such, for love of God. And this did not prove difficult for us, considering the purpose for which we were undertaking it, and we did not consider it a hardship to be separated and depart so far from our native lands for another so foreign, travelling to get there close to seven thousand leagues' distance; for there are that many leagues to sail and a certain number to walk before reaching that town or village of Maigoga, where we had entered when I began this digression to write of these kingdoms and their inhabitants, in the account I have just given.

This village of Maigoga is so called because of two streams which run through it at the foot of an eminence on which it is located, one of which, because of the many pebbles with which it is provided and over which the water breaks, making its continual noise, which the Abyssinians, imitating with an expressive sound the noise of the natural water, call 'guagua', and as 'may'[1] in the language of Tigré, the kingdom in which this village is located, means water, the name 'Maigauga' comes to mean water which makes noise among the stones. The proper name of this land is Fremona, for that of Maigauga is modern, given to it by those who made a town there.[2] This was the first village and land that we had in this empire, given to the sainted Patriarch Dom André de Oviedo and his companions for them to live

[1] Eth. and Tigrinya, 'water'.
[2] Salt stated that the name Fremona 'if ever adopted by the inhabitants is now wholly unknown'. George, Lord Valentia, *Voyages and Travels to India, Ceylon, the Red Sea, Abyssinia and Egypt* (London, 1811), III, 74.

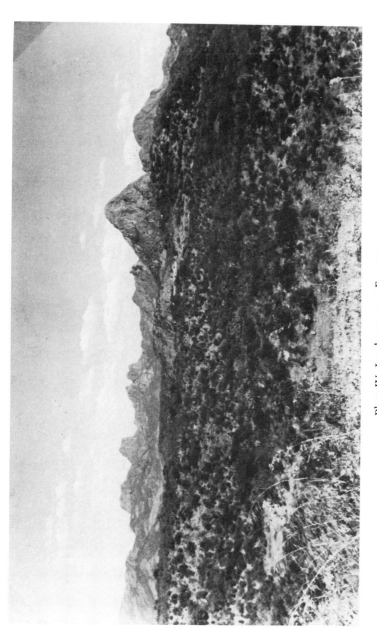

Plate IV. Landscape near Fremona

in as exiles from the court. It was in fact with this title that they were sent away from the court by Emperor Adamas Segued, a cruel enemy of the Catholic faith, both schismatic and a Muhammadan.[1] For, since it is closer to the sea, it is located at a greater distance from where the emperor had his court; and because of the little communication its people had with the people of the court, its inhabitants are considered in the same way as the Galegos are considered among us, the particular language they speak differing from the language of the court, just as that of Galiza differs from the common language of Portugal.[2] This village of Fremona or Maigoga, for it has both names, and I shall use either one in my relation is approximately five days' journey from the Red Sea[3] which, lies to the south-east of it. It was always the place of residence of the Fathers of the Company since they first entered that empire and also of Catholics and Portuguese who sought shelter there to live as such under the shelter of the church and teaching of the Fathers. However, as long as the Catholic faith was not received or favoured by the emperor and the great lords of his empire, Fremona remained a poor, scorned, small village, and its inhabitants were even persecuted by the heretics. When the faith came into favour and acceptance, however, it grew and was a great thing in those kingdoms; so that we can refer to it as the principal city of Ethiopia when the empire was converted to Catholicism.

When we arrived, three Fathers of the Company were living in it[4] in some small houses of stone and clay, the best material used, until that time, in the building of the most esteemed houses in all of the kingdoms. The material of which the church was built was no better as much straw and sticks were added, with which it was covered and of which it was composed. The veneration in which it was held, however, among the Catholics, numbering approximately three hundred, both native and Portuguese who were inhabitants there, and even among the heretics, was great because of the tomb and the holy relics of Patriarch Dom André de Oviedo which it contained. Here they received us with great applause and many tears of happiness on seeing the state in which we arrived, both in our physical condition caused by the sufferings from such a long, hard journey and in the condition

[1] Admas Sagad I, the throne name of Minas (1559–63). He was strongly opposed to Rome and, having spent some years as a prisoner of the Muslims, was accused by his enemies of Muslim sympathies.

[2] Galician, 'Gallego', differs from standard Portuguese, though much more from Castilian.

[3] Le Grand says five leagues, which is obviously wrong.

[4] Manoel Lameira, who was Father Superior, Tomé Barneto and Manoel Barradas.

of our clothing, which was in an equally sad state. We were in need of all possible hospitality and care in order to get well, and as the winter had already begun, we had sufficient time to rest. This was in June, and, although the Emperor and his brother, as I say further on, with many persons already Catholic, illustrious persons and great lords as well as the rest of the common people, [were waiting to receive the Patriarch and his companions], for which it was necessary to travel ahead to the Emperor's court, the winter season placed an impediment in our way and caused us to defer departure until November, when the rivers and roads are passable and there is less danger of sickness. I say this because winter comes to this region in the middle of May very suddenly and with great force, heralding its approach a few days beforehand, however, by some extreme changes in weather caused by the sun coming closer to those lands as it brings forth many vapours, storms, and thunderclaps by which it causes sundry rains. When, however, winter reaches its full force, which it retains throughout its duration, it does so with an extraordinary change in the air, opening up with a torrential storm, lightning, thunder and rain, so that it seems that the world is dissolving and the composition of nature is decomposing and melting together. This is always after two o'clock in the afternoon, and continues in the same way through the remainder of the winter, always leaving the mornings clear, with serene weather and beautiful sunshine, until two o'clock in the afternoon, so that people can travel and farmers can work. At about two o'clock, the sky begins to become overcast in the distance, flashes of lightning are seen from afar, the rumble of thunder is heard, the air becomes laden with black, heavy clouds filled with rain so violent, heavy and copious that if not finished quickly, another Flood will begin. At this sign, travellers seek shelter, crowding into the nearest villages, and, if in an uninhabited place, they pitch their tents which they always carry with them; the farmers cease working, taking refuge in their houses. The fury of the storm lasts for two or three hours, being all over and the air returning to its former serenity, so that it would appear that there had been no such storm if the fields remaining covered with water did not bear witness to it. This regular occurrence of rain is true of almost every day during the winter, which lasts for three months, from the middle of June until the middle of September, there being very few days on which this does not happen, none, however, when it does not rain and very few when it continues to rain the entire day continuing also at night as we see in our lands.

This land has a great affliction due to its excessive dryness caused by nine months of continual sun in summer and some hard winds that blow uninterruptedly for long periods, which are very frequent there, frightful thunderstorms, and repeated lightning, there not being a winter when some bolts do not strike, killing people and cattle. On one occasion one struck in the house where I was and, hitting the wall against which I was leaning as I was writing in a sitting position, it made a hole exactly two spans away from the place where I was sitting; and since it was so close, it left my left arm, as it struck in that direction, in great pain, which lasted for some time. It threw to the ground, as if they were dead, three children who were next to me, and going inside the house where I slept, it made some holes in the floor and the wall, also melting in three places inside its sheath, without damaging the sheath, a dagger belonging to a Portuguese who had left it there. And as it had already come from the house above, where it left everything within its walls all topsy-turvy and destroyed and a Father on the ground and two young men out of their senses, with the same swiftness that it did all this, it went out and killed a woman, three hundred paces from there, who was grinding with a hand grinding stone and a man another three hundred paces away who had gone out to bring back from the field his son, a small child, who was watching over a flock of goats. The damage was not great compared with what it had done and did at other times. I could have been at least seriously injured if God had not spared me in His infinite mercy.[1]

As long as the winter lasts one cannot travel to the court because of the large rivers existing in the central part of the empire. Since these rivers do not have bridges or ferries, it is very difficult to cross them and impossible to ford them. One, two, or a few more persons can pass by means of some stratagem, either by swimming or with the help of ropes when the distance permits them to be fastened on both sides of the river. In case of extreme necessity when it is urgent for important persons to cross, others make use of the following procedure: They make two strong leather bottles from the hides of two cows, on which, after they have been fully inflated with air, tied to sticks, and put into the water, the people ride and, with a certain way of rowing, pass to the other side. There is, however, danger from the hippopotami and crocodiles which from time to time attack such rafts or other boats

[1] A letter of Barradas, published by Beccari, 1903–17, XII, 483, confirms this story and proves that the incident occurred in 1631. The other priest was António Fernandez the younger; the young men were pupils at the Jesuit seminary.

made of great bundles of thick planking, and, tipping everything over, eat the people who go on them. I should say that only the crocodiles eat them, for the hippopotami do not, but tear them to pieces with their teeth, their food being on land and consisting of grass and tree branches. When the winter is over, one still cannot travel to the court, both because of the rivers which are still too swollen and most particularly because of the mortal sicknesses to which people are subject in certain low marshy places like bogs. Since the grass grows tall enough in those marshes to cover a man and gives off noxious vapours as long as the water has not dried up, those who venture to go through them suffer serious illnesses. People wait, therefore, until the middle of November, from which time forward they can travel safely through those places. And since we were waiting during that period, we had enough time to rest from the ill effects of our travels, spending five months in our village and house in Fremona.

However, since we were very desirous of employing ourselves in some opportunity to serve God and the land was ready for great accomplishments in His service, the governors of the neighbouring districts had asked that Fathers be sent to convert, confess and give Communion to the people of their lands after they had been baptized, for it was necessary to do all these things: to instruct them in catechism first, then baptize them, then confess them, and finally give them Communion, being Christians in full knowledge of the value and substance of this sacrament. The district of Sire fell to my lot and to that of another member of the Company.[1] It was two days' journey from the district where we were. We took all the things necessary to celebrate the sacrifice of Mass and to give Communion, and as many people would be gathering we carried a tent to set up in the field and of which to make a church. The Governor of the land was a good Catholic, his wife a confirmed heretic, so blind and obstinate in her errors that she was unwilling to listen to any discussion of the Catholic faith or any true information concerning her heresies.[2] We remained for several days in their community, which was on the top of some high mountains, a location ordinarily chosen by these lords for their dwelling places. Most of the houses were straw huts, some tents set up, others of stone and clay. These are the famous tents of Ethiopia which the prophet Habacuc so greatly abhorred and about which he

---

[1] A district west of Aksum and south of the Mareb river. Lobo's companion was Bruno Bruni.

[2] The governor was Mazera'eta Krestos, Eth. 'the Arm of Christ'.

was so scandalized in his canticle *Pro iniquitate vidi tentoria Ethiopiae*.[1]
And they truly are nests and breeding places of all evil, and the prophet
was not unfounded in so much lamenting their vicinity. The governor
gave us kindly hospitality, treated us courteously, and, on the first days,
provided us abundantly with what was necessary. And as the greatest
thing one can do as a greeting and welcome is for the host to order
immediately a live cow, which they call *feridá*,[2] and this is given only
to persons to whom they wish to do great honour, saying that it is
for the servants. We also did honour to him by having it killed
immediately and sending him a leg of the same cow with the entire
gall bladder, which I very willingly gave him, for all the use it was
to us. To him, however, it was a great courtesy, sent from such a person,
and very tasty; for they pour it over that meat when they eat, as if
it were an oil and vinegar dressing. The unbelievable thing is the relish
with which they eat it, so that I seriously doubted that it could be as
bitter as that found in our lands. I found, however, that the only
difference was that they were larger, nature apparently responding to
their taste for it and the great value they place on it. This was so much
the case that on one occasion when I had set aside one of them,
intending to use it to remove a stain from my hat, and asked for it,
I was told that a young Ethiopian who served me had taken it. When
I sent for him and asked him if he had taken it, he told me he had
done so and that it was because he wanted to drink it for certain
medicinal purposes. I answered him that I would believe it if he drank
it in my presence. He fetched it and, putting it to his mouth, he drank
it so rapidly and with as natural a facial expression and as composed
a manner as if he were taking a swallow of good wine, the gall being
almost the equivalent of two fingers in quantity and, if poured into a
goblet could serve as a goodly draught. As to the matter of his taking
this for his health, I know not whether as a treat or out of necessity,
I can vouch for the fact that I saw it with my own eyes and that they
do this every time they have the opportunity.

The results we obtained in the conversion of heretics in this
community were very meagre. The greater part of our labours were
expended with the governor's wife as we preached and taught the
elements of the faith, but since she heard it all with ill will and worse
predisposition, the only result we obtained was to learn that she
apparently was not among those predestined for eternal life, and also

---

[1] Habakkuk iii. 7. The Authorised Version reads: 'I saw the tents of Cushan in affliction'.
[2] Amh. *fĕrida*, a young, fat heifer or bullock.

to justify her damnation before God since she refused to open her heart and receive the news and counsel of her salvation, saying that her hour had not arrived and she would ask God to enlighten her. Although we told her that she should set forth her doubts so that we could resolve them for her, she would reply that she was an ignorant woman. In this she was speaking truth, but she was lying in her subsequent statement that she was young and inexperienced and did not know how to set forth a proposition, make a refutation, and reply to a refutation, the truth being that she was so old that she no longer had any children and so fat that she could not pass through a doorway, appearing to be over forty years of age. The real reason for this silence of hers was bad advice given to her by their heretic priests, whereby she and the rest of the people there, all of whom were so advised, were persuaded not to answer anything which was said to them under penalty of excommunication, pretending to be ignorant, though they truly were so, with the result that they completely closed their ears and doors to the light and the truth. From another locality in the same land we received a call and went there. It was located at the foot of a mountain and consisted of three communities, one at the bottom of the mountain, which was very high, another half way up the mountain, where there were beautiful fields and small villages rising in tiers up to the top. The largest community was at the top, where there was also a church, with various monks and clergy, which church served as a burial-place for the lords of that land. Having passed the two towns, the one at the bottom of the mountain and the one half way up, and beginning to climb toward the one at the top, we heard great weeping and shouting by all the people, large and small, which did not fail to disconcert us. Our perplexity was much increased by the explanation given us by one of those accompanying us. When I asked him why those people were weeping, he answered that it was because we were going to preach to them. I clearly saw that this was a result of fears harboured by the devil, who regretted having to lose some of the people there whom he had so much in his power. This weeping and tumult with which the devil intended to frighten us made me more determined than ever to work for the good and help those souls, so blind and deceived as they were, on the road to their salvation, continuing on my way until I reached the top of the mountain, where I found a goodly village with its church, but its people so unsociable that they showed very clearly at close hand what was prefigured by the sounds of weeping we heard from afar, receiving us with little enthusiasm and avoiding us as if we were excommunicants. The priest of the church, however, and the one who was head of the village, with a few others, gave us some hospitality. And, although we were there for a few days preaching every day to the people, explaining the mysteries of the faith to them, the false doctrines under which they were living in theirs, the good of their souls which we were striving for there, along with everything else we could think of for this purpose, nothing was sufficient to persuade them. Five or six, nevertheless, were converted, so that our work was not entirely in vain, and the devil could not keep all of his own behind closed doors. Because we had nothing further to do there and we were being called elsewhere, we left that place for the time being, waiting for a riper occasion, which was to present itself at a later time.

The village to which we were called was at a distance of half a day's journey. On the way to it, we traversed a region of beautiful, fertile plains, like the best of Alentejo, though not so sultry.[1] As the land is open and varied in places by some mountains which seem to have been raised there only for the sake of variety and beauty, as it would seem from their harmonious placement in the landscape, in addition to the diversity of trees, also gracefully and symmetrically arranged, although all natural, the various elements of this landscape help to make a beautiful sight for the eyes. The village was populated by the worst people of that whole district, confirmed heretics, violent people of evil disposition, and, if it were not for the lord of the land, though evil and like his subjects, having a better respect for courtesy and restraining his people, we would not have fared well there. And thus they received us with a greater show of hostility than the ones on the mountain, for they were more silent and cunning, whereby they hid their evil intentions. The courtesy of the lord of the land extended only to giving us good hospitality and advising us to keep people on guard at our door at night time and to leave the house only with extreme caution because he knew that his own people were ill disposed toward us. And although despite all this, we did our duty by preaching to them and informing them of the errors in which they were living, having several debates with some of them, in which they displayed much ignorance, frightful malice, and deadly hatred for the Catholic faith, nothing, however, was sufficient to convert a single one of them; the lord of the land telling us that later on things would ripen so that we could then gather the fruit we desired and now could not reach.

[1] Most of Alemtejo is rolling country with cork forests.

Taking leave and returning again to the mountain village where we were first, where the people, in a better mood and moved by Heaven, were wishing for our arrival with feelings of good will toward us equal and more intense than the hatred with which they had first received us, we arrived that night at the foot of the mountain, and, taking shelter in a village there, setting up our tent and altar on the following day, and starting to preach to them, there was not one of them who did not submit himself to the Catholic faith, large and small. This success was a good foundation for the success we were to have later, for, soon finishing our conversion of the people in this town, we climbed to the half-way point of the mountain, because it was the most suitable place for people to gather from both the top of the mountain and from the immediate surroundings. Nature made in the middle of this mountain a beautiful succession of level areas rising in tiers. These fields were of varying size, all of them fertile, and, on the highest and off to one side was the village, composed of a rather large number of people. In various other places were beautiful, thick trees providing sufficient shade for many people. And because many more gathered than we were expecting, we set up, in a more suitable place, a tent which served us as a church. And as we brought everything needed to say Mass, we set up our portable altar here, and, under the shelter of the shade of the trees we spent several days there with excessive work but great results in saving souls, for we were only two Fathers and the people were many. Before sunrise, we would sit down, each at the foot of his tree and, when the people had gathered, we would instruct them in the mysteries of the faith, and afterwards we would have them renounce their heresies and do acts of faith, hope, and charity and acts of contrition, because they were adults. We would then baptize them by the hundreds, having them kneel one after the other, the men on one side and the women on the other, and giving them their names in groups because we could not do it individually for each one; but, for example, a certain group of men were named Pedro or Antonio and a group of women were named Maria or Anna, etc. Afterwards, we stood up, those being baptized remaining on their knees, and a young man carrying a large pitcher of water kept filling my hands with water, which I poured on the head of each one saying the words to them and baptizing them. Because of the great numbers of people the work was great, so that my arms became tired from baptizing. However, the joy and consolation of seeing so many leaving the blindness of their heresy and the bondage of the devil gave me strength and lightened my task and urged me on to better things; for we then sat down to confess them, instructing them briefly as to how to do it, as it was a confession of their whole lives. Even though the baptism was enough to cleanse them of their sins without any other confession, since this was done conditionally and we were in doubt as to whether they had already received it or not, and although it seemed to us that none had been baptized correctly, in any case, to be more cautious and completely certain of the felicity and salvation of those souls, we performed both tasks, even though it cost us greater fatigue. After this was done, we said Mass, giving Communion to all those baptized and confessed, who were by no means small in number because of the addition for this act of faith of those whom we had baptized and confessed from the time Mass was over on the preceding day until the following day at the same time, which would be from eleven to twelve o'clock. After all this was done and those people were sent to their houses, we started with a new group of people who were already waiting for us, continuing in this way until dark, when we retired to our straw huts to rest a little, to read our breviary, and to eat a poor mouthful which could serve as a severe fast. We ate only once a day at that time, which was always late at night, and returned immediately at daybreak to the same place and labour. And as the days were many and on one of them a person was confessing with devotion and good will, at which I was much pleased, knowing that he was from the village on top of the mountain which had received us so badly, I asked him why he and all the other people from his village were coming now so willingly to be converted, having received us a short time before with so many tears and demonstrations of hatred. He answered that his monks and clergy had told him that as soon as we entered any land to preach, there immediately followed a plague of locusts that destroyed that district as a sign of the falseness of the doctrine we were preaching and of God's wish to punish in that way the land which receives us, and as they saw us entering theirs, they feared the punishment that was soon to come to them; but seeing, however, that this did not happen, so many days having passed since our departure, they all considered what was said of us to be false, and since the doctrine we were teaching was that of salvation, they were joyfully coming to receive it, regretful that they had at first rejected it.

This means of inducing the people to hatred of the Catholic faith is and was very often used by these heretic monks, sworn enemies of the Roman faith. Because they saw that in their ignorance they could not debate with us and convince us, as they attempted to do on occasion and came out confounded and ashamed, realizing that by this means they could not discredit us as they desired, nor with their lives could they give authority to their falsehoods because they were ordinarily corrupt, self-interested, arrogant, and very ignorant, they resorted to false testimony, persuading some with it, causing others to doubt, and causing universal trouble, alienating many from the Catholic faith, proclaiming the business of the locusts and that we were enemies of Our Lady, as the Abyssinians believe, because of the great love and devotion they have for her, that they are alone in praising, knowing, and esteeming the sovereign Virgin, adding that our words were deceitful, containing heretical poison which we would not reveal immediately but at a later time, and that the communion we gave was made of brains of camels, hares and dogs and even of small pieces of their flesh, these being animals held by the Abyssinians to be extremely unclean and detestable, so much so that if anyone were to eat a hare or drink camel's milk, they would consider him a Muslim and would no longer speak, eat or drink with him, all of this because of Judaic legal ceremonies, to which they are very much inclined. This practice is a very ancient one and very peculiar to the heretics, who, when unable to do so with truths, resort to calumnies to try to degrade and cast suspicion on the ministers of the Gospel and their doctrine, throwing up a smokescreen, when they can do nothing else, among the common people and the ignorant. As for the plague of locusts, they seized this opportunity because of the great number of these insects which come every year into several provinces, originating in some large uninhabited regions through which I travelled, where I saw so many of them, still small in size, that the ground, being covered with them, seemed to be moving with them. At the time when the seeds sown have sprouted, this plague appears, filling the air and blocking the light of the sun, which, a few days before this plague appears, is seen to be a darkish yellow as it is when it is beginning to rise, and since they fly high in the air, one cannot see them but can observe the indications of how numerous they are by the change in the sunlight. With this evidence that the locusts are coming, all the people begin to set up a cry, imploring God's mercy; for, since the shoots are tender, wherever they light they destroy all of it down to the roots. And since they are so numerous that they occupy the land for many leagues around, they take everything irremediably, leaving the lands, which now were seen to be green and beautiful, dry and bare without a single blade of green grass to be seen on them. The danger of this plague coming and the damage it does lasts until November, when, according to the reckoning of the Abyssinians, the September festival of Saint Michael is celebrated;[1] for after this day, no matter how many of these locusts appear, they do no harm, according to what experience has shown us. They fly very high and make their way to the Red Sea, where, falling either into the sea or on the sandy plains and wastelands that are on the shores, all of those of that year are destroyed.

[1] 29 September. He is commemorated on the 12th day of each month of the Ethiopian calendar. 12 Hädar is 18 November.

CHAPTER 18

[Concerning the calamitous state in which the locusts left the Abyssinians and the conversions made among them]

Although God apparently inflicted this incessant plague on the Abyssinians as a punishment for their wilful perfidy, He reaped some benefits from this misfortune, as is His wont; for, since many provinces were destroyed and the people were perishing without any recourse, the majority of the people abandoned them and went to seek sustenance in regions where this plague either did not extend or was not inflicting so much damage or where they found among the inhabitants some relief from their sufferings. Bands of these people were thus to be found on the roads, which were peopled also with dead bodies; and those who were alive were in such poor condition that they resembled the dead. And as we in the village of Fremona, I along with the many Ethiopians who were all Catholics there and the many Portuguese whom I had there with me, tried to help them, the news of the help we were giving brought many of these poor people to us in search of sustenance for their bodies and at the same time they received sustenance for their souls, for many were converted. Many children were baptized and, shortly consumed by hunger, went to Heaven, God, by his preordination, inflicting this punishment and suffering. Parents left many of them in our village and went elsewhere for shelter, abandoning them there in the knowledge that we would have to take them in. Many of these children died because they had arrived in too advanced a state of starvation; others were reared with the milk of the Catholic faith. One time among others, as I was going out on a matter of business, I met several bands of these wretched people, men, women, and children. I dismounted as I did on other occasions, and, making them stop and sit down, I indoctrinated and instructed them all in the mysteries of the faith, baptizing them afterwards; and since the village where I was was the usual route through which everyone passed, I ordered that they be given alms sufficient for a few days. One of the groups I met on these roads consisted of about thirty persons, large and small. I performed the same services with them, and when I was to baptize them, all of them submitted and received the baptismal water except for one who moved away from the rest, not wishing to be baptized. I called him, and when I asked him why, he said that it was because he was a Muslim; and no matter how hard I tried to persuade him to be converted, it was all to no avail. I left him to his obstinacy; but one of his companions, wishing to save that soul, with great Christian piety and charity, came to me and told me in secret that he was not a Muslim but that they were all from the same village and Muslims and Christians cannot live together. I again urged the stubborn heretic and no matter how strongly I insisted, despite his admission that he was not of the Muslim people, he affirmed that he was a Muslim because he had eaten some of the locusts that had come in this plague. Locusts are a common food for the Muslims; they make large drying-places for them, and when the locusts have been dried in the sun, they grind them and, from such a flour they make an extremely revolting, foul-smelling meal or pap, which they eat with much relish as a great treat, partly through custom and partly through devotion for Saint John, from whom they say they learned to eat them.[1] During this discussion, I still had in my hands a container of water left over from that with which I had baptized the rest of them, and as the heretic was stubbornly resolved not to be baptized, I said to him, 'You'll be wet at least'. I soaked him all over with it, to the great amusement of his companions, who saw him resisting the salutary holy water, but unable to escape the water, remaining very wet and mortified as part of the punishment which his obstinacy and perfidy deserved. I had better success in the instances I shall now relate.

During that period, it was my custom to travel every Sunday and holiday through the neighbouring villages, now some, now others, usually finding some people who apparently were waiting only for this visit for their salvation, as God went to seek them out, since they did not do it or know it, being rustic people and weary from hunger. It occurred to me to go to a certain village, where, from several previous visits, I was sure there was no one in need of holy baptism. Deciding, however, not to go there, I again felt a strong impulse to do so, and no matter how hard I tried to persuade myself not to go, I was

---

[1] St John the Baptist (Yahya) is mentioned in the Qur'an and revered by Muslims as a prophet. Locusts have been eaten in Arabia since pre-Islamic times and are regarded as lawful food. Like fish they need not be ritually slaughtered before being eaten.

unsuccessful, with the result that I finally resolved to go there. Lo and behold, as I was travelling, I met, in a certain place, a mother with two children who were crossing the road, whom I would not have met a few moments earlier or later. All of them, especially the children, were in such a woeful state that they were barely able to keep themselves on their feet and were the very picture of death. I went on my way without saying anything to them, saying, however, to myself: 'These people must already be baptized.' I was soon, however, so overcome by doubt that I turned back and, causing them to stop, asked them who they were, where they came from, and if they were baptized; to which the mother replied: 'Hunger has brought us to the state in which you see us, exiled from our home until we finish our lives wherever death takes us, which will be soon.' And their appearance bore witness to the truth of her words. She continued, saying, 'As for baptism, I have already received it, but these children have not.' I baptized them immediately, and giving them alms, I continued on my way, wondering if that was the reason why God had wanted me to make that journey, considering the impulses and reluctance I felt, and I became surer that that was the case, because, in the land where I was going, everyone was already baptized and there was nothing for me to do there, persuading myself because of this that God had brought me there only because of those souls; for, if they had missed that opportunity they could not have found another on the road they were following, nor could life have remained with them for many days during which a similar opportunity could be offered them. An even more urgent case was that of another child. One evening, as I was trying to equip a church, I saw that a woman was hurriedly coming toward me, and, when she was within earshot, she began to shout for help because she was exhausted and almost out of breath. Carrying a child in her arms and arriving as best she could, she asked me to baptize it, for she had come a distance of two days' journey only for this purpose. On seeing the child, I saw that it was struggling with death, already in the last throes, and, since I did not have water at hand, I sent a young man to go and moisten a handkerchief in the first water he could find. And because, although he was assiduous, the child's last convulsions were already failing and with this all hope for eternal life, I shouted for him to hurry, which he did just in time; for, as I was wringing out the handkerchief over its head and saying the baptismal ritual, it gave no more than one or two shudders, showing me that it was still alive, after which that pure soul flew toward Heaven with a felicity as great as the danger in which it had been of eternal damnation, since, if there had been a few minutes more delay, it would not have enjoyed the blessed state it now enjoys, losing it, even though so surely without any sin of its own, because of the most mysterious but most holy decrees of God Our Lord.

Returning then to the village where I was when I began this digression concerning the plague of locusts attributed to us, after we spent a few days in that occupation, leaving the three villages at the bottom, middle and top of the mountain converted, along with many other people of that district, returning again to the house of the lord of the land who gave us hospitality, and from which place we had gone out to do what I have just related, we again attempted the conversion of the aforementioned lord's wife, whom we found as blind and stubborn as before. And since she refused to give up the battle in any of the many bouts we had with her, we had to return again to Fremona where the rest of the Fathers were with the Patriarch. Before we arrived there, however, I received a letter from the Father Superior of the Mission that I was to change the name of Lobo to some other name because, since all the names that the Abyssinians have are of special significance, almost always very sacred, like Possession of Christ, Resurrection of Christ, Beautiful Christ, Food of Christ, etc., they immediately ask each person's name and its meaning or what the name means in their language; and, since *lobo* is the same as *gib*, and this word means a thousand bad and infamous things, so that such meanings as thief, highwayman, murderer, and three hundred others do not escape it, so that anyone who calls another *gib*, *lobo* is obliged to pay a heavy penalty, just as though he had said a great insult.[1] If they knew that I had that name of *gib* or *lobo*, they not only would think it strange and abominable but would believe that I had been given it because I embodied the evils it signifies, so that it was necessary for me to change it and I returned to the village of Fremona with a different name from that with which I had left it.[2]

Since the winter was coming to an end, we made preparations to travel to the court, where the Emperor and his lords were waiting for the Patriarch and his companions with excitement and devotion, good

---

[1] Lobo means 'wolf' in Portuguese. There are no wolves in Africa, but the Amharic word *zhĕb* or *jĕb*, which is cognate with the Arabic word for a wolf, is used for the hyena.

[2] He adopted his mother's name, Brandão. Le Grand adds: 'I had some difficulty in agreeing, and I represented to my Superiors that this name I bore suited me only too well; but as I had to obey, I prayed God that He would at the same time create a new heart in me, and that I should become a new man in fact as well as in name'.

Catholics that they were. As we were about to leave, an order arrived for me from the Superior of the Mission to the effect that I should remain in that house and village and take care of it and of the Ethiopian Catholics and Portuguese there.[1] That residence, being the oldest and largest of those we had at that time or at any time in Ethiopia was always considered the capital and principal city of the other residences. It was also the largest in the lands and church revenue it had; for the past emperors, as well as the present one always favoured it and were very generous to it, even when they were heretics. I took the responsibility for this work, which was by no means negligible, because whoever was there had to satisfy and render aid to the entire kingdom of Tigré, the largest of those possessed by the Emperor and, as I have said before, somewhat larger than all of Portugal. The Emperor had given this residence nine lands, which they call *guste*,[2] meaning something like 'large country estates', although some of them could be the equivalent of a beautiful county or earldom as far as the lands are concerned if those lands were all here in Portugal or if those of Portugal could be transported there, the latter being no better than the former, except in being better cultivated. Despite the great extent of these lands, they barely provided us with food for the people of the residence; for, although they produced a great quantity, the amount was not in proportion to the size and number of the lands, and much was consumed by the people of the residence, who necessarily were many because of the territory under our jurisdiction, the people under the protection of the Church as well as those outside because of the existing custom of giving hospitality to travellers, of which the Abyssinians avail themselves to a very great extent. With both categories of people, the crops are used up, not only in eating but in drinking, for they make of it a certain kind of beer of which they are very fond and they plant a great quantity of a grain called *sava*[3], especially if it is not a crop which one person has cultivated by someone else, for if it is cultivated by another, the work is not done well and the harvest is poor. In the case of those fields not farmed by the owners themselves, a very peculiar custom is observed with respect to their manner of collecting rent. When the grain is ripe, the man who takes

---

[1] The Patriarch left for the court in February 1626, accompanied by P. Juan de Velasco and F. João Martins. PP. Lameira and Barneto stayed at Fremona with Lobo. The first was Superior, the second responsible for the building of the church, and Lobo for the management of the property.

[2] A copyist's mistake. Amharic *gult, guelt*, Tigrinya *gulti*, a grant of land, free of tribute, to an individual or church.   [3] See p. 171 n. 2.

care of the land, called *xumo* and selected as his tenant farmer by the owner, without whose authorization he is not permitted to harvest the crops, goes to the owner and requests him to go see his lands and to impose on them the rent he considers appropriate. For this visit, the tenant prepares a good banquet for his landlord one day, and, after the latter is well satisfied with what he has eaten and drunk, for if he is not the poor tenant pays for it by a huge over-assessment imposed by the landlord, but if he is well satisfied with the food and drink provided him, he visits all of the fields and, by himself, imposes on each one what seems appropriate to him, so that a land which can yield four Portuguese *moios* or so of grain could be expected to provide a rent of four or five *alqueires*;[1] when the crops are very extensive, the rent consists of a fixed amount which they call *chan*.[2] This is the maximum rent imposed and even after imposition of this, they exempt the tenant from some of it, giving a much larger exemption because of certain tributes he is assessed, all of which worked to the disadvantage of the landlord, who because of this received so little that, although his lands may be very extensive, he is barely able to live on the incomes he receives from them. I, at least, was always buying food. It is very true that grain is sold very cheaply; for, when it is scarcest, it sells for the equivalent of one Portuguese *tostão* and six *vintens*,[3] and when it is in great abundance, from thirty to fifty *alqueires* of grain can be bought for the equivalent of one *pataca*.

In this village then and in this employment, I was beset by difficulties and cares which were very onerous to me because of the size of the kingdom to which I had to minister, both in the spiritual affairs of the entire kingdom and in the temporal affairs of the many people for whom I was responsible, as each Father in his residence served as the Patriarch's Vicar-General, curate for the Catholics, and a thousand other necessary things to be attended to. Since the famine continued for a few years, the sufferings of the poor people increased; and helping in the poverty I was in was no small task, not because of what was given them but because of what they needed and what I lacked to help them with. The fields and roads were covered with these wretched people, more dead than alive. Morning and night, they appeared in great numbers in my village; and since they found some help there,

---

[1] 1 *alqueire* = 13 litres; 1 *moio* = 60 *alqueires*.

[2] Amh. *çhan*, defined by Guidi, *Vocabolario amarico-italiano* (Roma, 1901), col. 850, as a measure of grain equivalent to about 280 litres.

[3] *tostão*: 100 *reis*; *vintem*: 20 *reis*.

they had difficulty in leaving it; and, as they took shelter wherever night
overtook them, outside in the fields or in the streets within the village,
many were found dead in the morning; and, as the same thing
happened to them in the fields and roads, they stayed there to be eaten
by wild animals, among which the wolves came to fall upon them and
multiplied so much because of this food that we could not be free of
them whenever it was dark.[1] At nightfall they surrounded the village
in a number of packs of ten or twelve so that no one could go out
without serious risk because of the many he would meet and by which
he would be attacked. They afterwards came into the streets of the
village for more slaughter, preying upon the people who were lying
there, found in the morning torn to pieces and half eaten. They even
attacked people in their houses, biting and wounding them, being so
very starved and bold that two or three times they entered our residence
so boldly that once or twice they drove us out of it. They even went
into the churchyards for prey, digging up the dead and feeding on them.
What caused me greater grief was when a child about ten years of age
went out of his house and was set upon by a pack of wolves. Taking
hold of him, they carried him off with much noise, the child crying
for help; and, although people ran to him as soon as possible, they found
him already torn to pieces, each wolf carrying off his portion, leaving
behind a few pieces of legs and arms, which we gathered up. All of
this happened so quickly that as soon as they fell upon their prey they
were dividing it up on the road where they were carrying it; and we
were chasing after them, totally unable to help the unfortunate boy.

---

[1] There being no wolves in Africa, hyenas are probably meant.

CHAPTER 19

[Concerning Dom Christovão da Gama and how I discovered his bones]

A few months after being in this residence, an order came from the Emperor to the Viceroy that he should go to a certain place, at a distance of twenty days' journey, to recover the bones of Dom Christovão da Gama, which were buried there. So that the reader will understand the events responsible for his bones being buried in that place, I must recall in some detail the invasion of Ethiopia by Mahameth Granhe, who had come from the kingdom of Adel, a neighbouring kingdom to that of Abyssinia, located in the interior of the Cape of Guardafui. Mahameth Granhe was a Muslim, whose name meant Mafamede the Left-Handed, *granhe* meaning 'left-handed',[1] which he was, and as superstitious in his sect as he was arrogant and cruel. Favoured by conditions of the time and with the assistance of many Turks and Arabs who came to him from Moca as mercenaries, he entered that empire, conquering, destroying, and subduing all the territory in his path. Unable to resist his advance, the Emperors Alexandre, Nahun, David, and Claudio[2] sought to place themselves in safety, leaving the field to the victorious Muslim, who became lord of most of that empire and its best parts, roaming through it without opposition, robbing and destroying everything that was sacred, killing many people and forcing almost all the rest to follow his sect. He had been doing this for fourteen years when Emperor David sent a request to the Portuguese king, which went first to Dom Manoel and then to his son Dom João the Third, asking him for help in recovering his empire and offering in exchange for this act of friendship his obedience to the Roman Church and one third of his empire for the Portuguese

[1] Amh. *grañ*, left-handed.
[2] Alexander (Eskender), 1478–95; Nahum (Na'od), 1495–1508. Both of these emperors lived before Grañ's invasion. David, 1508–40, is more usually known by European writers as Lebna Dengel, 'Incense of the Virgin'. He received the embassy of Dom Rodrigo de Lima, described by Francisco Alvares. In his later years he was a fugitive from Grañ, who invaded Ethiopia in 1528. Claudius (Galawdewos), whose throne name was Asnaf Sagad I, 1540–59, fought vigorously against the invaders. Grañ received help from the Ottoman Pasha of the Yemen, in particular a contingent of musketeers.

201

if they would recover his empire for him from the hands of the Muslims.[1] Although the most serene kings did not approve the temporal offer, they did accept, however, the conversion of those great kingdoms to the Catholic faith and considered it a great project and gain for their Catholic zeal, something which they very much desired and had attempted on several occasions at great expense and effort. They consequently ordered the aid to be given, which Emperor David, who had requested it, did not see or enjoy, but rather his son Claudio, who was still a child under his mother's tutelage.[2] Dom Estevão da Gama entered the Strait of the Red Sea with a powerful fleet to burn the Turkish galleys at Sues, as his king ordered him to do, and to give the promised aid to the Emperor.[3] Although he did not implement the first plan, he did implement the second by casting anchor in the port of Masuá and putting ashore his brother Dom Christovão da Gama — both were sons of the Conde Almirante[4] — with four hundred Portuguese and all the arms and ammunition necessary for the undertaking. The Captain set out for the interior, accompanied by a few Abyssinians and by Empress Ellena, who came to meet him on the road as her liberator, as she hoped.[5] Conquering various lands with great difficulty and some mountains that appeared impregnable to human forces,[6] he finally arrived at a beautiful, level plain called Bellat,[7] many leagues long and two or three leagues wide. Our Captain was unable to meet with the Emperor, although both wanted this very much, because the Emperor was travelling in the remotest confines of his empire, accompanied by the few who were following him, defending himself with this small force, more by the cragginess of his

[1] Lebna Dengel sent two ambassadors to Portugal. The first, Saga za-Ab, Zagazabo to the Portuguese, accompanied D. Rodrigo's embassy when it returned. He had at first been accredited to King Manoel, but before he had left Ethiopia, the news of the King's death and the accession of João III in 1521, had reached the country from India. In 1535 the emperor sent João Bermudes to ask for help against Grañ, whose invasion had begun two years after D. Rodrigo's departure. For the terms of the offer we are dependent on the insecure testimony of Bermudes himself. His narrative is translated in R. S. Whiteway, *The Portuguese Expedition to Abyssinia, 1541–3* (London, 1902).
[2] Claudius was eighteen at the time of his accession. Lobo is probably confusing him with his father Lebna Dengel who had come to the throne at the age of twelve. The effective regent was then not his mother, but his step-grandmother Helena (Eleni), the widow of Ba'eda Maryam, 1468–78, mother of Alexander, and step-mother of Lebna Dengel's father, Na'od.   [3] In 1541.
[4] Dom Vasco da Gama, Conde da Vidigueira.
[5] The Empress Helena had long been dead. Lobo refers to Sabla Wangel, 'Harvest of the Gospel', wife of Lebna Dengel.
[6] A reference to the *ambas* characteristic of northern Ethiopia. They are steep-sided but flat-topped hills, which, until the Portuguese contingent arrived with mortars, were almost impregnable.
[7] Belat, near Antalo. It is marked on the map in the *Guida dell'Africa Orientale Italiana* (Milano, 1938), between pp. 304 and 305. Le Grand has Bellut.

location than by the force of his soldiers. In addition, since the winter was becoming severe, it hindered our people in their progress, and since its full fury would soon be upon them, it did not allow time for the two armies to join together for the benefit of all. Dom Christovão had tents pitched and the Portuguese remained encamped while preparing to meet the Muslim king, who was coming in a proud, arrogant manner, making light of our people, both because of their small number, for there were not four hundred of them while the Muslims numbered many thousands, and because of the victories which had made him insolent. Dom Christovão set up camp, as I was saying, on the slope of a mountain, with a small area of undergrowth behind it, where he placed some pieces of artillery that he brought, mounting them so that they would be manoeuvrable. The soldiers rested and gathered strength for the encounters with the enemy, close at hand, who soon appeared, covering the fields with his multitude of cavalry and foot-soldiers. Seeing by the number of tents how few people appeared to be there, he sent this message to the Captain Dom Christovão da Gama: 'I know very well that you are monks (meaning people of little worth, according to a particular use of this word in the speech of that land) and that you have been deceived by these Abyssinians, who are evil men. Return to your lands, for I shall give you safe conduct and provisions for the journey. Take good advice, trust me, take advantage of this good opportunity and friendship I offer you before this benefit changes to your loss.'

After this message from the arrogant Muslim was given to our Captain, the first reply was to give a good suit of clothing, according to the usage of the land, and a few good gifts to the emissary, replying for himself that he had not come to Ethiopia to leave it without concluding the business which brought him there, which was to expel him and his soldiers from what he had tyrannically usurped; that, as for the deception or truthfulness of the Abyssinians, this all mattered little to him since he had found him, the one whom he was seeking and with whom he had to deal; that he certainly would not return until he had routed him; that he should keep his provisions so he could use them when fleeing for his own lands if by chance he should escape with his life from his hands; that he would make his own safe conduct with the force of his arm and his soldiers, trusting in the divine favour for whose sacred law he was fighting against an enemy who was persecuting it; that, however, it was not to be a safe conduct for the lands he had come from, since the way was always open for him, but rather for the Muslim's lands which he had left to come conquer those which did not belong to him; that he should follow the good advice he had been bold enough to give him; that if he did so and withdrew to his own lands, he would leave him in peace; and that, however, since he showed such good will in giving him advice, he was sending him that mirror and tweezers as gifts appropriate to him, informing him that now was the time when he could see whether or not he, Dom Christovão, was in the company of monks. The present of the tweezers and mirror, according to the usage of the land, is extremely insulting; for, with these gifts, he was calling him a woman (in recompense for his being called a monk) and, being such, could see himself in the mirror and make his face pretty with the tweezers.[1]

The message and the affront it contained threw the Muslim into a terrible fury; for, being at table when he received it, with the dishes served and ready to eat and in the company of his lords and captains, he rose from the table, ordering the call to arms and commanding that the entire army be made ready for battle, saying that he was going to seek out and capture those monks and that after they were promptly captured he would immediately return to continue his dinner; for he was so very certain of his victory and the rout of our men that he ordered the food to be left on the tables as it was. Our men also went out immediately, ready to do battle, and, as the plain was surrounded by continuous mountains on its western and southern sides, those mountains were covered with Abyssinians, seeing the unequal size of the two armies and awaiting the outcome of the conflict, daring neither to side with our men, because of their fear of the Muslims and their belief that the odds were against us, nor with the Muslims, because of their fear of offending our men who were coming to defend them, waiting to throw in their lot, as they did, with whichever army should be victorious. I learned of all this in the year 26, when on the journey I took, which I am presently relating, I found myself in this very place, mountains, and plain and made inquiries about the events to some sons, who were still alive, of people who were present on that occasion. The Muslim opened the battle by sending out ten Muslims on horseback to begin the skirmish.[2] In this first sally they met ten of our men who came out to them on foot. Our men aimed their matchlocks at the Muslims so successfully that, for a good beginning, nine of the ten were

[1] Le Grand adds that, fearing that the messenger might not deliver his reply, D. Cristovão had it written in Arabic by a slave in his company.

[2] Le Grand says that Grañ had a large body of cavalry and 15,000 infantry; Dom Cristovão had 350 men, having lost eight in forcing certain defiles and having sent forty to Massawa to maintain contact with India.

left dead on the field, one escaping, who in great haste because of the danger he was in, went to report to his own people what had happened to the rest of his companions. But, as the Muslims were many and had not yet experienced our artillery, they came out in double strength, sending out more people each time, even though their losses were great from the matchlocks and artillery. There is still preserved a large rock, which they showed me, split in two by a cannon ball that hit it and the hollow place in it. Finally both sides were fully engaged in battle, but the Muslims were already so confounded with fear of our fire power, because of the havoc they saw it cause among their people, that after a few hits they turned tail and that entire numerous army was put to flight by four soldiers, such was the comparative size of their camp and ours. The inhabitants of that land still celebrate today a saying which King Ameth Granhi was supposed to have said as he was fleeing. Earlier, at the time when he was about to do battle with the Portuguese, he had chanced to meet an uncle of his, whom Dom Christovão had driven from a mountain. Taunting his uncle for his cowardice, he had refused to accept his excuse that the Portuguese were all men of fire, because of their matchlocks, and had refused to heed the uncle's advice to turn back and avoid joining battle with our men, replying, 'Mountains do not retreat', by which he had meant that such was the behaviour of kings. On this occasion, however, when the king was fleeing the battleground, his uncle caught sight of him and said to him, 'My lord, how is it that you, being a mountain, are retreating?' The king answered, continuing on the road he was following, 'My friend, there's a lot of fire here.' And so it is, to this day, that when they want to say that something is difficult or that things do not look well, they say, 'So and so, there's a lot of fire here.'[1] Our army was left to enjoy rich spoils belonging to the enemy camp, finding the food still on the table, which they ate with no one to oppose them. In the meantime the Abyssinians came down from the mountains to rob those things which our men could not or did not want to pick up because they set out immediately in pursuit of the enemy, whom, four more times in different places, they conquered in pitched battle; for the enemy turned to face them that many times, trying their fortune, which on each occasion was the same as the first, until they arrived at Manbret field, a beautiful, spacious plain, where the Muslim continued his retreat toward his own lands.[1] Because the winter had begun, however, he

---

[1] Le Grand has: 'They say mountains do not go to fire, and there is plenty of it there'.
[2] Le Grand's text says that Grañ camped 'near Membret, a naturally strong place'. After his defeat by D. Cristovão near Antalo Grañ withdrew for the rainy season to Zabl, south-east

was obliged to stop and our men could not pursue him. Both armies remained encamped at a short distance from each other and within sight of each other on two hills, which I saw, each army resolving to gather strength to put an end to their controversy when the winter was over, which was what later occurred.

During all this time, Granhi obtained reinforcements for his army, bringing, as mercenaries, two thousand Turkish musketeers, along with many horses, arms, munitions and provisions,[1] all of which were lacking in our small camp, as the Captain and his soldiers were left with their valour and confidence in God, for whose cause they were fighting against the enemies of His holy law and name, by order of their king, for the reputation of their nation, and for the liberty of those peoples, among whom were recognized and venerated the sacrosanct name of God Our Lord, the Cross and the Saints. There were little more than three hundred of them. Their provisions and ammunition were in short supply because there was no source of supply other than India, for which reason the Captain had sent a detachment of his soldiers to Masuá to see if they would find word from India. Even though this detachment was small in number, they were very much missed in a camp where all of them together came to a small number and a small military force. With the news of the reduced state and capacity of our men, for the Muslim was well informed of it all, and with the strengthening of their camp, the Muslim came out of his entrenchments and offered battle to our men, whose valour caused them to accept the challenge, even though it was under unheard-of conditions of inequality. Both sides joined in battle, and it lasted for many hours, with the usual losses of the enemy soldiers in the skirmishes by which they were trying to fatigue and diminish our small numbers of people. And as their people were so numerous, those who died made no impression in that multitude, while those missing from our forces were a very great loss indeed, until the enemy made a final charge, breaking through the entrenchments, so that our camp was invaded and put into confusion, especially because the valiant captain Dom Christovão had been shot

of Lake Ashangi; the Portuguese encamped in Wafla, south of the lake, and the battle took place on a plain near here, C. F. Beckingham, 'A Note on the Topography of Ahmad Grañ's Campaigns in 1542' *Journal of Semitic Studies*, IV, no. 4 (Oct. 1959), 362–373. The name used by Lobo probably represents Mambarta. Ludolf, *Historia Æthiopica* (Francofurti ad Moenum, 1681), lib. I, cap. iii, sect. 27, lists it among the prefectures of Tigre; the Patriarch Mendes, *Expeditio Aethiopica*, lib. IV, cap. xv, in Beccari, IX, 1909, p. 340, calls it 'the limit (*meta*) of Tigre', probably meaning the most southerly part of the province.

[1] Le Grand says that Grañ appealed to the Arab princes and received 2000 musketeers, who embarked at Mocha, while the Turks sent a considerable train of artillery and 900 picked men.

in the right knee and was fighting with his sword in his left hand, for his right arm had been broken by another shot; whereupon, the few giving way to the multitude and valour to the good fortune of the victorious Muslim who was now master of the field, killing, capturing, and robbing, our Captain went off with ten men who accompanied him, taking the road to some mountains covered with a thick growth of trees, where, resting from his toil and treating his wounds, he was discovered and captured by the Muslims who came looking for him, and was taken to King Granhi, who was already encamped in a spacious field below the one where the battle was fought, at which one arrives by a descent of half a day's journey. The Muslim was overjoyed at the capture and, because he had an uncle of his and a nephew who were both wounded, he ordered Dom Christovão, for a good beginning, to treat them for their wounds, which he did in such a way that both of them soon died. When the Muslim complained that he had killed them, he replied that he had not come to Ethiopia to give life to Muslims but to get rid of them all and, since he had handed them over to him, that that was the treatment he knew about and that he had to give them. With his grief at the death of these relatives and the hatred he had for Dom Christovão because of the ill-treatment he had received from him in so many battles and his resentment because of the message and present he had sent him in the beginning, and above all because he was a Christian, of whose name he was a mortal enemy, as he had at times declared in speech and much more often by deeds in the fury with which he destroyed every sacred thing that he found, he ordered him to be cruelly tortured. He first had him stripped and a large hand-millstone placed on the back part of his head, a great insult in this land. He ordered him to go up and down the whole army with the millstone on his head, with great contempt, derision and insults given to him by the people in word and deed, as they all gave him blows with the shoes they removed from their feet. Then he ordered large plates of iron to be heated and his back and chest to be burned with them, and with the tweezers Dom Christovão had sent him he ordered them to torment him by pulling out flesh and hair. Finally, sticking wax on his beard and on the hair of his head, he ordered him set afire. The valorous Christian gentleman suffered all these torments with admirable constancy, continually speaking the holy name of Our Saviour Jesus Christ, offering Him all these torments in compensation for his sins. All of this was told me, in the same land where it happened, by a Muslim, then very old, who was present as all this happened.

Finally, the Muslim Granhi ordered him brought into his presence, and, speaking to him with fair words, told him that if he would disclose the whereabouts of his Portuguese soldiers and deliver them to him and if he would become a Muslim, he would not only spare his life but would do him the kindness of sending him to his homeland. The soldier of Christ well understood the deception of these words; but, whether there was deception or not, he answered him, with zeal, valour and Christian freedom, that not for all the kindnesses he could do for him, nor for all the tortures he could inflict on him, would he disclose the whereabouts of a single Portuguese; and as for exchanging the true, holy faith he professed for a false, impure one like that of the Muslim, he should know that he would not do it for anything in the world, adding a thousand insults against Mafamede, extolling, on the other hand, the excellence of Christ Our Lord and His law. These words and their frankness were fire inflaming the Muslim with fury and rage; and, blind with passion, seizing his scimitar, with his own hands he cut off his head then and there in reward for such an illustrious confession of faith; whereupon that victorious soul flew to Heaven, carrying the palm of the conquest of glory, which God declared on the spot; for, from the place where his head fell, a fountain burst forth which served for many years as a miraculous cure for all kinds of sickness and for all those who sought cures, without distinction among Muslim, pagan or Christian; and from that time forward, his body, which was buried there, provided the same effect for the same people. The Muslim ordered the body to be quartered; and, leaving one quarter of it and the skull there, he sent the other three quarters and the skin from the head, according to his custom, to various places to solicit rewards for good news as a token of his victory. He ordered a dead dog to be thrown into the miraculous fountain, as they customarily do on similar occasions, to dull its miraculous powers and discourage worship of the place, because of the loathing the Muslims have for this animal; and on the quarter and head remaining there he ordered everyone to throw a stone, as is their custom, the Christians crying out the name of Our Lady the Virgin, saying in a loud voice *Sera Mariam*, 'enemies of Mary',[1] which anyone would be who did not throw a stone there, and the Muslims saying *Nebii*, meaning 'prophet',[2] a name they use as an epithet to refer to their deceiver, with whose name, all of them saying Nibii, Nibii and throwing stones, they made so high a pile that it cost

[1] Eth. *tarä Maryam*, 'affliction of Mary'.
[2] Arabic *nabī*, prophet, and especially Muhammad, 'the Seal of the Prophets'.

me many hours unpiling them when, as I shall presently relate, I went to recover those sacred bones.

Heartened by the happy outcome of his victory, Granhi turned back to recover what he had lost and kept regaining control over everything as far as Dambia, which is the province where the Emperor's court is located.[1] Emperor Claudio had already arrived there and had assembled there all the Portuguese who had escaped from the rout, who again incorporated in a company and petitioning the Emperor, who was extremely aggrieved at the death of Dom Christovão, whom he had journeyed so far to find, that they be permitted to go fight with Granhi with none other than the Emperor himself as their Captain, for they wanted no other. Since Claudio was a valiant, courageous young man, he accepted the offer, and giving battle to the Muslim, the Portuguese, forming a tightly-knit unit, boldly forced a path through the enemy's army, the Muslims giving way before the strength of their onslaught. When they sighted the king, who was the object of this manoeuvre, they aimed and fired at him until his chest was pierced by a musket-ball from which he fell dead on the front bow of his saddle and shortly on the ground, with Pero Lião[2] in hot pursuit; for it was he who knew for a certainty how well he had aimed and hit the mark and, sure of the outcome, followed the horse to enjoy his victory; for, as soon as the Muslim fell from his horse, he cut off one of his ears and, putting it in his pocket, kept on killing Muslims, as all the others, both Portuguese and Abyssinians, were doing, because the Muslim army was now in a state of disarray on learning of the death of their king. The latter, before expiring, feeling himself wounded, in great pain and rage, took the unsheathed scimitar with which he was fighting and struck a blow on the trunk of a tree near him. The mark, tree, and place are still in existence today. I saw them and learned that it is called *Granhi Berr Jaaf Granhi*, Granhi's Gate, Granhi's Tree.[3]

After Pero Leam, other Abyssinian soldiers arrived, one of whom, not noticing that the ear had been cut off, cut off the dead body's head and went to present it to the king, saying that he had killed him and asking for a reward for his deed; for it is the custom among these people, as a sign of their triumph, to cut off some part of the vanquished dead man. Some cut off noses, others one of the ears, some the heads, others also the foreskins following the Judaic custom, which is, I should say,

---

[1] The country N and NW of Lake Tana.
[2] Le Grand adds that he had been D. Cristovão's valet de chambre.
[3] Amh. *Grañ bärr, Grañ zaf*. The meanings given are correct.

of less decency than modesty requires, and taking all of these things to their general, throw them at his feet, making various heaps, some very filthy and abominable. And in proportion to the number of pieces he throws down each one thus proves his valour, except that some, in order to avoid appearing empty-handed and having less of a reputation for bravery, do not shrink from taking such tokens even from their own friends and servants, leaving them dead, without many pangs of conscience, in order to gain credit for themselves and obtain the reward which they always receive. This is what was done by the Abyssinian who presented the king's head. Since this was such a remarkable accomplishment, because of the person involved, he was, to an equally remarkable extent, the recipient of applause, esteem, and rewards such as rich clothing, valuable weapons, a sword and dagger, lands, etc. As everyone was rejoicing at the victory, marvelling at Granhi's death, from whom they had received so much woe, casting a thousand imprecations and curses on his head there present and on his soul that was in the devil's power, extolling the valour and good fortune of the Abyssinian who had killed him, Pero Leam entered without saying anything, having just returned from the slaughter in which he had been occupied in pursuit of the enemy soldiers; and, as he was known as a brave man, they let him through and almost commiserated with him because another had done what he had not done in killing the Muslim king. Arriving, however, near the head that was in front of the Emperor and taking it in his hand, he asked who had killed the Muslim king and had cut it off. The Abyssinian responded boldly and firmly that it was he who had done it, to which Pero Leam replied, 'Then what is this? Did the Muslim not have two ears? How is it that he is lacking one of them, or who cut it off?' The Abyssinian was somewhat perplexed and gave no reply, while those present were suspending judgement; whereupon Pero Leam added, 'Without doubt whoever cut off the ear from this head must be the one who killed the Muslim and not you, since you do not have it and cannot account for it,' to which all shouted their approval that this was so. 'Well, *I* killed him,' replied Leam taking the ear out of his pocket, 'since I cut off the ear which you see here.' The Abyssinian was confounded and everyone applauded Leam's trick. Since they now had proof that he was the one who had killed the Muslim, they praised his valour, all of them then heaping abuse on the dissembler; and the Emperor ordered him to give up the prizes he had falsely usurped, along with the honour of the deed, and that they all be given, along with other additional ones, to the said Pero Leam, who, because of this and other similar deeds in arms, became so highly esteemed and so famous that when anyone wanted to praise a man he would compare him to Pero Leam. This was also true of praises for the Emperor; for, when they sing songs to him in his praise, as is the custom in those kingdoms, they give him no other praises than those comparing him to Pero Leam, which in their language and with their metre and phrases have a pleasing gracefulness, as they say to him: 'You are as valiant as Pero Leam, as great a horseman', etc., continuing with praises of his body, his strength and everything else for which they wish to praise him.[1]

The fate of Granhi, following the death of Christovão da Gama, has been a digression from the thread of my relation up to this point. Returning therefore to the point where I interrupted it and continuing the journey to recover the bones of Dom Christovão, which gave rise to the digression, I say that at the Patriarch's request, the Emperor ordered his son-in-law, Tecla Gergis,[2] Viceroy of Tigré, to recover and bring back the bones of the said Dom Christovão; and, as the royal instructions came to me for transmittal to the Viceroy, I gave them to him all the more gladly because of my delight that this undertaking was being realized, a project which I had strongly urged because of the promise I had made to the Viceroy of India, the Conde da Vidigueira, who, when I left Goa for the coast of Melinde in the year 1624 to open a way, by that route, to those kingdoms, which was very much desired, as I have related earlier, requested that, if, in that vast interior and barbarous lands I was to traverse, I should have news of the tomb of this valiant nobleman, who was his uncle, I try to obtain and send him some of his bones. And since now there was not only definite news of where he was buried but also an order from the Emperor to recover his bones for him, I was delighted at the opportunity not only to persuade the Viceroy to do it, who was a friend of mine, but to accompany him myself and, to be surer of the outcome,

---

[1] The most detailed and reliable account of the battles of the Portuguese against Grañ and of the death of D. Cristovão, is that of Miguel de Castanhoso, translated in Whiteway, 1902, pp. 1–103. Castanhoso, who was himself one of the Portuguese contingent, says that the Emperor had promised that whoever should kill Grañ should marry his sister, if he were an Ethiopian, and should receive great rewards if he were a Portuguese. In the battle the Portuguese matchlockmen recognized Grañ and concentrated their fire on him. One of them wounded him mortally. An Ethiopian then cut off his head and brought it to Claudius, who enquired into what had happened and decided that the Ethiopian did not deserve to marry his sister, since Grañ had already been mortally wounded; 'nor did he reward the Portuguese, as it was not known who wounded him; had he known he would have fulfilled his promise', Whiteway, 1902, p. 82.

[2] Takla Giyorgis, 'Plant of (St) George'.

to participate in the search and discovery of the tomb and of the bones, all of which happened as I desired, as the Viceroy assented to the journey and was pleased to have me accompany him. We soon set out, and because the place where the tomb was located was at present a vast province occupied and inhabited by Galas, a barbaric, cruel people and the terror of all the Abyssinian kingdoms, there was no one who did not consider that I and all those going on the journey were doomed, as everyone wept over us as if we had died. We started out, however, the Viceroy having many soldiers in his company which was continually being reinforced with greater numbers because every precaution was necessary in view of the danger of the journey and ferocity of the enemies whose lands we were to enter. This Viceroy was twice the son-in-law of the Emperor, against whom he rebelled a short time afterward, for all of which he paid the due penalties as I shall later relate. At this time, however, he showed himself to be a good Catholic, taking pleasure in favouring matters pertaining to the faith. He honoured the ministers of the Gospel and was very kind to me, being on very friendly terms with me, all of which soon changed, in the manner which I shall shortly relate.

The land toward which we were travelling was at a distance of fifteen days' journey from the one we had left. It is the custom, however, for the armies not to travel very far at a time and to make short journeys each day because of the baggage trains, women and children and beasts of burden which follow the army and because they take with them all the provisions they need both those of each individual and those for sale; for, when the army pitches camp, they immediately set up a city with streets, churches, a market-place and courts in which justice is meted out, the court officials always accompanying the king or the viceroy. In each district they enter it is obligatory for the inhabitants to provide sustenance for the army, giving them bread, wine, beer and meat, all free, as long as it is travelling in the district, the lord of the land first warning all the inhabitants to be prepared. After the viceroy has pitched camp, with each person in it lodged according to his rank and station, which is done without any confusion or dissension because the distribution of everything has already been done and each person knows his place because of a lance that the captain of the vanguard, who is also the master of ordnance and the quartermaster, fixes wherever he thinks best, selecting that place for the prince's tent, so that all the others arriving know that the place marked by the lance is where the viceroy's tent is to be pitched; and each one, by prearrangement, then takes his own place. After everyone has set up camp, as I say, the present, large or small in proportion to the abundance of the land is brought in, consisting of so many live cows, so many thousand cakes of bread, so many thousand jugs of wine, so many of beer, keeping this proportion that for every hundred cakes of bread, called *apas*, they must add twenty jugs of beer and ten of wine along with one live cow. All this is presented to the viceroy with a statement of what is being brought to him – a certain amount of bread, a certain amount of wine, etc. – all of which is delivered to the viceroy's steward for inventory, and if anything is lacking from what has been stated, a heavy payment is made. But even after presenting this gift, the people are still not free of obligation; for on the next day, without fail, the viceroy imposes a certain penalty on the entire land for not giving sufficient food. They must pay this penalty, whether they have given already or not. They bring more for the important people in the army, whom they immediately identify, and it is an inviolable custom for them to include in their gift for each one a live cow, bread, wine, and beer. This is what I ordinarily received, in addition to which the viceroy, from what came to him, would always send me a present, so that on some occasions I would be given two or three very fine cows on one day for the consumption of the people who were accompanying me. It is very true that, despite this, they always carry with them, as did I, the necessary provisions for the people that each one has in his charge. Another obligation of each district is that they must clear the roads, cutting the undergrowth and trees, so they will be open and will in no way offend or bring harm to their prince; and if they do not do this, they pay a great penalty. It is really necessary that this be done because of the great quantity of undergrowth which abounds there and some trees with large thorns, which we found very frequently.

Receiving hospitality in this way, we travelled until we were close to the field we were seeking; and, because, for the better implementation of our purposes, we needed people well-informed concerning the land and the history of Dom Christovão, the Viceroy caused to come with us the Muslim of whom I have spoken earlier as an eye-witness, and a Christian who had heard about the whole affair from his father who had been present at it. Both were natives and lived near the said land. We questioned each of them separately concerning the signs by which we could find the tomb. Although their stories were in complete agreement, I took both of them with me to be on the safe side, the Muslim being carried on men's backs because of his extreme age and the road being unsuitable for horses, asses or mules, and the Christian travelling on foot. We reached the top of the slope, with all the soldiers in battle order ready for any event, a precaution made necessary by the proximity of the barbarians. We went down the mountain and, in a certain place, as had been indicated by our two informants, we found three graves, one of which, the one in the middle, they affirmed was that of Dom Christovão.[1] The two others were those of the Muslim Granhi's uncle and nephew, the latter a young boy. That these were in fact their respective graves was borne out when we found identifying signs in each of them. For, in addition to the general description of the place which had been given us, right in the pile of stones in the centre was a hole from which they said the people took stones as a remedy for their illnesses, God Our Lord responding to their piety and devotion by doing marvellous works – a very strong indication that this was the location of the spring they say burst forth as soon as the head of the valiant soldier of Christ fell to the ground and which ran for many years. In the same tomb we also found teeth which appeared to be those of the dog which was the one they said the Muslim had had killed and thrown into the spring and hole. Since the pile of stones was large, and had been covered with earth for nearly a hundred years, it was very difficult to open it up. In it we found the bones of one leg, for only a quarter of the body was buried here, and the lower jawbone with some teeth, all of which I kept with veneration.[2] And to be absolutely certain, we had the two other graves opened, in which I found bones of a large man in confirmation of their statement that the Muslim king's uncle had been buried there, and in the other those of a child, because the nephew of the same Muslim was also buried there in his own grave. The sight of this and the proof provided by these particulars made what they affirmed more likely, namely, that this was the tomb of Dom Christovão and these his bones.

After our work was finished, and again climbing the slope, which took us several hours, we continued our journey, withdrawing with haste, good order, and watchfulness because the whole land was suspect. The soldiers were divided into squadrons on the plain but kept close to the mountain in order to take advantage of it in case of any attack

[1] Almeida, in Beccari, 1903–17, VI, 501, states that D. Cristovão was buried at Wafla, which is near Quoram, to the east of Lake Ashanghi.

[2] Le Grand adds: 'I cannot express the emotion I felt when I saw these relics of so great a man, and when I thought that God had been pleased to make use of me to preserve them so that one day, if it should please our Holy Father the Pope, they could be exposed for the veneration of the faithful'.

by the enemy. Since the enemy concentrates all his strength in cavalry, which is effective to the extent that he has it on a level plain, he gives the advantage to his opponent if he attacks him on a mountain. The Viceroy and his party travelled along the middle of the slope, from where we saw a squadron of these barbarians, who were, however, friends of one who was travelling in company with the others in our army. I noticed that this man, although tamed, demonstrated his great ferocity and thirst for spilling human blood by indulging in many mock skirmishes, brandishing his lance and being barbarous in his appearance, gestures and voice, bursting out on occasion with wild, uncouth shouts. When I asked what that barbarian was doing and saying, I was told that he was beside himself with rage, shouting and asking how it was possible for him to be among so many people and not be permitted to kill a single one because they were friends. This pained him terribly and he worked himself into such a barbaric fury that a vein burst from his chest because of his fury and rage. He was with us in this state until we arrived at the place where we had left our supplies and mules, whereupon we set out for our homes, and after a few days we stopped in a field at the foot of a village in which, when we passed through there, two men of that land killed one of the Viceroy's soldiers to rob him, which they did, but were immediately captured and placed under guard until our return. Their case was decided very quickly, both of them being condemned to death. Justice is meted out without delays of briefs and clerks of court, everything being done verbally except when time is needed to make some investigation. In this case little was needed because the facts were evident and they had confessed. They were both handed over to their adversaries, according to the custom of the land, so that they could execute him as best they saw fit. On such occasions the relatives of the dead man join in, and after having a great feast because of their satisfaction at having in their power the person who had shed their relative's blood, they spend the night in celebrations, playing musical instruments and dancing, and when morning has arrived, before which the wretched condemned man has seen and heard all these things as preludes to his death, they all arm themselves and, taking him to the field, with both of his arms tied, they put him in the middle where they kill him cruelly in one of three ways. The first way is as follows: They make a small hole in the ground large enough for the condemned man's mouth and nose to fit in it. They then throw him to the ground with his face and stomach on the ground and his mouth and nose in the hole and, putting a heavy stone on the back of his head, they have effectively seen to it that his life is soon finished. The second way is for all of them to come at him with clubs, one *covado* in length and the size of two fists together at the end, and club the unfortunate condemned man until they break in his head and finish him off. The third way is more common: They all come toward the poor fellow with his hands tied and strike him with their *zargunchos*, the first to do this being the closest relative of the dead man – father, son, or brother; after them the rest enjoy their turns, each one giving his spear-thrust until they kill him, piercing him through and through. And if someone comes too late, he either strikes the dead body or moistens his spear in the blood that has been shed; and it is necessary to do this ceremony as one who is affirming that he too has killed, avenging the death of his relative and participating with the others in the defence of each one; for the relatives of the condemned man customarily avenge the death inflicted on their relative by killing any one of their adversaries who is caught unawares. And whenever someone from one family has killed someone else from another, each one stands on his guard because the first person the dead man's relatives come upon, even though he may have had nothing to do with the death, pays for the aggressor, with which payment they say that the blood of their relative has been avenged. In conformity with these customs, the wretches of whom I have spoken were condemned and handed over. As they were being taken to be executed, I was brought a message telling me what was happening. I immediately sent another message to the Viceroy asking that he not permit those men to die without my confessing them, which he immediately ordered, commanding that the execution of the sentence be stopped. However, when the message was given to the condemned men, one of them was so stubborn a heretic that he refused to wait to be confessed so as not to receive the Catholic faith, and, continuing forward, was soon killed by the spear-blows, in the very sight and almost in the arms of his mother, who had come to be present at her son's misfortune, but was unable to help him. The second man had better sense, for he stopped and I had him brought to my tent, where, while I was confessing him, I had people negotiating with his adversaries for them to pardon him in exchange for such merchandise as I would pay presently. Since they had killed one of them, they were easily persuaded to pardon the other in exchange for money. How much it was to be, however, was the difficulty. They at first demanded a thousand cows as the price for his life, but since this was excessive, as was also the five which I promised them, after much haggling we finally settled on twelve, provided that I would give them this number immediately or the equivalent in money. On such occasions, the Abyssinians are accustomed to come forth liberally with contributions, the women even giving their ear ornaments. This happened in this man's case; for, after I had made the contribution I was able to make, I caused the remainder to be solicited, which was then given to him in the encampment, with which his adversaries were satisfied and he was free or, as one might say, resurrected from death to life.

After this episode, we continued our journey, and before it was over, I parted company with the Viceroy, as he went off for an attack on certain enemies and I went to my residence, where the Portuguese received the bones of Dom Christovão with many tears, as the sight of them revived their memory of the victories he had achieved, the loss of his valour and person for the benefit of those kingdoms, the abandonment in which their fathers remained there, as well as that in which they, their sons, now found themselves to a much greater extent. Putting the bones in a decent place, I sent them the following May six hundred and twenty-seven, having recovered them in October six hundred and twenty-six to the Viceroy, the Conde da Vidigueira in India, not a relic of them, as he had requested of me, but all those that were in the tomb, and, along with them, Dom Christovão's helmet, which a great lord of lands had preserved with great esteem along with an image of Our Lady, which had belonged to the same Dom Christovão, both of which he donated because he was a friend.[1]

[1] The relics were taken by P. Barneto who went to Goa on the business of the Ethiopian mission. A. Braga MS. cited by P. da Costa gives the name of the donor of the helmet as Mariam Azagebeda, presumably Azaj (judge) Ba'eda Maryam, 'By the Hand of Mary'.

CHAPTER 20

[Concerning the rebellion of Tekla Georgis and how he tried to get me in his power]

In the journey the Viceroy made that summer,[1] he arrived at the Emperor's court and found there such bad news concerning the behaviour of his wife, the Emperor's eldest daughter,[2] that he was on extremely bad terms with her, and on much worse terms with the Emperor because the latter would not permit her offence to be judged, as is the custom; for such matters are decided by legal means, as I have said previously, and they do not try so much to keep this sort of thing from being known nor do they avoid the bad name that results from this when the said woman is not condemned and the adulterer not fined; but things have become so scandalous that the more illustrious the women are the less attention is paid to their licentiousness; and, if they are ladies of royal blood, called *ousoros*, meaning princesses, the husband has no right at all to take legal action against them nor can they say to them, 'You have behaved well or badly,' but must endure everything in a good spirit; and if they are true Catholics, they have an exceptional opportunity to prove their great personal merit and to practice the virtue of patience and rare tolerance. I recall that we spoke earlier of certain oxen of huge size, whose horns are so stupendous that they serve as wine casks, each of which holds ten to fifteen *canadas*. These poor husbands and those oxen are both called *gueches*.[3] By this I do not mean that there is any relationship between them, but I do say that if they were to grow, as the common people mistakenly proclaim, the husbands and the oxen would be in close competition, there being doubt as to which of their horns were larger. And because our Viceroy publicly took much greater offence at the wrong done him than is usual in that land, seeing that he could not punish his wife as she deserved, he let himself sink so deeply into resentment and melancholy that he decided to make an excessive show of it, for which

---

[1] 1627.
[2] Her name was Wangelawit, Evangeline. Takla Giyorgis was her fourth husband. When he was made Viceroy of Tigre she refused to accompany him.
[3] Amh. *gosh*, buffalo.

purpose, returning to his viceroyalty, he formed a plan to put into effect an unusual rebellion which he had worked out beforehand with the best and most powerful people of the kingdom of Tigré against the Emperor, who was twice his father-in-law and had invested him with great powers and responsibilities. This man was of an illustrious family, the lord of great lands, and of very high birth. Many heretics, displeased with the progress the Catholic faith was making, especially their monks, who were its mortal enemies, seized upon the opportunity presented by the Viceroy's displeasure, and, perceiving his disposition of mind, so stirred up the fire and wove the web that they obtained their desire, so that the Viceroy revolted, seconded by all the rest, invoking their ancient faith of Alexandria against the Roman faith, so that the malcontents would have reasons to join them, and the wicked people and vagabonds could gain from the rebellion; for, being so numerous, these people are easily stirred to much rebellious activity and to attempt any kind of trouble. The only uncertainty was how the conspirators could be assured that some of their number would not go back on their promises, especially the Viceroy, several of whose sons were nephews of the Emperor and frequented his court. They were also aware of the natural inclination of the Abyssinians to forgive easily, even in the case of offences like these. If the man who is a cruel tyrant today asks for forgiveness tomorrow, everything is forgotten and he remains a great lord. They were therefore afraid that the Viceroy might be pardoned, picking up the best cards for himself and leaving them all in the trap; so they agreed that a Father should die at the hands of all the conspirators, with the Viceroy being the first to strike him, so that it would be impossible for the Emperor to pardon any of them and they all would be under greater obligation and more diligent in carrying forward their conspiracy, having no hope of achieving pardon. Since I was alone in that kingdom, the death sentence was given to me. For this purpose the Viceroy immediately had a strong fortress made, where he could fortify himself in any battle when the Emperor sent soldiers to attack him. When this was done, he sent me a message to go and see him, saying that he had an important matter to discuss with me. At that time I had already heard some rumours of the Viceroy's disposition of mind, concerning both the rebellion and his plans against me. Although I was inclined to credit the first, I could not believe the second because of the friendship he had for me. However, I sent a Portuguese who served me, an intelligent and trustworthy man, under the pretext of sparing me the journey, with instructions to look about him diligently to see if he could detect anything to corroborate the rumours. Although he made every effort to discover the truth and was a very resourceful man, the Viceroy was so skilful in hiding his intention and keeping it a secret that my servant wrote to me that I could go in complete safety, whereupon I resolved to make the journey, which would take as much as five days. Since several days had been spent in messages being sent back and forth, I had written to a Father who resides in the Emperor's encampment of how I was making that journey at the insistence of the Viceroy. The Father reported this to the Emperor, who asked him if he was aware of the reports that had reached him from Tigré concerning the Viceroy's intentions and insisted that he send me word that I should not leave and that if I were already on the road, I should turn back wherever the message might overtake me if it found me alive. The message came with all speed, but it arrived several days after I had left, and, immediately sent in pursuit of me, it reached me as I was already returning without having had the interview with the Viceroy, which, if it had happened, would have cost me my life; for the Viceroy, wishing to carry forward what he had begun and to give assurance to the conspirators, made so many entreaties that I should go and was so skilful in concealing his intent, that he completely bemused my spy, who wrote to me that I should go without any fear, which I did. In my four days of travelling I was continually warned not to go any further because the Viceroy was determined to kill me. They were so earnest in telling me this that they considered me excessively trusting in going ahead, which I did because I did not believe that without cause the Viceroy would commit such a betrayal of our friendship. But God who disposes all things, saw the good intention with which I was travelling, confident as I was in the little reason there was for such treachery and in the many reasons for the very opposite, penetrated the perfidy and cruelty with which the Viceroy was hastening to kill me, and so ordered things that, as we were about to meet, there remaining only a half-day's journey before the two of us would arrive at a certain predetermined place, which was to be the site of the conspiratorial sacrifice, the Viceroy suddenly went off to conclude certain business he had with a group of Galas who were to help him in the treasonable uprising, sending word to me to go ahead to a certain place where I would be entertained until his return, for which purpose he was sending one of his overseers. However, as soon as I received the message, being confirmed in what I was hearing by new indications I had received, I turned around and, with less assurance than I had had up to that time, headed back again toward my residence, meeting on the way the bearer of the Emperor's order and message, in which he was ordering me not to go out in response to such messages from the Viceroy. The warning, however, would have been too late if God had not first countermanded the designs of that tyrant.

When he learned that I had turned back, the Viceroy was, of course, considerably annoyed at my having escaped from his hands. He concealed his displeasure, however, waiting for a better opportunity. In the meantime, I was continuing my journey, during which one of his monks came to see me. The monk was blind but a great talker and was considered a man of learning; and he truly could have a greater reputation among them for his babbling than for any fund of knowledge he might have had, although he was fairly conversant and knowledgeable in the Scriptures, with which knowledge he caused himself to be respected.[1] Although he was physically blind, he could also be king of those in that land who were blind in their souls and in knowledge of divine matters. He made a show of being a good Catholic and a great show of friendship for us. I gave him shelter and supper one night, which was permitted in the country and on the road, particularly in an unpopulated region such as the one in which I found myself at that time.

When travelling, I took with me servants and necessary provisions, since inns do not exist there and I did not want to cause hardship to the people in the places through which I passed; for, although they were under obligation to give free shelter and food to guests, this was still a burden, especially for the poor, and a very heavy one. Someone, however, came and gave me some of his honey wine, which was a great fortifier for the monk. That wine is very much of a fortifier for these people and it is considered a great kindness to have an abundance of it, which is all their entertainment and courtesy, because in this land drunkenness is cultivated to its highest degree. The more intoxicated a guest becomes the more courteously he considers himself to have been entertained. The monk was so well entertained that he had to unburden himself of the excessive quantity of wine in his stomach but still remained in such good disposition that he spent the whole night in a state of total oblivion, for which he was so grateful that he came to thank me in the morning for the courtesy I had extended to him. One

[1] Le Grand: 'He knew the whole of Holy Scripture; it seems that he had taken more pains to learn it by heart than he had to understand it. As he talked much he quoted it often and nearly always inappropriately.'

of his several ways of expressing his thanks to me was to tell me of the great marvels and miracles wrought by the founder of his monastery, named Tekla Aimanot, meaning 'Plant of the Faith'.[1] The following is one of a number of fables told about him: that a devil, who went into a spring where Tecla Aimanot's monks went to get water, disturbed the monks and mistreated them, playing pranks on them, some of which were amusing and others troublesome. Provoked by this, and by the annoyance it caused his monks, the said Tecla Aimanot went to the spring, where he rebuked the demon for what he was doing and, after various arguments and excuses, was finally able to persuade him, as penance for his sins, to become a monk, in which he was ill-advised and ill-intentioned. However, since circumcision is so absolutely necessary among the Abyssinians, he was unwilling to accept him without his being circumcised first. The devil agreed to it because of the advantage he was hoping to gain if he submitted to it, since the same monk was to perform the operation. When the work was done, he dressed him in the monkish habit, and the converted devil lived among the other monks in exemplary and edifying fashion until his death ten years after donning the habit. His death was so blessed that he went off to Heaven, where those poor barbarians believe he was admitted and still remains without any difficulty whatsoever. It is very true, however, that the more intelligent among them ridicule these fables, but the idiots consider them sacrosanct, convinced as they are by these monks of theirs. They recount thousands of these fables, like the one about another demon who had a son called Abbot Mamas,[2] whom they hold in veneration as a great saint of the monastery of Abagarima,[3] which was one league away from my village and to which I went on many occasions; or like the story of another demon who was killed by a great saint named Guebra Manifes Kedus, meaning 'Slave of the Holy Ghost'.[4] This monk is said to have killed the said demon whose body was one hundred *covados* long and two *covados* wide; and, although not very much in proportion, unless he were to be considered a pillar or column, the demon nonetheless paid the

[1] Takla Haymanot, 'Plant of the Faith', probably the most famous Ethiopian saint, founder of the monastery of Dabra Libanos, and reputed to be the intermediary who arranged with the ruling Zagwe dynasty the so-called restoration of the Solomonic line in 1268 or 1270.

[2] According to the Ethiopic synaxary St Mamas was an orphan, but had human parents. It is not stated that he was an abbot, E. A. W. Budge, *The Book of the Saints of the Ethiopian Church* (Cambridge, 1928), 1, 18.

[3] Abba Garima, a monastery about four miles east of Adwa.

[4] Gabra Manfas Keddus, 'Slave of the Holy Ghost'. Lobo's story does not occur in the synaxary, Budge, 1928, pp. 755–72.

Plate V. Takla Haymanot forbids the wild animals and birds to eat the monks' crops; they obey

Plate VI. Takla Haymanot miraculously grows wings when a devil cuts
the rope by which he is descending a cliff

penalty for some evil deeds he had committed in that district; the people gathered to throw the dead body down from a high cliff but were unable to move it until the same saint came and dragged the body with his friar's rope and hurled him over the cliff.[1] The people are so trusting and gullible concerning these fables that their blindness is pitiful to contemplate.

Returning, however, to my itinerary, after I arrived home, I had more definite information about the Viceroy's intentions concerning me, and so I thanked God for delivering me from such danger. I was required to leave that kingdom for another kingdom further into the interior at a time when the said Viceroy was already coming after me, in secret however. When he learned that I was leaving, he sent me many messages making every effort to have us meet before my departure; but it was too late for this, and, better informed and no longer in doubt about his intentions, I went ahead without seeing him. Foiled in his evil intent with respect to me, he decided to accomplish the same end by killing five Fathers who had arrived from India at that time[2] and one other who had remained in my place at our residence.[3] In order to be surer of it, he went to meet them on the road and doubtless would have executed the sentence and evil intent he had decided upon if he had not wanted to be still surer of his advantage by not letting a single one escape and, therefore, by seizing at the same time the one remaining in Fremona. He therefore desisted from killing the five Fathers, wishing to have a catch of six, for which purpose he asked all six of them to come see him one day. They all went innocently except for one who happened to be ill and remained in the house, which was another circumstance, possibly created by God, preventing the occurrence of so dreadful an evil. As the five Fathers were returning home, they all discussed what they had seen and what they had been told them. With this and further information which they received shortly thereafter, the treachery was discovered. Because the tyrant now realized that he could

---

[1] Le Grand: 'The good Father was in a mood to tell me more stories, had I been willing to listen to him. I interrupted him and said that all these tales bore out one thing we had experienced. It was that there were plenty of Devils in Abyssinia hidden in the habits of Religious and that they were no less wicked for being monks.'

[2] PP. António Fernandez the younger, João de Sousa, João Pereira, Francisco Rodrigues and Damião Colaça, who had reached Massawa on 5 May 1628.

[3] Gaspar Pais. Le Grand's text reads: 'He decided to direct his entire vengeance against Father Gaspar Pais, a venerable man, who had grown grey in the Ethiopian missions... One luckily fell ill, another stayed to look after him, so that only four went to the Viceroy'. An unpublished letter of the Patriarch, Academia das Ciências, MS. Azul 534, f. 6, cited by P. da Costa, makes it clear that Takla Giyorgis wanted to be sure of killing all the Jesuits, because, if he did not, the survivors would fortify Fremona against him.

not lay his hands on them, he went off two days' journey from there; and, since his designs against us were turning out so badly and he could no longer conceal his intentions, he dropped all pretence and clearly revealed himself as a rebel against the Emperor by capturing, for better evidence of his own commitment and that of his fellow conspirators, a Catholic cleric who was his confessor.[1] Tying the cleric's hands and feet, he and all the conspirators took him to the field, where they stood him up so that the sacrifice could be made there and all of them could confirm their adherence to the conspiracy with the blood of that priest, which was what they had planned to do with me the first time they summoned me. The Viceroy was the first to strike the cleric's chest with his *sarguncho*, followed immediately by all the rest who pierced his body through and through with wounds. Those who could not strike when he was still alive moistened their *zargunchos* in the blood which was dripping from the body, after which they threw the body to the dogs and wild beasts, stripped of its clothing as a greater outrage and cruelty. There followed another brutal event and an even greater evil, for the Viceroy issued a public proclamation that everyone should give up the Roman faith and return to that of Alexandria, for which purpose they were to collect all crosses, medals, rosary beads, reliquaries and all other religious objects they had received; and, making a great pile of all these things and heaping a thousand insults on the sacred images, he ordered them all to be burned. However, the apostate soon experienced divine punishment; for, being informed of everything, the Emperor sent against him a great Catholic named Keba Christos, whose name meant 'Anointing of Christ',[2] making him Viceroy of the same kingdom the tyrant had. They joined battle and, although the tyrant had many more people, among them a squadron of Galas, since the cause of the new Viceroy was just, because it was the cause of God he was defending, the Catholic Viceroy, unarmed, led all the others into battle, with exemplary faith and confidence that without his throwing a lance he was sure to be victorious, which he was; for miraculously almost at the beginning of the first encounter, the tyrant was defeated with great slaughter of his men.[3] He was captured with

---

[1] Le Grand's text reads: 'He turned all his wrath against Father Jacques, his confessor, whom the Patriarch had given him, as one of the finest masters of the spiritual life that there was in the whole of Abyssinia'. He was Jacobo Alexandre, a native of Fremona and a pupil in the Catholic seminary there.

[2] Qeba Krestos, 'Oil of Christ'.

[3] Le Grand says that the Gallas made some resistance but that the Viceroy's other troops abandoned him; 300 Gallas and twelve monks were killed.

many of the conspirators, some of whom were killed.[1] He was finally taken in irons to the Emperor's camp, where he had his sons and his wife and the Emperor who was twice his father-in-law. All these reasons were not sufficient to prevent his being sentenced to an infamous death by hanging from the branch of a tree, and two weeks later a sister of his, who was extremely active in the rebellion and uprising, suffered the same fate on the same tree, both of them justly paying, in this way, for the evil they had done.[2]

[1] Le Grand says that the Viceroy hid in a cave where he was found three days later along with his favourite Zoalda Maria and the monk Zebo Amlac, both of whom were at once decapitated. Zoalda Mariam is Za Walda Maryam, 'he of the Son of Mary'. Amlac is Amlak, 'Lord'; Zebo is unintelligible.

[2] Le Grand: 'Tecla Georgis was taken to the Emperor; his trial was soon done: he was condemned to be burnt alive. He thought that if he were converted, the missionaries, his wife and his children speaking on his behalf, he would have his pardon. He asked for a Jesuit to hear his confession and abjured his errors. The Emperor would not yield, either to his daughter's entreaties or his grandchildren's tears. He only mitigated the sentence and condemned him to be hanged. Tecla Georgis retracted his abjuration and died in his old errors. Adero his sister, who had had as much as anyone to do with the rebellion, was hanged from the same tree fifteen days later'.

CHAPTER 21

[A brief and very reliable account of the River Nile]

A little before this tragedy, I had arrived at the Emperor's court to pay my respects to him, which I did and then went to a province of the kingdom named from the Damotes. As I was on my way there, I almost fell victim to a fatal misfortune. There are, in that province only, certain herbs very similar to our water parsnips,[1] both in their appearance and in the fact that they grow close to water. These plants, however, are so poisonous that if a mule eats them it soon dies. Although I knew about the nature of these herbs, I did not know what they looked like. I happened, then, to be on the banks of a river, doing without a siesta, when I saw one of these herbs so fresh and green that I was sure it was good to eat, for I thought they were water parsnips. I picked some of one of them and put it in my mouth and started to chew it. Nature then stirred in me the sudden fear that this might be the herb I had heard about, but since I was persuaded or the devil willed it, I banished the thought from my mind, saying to myself that that could not be, and I continued to chew; but as doubt and fear were still working in my mind, I spat out what I was chewing. Just then a man arrived who knew the herb. He shouted to me to spit it out, saying it was poisonous. I finally knew the truth of the matter and thanked God for delivering me from so obvious a danger.

Continuing my journey, I arrived at the famous River Nile, so much celebrated in history, so mysterious as to knowledge of its source, and so far removed from the common knowledge of civilized people; and all these considerations came to my mind when I saw it. The place where it passes is in some broad fields over which it spreads its waters when it carries a greater abundance, and, being at this point a little more than two days' journey from its source, it is already so mighty a river that a musket-shot could barely go from one bank to the other. It is

---

[1] *rabaças, Apium nodiflorum*, L. The Department of Botany at the British Museum (Natural History) informs me that, as a systematic Flora of Ethiopia has not yet been compiled, it is not possible to identify with certainty the plant which Lobo so nearly ate.

quite deep here and has a great abundance of hippopotami. People, however, ordinarily swim across it at their risk because many are so badly treated by these animals that they do not reach the other side alive. Those who have a better chance are the ones who get into some boats made of timber as thick as a man's bare arm, or rather many bundles of it joined together, with a kind of stern and bow, rowing with some long round pieces of wood, by which means they pass to the other side; but even in these boats the passengers are not safe because they too are attacked by the hippopotami, which capsize the boats and kill the people in them, although they do not eat them, for they feed on grass and branches on land. The crocodiles do eat people, for they are very carnivorous and flock to this plunder of the poor swimmers, glutting themselves ferociously upon them. Since we have reached the point where we are crossing this illustrious river, beyond which was the land and residence toward which I was travelling,[1] it will be well for us to give a short and very trustworthy account of it, which certainly will be all the more precious because such reliable information has always been repeatedly desired by those who, by so many ways and means, have investigated its secrets, always unsuccessfully, giving rise because of this, to as many fables concerning this river as there were authors discussing it, which fables have been spread abroad in many books.[2]

The famed Nile, called Abaui by the natives of the land, meaning Father of Waters[3] because of the great abundance of them it carries in its current, has its source in a province of the kingdom of Goiama called Cahala,[4] one of the best in the empire, populated by a certain group of people called Agaus,[5] Christian in name and pagan in their customs and ceremonies because of their proximity to many pagans, also called Agaus, with whom they have blood relationships. Both groups are numerous and barbarous, difficult to subdue, both because of their fierce, rebellious nature and because of the terrain which is craggy in the mountains, difficult to travel in because of the dense cover

[1] Lobo was on his way to the Jesuit residency near Kolala. The Nile he was crossing was therefore the Little Abbay, the name given to the stream between its source in Sakala and its entry into Lake Tana.
[2] Le Grand: 'Since I have arrived at the banks of the Nile, and as I have crossed and re-crossed this river so many times, and as all I have read about the nature of its waters, and the causes of its overflowing, is still full of fables, I want to report what I have seen with my own eyes and what I have learnt on the spot.'
[3] Abbay, the Blue Nile. The folk etymology, which is untenable, arose because ab is Ethiopic for 'father'.
[4] Sakala. As often the cedilla has been omitted under the C. Le Grand has Sacahala.
[5] See p. 159 n. 3.

of many trees, and much more impenetrable and ungovernable because of large impregnable caverns with which it is fortified, where they take refuge in case of need, so strong that no force can overcome them, so large that they hold inside of them three hundred and more cows with two or three families of many people; for these savages have many wives, one for every hundred cows they possess, sometimes more. The source of this famous river, the object of so much searching but hidden for so long, is discovered almost at the eastern boundary of this kingdom of Goiama on a very gradual slope made by a certain mountain, seeming more like a rather irregular field than a mountain slope with quite an expanse of open, flat ground, where one can see for a fair distance. In this gradually rising plain, one discovers, in the driest part of the summer, two circular pools or wells of water, which we can more appropriately call pits four spans in width and separated from each other by a distance of a stone's throw, one of less depth than the other; for, in the shallower one, with a lance eleven spans in length one could touch bottom, although some claimed this was not the bottom but rather certain roots of some bushes which are in the bank next to this somewhat smaller pool. The second one lies to the east of the first in a lower place on the said slope or plain. It is so deep that with a measure of more than twenty spans the bottom could not be found,[1] nor had the local pagans been able to find it at any time before then. The whole plain, especially the part near the said wells seems to be a subterranean lake, because the ground is so swollen and undermined with water that it appears to bubble up when a person walks on it, which is seen more clearly when there are large rainfalls, for then the ground yields and goes down at any step one takes on it; and the reason it does not swallow up anyone who walks on it is that, since all the land is green and this part had many various grasses and herbs, the roots are so intertwined that, with the little soil that holds them together, they can support anyone who walks on the field, which at its widest point can be crossed by a stone's throw, but only if shot by a sling.[2]

The area near the source is populated by pagans of the land, who have a village there from which one climbs a moderate, gentle slope for above half a league to the top of a hill called Guix;[3] and because the ascent is so gradual and so long, one does not realize he is going

---

[1] Le Grand states that Lobo tried himself.

[2] The best description of the source of the Nile, which confirms Lobo's accuracy, is given by R. E. Cheesman, *Lake Tana and the Blue Nile* (London, 1936).

[3] Gish, Bruce's Geesh.

228

up until he reaches the top, for he then sees how far down it is on the other side and how the hill overlooks all the rest of the land that can be seen from there, although one can climb up there from all directions without difficulty. On the crown of the hill rises a hummock, a place of superstitious veneration for the pagan Agaos, for it is given over to many sacrifices they make there of many cows; and it was the custom for many centuries up to the century preceding the present one for their great sorcerer, venerated among them as a High Priest or Pontiff, to come there, and, on a certain day of the year when many people gathered as if for a very solemn celebration, he would sacrifice a cow near the said source and, throwing its head in it, would then make many other sacrifices of a great number of cows which the crowd would liberally offer him on that hummock, all of them eating the meat as a sacred thing; and with the bones of these cows there were made two immense piles nearby, which, judging from the abundance of bones, represent a great multitude of cows. These bear witness to the abundance of cows which they offer to this source of the Nile, whose greatness gives occasion for so many fables and so much profane adoration. This minister of the devil exerted himself even more, for the greater fascination and pitiful deception of these poor people; for, ordering a magnificent bonfire to be built in the same place, and greasing himself so thoroughly with the tallow and fat of the cows that he remained little less than a candle of tallow, considering the many layers of it he put over his whole body; and, sitting down on an iron chair[1] in the middle and at the top of the bonfire, he would order them to set fire to it on all sides; and he kept discoursing with them and preaching to them until all the wood was burned up without his being burned or the tallow even melting, all through art of the devil, permitted by God as a punishment for the brutish blindness of those wretched idolaters, who, because of such marvels, worship in their deceiver a certain counterfeit divinity and true hypocrisy, deceit and pride, and at the same time he satisfied his greediness with the great quantity of merchandise given to him by those blind people.

The whole area, both where the sources of this famous river are located and a plain lying to the south, east and north of them, which must be a league in length, cultivated in some parts and in others covered with low brushwood, is so high with respect to the surrounding land that from whatever direction one approaches it, he is always climbing upward; and from the very top of this high field, the Nile

[1] Le Grand says the chair was made of straw.

229

has its origin and derives its current. Since it is so high and dominant and all the surrounding ground is so underlain with water, as I have already said, it is apparently also the source of the other river which on the southern side springs from the bottom of this hill and carries its current through a wide, deep valley, and, flowing for a short distance, soon enters the same Nile, carrying to it its own waters which, because of the slope of the place toward that southern part, had been diverted from it.[1] The Nile does not show its current immediately upon leaving its source but, carrying it hidden and underground, following the path indicated by the rich green grass which follows along eastward for a matchlock shot's distance, turns immediately to the north in a wide bend; still hidden, muffling its waters and following the same thread of green grass for the space of a quarter of a league, the famous Nile appears for the first time among a few rocks; and it does not fail to cause joy and astonishment in those who observe it with more curious attention than do the barbarous natives, whose discussion and esteem of it is limited to their fabulous and false superstition about it, the Europeans being concerned with more curious, profound discourse, their books being so full of the greatness of this river. The notable efforts made by great monarchs to discover its sources, all however to no avail, to discover the secrets of its current, waterfalls, and increases, without ever finding the prime reason, all of this now being so clear and obvious to us that we can measure the spans of it and give testimony as eye-witnesses to everything that the Ancients wanted to know and about which they invented so many fanciful tales because they were unable to reach it.

As the discussion went deeper into this subject, we recalled the opinion, so long accepted, that this river was the famous [Gehon][2] encircling the whole land of Ethiopia, as the divine Scriptures attest, which the Nile certainly does; but since the [Gehon] is supposed to have its source in the Earthly Paradise and we discovered the Nile's source in the province of Cahala in the kingdom of Goiama, both of which have been named above, the authors agreeing that both refer to the same things, differing only in their names, it now remains to be seen if this curious discussion permits reconciliation of these two

[1] Le Grand names this river Gemma. There are two rivers called Jimma or Jamma in Ethiopia. Lobo here refers to a tributary of the Little Abbay which joins it about 40 miles S of its entry into Lake Tana. The other, larger, river is a tributary of the Abbay after it has left Lake Tana, joining its left bank about 80 miles NNW of Addis Ababa.

[2] There is a lacuna in the MS. Lobo is referring to Genesis ii. 13: 'Gihon; the same is it that compasseth the whole land of Ethiopia'.

sources so distant from each other, with such different locations, that of Ethiopia being so high that by reason of its height it is called 'above Egypt' and is the real source of this river, Egypt being located much lower with respect to Ethiopia as deep valleys are with respect to the highest mountains, as I observed many times, casting my eyes over the vast area from Dambia toward where the Nile flows toward Egypt; and the location of Cahala, fatherland of Egypt, is even higher than that of Dambia. What is more, if the authors place the Earthly Paradise in Palestine and provinces near Arabia, according to what human understanding can conjecture in so mysterious a matter, all this land lies so much lower than Egypt itself that for that reason its princes and sultans were unwilling to open, as they had intended, and drain the Mediterranean Sea, connecting it with the Red Sea, cutting through approximately thirty-four leagues of land from one sea to the other, as they could have done, fearing that they would inundate all of Arabia and thus destroy it. This demonstrates how much lower Arabia is with respect to Egypt, which itself lies, as it were, under the feet and very much in the shadow of the loftiness and height of our Ethiopia. And if this source, by means of an occult property of attraction peculiar to the land, draws the Nile's waters to itself from the Gehon in Arabia through underground passages and hidden springs, bringing them to the lofty place where it reveals them to view, the windings and turnings by which it attracts them to itself are indeed extremely long; for, unless the source in Cahala draws these waters to itself by a course under the Red Sea,[1] which lies opposite it and separates Ethiopia from Arabia, for [the Gehon] flows in the middle of Arabia and Palestine and the other surrounding provinces, where God, as it appears, situated the Earthly Paradise, corresponding on the other side of the sea to the lands of Ethiopia of which I speak; unless, as I say, that source in Cahala attracts the waters of the Nile to itself in this way, which it most assuredly does not do, it must necessarily bring them by that isthmus of thirty-four leagues from sea to sea, of which I was speaking, all of which is extremely barren, sandy and waterless land. However, if we should wish, in spite of all these difficulties, to say that this river Nile is the famous [Gehon], one of the four mentioned in the Scriptures, let each individual explain for himself the difficulties that arise from

---

[1] According to Genesis ii. 10–15 the Nile, if it was to be identified with the Gihon, the Tigris and the Euphrates were three of the four branches of the same river which 'went out of Eden to water the garden'. The notion that the Nile went underground and emerged again elsewhere was an attempt to explain the geographical difficulties occasioned by the identifications.

all of this and come to whatever conclusions may seem best to him. I, for my part, am continuing to follow the course of the Nile, which we see now at its source, but so slight and lacking in water that it certainly seems to have just been born of its mother, as narrow as the body of any man and so shallow that it is little more than one span deep — a very slender stream, very much lacking in water in the greatest heat of the summer. Soon, however, it swells with the waters of various springs which rise in the midst of its current, other waters contributed by nearby springs, and particularly from various streams and small rivers which very quickly come to contribute their waters, unwilling that it should be so much in need of them. To cover up this lack and to cause it to have the abundance of water corresponding to the Nile's reputation, they give it all they have, swelling it with all they can, considering it better to support the greatness of this famous river, to their own total loss, than to preserve their own names and little water, so that the glory of the illustrious Nile should not be diminished. The river which most noticeably increases it a little below its source is the one the natives call Jama,[1] with which, in little more than a day's journey, because it is then a mighty river, the Nile begins to deserve its reputation for greatness.

At about twenty-three leagues from its source, it spreads out so much over a flat terrain, which is the usual passage from the kingdom of Goiama to the province of Dambia and is called Baad,[2] that a shot from an overcharged matchlock has difficulty crossing it. Running approximately seven to ten leagues from this place toward the north and turning to the east, it enters the famous lake of Dambia, called Bahar sena, meaning Likeness of the Sea, or Bahar Dambia, Sea of Dambia.[3] It crosses a small portion of this lake with such fury that one distinguishes the thread of its current from the rest of the water of the said lake, from which, after traversing this lake for a distance of approximately six leagues from its entrance to its exit, it resumes its course with a greater supply of water than it had before it entered. Continuing for a little more than five leagues, and reaching a land named Alata, the Nile makes one of its famous cataracts.[4] Because it

[1] Le Grand mentions the Gemma, Keltu, Bransu and other streams, i.e. the Jimma, Kelti and Branti.

[2] Bad in the Ethiopic sources; the plain across which the Little Abbay flows to debouch into Lake Tana.

[3] The Portuguese name for Lake Tana was Lake of Dambia. The etymology 'Likeness of the Sea' is untenable; *sena* merely represents a different pronunciation of Tana, formerly Tsana or Tsena.

[4] The famous falls of Tisisat. Alata is the name of a tributary which joins the Abbay a little above the falls, and of a village at the confluence.

Plate VII. The falls at Tisisat

rushes down with all the weight of its water from a high rock, causing with the crashing and fall it makes into a wide, deep pit so thunderous a noise that it is heard from very far away; but from a much greater distance one sees the mist and foam it raises, looking like the smoke of a fire or rather of many fires together. Since the fall it makes as it plunges down from this precipice is extremely furious and the rock goes straight down to the bottom, the water rushes so far out from the vertical rock that it leaves room for travellers to walk at the foot of the rock with no danger of getting wet, but rather with the great treat of the delightful, beautiful view which so much water together makes as it hurls itself from the high rock, and, serving as a parasol which in that place protects people walking there from the sun's rays and heat, the most beautiful, cool, and crystalline place and the most pleasant shade to be found anywhere in the world; for, with the reflection of the sun's rays striking the water, it displays a thousand colours like those of the rainbow. The waterfall, with the sun's rays striking it, is similar to the rainbow in another way, in that it forms an arch because of the fury with which it falls and the height of the rock, which is so wide, because of the river's width at this place, that a person with a strong throwing arm would have difficulty throwing a stone from one edge to the other.[1]

It is appropriate at this point to mention the widely circulated and much believed fable celebrated by authors that those who live near these cataracts are deaf because of the continuous thundering made by the river as it falls. What I can say is that I have seen none of these deaf people. Those who inhabit the surrounding areas are not deaf nor is there any report of such a marvel, although I do confess that the thunderous noise is great. A little beyond this place, two rocks so constrict the width and water of this river that they provide a convenient place for crossing, using logs to pass from one side to the other, forming so safe and sturdy a bridge that the whole imperial army passes over it. Because the rocks constricting the river continue to be close together, the river soon reaches a place where the rock, arching on both sides toward the middle, brings the two edges at the top so close together that, because the distance is so short from one side to the other, some of the boldest people dare to cross the great Nile here in one jump, not without fear on the part of those who watch them

[1] Cheesman confirms the essential accuracy of Lobo's description. Bruce commented: 'It was one of the most magnificent, stupendous sights in the creation, though degraded and vilified by the lies of a grovelling, fanatic priest', sc. Lobo, *Travels to discover the Source of the Nile*, 2nd ed. (Edinburgh, 1805), v, 106.

and those who jump, caused by the height of the rocks, the depth of the river, the abundance of the water collected there, and the thunderous noise it makes. With the convenience of the place and the availability of stone workers who had come to him from India, Emperor Seltan Segued[1] had the opportunity to build here a bridge forming a single arch in the most suitable place for communication between the kingdoms bordering there. This bridge was the first permanent one that the Nile saw over it and the first master to disdain and, as it were, to subjugate the pride of its mighty current.[2] In the course it makes here toward the south, it touches the borders of various kingdoms lying to the east of it: that of Begmeder, whose name means land of sheep – so named because there are many good sheep in that kingdom, for *beg* means sheep and *meder*, land;[3] after this comes that of Amhara, then Olaca, Xaoa, and Damot.[4] As the river's course runs along the borders of these kingdoms and provinces I have named and which it touches with its left side, its right side is bathing and encircling the borders of the kingdom of Goiama, for it keeps circling around it until it reaches two lands which it separates: one in the kingdom of Damot, called Bizan, and the other in that of Goiama, called Gamarcansa, at which place it returns so close to its source that, by travelling across to the source, one can reach it in a day's journey.[5] Up to that point it has run for a distance of a little more than twenty-nine days' journey,[6] if anyone, out of curiosity, wanted to go over the whole distance the Nile travels from its source to that place, collecting water

[1] One of the throne names of Susenyos, 1607–32.
[2] The bridge was built in 1626 by a craftsman who had come from India with the Patriarch, *SRE*, pp. 26, 27. Cheesman wrongly attributes this bridge to Fasiladas, who also had Seltan Sagad as one of his throne names.
[3] The meanings given for the two words are correct, but this is another instance of folk etymology. It has been suggested that the name is connected with Amh. *bäga*, 'dry season' because of the aridity of this province. *beg, meder*: Amh. *bäg, mĕdĕr*.
[4] Amhara, Wollega, Shoa, and Damot.
[5] Bizan is the district more often called Bizamo by the Portuguese and in the Ethiopic chronicles, and in the latter sometimes Bizama. The name does not occur on modern maps. On Almeida's map it is marked Reino Bizamo between the Abbay and the Angur, *SRE*, opp. p. xcvii; Ludolf's map shows it in the same position. The whole passage is evidently based on Paez liv. I cap. xxvi. He spells the second name Gumâr Çancâ and this corresponds to the spelling in the Ethiopic chronicles. The name may survive in the market town of Gumar, shown on Cheesman's map. The Abbay makes a large loop to the north and at the Zakas ford is only some fifty miles from its source. On Cheesman's map this is shown as the border area between Damot and Agaumedr, the western border of Gojjam being far to the east. Lobo, like Paez, here clearly regards Gojjam as occupying the right and Damot the left side of the Abbay. Elsewhere, e.g. p. 226, he treats the country on the right bank here as part of Damot.
[6] According to Paez, *loc. cit.*, he himself asked Ras Se'ela Krestos about the distance in the Emperor's presence and was given this estimate after several of the dignitaries had consulted together, 'if I remember rightly'.

as it describes its famous arc and curve and, with its course, sets the boundary of the famous kingdom of Goiama. After it has passed the land of Gamarcansa, the Nile with its current does not yet make its exit from the territory presently under the dominion of the Abyssinian Emperor, but, after a few days' journey, it then separates this empire and the kingdoms of Fazulo and Ombarea,[1] inhabited by pagans with frizzled, curly hair and of very dark colour, whose lands are so extensive that when Ras Selanios went to attack them in the year 615, he gave it the name *Adisalem*, meaning New World because of the immensity of its vast regions, unknown until then.[2] Since the Emperor's dominion over lands he possesses today ends at this place, we shall not follow further the Nile's course, which from here onward goes in search of the plains of Egypt in order to fertilize them. It is known to us, however, that it passes through countless barbarous and extremely hot provinces. It flows through deepest valleys between very high craggy mountain ridges, adding more and more to its stream with the tributes of new waters which various rivers flowing into it come to pay to it. Since in all this distance it makes several cataracts similar to the one of which I have already spoken, I am not repeating anything about these. I shall only say that the small quantity of fish bred in this famous river is apparently because of the crocodiles and many hippopotami that inhabit it and also because of the cataracts where, as it hurls itself down, it doubtless kills the fish by the impact and weight of its waters. And although the hippopotami do not eat them, because they feed on grass and tree branches like any other land animal, the crocodiles, however, do not spare them, nor do they spare any other living thing, be it man or animal, because they are exceedingly voracious animals.

[1] Fazulo is Fazogli or Fazughli, a region now included in the Sudan, on the Ethiopian border. At this time its ruler was subject to the Fung Sultan of Sennar. Ombarea was a name applied by the Jesuits to an area on the right bank which they believed to be opposite Fazughli. This it cannot have been; it may be the modern Innabara, *SRE*, p. 241.
[2] In 1615 Ras Se'ela Krestos, 'Image of Christ', made extensive conquests on the right bank of the Abbay to the SW and W of the Emperor's dominions. P. da Costa suggests that Lobo may have written *Sela xios*, which the copyist misread. Amh. *äddis aläm*, 'new world'.

CHAPTER 22

[Other curiosities concerning the River Nile including the reason for its floods]

Since I have spoken of these two animals, I want to satisfy any who are curious about them by giving brief and authentic particulars. The crocodile is an ugly animal, disproportionately wide for its length, with short, thick front and back feet, its tail similarly short and thick, dark brown in colour, its body armed all over with scales, an extremely ugly head because of the scales it has on it, making it look like a rough rock; large, fiery, frightful eyes, an enormous mouth and teeth in two rows like sharp, cutting saws. With the hardness of the scales it has as armour all over its body it can resist any musket ball. The ease with which they cut with their teeth is remarkable, for they either carry off their prey whole or instantly take in their mouths the part they have seized, be it a foot, arm or leg; in which latter case, a person is relatively fortunate if, in his misfortune, he feels himself missing that part which the crocodile has seized. Its vision is so acute that it sees from a great distance anything entering the water and moves up to it with remarkable swiftness, and a man's or animal's hand or foot, if incautiously put in the water to be cooled or to get water to drink, does not escape them, for they swim extremely vigilantly in search of prey, especially in a place where people cross. As for the commonly alleged artful practice of simulating the weeping of a child so that they may, by this deception, make a better and surer catch among those who, moved by natural compassion and curiosity, wish to investigate, to their detriment, and come to the aid of the weeping person, I say that, although I saw some and was in a place where there were many, both in and out of the water, I never heard such weeping nor do the inhabitants of that land have any report of this.[1]

The hippopotamus is about the size of two ordinary oxen, but longer, fatter, lower and more out of proportion. Its members are more robust,

[1] Le Grand: 'Neither I nor any of those to whom I have spoken about the crocodile has ever seen it weep, and I regard what is said about its tears as one of those fables with which one amuses children'.

its colour dark brown, almost without any hair, a very small tail with few bristles on it, an enormous mouth, teeth more than a span in size with sockets for them inside the lips. Two tusks protrude from its mouth, curved like those of the wild boar but larger and as thick as a man's arm; its feet are short and almost round with four toes with hoofs. From this description of its composition, one can see how dissimilar it is to the horse and how inappropriately the name and shape of the horse is attributed to it, except for its ears because they are pricked up and small and much like those of a horse, and also in its way of neighing, not as free and continuous as that of the horse; also, like the horse, it expels air forcefully from time to time, especially when it becomes furious or it comes out of the water, clearing its head of water. It finds its food on land where it ordinarily lives, and it cannot stay under water for a long time. Its hide is so thick and hard that in many parts it is impervious to a one-ounce musket ball. It runs little and in a straight line without turning to one side or the other no matter how much people pursue it. It is very true that it tears to pieces any people it may meet in its path, so that when one seeks safety, no matter how fierce it may appear, to avoid danger it is enough to move, even slightly, to either side of its path. I had occasion to experience this when I met two of them in a certain place where many people were coming to kill them. No matter how many musket shots were fired at them, they made only a slight scratch in the hide. One musket ball did pierce and kill only one of them, which was hit in a vulnerable place. The other, which was seeking safety in the water, happened to come where I was. I followed it at the same speed with which it was moving and at a distance of three or four paces from it. A young man was going along on its other side striking it with his spear with all his strength with me urging him on to greater efforts. None of his spear thrusts could penetrate the animal's hide, the spear being bent and twisted as if it were made of wax, and although we kept so close to it, pursuing it closely with shouts and wounds, and by turning it could have quickly seized either one of us, it neither did it nor attempted it. The meat of these animals is very coarse and in no way different from that of a cow except that it is darker and bloodier and therefore quite indigestible and bad for the health.

In addition to the information I have given up to this point concerning some curiosities relating to what authors report about the celebrated Nile, it seems necessary to satisfy the doubts of some dissatisfied persons who still doubt what experience and extensive travels in such strange lands have discovered about the origin and secrets of this river and put all their belief in the trustworthiness and authority of the Ancients. Although they are very deserving of veneration and credit, some certainly should be left for the experience and truth of the Moderns, especially in the proofs they bring, with which they show the reasons why Antiquity was ignorant of the origin and source of the River Nile, which has now been discovered, with less elaborate but more appropriate efforts than those of the Ancients, although we must confess that they were all fortuitous and completely unplanned for the purpose of this discovery. Certainly not the least of the reasons for the universal ignorance of the Nile's source until now was the remoteness and cragginess of the province where it springs forth and the barbarousness of the people who inhabit it. For, if even their own prince has difficulty, or rather has to use extraordinary efforts and great armies to keep them temporarily under his control, it is obvious that foreigners and outlandish discoverers would not be admitted into the interior of their lands. The principal reason, apparently, that great monarchs of ancient times did not find what they sought in so many ways and with so much care was because, as the authors affirm, those who wanted to discover its source and origin sailed up the river itself; and what with the many twistings and turnings this river makes and the great distance and time expended in navigating it, the discovery was made extremely difficult. They finally came upon its mighty cataracts, and since they were unable to conquer them or continue further, they turned back, with their efforts wasted, and spread an attitude of defeatism, with which they discouraged others who wished to imitate them and follow their example. In addition, they could not travel by land because of its asperity, the craggedness of the mountains, the excessive heat of the valleys, and entire provinces, through which the Nile flows, inhabited by barbarians as untamed and fierce as the very beasts, as cruel and ferocious as the wildest animals, without communication or any civilized contact whatsoever with foreigners, there being an infinite number of tribes of these people populating the interior which the Nile cuts through, irrigates, and visits with its current. It is certain that many times one must encounter vast, extremely rugged wildernesses virtually uninhabited by wild animals to say nothing of human beings. All of these difficulties together made this discovery so difficult, both for those who attempted it and for those who only wanted to do so, that, some having failed in their efforts and sufferings and others having been disappointed in their desires and hopes, they all, in common accord, came to the conclusion that the said source was utterly unknown and, as it were, enchanted. There was, however, an easy way to obtain this information, and that was the one which offered and declared it to us, which was by entering that land from the Red Sea and travelling in a somewhat more southerly direction than due southwest about twenty days' journey. By so doing, with a minimum of difficulty, they would have reached the place we reached, where they would have seen what they desired so much, the very source which we reached, the intensity of our joy in discovering it being no less than that of the Ancients' desire to know about it; but since the ancient monarchs, both Greek and Roman, the Alexanders and Caesars, never got to the Red Sea,[1] penetrating its ports and gulfs, to say nothing of conquering the tremendous navigation to the East undertaken and successfully accomplished by the valiant Portuguese who, sailing to the said Red Sea and penetrating the provinces of Africa which border on it, where nature had hidden the noble source of this famous river, not penetrating these places, as I say, abandoning all hope after so many frustrated efforts and sufferings, they preferred to consider this source as beyond the range of human knowledge rather than cast discredit upon that power which was able to conquer mightier things, frustrated as they were in their attempts to attain this discovery.

It was easier to understand the reason, so little known and variously imagined, for the inundation of the Nile in the plains of Egypt, with which it fertilizes them; but since the Ancients were also unsuccessful in attaining this, their lack of success gave rise to the variety of discourses published by authors on this subject. Since these discourses were founded only on what each author drew from his own mind, and since nature does not adapt its works, or rather the rules of them, to the rules of human understanding and discourse, it is not very surprising that some go off on tangents, giving reasons so far removed from what happens in reality, while others, more prudent, take shelter in the usual place of refuge, the sanctuary, as it were, of occult causes and qualities; it being known without any question that the reasons for the floods are not furious, contrary winds blowing in the mouths of the Nile and making its waters turn back so forcefully that, by stopping the waters following them from flowing further, they overflow the banks of the river and spread out over the vast Egyptian

---

[1] Several Hellenistic and Roman authors had considerable knowledge of one or other of the Red Sea coasts, e.g. Agatharchides, Strabo, Ptolemy, and the author (or authors) of the *Periplus of the Erythraean Sea.*

plains; nor are they what another more speculative than reliable author has to say, which is that the waters of the Indian Ocean, driven by furious tempests, send by mysterious means such a great abundance of water to the lake where the author in question imagines the River Nile has its source that it causes such floods that the river overflows and lays under water the fields of Egypt where it keeps spreading out. To say that the snow covering the mountains of Ethiopia near the Nile melts at those times is an even more ridiculous fantasy, since it is certain that in a place where the heat is considered so intense that it makes the lands uninhabitable and the nearest inhabitants are burned by it in such a way that we can see the results of it in the negroes' skin, so much coldness cannot coexist and be maintained along with so much fiery heat. And even if there were snow, it would only be in the very highest regions of the Abyssinian empire, where snow appears only in two places in some years, namely on the mountains of Semen in the kingdom of Tigré and on those of Namora in the kingdom of Goiama.[1] Even if these, at the places where they are closest to the Nile, could send their waters to the Nile when their snow melts, the mountains of Semen, because of the distance and the intervening mountain ranges, could in no way pay this tribute by using this snow to augment the river's current, to say nothing of the fact that the said snow does not appear every year in these places, while the said inundations come every year without fail at certain times, as I shall relate and as all Egypt can testify; and when there is snow, there is so little of it that, when melted, it can hardly water the roots of its own mountains, much less make mighty rivers with which to increase the Nile or its waters. In attempting to explain this mystery, Aristotle places along the Nile certain springs, which he claims are regulated by the heat of the sun. He states that these springs are naturally confined by the cold weather of winter, so that they gather and store up the abundance of water which, when released by the action of the sun's heat in summer, spreads far and wide and causes the said inundations. This great philosopher maintains that this is the sole cause of those mysterious floods, at which so many are amazed and of which few have any certain knowledge.[2] This being Aristotle's contention,

[1] Semien is a mountainous region lying NE of Lake Tana; it includes many peaks over 13,000 ft. Janamora is in Semien near Socotà, *SRE*, p. 238. The reference to Gojjam is certainly a mistake. There has been much discussion about the occurrence of snow in Ethiopia. Bruce, 1805, v, 256, wrote: 'snow was never seen in this country, nor have they a word in their language for it'. Rüppell often saw snow on the Semien mountains, *Reise in Abyssinien* (Frankfurt a.M., 1838, 40), I, 356, 402, 403, II, 14, 243, 244, 249, 251.

[2] Lobo refers to the pseudo-Aristotelian tract *De inundatione Nili*, fragments of which are quoted by Greek authors, including Strabo and Photius, and of which there is a Latin version, *Aristotelis qui ferebantur librorum fragmenta* (Lipsiae, 1886), pp. 188–197.

I say that he is right in affirming that it is springs which cause the said inundations but it is not those he indicates but rather those of the abysses mentioned in the Holy Scripture, as I shall explain presently. The Church Fathers, such as Saint Ireneo, Theodoreto, and Abulence have recourse to surer principles when they refer all this to mysterious secrets of nature and to the knowledge God has of this truth, which was investigated and discovered, along with many other secrets of nature, through the valour and tireless diligence of the Portuguese nation.[1]

In brief, the true and only cause for the inundations of the Nile in Egypt is as follows: The rains in Ethiopia occur in the months which are summer for us and winter for the Ethiopians, and these are the very months when the Nile appears so swollen with water in the fields of Egypt and causes them to be fertilized with its marvellous inundations, from the middle of June through all of September. Since Ethiopia is a land of high mountains rather than extensive plains, all of its rain water immediately flows in abundance down to the valleys, forming turbulent rivers and streams, all of which empty into the Nile. As the Nile wanders over all of Ethiopia, encompassing vast provinces of it in its long course, it keeps receiving an infinite number of rivers. The great swelling of the Nile by the many contributions it thus receives is what causes it to bring about the effects observed in the fields of Egypt. Because it carries the richest soil from the lands through which it flows, it collects all that of Ethiopia and fertilizes the Egyptian plains with it, just as the Mondego does in the famous plain of Bolão and the others it irrigates in its course toward the sea.[2] Since the rainy seasons are long and during those times the rivers are always turbulent because of the water coming down from the mountains, it is not very

---

[1] P. da Costa sees here a veiled allusion to the enquiries made by D. João de Castro at Massawa in 1541. He enquired about the cause of the annual inundation and learnt that it was the result of the rainy season in the highlands of Ethiopia, J. de Castro, 1971, II, 236. The references to Irenaeus etc., are taken from Paez, liv. I, cap. xxvi, 1945–6, I, p. 217, who took them from Urreta, 1610, p. 303. The last quotes Irenaeus as saying: 'Many things have been written about the risings of the Nile, some probable, some improbable; some that have the colour of truth, some without a trace of it. The truth is known to God'. He gives a reference to 'lib. 2 adversus Heresas cap. 47'. I am indebted to Professor Henry Chadwick for the information that, in the division of the *Adversus Haereses* now accepted, this represents II, xxviii, 2. The other references are to Theodoret, *Graecorum affectionum curatio*, in Migne, *Patrologia Graeca*, tom. 83 (Paris, 1859), col. 920, and Alfonso Tostado (Bishop of Avila and hence called Abulensis), *Opera omnia*, Coloniae Agrippinae, 1613), I, 87.

[2] We are indebted to Professor P. José Geraldes Freire of the University of Coimbra for the information that this plain lies to NW of Coimbra, between what is now called the Estação Velha and the Rio Velho, extending from the Choupal to the Adémia. It is no longer subject to flooding by the Mondego as the course of the river was rectified in the eighteenth century.

surprising that this is the entire reason that the Nile's water flows in
these months with its muddy increases, which, as I say, are from June
to September, the time when the Egyptians experience the cause of the
fertility of their soil. And if we ask the people of Egypt at what time
the increases of the Nile begin in their fields, they will say that it is
from the middle of July onward, and as the winter or rainy season in
Ethiopia starts in the month of June, the period from then until the
middle of July is the time during which the Nile swells its current with
the waters it receives and reaches Egypt as so mighty a river.

Concerning this discovery, it is appropriate, by way of corroboration,
to report what happens every year in Cairo and is experienced by its
inhabitants, which is that, since all of Egypt's fecundity and the fertility
of its fields depend upon the increases of the Nile and vary in quality
in direct proportion to the extent to which its vast fields are inundated,
one rightly comes to the conclusion that the source of their good
fortunes is our Ethiopia, since it is the cradle of the famous Nile, born
in the most interior of its provinces, growing and enlarging itself with
the waters with which from every direction, by means of abundant
rivers, it keeps enriching and enlarging itself. In respect to this, it has
been the custom up to the present time, witnessed by foreigners and
preserved by the natives in that great city, to inform all the people,
since all their hopes hang on these inundations and the fertility of the
year, to inform them, I say, as to how much the river is swelling, for
a tower to be contrived at the edge of this river, so proportioned that,
as the river makes it course to the Mediterranean Sea, it also enters the
lower part of the tower which is open on the side facing the river's
current; and each day, according to how much it increases, certain
marks are put there or are already made on the wall. These marks are
called *picas*.[1] Every night announcement is made in the principal streets
of Cairo of how many marks have been covered; for, as the water rises
and covers these marks, the fertility of their land keeps increasing.
When, however, it does not reach sixteen of these marks, they fear there
will be a famine because of dryness and lack of crops. When it rises
above this number, however, the closer it comes to twenty-five, the
greater is the fertility of which they are assured by the increase,
according to what experience has taught them. However, just as the
lack of water and its failure to cover sixteen *picas* is a sign of drought
and consequently a sterile year, so an excess of water covering more
than twenty-five *picas* is equally harmful; so that a greater number of

---

[1] The Nilometer is marked in cubits, Arabic *dhirā'*.

marks both below sixteen and above twenty-five are sure indications of a famine of greater and greater proportions because of too little or too much water.[1] These public announcements begin in Cairo, as the capital city of all Egypt, on the 25th of July, at a time when, because winter has been in progress in Ethiopia for approximately one month, the Nile is already carrying an abundance of water with which to cause the increases. The announcements end at the end of September because winter is already over at that time in Ethiopia and the Nile is no longer receiving the waters contributed to it by the rivers and mountains. Since the Egyptians are so dependent upon this river for their crops, it has come to be said of their country that it knew no Heaven or God other than the Nile; for, since the Heavens never refreshed them with rain and they, as barbarians and blindly ignorant people, did not ascribe to God, author of all good, what they received from the Nile, they looked upon the Nile as their only God and benefactor, from whose inundations their fields received refreshment and fertility and they themselves received the fruit of the land and happiness.

[1] Lane states that the daily announcements of the height of the Nile began about 3 July, and that there was 'an old law, that the land-tax cannot be exacted unless the Nile rises to the height of sixteen cubits of the Nilometer', *An Account of the Manners and Customs of the Modern Egyptians*, 3rd ed. (London, 1842), pp. 454, 455.

CHAPTER 23

[How I went to the province of the Damotes and returned to the kingdom of Tigré. Beginning of the persecution]

We have strayed far from the thread of my narrative, which I interrupted at the point where I was at the edge of the River Nile, to include the digression just concluded concerning its secrets, source, current and inundations. Since we are about to cross it, I must report that I was of use in giving a name to a place where people can cross; for until that time the people had discovered no passage other than the ordinary one called Baad, named after the province of the same name, where it was located. Since I arrived there with many other people who had also come to cross the river and as some were starting to cross it and there was only one of the boats made of bundles of thick logs, which I have mentioned earlier, I became tired of waiting while the others were crossing and walked off with three or four men, going upstream along the edge of the Nile; and, because of the advantageous placement of stones I observed, I went through the trees there were along the river and, passing from one stone to another, the Nile lending itself to this all the way across because the water stayed below the tops of these rocks, I kept making progress across the river, so that I, along with the others I was taking with me, reached the other side with my feet as dry as they had been when I started, much to the amazement of those who saw us already there and had no knowledge of the said passage. Some of them immediately went to find it and were also able to cross there. From that time forward the passage has been known and named as the passage of Father Jerónimo.

This province of the Damotes, where I went to live in a residence we had there called Ligonous,[1] has an excellent climate, extremely

---

[1] *Lëjä Nĕgus*, 'Son of the King'. The name does not occur in the Ethiopic chronicles or on modern maps. It is marked on Almeida's and Ludolf's maps, but these are so inaccurate that it is not possible to determine its position with any precision. The Jesuit mission to the Damots was moved to Leja Negus in 1626 from a site near the source of the Nile, Mendes, 1909, Lib. II, cap. v, pp. 193–4, and Almeida, lib. VIII, cap. xxiii, in Beccari, 1903–17, VI, 493.

healthy and wholesome, as delightful a place to look at as can exist because of its terrain composed of fields, valleys, and mountains, all as perfectly proportioned and as beautiful as anything that could be imagined by a person of curious mind and described by his fine words and ingenuity. This beauty was enhanced to no small degree by the coolness and beauty of the woods of excellent trees, especially cedars, which abound on the mountains and in the valleys. The climate is so temperate that at the same time I saw in some places ploughing and sowing and in others the wheat already sprouting, while in others it was full-grown and mature, in others reaping, threshing, gathering and again sowing, the land never tiring of continual production of its fruits or failing in this readiness to produce them. Among the notable trees that grow there is one native and peculiar to that place called *ensete*,[1] unlike any tree found in our lands. Its leaves, however, are so large, both in width and length, that two of them are more than enough to cover a man from head to foot if both are hung one under the other from his neck. This plant is admirably profitable to man, for there is no part of it which is not used advantageously in his service. In addition to the fact that a small number of its leaves furnish and carpet a house with its sprightly green colour, it also serves pleasingly as clean plates when one wants to eat rustically with much freshness, cleanliness, and delicacy. After it is dry, it is woven and they make from it a certain flax, from which they weave not only rope similar to that made of hemp but also various tapestries of different colours. From the branches or stems in which the leaves are set they make an extremely fine, white, pure flour, than which there is no finer milled anywhere. When it is eaten with milk, for only with milk does it have its full flavour, it is a very delicious and delightful food. The trunk and roots serve as something like turnips or potatoes, although more substantial since they are as thick as any man. Travellers provide themselves with this food which, previously cooked, lasts them for several days. When cooked it resembles the flesh of our turnips, so that they have come to call this plant 'tree of the poor', even though wealthy people avail themselves of it as a delicacy, or 'tree against hunger', since anyone who has one of these trees is not in fear of hunger. The best thing about this tree is that when one cuts it down about one span from the ground and cuts criss-crosses into the remaining stump, four or five hundred

---

[1] Amh. *ensät*, sometimes called the wild banana, formerly known as *musa ensete*, now *ensete edulis*, a staple food in parts of south-west Ethiopia. The root and lower part of the stem are eaten, not the fruit.

sprouts come out of the stump, which are then planted and grow into trees like the one from which they sprouted. When the tree is cut, it makes such grievous and human-like moans that it gives the Abyssinians occasion to say: 'We are going to kill an ensete' instead of saying 'We are going to cut it down', because of the way the tree appears to be affected by the blows they give it. Finally, at the very top of the tree, from among the leaves, there blooms a kind of spike or cluster so large that it must produce 500 or 600 figs, which from green turn yellow when ripe, the size of small *beberas*,[1] each one of which has its stone which, when planted, produces another similar tree, so that this tree is the most productive and useful of any I have seen, since everything it has serves for human sustenance, even to these figs, although their taste is not as good and is bitter like unripened berries.

I lived in this province for nine months[2] and completed there a beautiful church of freestone lined with beautiful cedar, so good that, being for that place one of the famous churches in the land, it could appear without shame in ours, where such buildings are more elaborate. The people are noble and of excellent temper and natural inclinations. They were at first stubborn in their errors and great enemies of the Catholic faith, so that, because the Emperor ordered them to receive it, more than seventy of their monks, obstinate in their false beliefs and practices, rather than abandon their errors, preferred to enter Hell ahead of time, all of them casting themselves, helping one another to do so, from a very high cliff and being broken to pieces on the steep rocks before reaching the ground at the bottom of the cliff, wishing to jump to Hell from so high a place, since they could not and it would not have been well for them to take their lives in the middle of a field. Others, more than six hundred monks and nuns, died in a battle as all of them came in the vanguard of the army of heretics with altar-stones[3] on their heads, assuring their followers that at the sight of the said stones the Catholics would be defeated without a blow of a sword or a thrust of a lance. All of this was because they would not abandon the observance of the Sabbath.[4] They were not only defending the observance of the Sabbath but were also attacking the Catholic army

---

[1] A kind of early fig, black outside with red flesh.

[2] Le Grand says two months.

[3] Lobo refers to *tabots*, which are consecrated, inscribed, rectangular slabs usually of hard wood, sometimes of stone, which represent the Ark of the Covenant. They are kept in the inner sanctuary of the church and may be touched only by priests.

[4] The Ethiopian Church observed the Jewish Sabbath as well as the Christian Sunday. 'The history of Sabbath observance in Abyssinia is fairly chequered, and the sources are often ambiguous and even contradictory', Ullendorff, 1960, p. 105.

because the Catholics did not observe it. Their vain presumption deceived them, for they were the first to experience the falseness of their pretensions and the futility of their heedlessness of the Catholics' lances and swords.[1] Being, as I say, such cruel and obstinate enemies of the Catholics, they afterward submitted in such a way to the truth of the faith that there were no more devout or better instructed Christians than they. I lived among them, as I say, for nine months, going up and down the principal districts of this land, penetrating far into the interior of it, very close to the barbarous pagan Gallas, where a great Catholic viceroy of the land was on the frontier to protect the entire land, a place so dangerous and the barbarians so bold that they not only had killed this viceroy's predecessor in battle but soon killed this one also in another battle.

Every year, all of us who were working in those provinces, had the custom of gathering together, not only to meet and console one another with the presence of those who lived as brothers united in fraternal love and so far removed not only from our own provinces, so distant from these so foreign and remote, but also to discuss the spreading of the faith and preaching of the Gospel and ways and means by which it could be further extended. Since it was the Christmas season, after Christmas had arrived, I spoke of returning to Dambia to the Emperor's court, where the Superior of the Mission and the Patriarch were in attendance. In the company of other Fathers who lived in residences two or more days' journey away from mine, making a party of five, in addition to people who accompanied us, we travelled without mishap until the very last night of the journey, when God miraculously delivered us from the death which some heretics very carefully planned for us through a stratagem very much to their liking: as we came into a place which was a veritable stronghold of heresy, because the Empress[2] was a great patron of these people and their beliefs, they saw an excellent opportunity and wished to kill all five of us, for which purpose they gave us some large round houses with walls of stone and clay and roofs of wood and straw, into the largest of which all five of us withdrew for the purpose of sleeping. Because these houses were not inhabited, they had become infested with reddish biting ants of a certain species existing in all of those provinces, which, with their biting, wanted to drive us outside, unless it was a warning from our

[1] These events had occurred in October 1621, the imperial commander being Ras Se'ela Krestos, Pêro Pais (Paez), *Historia da Etiópia* (Porto, 1945, 46), III, 153.

[2] Seltan Mogasa.

guardian angel wanting, by this means, to remove us from danger by causing us to leave the place where it was being prepared for us. Lying in bed, then, as we were, we felt the enemy, meaning the ants, which, as if launching a sudden assault, attacked us in such a way that we had to get out of our beds, light a fire, and call our people to help us, who, with the light of the fire, freed us from this kind of enemy, now strewn all over the floor of the house. As the more dangerous enemies were keeping a careful watch, the contest with the first ones now over, the servants back in bed, and we were again comfortable. My bed was next to the door, the house having two doors, one of which they had closed up so securely that we could never open it even before the danger, from which circumstance we afterward concluded that they had secured it intentionally to leave us fewer means of escape; the other one was merely locked when those who were observing us at a distance, in anticipation of their evil deed, set fire to a hedge twenty feet long that ran from another house toward the one where we were. God willed that they did not set it closer to our house; for, if they had or if they had thought to close our door from the outside, we should certainly have all perished in the fire. By chance, a young man was watching, who saw the fire beginning to burn and ran quickly to inform me of it. Getting out of bed, I only had time to shout to my companions warning them of the danger. When they were outside the house, the fire was already spreading in no time at all with such fury that there was scarcely time for all of them to get out and to drag out their poor beds, the house immediately going up in flames along with three others with whatever was inside them, the servants escaping and the heretics foiled in their wicked intentions and we acknowledging the favour God had shown us and now in full knowledge of the will and intentions of our hosts, who did not appear in the village until after we left, which was on the next day after the night of the fire.

Reaching the place where the rest of the Fathers were waiting for us, which was in the house of Gorgorra[1] where the Emperor was kind enough to be, staying there a few days and, on his departure, declaring by a message his desire that I should return from there to the kingdom of Tigré, where I had come from, which the Superior had to authorize despite the fact that he had destined me for another residence further into the interior of that empire. Leaving therefore for the one to which

---

[1] Gorgora, on a peninsula on the north side of Lake Tana, about 30 miles SW of Gondar. Susenyos had a palace there, the ruins of which Cheesman visited. Almeida wrote his *Historia de Ethiopia a alta ou Abassia* at Gorgora.

I was assigned, I went by way of Ganete Ilhos, which means Paradise of Ilhos,[1] where the Emperor was in some fine palaces and a garden built for him by workmen from India and where he had had us build a fine church and house. I spoke to him there and he ordered a large gift of money to be given to me to continue the work of the residence I had begun in Tigré and which I had had to discontinue. On the way, we had to pass through a desert for two days' journey, where I was to experience a painful vexation with a spitting cobra.[2] If, instead of ejecting its venom toward me from a distance, it had done so from close at hand, it undoubtedly would have killed me, as it often does kill people; but God willed that it was at a distance, so that, although I felt, in the symptoms I experienced, the effectiveness of its poison, I was fortunate enough not to experience the full force of it; but it was enough to cause me a restless night as I availed myself of the bezoar-stone.[3]

These snakes are not very long but have a large belly. They are beautifully coloured with black, gray and yellow, with a large mouth, and, receiving much air when they want to do harm, they expel it very furiously, causing their deadly effect at a distance of three to four spans, poisoning all the surrounding air so that it is enough to ruin the eyes of anyone who receives it without taking precautions. However, since I was further away, the poisonous air was not so strong. Although I did escape this cobra I was not, however, so fortunate with another which placed me at the gates of death. The other one caught me totally unawares as I was going to pick up a leather bag that was inside a house. It bit me on one finger and I believe it left a piece of a fang in me since I saw and drew from my finger something like a little hair. In any case, it certainly spread up my arm so painfully that at moments I felt the pain rising to the point where, reaching my armpit, it went into my body and I soon felt my heart affected by symptoms of approaching death, so powerful that I was already losing my eyesight, many extremely effective antidotes which I took being of no avail, such as bezoar-stone, creating flesh sores by irritation, and unicorn. None of these could counteract the poison because it was very powerful, so

[1] Ilhos is a copyist's mistake for Jesus. Ganneta Iyasus, 'the Paradise of Jesus', was the name of the Emperor's palace at Azazo, four miles south of Gondar. The plural 'palaces' is probably used because, like so many palaces in India and the Middle East, it was a series of pavilions in a garden, rather than one large structure.

[2] Several species of cobra are able to spit venom, sometimes for a distance exceeding their own length.

[3] A concretion found in the stomach or intestines of certain animals, especially ruminants; it was highly valued as an antidote to snake-bite.

I was forced to take hastily the last and most effective, although most repugnant, medicine, which proved, with the help of God, to be effective,[1] even though I remained very weak throughout the night, with attacks from time to time, indicating that some of the poison and its effects were still inside me. However, by chewing a garlic clove at each of these attacks, I felt better; but both the garlic and the effects of the illness so damaged my capacity to taste that I was unable to taste anything for a month thereafter, no matter what I ate, until little by little my taste was gradually restored to its natural state.

For approximately two years I lived in this land, somewhat more tranquilly on this second occasion, busying myself with the ordinary tasks of conversion of souls, baptizing, confessing and catechizing those newly converted to the Catholic faith. It happened during this period that I was obliged to accompany a Father who was on his way back to India because of poor health. As I accompanied him on a day's journey through an uninhabited area, where there were a number of trees the size of a plum-tree, the fruit of which was called *anchoy* by the natives and was the size of a plum, almost round, yellow in colour, pleasing to behold, having a tart taste like wild fruit, although there is so little wild fruit there, and eaten by the natives.[2] Since it was then in season, I picked some of this fruit as I was travelling and ate some, eating not only the fruit itself but also the skin and the stone inside, which I found as sweet and good as those of Europe. Although the fruit is not at all harmful, I was soon to experience the effects of the skins; for no sooner had I arrived at the place where I was to spend the night than I was struck by an illness more severe than I had ever experienced. The skins of these *anchoys* caused extremely dire symptoms which were the same as a healthy enema of antimony, this one being enough to purge me of the remaining days of my life, and I was brought to this pass in a very brief space of time, the same disturbance and danger continuing all through the night. At daybreak, I was in such a condition that I did not know what to do and managed only with great difficulty to return to the residence where I did not recover for a long time. I then learned that the skins are a powerful poison or purgative, eight or ten of them being enough to cause the effects of the most powerful purgative available; and I, in ignorance of their properties and efficacy, had eaten more than twenty, to satisfy my gluttony.

From this province I went to another, in the same kingdom of Tigré,

---

[1] P. da Costa suggests that Lobo may have resorted to goat's urine, which he mentions later as a medicine.   [2] I have not been able to identify this tree.

called Debaroa, near the sea, a little more than two days' journey in the province called Saraoe, a healthful, cool, fertile, pleasant land,[1] inhabited however by vile people – many Muslims as well as the schismatic Christians, identical with the Muslims in their customs. I did not have much rest there, however, because the devil soon began to turn things and the mood of the evil people against the Catholic faith by means of his ministers, the heretical monks, so that I once again had to take refuge with the other Fathers in the town and residence of Fremona, since it was a large village inhabited exclusively by Portuguese and native Christians, all of whom were good Catholics. The uneasiness and disorder soon increased with the illness of Emperor Seltan Segued, who, with his person, valour, zeal and piety of a true Catholic, not only sustained and propagated the Catholic faith throughout his empire but also repressed the fury and arrogance of the heretics. Losing, along with his health, his forces and power, which his son took from him almost by force, he could not restrain the heretics, who, seeing themselves freed of his presence, dared to harass that church throughout the empire, freeing themselves from obedience to it and rebelling, having become apostates against the Catholic faith because of a decree that all should abandon it and return to the ancient Alexandrian faith and to the schism and heresies they had renounced, thus reviving the ancient errors and abuses they had earlier abandoned. Even though many Catholics resisted and upheld the Catholic faith, as they are still doing at the present time, at the cost of much abuse, exile, loss of property, torture, and death, many weak people fell and the evil ones became more insolent; for, being many, they prevailed over the small band of Catholics.

The worst of this revolt and persecution fell on the Patriarch, the Bishop, and the Fathers who were there as ministers of the Roman faith, as the heretics avenged themselves and took up arms against us because of the hatred they had for it. On this occasion, wherever we were, we began to experience the violence and insolence of the heretics. A good share of these misfortunes extended into Fremona, where I was. Since they came upon us in a foreign land so distant from the lands where we were born, the most remote and easternmost corner of all of Africa, and we were surrounded on all sides by mortal enemies – Muslims, pagans, and heretics – and thrust among them with no means of

[1] Debarwa is now a village 18 miles south-south-west of Asmara; it was formerly the capital of the Bahrnagash, the governor of the coastal province. Serae, or Sarawe, is the portion of the Eritrean plateau lying N of the Mareb river.

communication with India other than through the Turks on the Red Sea, we being of white colour in a land where all were black, with no other protection than that of God and no place from which help and communication could reach us other than through their hands and through those of the Turks, all of this obliged us all the more to put all our trust in God since there was so little to hope for on earth. However, the Viceroy who was in that kingdom had been until then a great friend of mine, making a show of being a good Catholic, and although he still did so, his friendship cooled, so that his soldiers were emboldened to practise upon us a thousand annoyances and abuses, taking from us everything that belonged to the church, lands which provided sustenance for the poor and everything else they could lay their hands on, placing us, as it were, in a state of siege; they even tried on one occasion to come to attack and rob the town itself, starting their execution of the attack and robbery at another place, a small neighbouring village. A band of soldiers came upon that town, went into it and divided up the houses among themselves as authoritatively and confidently as if they were their owners. As they were starting to try to take possession of the spoils, a Portuguese with his four young sons[1] came out to meet them and attacked the whole enemy band so vigorously that they quickly routed them, without killing any of them because they had no desire to do so, but giving some of them more than they had bargained for. Fearing for their lives, the soldiers fled to their nearby encampment. After recovering from their panic, they gave the call to arms, whereupon the whole camp became stirred up against us; and those soldiers, now reinforced with a goodly multitude, came to attack our village and destroy it by fire and sword. And since this danger and the determination of those people were more and more obvious, about fifty of our people resolved to put up a defence, sallying forth so vigorously to meet the enemy forces on the field that they broke the impetus of their attack and kept them from moving further forward. Our men joined battle with them so courageously that they forced them to withdraw with more than sixty wounded, there being about thirty in the same state on our side, but with no one killed on

[1] An unpublished report by the Patriarch, of which several manuscripts exist in Portugal, has enabled P. da Costa to identify him as Manuel de Sousa, grandson of one of D. Cristovão's companions. Mendes says: 'He was more like his grandfather in courage than in language, for he did not get his Portuguese quite straight.' With three sons (not four, as Lobo says) and servants 'instead of São Thiago he called out Santago against these heretics and unbelievers. The apostle, though badly pronounced, responded so speedily that in less than a stone's throw ten or twelve soldiers had fallen well supplied with hits from stones and blows'.

either side, although the fighting had lasted for almost three hours. As a result of the disastrous outcome of this battle, the Viceroy broke off his friendship completely making great efforts to capture me, even laying siege to us by tightly encircling us. Since, however, our cause was considered just, even among our enemies, although the time was not a very favourable one for us, I was able to avoid falling into his hands despite the many expedients and tricks he employed for the purpose of using me as a hostage to force our people to do whatever he, the Viceroy, might want them to do. The affair gradually calmed down, especially when the Viceroy ceased governing and was succeeded by another Viceroy, with whom, as it turned out, however, our fortunes did not improve but rather worsened.

The new Viceroy's name was Isa Acem, a son-in-law of the old Emperor and a cousin of the reigning Emperor.[1] He was a bad man, deceitful, very lacking in judgment, without truthfulness or shame or fear of God or men. In the beginning, he made a show of good friendship with broad promises of great favours, protection of our possessions and our safety, all for the purpose of deceiving us. He proceeded in this way for a few days until, with the old Emperor's death, the interests of the Catholic faith were totally ruined, the heretics became uncontrollable, and we began to experience everywhere the rigours of persecution. I shall now postpone further discussion of our sufferings in Tigré to relate what happened at the Emperor's Court with respect to the Patriarch, the Bishop and the Fathers, whom I shall accompany until I bring them to our residence in Fremona, whereupon I shall return to our experiences there with the new Viceroy, Isaac.

[1] His name was Yeshaq (Isaac). By the old Emperor, Lobo means Susenyos, by the reigning Emperor, Fasiladas.

CHAPTER 24

[How we were exiled to Fremona]

After the Emperor's death, the heretics immediately entered into discussion among themselves as to what should be done with us, holding various councils and making various decisions. On some occasions, which were the majority, they condemned us all to death in order to satisfy once and for all their wrath and fury against the ministers of the Gospel, whom they considered, as indeed they were, sworn enemies of the Alexandrian stubbornness and perfidy they were then professing, intending to accomplish two things on this occasion: to satisfy their hatred and to bring down completely the edifice of the faith by destroying those who upheld it, depriving the Catholics of the support, advice and strength which they had in our Fathers, as in teachers from whom they had learned the Catholic faith. On other occasions they resolved to exile us either to an island they have in the Sea of Dambia, which we certainly could not leave without an order from them, or to some one of those low-lying lands that exist in Ethiopia, where those exiled quickly die. And in their decision to exile us they had no good intention of sparing our lives but rather were dissuaded from killing us outright by their fear that, if they did so, the Portuguese would come to them from India to call them to account for the evil they had done, an eventuality which struck terror into their hearts. And for this reason, the opinion and vote of the more temperate among them was that if they were to send us back to India, they feared that we would return with Portuguese forces to restore the faith to power and put the Catholic Church in possession of all it had gained in that empire and which it had lost unjustly. Following this line of reasoning, they thought that as long as they kept us alive and in exile we would serve them as hostages so that, if the Portuguese were to come, as they feared, we would be obliged to negotiate peace and agreements with both sides concerning their past offences against us and the present intended vengeance of the Portuguese. While they vacillated without coming to any final decision on what course of action to take, they exiled us from one place to another, with a thousand vexations, sufferings and afflictions and with a slow death, so that we could rightfully affirm that we were living a fatiguing and very afflicted life, keeping ourselves alive by eating the bread of suffering and drinking the water of tribulation; for, in addition to suffering in our persons, houses and poor belongings, being robbed and despoiled of them, we were witnessing the destruction of the faith and the damnation of so many souls, the affliction and abandonment of so many Catholics suffering for justice and truth; and doubtless all of us or most of us would not have escaped with our lives, considering the fury of the heretics, the power they had gained over everything, and the hatred and excesses they unleashed against the Church, if God Our Lord had not come to our aid at the opportune moment.[1]

What happened was that, the king of Monbaça having rebelled at that time against the fortress we have there, killing the Captain and perpetrating so many excesses and cruel acts, as everyone knows, the Viceroy of India took care to send a large fleet and forces against him so that his rebellion would not be left unpunished.[2] As the ships were setting sail for this purpose, they wrote to us from Goa informing us of the preparation and purpose of the fleet, with the number of sails which they said were eighteen, and adding that on their return from Monbaça they were to sail up that coast as far as the gates of the strait where Zeila is located, the port of Adel, and were to destroy it in punishment for the death inflicted by its king on two Fathers, my companions, who had gone there in the year 1624, an action which the Viceroy considered very necessary. And since this port is not at a great distance overland from the kingdoms of Ethiopia, those who were inexperienced believed that they could reach those kingdoms by that route. And since I had been informed of this, the Viceroy[3] asked me how many ships there were. I told him there were eighteen, having informed him a few days earlier that an India carrack sometimes carried a thousand soldiers. Being inlanders, they were unacquainted with the differences between one kind of ship and another and were under the

---

[1] Le Grand's text records the following prayer used by the Fathers at this time: 'You are able, O Lord, to dispose of our lives. Only grant us the strength and courage to endure the most cruel torments. We shall be overjoyed to die for Your Holy Name. But what is to become of the poor souls You have redeemed by Your blood? Have pity on them. Have pity on us. Do not permit Your enemies and ours to triumph over the truth, and to take corruption into the sanctuary. Let us, if need be, eat the bread of sorrow and drink the water of bitterness, but, O Lord, come to our aid, hasten to help us. The time has come.'

[2] D. Jerónimo Chingulia, King of Mombasa and a Portuguese protégé, reverted to Islam in August 1630 and massacred the Christians in the city. Ecclesiastical documents relating to this episode have been edited and translated by G. S. P. Freeman-Grenville, *The Mombasa Rising against the Portuguese, 1631* (London, 1980).

[3] i.e. of Tigré.

impression that those eighteen ships were all India carracks. Figuring the military forces aboard the ships at one thousand soldiers per ship and recalling what four hundred Portuguese had been able to do against more powerful enemies, which I have related in my account of Dom Christovão da Gama, they were appalled at the prospect of what eighteen thousand would be able to do now especially since the Abyssinian Emperor's forces were now reduced. Since they considered it a certainty that they were already coming by land, there being some who affirmed that they were already inside the empire and who reported the day's journeys and having heard shots from the artillery they were bringing with them, and because of their horror and fear of all this, this wild fantasy was enough to dampen their vehemence when their anger and hatred against us was at its highest pitch, not daring to condemn us to death according to the decision they had reached. They came to another barbarous decision, however, and that was that they made a secret agreement with the Turks that they, the Turks, would kill us, their own responsibility being limited to delivering us into their hands. And for greater assurance that their intention would be carried out, they emphasized two points to the Turks, which could serve as a strong invitation and stimulus for them to do as the Abyssinians wished: The first point was that, as they were exiling us and banishing us from their kingdoms for being hostile to their ancient religion, we were taking much gold with us. Their idea in telling them this was that the Turks would want to satisfy their greed for this gold and not finding any, as certainly would be the case, they would suspect us of hiding it and would certainly kill us. And indeed the device was almost certain to bring about the desired effect because of the insatiable greed of the Turks, who stop at nothing and commit every imaginable cruelty for their own illicit gain. The second point was even more persuasive in the minds of the Turks, who were distrustful and fearful in proportion to the greatness of their tyranny and the unjustness of their possession of those islands and the whole Red Sea and therefore were always fearful of some greater power coming and casting them out of those places they wrongfully possess; and because of this fear on the part of the Turks, the Abyssinians gave them to understand that if we were to escape alive from their hands and reach India alive, we would return with Portuguese forces to conquer the Abyssinian empire and expel them, the Turks, from that island of Maçuá and from the port we would use to gain access to Ethiopia. It was easy for the Turks to believe all this and to promise to put us to death, making arrangements to do so and waiting only for them to hand us over to them.

After the agreement was arranged and concluded, we were informed that we were to leave our houses to be exiled to the kingdom of Tigré and that from there we were to go to the Red Sea. And since their intent was only that we should be killed, it mattered little to them that there was no ship in which we could do so. However, they discussed arranging executions, which they had planned to have accomplished at so great a distance, as some of them offered to put them into effect closer at hand, for which purpose, in addition to their taking from us what they wanted of the poor belongings we still had, they left the rest to be taken on the road by those who would attack us in an uninhabited place, as they did, and would obtain from the robbery of what was left some reward for their wickedness as well as our deaths, all of which happened as far as the robbery and attack were concerned. For, as the Patriarch and other Fathers were coming through a deserted area, they were attacked by approximately six hundred brigands armed with lances and *adargas* and much more so with hatred and greed, who robbed them of everything they could lay their hands on. Our people immediately took refuge on the top of a hill, at the bottom of which the robbery was boldly accomplished. They began climbing the hill shouting that they wanted the heads of everyone, and they undoubtedly would have cut them all off if about thirty Catholics accompanying the Fathers had not opposed their frenzy, resisting the brigands' fury with courageous vigour and with such success that they not only stopped them from moving forward but, attacking them with extraordinary courage, put them to flight, wounding some and killing the captain of all of them, upon whose death they dispersed, leaving our people free to continue their journey. Further on, however, other brigands in greater numbers and strength were waiting for them in another uninhabited area similar to the first; but, since I was informed of the robbery that had taken place and of the one being prepared further ahead, I gathered together some friends from among the most important people in the land, along with many Portuguese from my residence and town of Fremona,[1] and went out to meet the robbed, exiled travellers, taking them some refreshment and food, of which they were in great need. And as I came upon them just as they were approaching the danger of which they had been informed and were

---

[1] Le Grand: 'I assembled all my Portuguese and Abyssinian friends to the number of eighty-four men'.

fearful, they were overjoyed at our coming and at the prospect that the rest of their journey would be in safety, which was the case as we arrived at our residence of Fremona, exiled, persecuted and robbed, there being assembled in the same house a Patriarch, a Bishop and eighteen religious of the Company who were there at that time, with four hundred Catholics, both Portuguese and people of the land,[1] who also had come as exiles and wished to share our fate for the cause of the Catholic faith. It was my responsibility to find food and sustenance for all of these people, a difficult thing on that occasion both because we did not have it in the house and because it was the winter season, our enemies were many, our situation was extremely precarious and there was no source of food for us. However, since I had friends in that kingdom and our necessitous state demanded it, we had to place our trust in God to see that we would not all perish. The chalices and vestments and other church decorations that escaped the brigands and which finally were to come into their possession were dismantled into various pieces and sold to help us through our sufferings, in which the Viceroy, Isaac, was of assistance, the same Isaac who was beginning his viceroyalty at the point where I broke off my narration, delaying till now the continuation of my discussion of him.

The new Viceroy, then, with false words, tried, and was successful in his attempts, to seize for himself some poor belongings still in our possession, and, taking advantage of his friendship with me, came to see us, expressing pity for our sufferings, offering his favour and promising great things so that we would not be in need. All of this, however, was for the purpose of gaining a few items for himself, which he took away with him. Since we were uncertain as to whether we would all be sent or we would remain and being sure that if we all went together we would not escape from the cruel hands of the Turks, we wished to send someone ahead to relieve us and also to procure help in India for that Christianity and for those who remained in such great suffering. It was first necessary to obtain permission and safe conduct for the travel, which I undertook to obtain both from the Viceroy, to permit only [lacuna in MS.] to go, and from some friends through whose lands they were to pass, so that these friends would protect them from the heretics and highwaymen who were doubtless lying in wait to attack them and take their lives. This was all easily negotiated. And in the discussion of those who were to go, I was chosen

---

[1] Le Grand says 400 Portuguese.

first, not only to discuss in Goa the help we were seeking but also, if necessary, to go to Portugal and Rome for the same purpose. However, after being chosen, I was to stay behind since the others remaining in Fremona were unfamiliar with the people and the particularities of that kingdom and I would be very useful to them in these matters; and, as it turned out, I was certainly of use to them.[1] Four other Fathers left[2] while all the rest of us remained in all the dangers and lack of necessities of life I have mentioned up to this point, having to struggle from that time forward against the greed and cruelty of the Viceroy, for it was soon revealed that the heretics' thirst for our blood was no more intense than his for our poor possessions.

When I went to visit the Viceroy in his encampment, there was a man there, whom I knew, who was condemned to die and was about to be handed over to his enemies to be killed by them, according to the practice I have described earlier. As he was considered a Catholic and was asking for confession, I wanted to help him in his hour of need. The whole encampment, however, was swarming with heretics, some of whom were the very craftiest and deadliest enemies of the faith. As soon as they learned that I would be confessing him, they bellowed with rage. Because the confession was to take place in the field where they held him prisoner with two chains, each two *covados* in length, attached at one end to a large iron ring on each of his arms and attached at the other end to a similar iron ring on the arm of some trusted friend of the plaintiff, according to the custom of the land, I had him released from his two guards and, remaining alone with the condemned man, I proceeded to prepare him to die well. I was completely surrounded by an infinite number of heretics, very unhappy with what they were witnessing and with the prospect of that man dying in the Roman faith. All of their hatred, however, was against me, and they were gnashing their teeth and giving strong indications that they were on the point of attacking me. Although I saw the danger I was in and how difficult it was for me to escape it, the cause, however, for which I was suffering was so worthy and the means of escaping the danger was so difficult that I placed the affair wholly in God's hands, continuing my ministrations so that that soul would not be lost. Since his soul was not among the chosen ones and the sinful life he had lived made him

[1] Le Grand: 'But as it was considered that I knew the language of the country better than my companions, the decision was changed and I stayed in Abyssinia'.
[2] Manoel de Almeida, who had recently been appointed Provincial at Goa, Manoel Barradas, Damião Colaça, and José Giroco, together with two of the Patriarch's chaplains.

worthy of the fate reserved for him, he failed to take advantage of that most important occasion and thus lost his opportunity for salvation; for, after I had confessed him to my satisfaction and as I was about to give him absolution, which certainly would have been followed by my own death, as indicated by the furiously agitated state of the heretics, one of the boldest and rashest of them pushed his way to the front of them so as to be seen and shouted to the prisoner: 'So-and-so, if you think that you will escape death by confessing in the Roman faith, you are deceiving yourself. By doing that you are making it more certain.' Hearing those words and thinking that they meant there was some hope of their letting him live, the wretch got up from where he was kneeling at my feet, without waiting for the absolution, and said, 'No, no, I'm not confessing.' As soon as he had said these words, his enemies, the plaintiffs, rushed to him and, quickly taking him less than twenty paces away, gave him eight spear-thrusts by which his life was drained from his body as well as from his soul, because of his inconstancy, which was enough for the satisfied heretics to abandon their intentions with respect to me, since this man had not escaped from their hands as they had feared.

Since the Viceroy was now aware that he no longer had anything to hope for from our poor possessions because they were non-existent, he wished to derive gain from our persons and was thus very anxious to have me in his power, which he doubtless would have done if I had not been warned of his treachery and perfidy by a close acquaintance of his, who gave me signals of his intent as I approached, so that I had time to withdraw. If the Viceroy could get his hands on me, he intended to extract a heavy payment from my poor companions and the Catholics who would have had to provide it by denying themselves necessities of life. He also intended to hand me over to a rebellious heretic in exchange for his father, whom the heretic held captive. The rebellious heretic would doubtless have been overjoyed at the exchange because the heretics, especially the monks who were with him, were very anxious to have one of the Fathers in their power so that they could inflict a cruel death upon him, as was his intention. The Viceroy tried many means and various stratagems to lay hands on me; since I was forewarned, however, and was constantly advised of his tricks, they were all in vain. He finally came with his entire camp, which he set up close to us, surrounding us and virtually laying siege to us for the purpose of capturing me, but this stratagem was also unsuccessful. He again tried protestations of feigned friendship with which to deceive me, but also to no avail. He finally pretended that he had a matter of importance to discuss with me, but, when I excused myself from going to his encampment, he proposed that we see each other midway between my residence and his lodging. However, since I did not have the necessary security for my safety, I agreed to it with the provision that he would come close to our residence with only three servants and I would go with the same number of Portuguese to speak with him. After this was agreed upon, he came and I went out cautiously with the three Portuguese, who were much more cautious and were resolved to repulse any attack. And because the Viceroy was soon followed by a goodly number of his people, who kept coming little by little to the place where we were, our Portuguese did the same, coming out of the residence and drawing closer, ready for any event. But the Viceroy, seeing that his plan could not succeed, although his intent was obvious, returned to his encampment without accomplishing what he had intended, nor did he make any further attempts, knowing how alert the Catholics were and how determined they were not to allow him to bring his evil plan to fruition. He was soon punished, however, for, a little over a month later, he was taken prisoner at the same place as a traitor to the Emperor, having tried to join the rebel who held his father captive, because he had not been able to bring about his release by exchanging one of the Fathers for him, and was taken in shame and disgrace to the Emperor's encampment.

At this time the heretics wanted to keep their promise to the Turks by delivering us into their hands, for which purpose the Emperor ordered a confidant of his to take us to the sea. Because we had definite news of this and pitied the abandoned state in which those Catholics were left to the fury and violence of the heretics, we resolved to scatter in various places, remaining hidden, with all the risk that such a decision threatened us with, both because of the efforts that the heretics were to employ against us and because of our white colour giving us away. For this purpose, since there was no other province any nearer to the sea than that one, it was necessary for me to go to the province of Saraoe to negotiate the matter with some powerful men in that land, friends of mine, as I did, leaving for that province, with a Father as my companion, where I discussed and concluded the matter to our satisfaction. Because there were sixteen Fathers remaining in Fremona, nine of them came to the place where I was, and for greater dissimulation the lord of that land,[1] not the one who was to keep us

[1] Le Grand's text identifies him as Yohannes Akay, 'who had been holding out against

hidden, treated us at first with courtesy and good words but afterward treated us very poorly indeed and, being a miserly, evil man, caused us trouble and suffering on many occasions. We built some thatched huts in a field where we lived close to a certain village of heretic country-folk, surrounding ourselves with brambles in order to avoid attacks by thieves and wild animals, since the land had an abundance of both, which obliged us to keep constant watch throughout the nights, dividing the quarter-watches among us. The season was that of Lent, during which our daily fare consisted of a few lentils made into a kind of mush and some cakes of a sort of poorly cooked rye-bread, of which we did not have enough for our needs; so that, to sustain us, we had to sell the very clothes we were wearing, making from them various pieces of cloth such as it was possible to make from such material. In exchange for these we procured a small quantity of grain, which we ate toasted over the fire, or a little barley, the flour of which was a tastier treat.

The common country-folk of the land came to hold me in high repute as a doctor, thinking that that was my profession, and coming to ask me for remedies, which I distributed liberally and authoritatively according to the instructions in a handbook I had; and I did not disdain the art of gaining some profit from it if those who sought my advice were returned to health because of it. On one occasion, a man suffering from asthma, very severely afflicted with it, came to ask me for a remedy, which he wanted to be one which would quickly make him vomit that encumbrance he felt in his chest and which was keeping him from breathing. It was very difficult for me to persuade him that the cure for that illness was a much slower one. For a good beginning he offered me a sheep and two *alqueires* of wheat, all of which served us for Easter and was a wonderful help to us in our trouble. As my part of the bargain I did the very best I could according to what the art had taught me and what the land could provide to restore him to health. Although there was a dearth of many of the things that could be of use to him, there was one item in abundance and very much available, namely, syrups of goat urine taken in the morning on an empty stomach, which he took for a few days, which could not fail

the Abyssinians for a long time in the province of Bar. He received us with every kindness and had us taken to Adicota, which is a steeply scarped rock three leagues from his residence'. Bar means the province of the Bahrnagash, i.e. the maritime province, of which the capital was Debarwa. Adicota is Addi Cotadù, a hill within sight of Debarwa, *Guida*, 1938, p. 233.

to bring him the desired result. He took them very well and I increased the dosage so that he knew he was taking something.[1] I do not know whether or not these dosages were of benefit to him. I only know that the payments did not continue, although I must say that what he had already brought was ample payment for the remedy. He disappeared one day and I saw nothing more of him, for which I was not sorry, for fear lest my professional skill be discredited, with which I know not whether he was well or poorly satisfied. I only say that as far as the remedy is concerned he should have been extremely well satisfied.

In the meantime, the said lord of the land, who had given us protection, was distrustful of us, expecially because we had not brought him the large bribes he wanted from us, and made us leave the place where we were lodged and go to the village where he lived, more than three leagues from there. The weather was the hottest of the year, the Lenten fast-days, during which they abstain even from water all day long until sunset, when they begin to eat, our fasting being what I have described earlier, which, added to the toil and heat of the road, was extremely troublesome and much more so because the shelter they gave us was in a stable, only half of which, unfortunately, was then inhabited by the cattle, so that half of it was for those animals and half for us. We spent many days in this suffering and affliction, changing from one place to another, never improving our lodgings, however, so that I know not how it was that the oxen and cows did not lodge a complaint against us for continually dispossessing them of their dwellings. The last one was even worse than the previous ones and we all surely would have ended our days in it if we had stayed there very long; for, without going into more details, this other stable was in a very remote location, lacking everything necessary to life and without any possibility of our buying anything anywhere. Because this change had brought us to an extremely desperate state, I prevailed upon my old friendship with the said lord and went to find him and ask him to provide a better, more appropriate stable for us. Since I found him engaged in a rather singular occupation, I shall take this opportunity to report it.

The man to whom I was to address my petition had many good and virtuous qualities, but one characteristic of his was that he was extremely greedy, and to satisfy this greed he would search for gold in any place indicated to him. Because it was a tradition that in a certain

---

[1] *não ficava em jejum*, a double entendre, meaning both 'He was not fasting' and 'He knew exactly what he was taking'.

place about three leagues' distance from his dwelling there was a certain treasure that many of his forebears had been unable to discover despite all their attempts to do so by digging there, he wanted either to determine that the treasure was non-existent or to satisfy himself of its existence, which latter alternative he considered more certain, for his heretical monks told him that now was the time to find it because the demon who had prevented the earlier searchers from discovering it was far away from there, had lost a leg, was blind in both eyes, was mourning the death of a son, had a daughter who was one-eyed and ailing, and thus was unable to come to prevent any work he might undertake to discover the treasure. To all these fables and this nonsense he lent so gullible an ear and was so thoroughly convinced by them that he not only considered it absolute fact but undertook the work with complete certainty that he would be successful – to such a state had this poor man been reduced by his barbarous greed, ignorance and stupid blindness. For the ceremony he assembled many monks who were to be in attendance and were to keep singing as long as the work was in progress. Among the monks he summoned there was one over a hundred years of age, reputed to be a great saint, a famous hermit, totally blind and so crippled that he was unable to move, his skin all shrivelled, nothing but skin and bones. He had only his voice with which to deceive, and arrogance and self-conceit to so high a degree that he supposed that he alone, with his prayers, was sufficient to obtain the hidden treasure from God. Consequently, when he learned that other monks had also been summoned to sing and perform the ceremony, he insisted that either he would not go if others were going or he would go alone because he alone was more than sufficient. And because he was respected as a great saint, they accepted the condition that he be taken alone; and he rode on a horse, enveloped in black sheepskins which served him as a suit of clothes. For the celebration they also took a great quantity of beer, toasted grain and a beautiful black cow, all of which were necessary for the purpose of the treasure, much more so, however, for blind superstitious people, diabolical sorcery, idolatry, abominable sacrifice and adoration of the devil; and their monks and blind schismatics found nothing in this work to prick their consciences but rather approved and authorized it with their presence and their music. When they arrived, two hundred men with their tools for digging were already waiting. The place was under a huge rock, and since it was on the slope of a mountain, they were to dig at the foot of it until it rolled down the mountain, after which, according to their books and the affirmations of their learned men best versed in them, gold was to flow down so copiously and impetuously that it would flow into a certain famous river which ran near there at a distance of half a league, so that they found no difficulty in the existence of a river of gold, as though it were flowing water. The most ludicrous thing about it was that rumour of the treasure brought countless people, each hoping to carry off his share in sufficient quantity to relieve him of poverty forever. The lord of the land, the convener and director of the celebration, was so apprehensive that those who had gathered would carry off a great quantity that he stationed himself on the rock and did not allow the people to come close to it, furnished as they were with leather bags, each of which, filled, would have provided its owner with enough gold to free him from poverty.

When I arrived, the work was in progress, arranged as I have described. The people were digging furiously, inspired by the hope of reward, the monk was off to one side, singing and chanting more valiantly than his age and strength should have permitted, the sun was doing its work and each of the workers was doing his, while the organizer of it all watched over them all and the old monk kept up his singing, sizzling in the sun. I was watching from the side, marvelling and feeling compassion because of the ludicrous mockery the devil was perpetrating on those poor people. The work continued until four o'clock in the afternoon with not a sign of what they all desired. And although I wanted to take leave of the Xumo, which was the title they used in referring to the lord of the land, requesting the desired answer to my petition to remove my companions from the place where he had exiled them, their continued presence there being certain to bring death to all of them in a few days, it was not possible to present my petition because his greed and delusion did not leave an opportunity for it. I did remind him, however, that if the treasure were not discovered, as he was certain it would be, the deceitful old monk deserved at least thirty lashes from a strong hand, since his age and physical condition would not allow more, because of his blame-worthiness in crediting so fictitious a thing and the dishonour he brought upon himself in authorizing and participating in the sacrilege of making sacrifices to the devil. His greed and blindness, however, did not allow him to observe or recognize any of these things. At about five o'clock there was great rejoicing among the diggers because at the very base of the rock one of the mattock blows uncovered a hole, which must have been the abode of some rodent. They immediately came forth with the black cow, beheading it in front of the hole, which was no less than sacrificing it to the demon, whom they believed to be lord of that place and its treasure. Quickly skinning it and cutting off a slice from a thigh, they singed it in the fire and perfumed the hole with its incense by placing it in the said hole in order to permeate it with that sweet scent. And since meat must be accompanied by bread and wine, they scattered toasted grain and beer over all of that place to the applause of the spectators, the rest of them eating the remainder of the black cow. The hopes for the gold increased and each person was in readiness, expecting the river of gold to burst forth at any moment. The Xumo was in a state of great agitation on the rock, watching with the utmost vigilance and ordering everyone to keep at a distance so that he could more easily have his share. As night was about to fall, lo and behold, the rock gave indications that it was going to roll down the mountain, which it did, and to this day no fountain of gold has sprung forth, to the amazement of all, the great regret of the Xumo, the shame, if they have any, of those who affirmed it, but none on the part of the old monk, for he saw nothing, having to attribute their lack of success to the lack of faith of those present, who, one after another, returned to their houses, their expenses having gone for naught and with their leather bags as empty as when they had brought them.

After the treasure had been shown to be non-existent, I undertook my mission of obtaining a decision concerning my companions and even an improvement over their having to go from one stable to another, for I found the Xumo in a receptive mood. I was fortunate enough to obtain everything I asked for, good fortune, in this case, being aided by a certain bribe we agreed upon, the nature of which was dictated by our poverty and our protector's ignoble greed, for he had to be content with one of our cloaks, which was not a very new one, two small silver communion vessels and two ounces of gold. In exchange for this he permitted us to return to the place where we had been first, in the first village and dwelling-place, where each one of us took up his abode again in his thatched hut which we found still standing, returning to those huts as Lent was coming to an end. The Lenten season was extremely difficult for us because the little food we had, as I have related earlier, could not be eaten before sunset, for the daily fasting is observed until that time among those people and is a very natural thing for them, as I have said before. They are so scrupulous in observing their fasting that they say mass and give communion to the laymen only after sunset, for they believe, in their ignorance, that they would be breaking fast with the sacramental species if they were to say mass and give communion any earlier. They placed us under guard, however, the inhabitants of the village watching us by day and people from the surrounding area taking turns guarding us at night.

CHAPTER 25

[Concerning the difficulties we experienced until being handed over to the Turks]

At this time the other companions remaining in Fremona had left that village and were now under the protection of that friend of mine with whom I had made arrangements for them.[1] The Emperor had been informed of this and, on the advice of the heretics, ordered a great minister of his, a zealot in his religion, who was coming with many forces in the company of the newly-appointed Viceroy, to seek out all of the Fathers in order to take them into custody and hand them all over to the Turks, all except for Father Jerónimo.[2] This person was, of course, my poor unfortunate self, and it was the Emperor's order that either I alive or my head should be brought to his court, for he feared that, if I were to reach India, I would return to Ethiopia bringing Portuguese forces with me, because his soothsayers had so prophesied.[3] The Patriarch and the Superior informed me immediately of the decision, for they had learned of it by an entirely trustworthy warning from some Catholics who were at court, and ordered me to keep myself in hiding. This was an easy matter as far as my own person was concerned, but the nine companions who were with me would suffer because of it. And although the danger facing me was more obvious, if I were to fall into the hands of the royal minister, than that which could be feared by my companions, I resolved nonetheless not to increase their risk for the sake of my own safety but rather to risk whatever might happen by not abandoning them, unless someone could be found to hide us all. And although the latter course was more difficult, God did not fail to reward the diligence and will with which

---

[1] The Patriarch and the other priests who had stayed in Fremona escaped by night on 5 March and placed themselves under the protection of Yohannes Akay.
[2] The Emperor ordered Yohannes, Shum of Sarawe, and one Melka Krestos to conduct the Fathers to the Mareb river, where they were to be handed over to the Bahrnagash who was to take them to the Turks at 'Adecamô', presumably the Addi Chianò of *Guida*, 1938, p. 234.
[3] The new Viceroy was ordered by the Emperor to secure Lobo, alive or dead, and Yohannes Akay was made Bahrnagash on condition that he handed over the Fathers to the Turks.

Plate VIII. Homestead in Tigre

I sought the accommodation. And thus, on the night of Low Sunday, the only night when we were not guarded, and when our guards in the nearby village were oblivious to the world from sleepiness and wine, for this is the principal feature of any and all holidays or celebrations, we all slipped away quietly to a certain safe place where the rest of our companions were. Each one left as best he could, while I remained behind to accompany one of the Fathers[1] who, being old, tired, and frightened by the weather and the darkness of the night, which made travelling very hazardous, especially in one place about half way to our destination, where we had to traverse an area of very thick undergrowth, this elderly Father, as I say, was much in need of company and assistance, which I provided, much to my own cost; for, as he was supporting himself on my shoulder and arm in order to be able to travel, I was unfortunate enough to fall headlong down a gully of undergrowth, stones, and thorns, praising God that I was able to come out of it with no more than lacerations and abrasions in many places and the skin torn from my right arm and hand, which was a great help for the dangerous situation and travel which we were beginning. The wound, although large and more painful and frightening than dangerous, could be treated only with a handkerchief with which I bound up the skin and hand, which sufficed to heal it, for there was no other remedy available, although it did not heal for days.

We reached the people who were waiting for us as best we could. When they saw that there were so many of us, for our group consisted not only of the Fathers but also some young men accompanying us, they set up a clamour for more gain than they had originally stipulated. Having first agreed upon one ounce of gold, they insisted that it now had to be seven ounces, a tent and one of the mules on which we were riding, all of which we had to give them. Setting out again on our journey, we travelled the rest of the night until 8 o'clock in the morning, always through thick undergrowth, at which time we concealed ourselves in the undergrowth to rest, as we did. And since we were in need of some relief, a drink made of water and a little barley flour was dropped to us from Heaven, as they say, for we were provided with this refreshment when we needed it. After a few hours of rest, we were beset by another greater trouble, which was that a brother [sic], as payment for what he was secretly bringing us, also demanded his reward. Unless we paid him, we could not continue our journey;

---

[1] António Fernandez the elder, who was 80. Le Grand: 'I obeyed and left on the night of 24 April with one companion.'

and, since we were in no condition for further quarrels, we had to give him another mule, another 7 ounces of gold and a small tent we still had in our possession.

From there we continued our journey, travelling at night and always keeping ourselves hidden in the undergrowth in the daytime, with tigers and lions and various other wild animals coming to visit us as though we were transient guests of theirs and they were giving us the hospitality of their land and homes. One evening we began to see a mountain from which a spacious valley could be seen, through which we necessarily had to pass. However, we could see about three hundred elephants, large and small, which were grazing in that field and were coming across the road we were following. The sight of those wild animals and the meeting with them certainly cast doubt upon our passing through there, which was all the more perilous because these animals are especially ferocious and cruel when many of them are travelling together and when they have their females and young with them, which was then the case. The worst of it was that there was no possibility of our turning back, for we were fleeing from the hands of the heretics who were at our heels. Remaining where we were was more disadvantageous because we had nothing to eat and no possible source of anything, in addition to which the distance we had to traverse was so great that, in order to cover it, it was necessary to travel from 4 o'clock in the afternoon all through the night until 8 o'clock in the morning of the next day without ever taking any rest. The obvious danger from those wild animals certainly caused us great fear, but considering all the alternatives, we judged that the least of the evils was to press forward taking all the risk and trusting in God, rather than delaying our journey, because it was essential that we pass through a land of hostile brigands that very night so that they would not learn how close we were and attack us, catching us on the road. Therefore, commending ourselves to God, we descended the mountain and took the road across the valley, approximately half a league wide, making as much haste as we possibly could, expecting at every step to meet the elephants and the fate reserved for each of us, but it pleased God that either they had passed through quickly, even though they had been very widely dispersed, or they had taken another road, failing to cross ours. And we were not yet completely out of danger, since we were still in the last part of the valley, when those who were accompanying us, as these people are extremely superstitious, made us stop, we being ahead of them, and ordered us to dismount. We feared that their intentions in giving us this order were more sinister than they afterward proved to be, for we thought they at least intended to rob us of the little we still possessed, both the people and the place giving ample reason for us to believe this or something much worse. When I asked their usual spokesman to tell us why we were stopping, he said they were doing so because they had heard a bird singing on the left and it is their custom to interpret this as such an evil omen that they will not continue on their way until they hear the same bird or another one singing on their right. We had to obey, all of us dismounting, not unmindful of the consideration that we could still be visited there by the elephants and experience the effects of their ferocity, from which until then, through God's mercy, we had escaped. We were forced, however, to be patient until we should be favoured by the second omen, because of the belief held by our masters. As we were being detained for a long time, it occurred to me to pretend that a bird had just sung on the other side, and my going joyfully to their spokesman and asking a reward from him for the good news of this fortunate happening was enough to allow us to continue our journey. At nightfall we arrived at some wells from which we drew water which served us as afternoon meal, supper and almost as an advance dinner, as this refreshment lasted us all night long until the next day at 8 o'clock without our accompanying it with anything else. When it was dark, we were traversing the dangerous land, all the more perilous because we went so close to the brigands' village that the dogs caught our scent and set up a clamour with their barking. Heaven willed, however, that no one came out. On the following day, as I say, we reached the place where the rest of our companions were, on a high mountain and a very inhospitable land devoid of all the necessities of life but safe from outside enemies if not from the ones who were with us, who spared us, not because of any good will they had for us but only because of their respect for the man who was keeping us hidden there.

We stayed for a few days in this solitary place. Because we had a presentiment of trouble, we began to pair off in various directions. When two other Fathers and I were about to go to a certain safer, more solitary place, the treachery of the man who was protecting us descended upon us and caused us to move to another place. As we were starting out for that place, we saw that a large number of people were gathering, carrying only walking staffs in their hands and leather bags under their arms. Moving hurriedly toward us, they were going to overtake us at a certain narrow place, through which we would have to pass. I curiously asked where those people were going; and I learned, by pressing my inquiries with greater curiosity, that they were going to wait for us and rob us, all the people of the land gathering to have a share in what they could get from us, each of them bringing his leather bag to carry off his share, just as they had done on the occasion of digging for the treasure. And they soon gave indications of their intentions as they began to harrass some people who were going ahead; and they doubtless would have despoiled us of everything including even our clothing, which they could have done with impunity, if some friendly people had not appeared and come to our defence. By arguing and entering into agreements, we settled that we would give them a certain amount and that they would allow us to pass unharmed, and we had to give it to them to avoid greater troubles. We finally reached a more convenient place, capable of providing us with some food and sustenance, certainly no more elaborate than was sufficient to sustain life. It was of such quality that, after we finished eating a little bread, we were intoxicated by it in such a way that it all was soon regurgitated, leaving our stomachs empty. One time I felt extremely nauseated because of the poor meal, and, as I was vomiting uncontrollably, one of the natives who saw me from a distance and professed friendship for me came up to me and congratulated me on the great quantity of wine I had consumed, since I had got drunk on it; for they consider any opportunity of that type a stroke of great good fortune. He asked me where I had got it, to which I answered truthfully what had happened and told him of the poor quality of the bread which had caused it. He did me the favour of inviting me for a tasty afternoon meal, which was truly the best one, as well as dinner and supper, that I had had for many days. It consisted of milk that was curdled but very sour and toasted barley flour, which was like bran, and, moistened as it had been with hot water, was half dry, half mildewed, which, with a little butter on it, makes an excellent food for geese, although I considered it a great treat, as did the man who gave it to me; and in truth it served us as a great feast for several days. The days were few, however, for our master soon sent us warning that we should prepare ourselves because he wished to take us to the sea to be handed over to the Turks, according to the Emperor's order. No matter how strongly we reminded him of the promise he had made us to keep us under his protection as his *Acobam*[1] according to the custom of the land, we were unable to deter him.

---

[1] Eth. and Tigrinya '*ĕquban*, 'those guarded over'.

The custom called *Acobam* is in very common use among these people. It provides that, when any person finds himself persecuted, even by the Emperor himself, he goes to one of those lords and tells him that so-and-so is persecuting him and so he is asking the lord to take him as his *Acobam*, meaning 'under his protection'. The lord must do this without fail and immediately inform his *Acobam's* opponent that he has become his protector and, as such, must act as the judge of the grievance between them and any persecution done to his *Acobam* is done to the said lord, and he may by no means hand over his *Acobam* to the opponent and is even obliged to defend him with his life. The protection of this man, finally, is like a haven and a sacred place of refuge. It was not so for us, however, as breaking all customs, he took us away to be handed over to the Turks. Our journey took us through a wilderness where some days were frightfully hot and the place extremely close and stifling, for we always travelled in valleys with many trees which, although they protected us from the rays of the sun, could not prevent its great heat from oppressing us. Our food, when at its daintiest, was the famous toasted barley flour, which they call *bessou*[1] and, which does, I must admit, provide refreshment and great nourishment. We slept on the ground and right on the grass so as to be cooler but with the fear of a possible visit from one of the large, loathsome, poisonous scorpions found there. In the daytime we travelled surrounded by soldiers and at night we were guarded so closely by them that, wherever we bedded down, we could not move ten or twelve steps outside of that place, for the soldiers on guard would drive us back with a volley of stones. And truly, I did well to escape a hefty charred log that was thrown at me when I least expected it, absent-minded and preoccupied at a short distance from where the others were and it brought me back to my senses more quickly than a rooster's crowing would have done, and I returned to our place more hastily than I had left it.

While the Turks were not arriving to take delivery of us, though they had already been sent for, our master kept relieving us of whatever poor possessions we still had so that when the delivery was accomplished we were so light and free of cares, as far as anything of any value was concerned, that the Turks had very little indeed they could take from us; for both he and his servants kept demanding things they saw or suspected we had and took whatever caught their fancy, even the mules on which we were travelling, so that we finally were all on foot. One

[1] Amh. *bässo*, toasted barley somewhat diluted, forming lumps rather than a single mass.

day before we met the Turks, we almost lost our lives to five elephants we saw by chance as they were sheltering themselves from the sun's rays in the shadow of a rock. One was of enormous size, while each of the four others, though smaller, was of good size. And as they were a stone's throw away from where we were travelling, we went closer to have a better look at them. As long as we did nothing to provoke them, they gave no sign of ferocity. However, as soon as one of the bolder youths intentionally hooted at them, they went into a diabolical fury. The large one raised his trunk straight up in the air, looking like a huge beam, and, as if it were playing a horrendous, fine trumpet, it began to trumpet with so thunderous a voice that it resounded through the whole valley and pained our ears. Meanwhile the four others kept turning around the large one as if to work themselves into a rage and, after a few turns, they all rushed to attack us, with such impetus that if it were not for some high riverbanks separating them from us, they would soon have been upon us, to our woe. We were running for safety as fast as each of us could, although, if they were to cross the river banks, we could never have reached safety if God had not favoured us with that impediment, giving us good warning never again to come so close to such tusks as we did on that occasion.

CHAPTER 26

[Concerning what happened with the Muslims of Massawa and Suakin]

On the following day after ten o'clock in the morning, we found ourselves in a relatively cool river-meadow, where the Turks were awaiting us. We had a short period of rest before being delivered to the Turks, which was done just as though we were cattle for slaughter, all of us being counted, for it was indeed for the purpose of slaughter that the Abyssinians were handing us over and the Turks were receiving us. We were well aware of the agreements, but placing our trust in God, we were awaiting the disposition of His divine will, happy to accept whatever fate was in store for us. At two in the afternoon, they put us on camels and we began to make our way to Maçuá.[1] There were about eighty Turks, all with matchlocks, who had come to receive the prize. They formed a vanguard and rear guard and kept us in the middle for greater security, although the territory through which we were travelling was so uninhabited that we had nothing but wild animals to fear. We stopped for the night at the place where darkness overtook us, where the captain of the Turks, called Sardali, taking pity on our wretched state because of his kindly nature or perhaps he was preparing some trick motivated by greed in hopes that we would courteously give him something in return –, he had a treat prepared for us, inviting us to drink cava,[2] which is a drink made from a certain seed like beans, which, toasted and ground, is put into boiling water which it changes into something much like chimney-soot water. This

---

[1] They were handed over to the Turks on 20 May, though the Patriarch protested at the breach of faith and reminded the Ethiopians of what they owed to the Portuguese. Besides the Patriarch and his attendants, those handed over were PP. Carvalho, Lobo, Marques, Matos, and the two Fernandez. Those who stayed behind, all of whom were to meet a violent death, were D. Apolinar de Almeida, Bishop of Nicaea *in partibus*, and PP. Bruni, Cardeira, Franceschi, Gaspar Pais, Pereira, and Rodrigues. Le Grand says the Turkish commander treated them with much kindness and humanity and seemed to pity their wretched state.

[2] Arabic *qahwa*, Turkish *kahve*, coffee, already well known in the Ottoman empire, but only just beginning to be known to Europeans. Among the first Europeans to drink and describe it were the Jesuits Pêro Pais (Pedro Paez) and António de Monserrate during their captivity in Hadhramaut in 1589, when they were trying to reach Ethiopia.

is poured into small china cups and must be sipped slowly because it is extremely hot.[1] The taste is slightly bitter, and it has the effect of fortifying the stomach and providing sustenance during the day. Their use of this drink and the attachment they have for it are so great that they can never be in conversation or do business without a *chávana*[2] at their mouths, for that is the word they use for the china cup from which they drink it. And when any guest comes, the first thing immediately following the first 'God save you' is that they give him one of these *chávanas* to drink. Sardali followed this custom with us, and, after he had entertained us in this way, which was no small favour considering our wretched condition, we spent the rest of the night awaiting what would happen to us on the following day when we would be entering Maçuá, where we arrived on camels at ten in the morning, the sorriest-looking, most ragged figures imaginable and, as such, were greeted with a thousand mockeries and shouts of derision, especially by the young boys, and it was only through God's mercy that they did not receive us with stones and old shoes. Although they spared us those, they did not spare us all sorts of bad names and other insulting words, which we the more willingly endured since they did not raise their hands against us or attack us bodily.

The place we entered is a stronghold, like a fortress, which the Turks have at a distance of two leagues from the island, made of stone and clay with its walls and ramparts and some small artillery pieces, all for the defence of certain nearby wells from which all the water used on the island is transported daily. Since the place is suited for it, there are some gardens there in which a few varieties of produce are grown: lemons, citrons, the best watermelons in the world and some sugar-cane. We entered the ground-plot of the fortress and, after we had dismounted, they ransacked all the rags we were wearing, thinking that all the gold in Ethiopia would be in them, according to the information the Abyssinians had given them. We went up to visit the Amir who is the governor of the island or lieutenant of the Baxá. In the meantime, by his order, they made a thorough search for what there was, and, despite all the diligence they could employ, they could find nothing more than two chalices we still had hidden, one mine and the other the Patriarch's, and, on the Patriarch they found two pectoral crosses of little material value but extremely valuable as relics, something in

---

[1] Le Grand says that the Turkish commander offered them coffee, 'which we drank and in which we took no great pleasure'.

[2] Also *chávena*, a tea- or coffee-cup, from Malay *chawan*.

which they were less interested. And since they were being so thorough
in searching everyone, I thought it politic, before I was frisked, to hand
over as many as six *venezianos*, which are gold coins like *escudos*,[1] that
I still was carrying with me as well as a few more that other Fathers
had and which we had been using for sustenance. The impression made
by my courtesy and liberality was so favourable to me that, when they
got to frisking our persons rigorously and minutely, they did not
concern themselves with me, saying that I had already given what I had.
The Turks were astonished at not finding what the Abyssinians had told
them to expect, seeing clearly that we did not have it. On the one hand
the frustration of their hopes for booty caused their greed to explode
into furious anger, while on the other hand they had obtained ample
proof of our poverty and of the deceit and wickedness of the
Abyssinians who had tried to make us appear odious to them and
irritate them against us. After they had completed their inspection of
us, they sent us to the house of a Hindu friend of ours, where we rested
for the remainder of the day until the next evening, when they made
us embark for the island for greater security until they could decide
what to do with us. We arrived at midnight, and they even frisked
us again, but this time with no profit whatsoever, after which they sent
us to a house where we were kept in virtual imprisonment. We retired
there in the company of so many poisonous lizards and vermin, in
which that climate abounds that, in addition to the nausea caused us
by their multitude and appearance, the noises they made kept us from
sleeping.

On the day following our arrival, I had a message from a Portuguese
lad who served me, whom I had sent on a certain errand and whom
they had waylaid and taken into captivity as a slave under contract for
25 years. They had taken him to be sold on the island and from there
to be resold to the Arabs, who were great traders in this kind of
merchandise. He was indeed on the point of being resold and was in
the meantime being held prisoner in a house when he sent to me for
help. I was able to procure his release, although it proved to be at greater
expense than I thought; for I had entrusted the negotiation to a Jew
turned Turk who was there and who spoke Spanish as well as I speak
Portuguese and I do not know what this man said to the governor who
had made himself the owner of the lad and who sent me word that
he was sending him to me and that I should immediately send him

[1] By *venezianos* are meant Venetian ducats or sequins. The gold *escudo* was worth four
cruzados.

sixty *patacas*. I found myself embarrassed by this decision and responded that the price was high and requested that he set a more favourable price and that he allow me time to seek the money in alms. This message, or whatever the Jew saw fit to say to him, was given to him in the fortress town[1] two leagues away from the island, where we first entered. As the Turk was extremely cruel and greedy, he flew into an uncontrollable rage, and, embarking for the island, came swearing to have me given two hundred lashes if I did not hand over the sixty *patacas* to him immediately. He sent me this message immediately upon his arrival with a fury and passion equal to the hatred for Christians and the greed that were always burning in him. That poor fellow that I was found himself in great difficulty over sixty *patacas*, for I did not have three *reis* to my name. The Turk's will and determination were well known to me and I could be sure that he would order the two hundred lashes and that they would be administered by a strong hand and would be well counted, more rather than fewer, in accordance with the liberality of both the one who ordered them and the one who executed them when it came to this kind of payment, as we had had occasion to observe a few days earlier, when a brother almost eighty years of age who had gone into exile with us rather than place his faith in peril, a native Abyssinian who for having requested, without exceeding the limits of justice and courtesy toward the said Turk, that the governor give him a servant of his whom they were taking from him to make him a Muslim, was given the reply by the governor, roaring with rage, that he wanted to cut off his head with his own hands. And because they calmed him down to some extent, he ordered that he be beaten with two hundred lashes and, moreover, that they be administered by two Turks who stretched him out face down on the ground, giving him lashes all over his body with much industry, multiplication – one on each side of him – and cruelty with a horse-whip, a cruel instrument they call a *chabuco*.[2] With this instrument used in the same way, they intended to administer charity to me, for which I was already preparing myself because the governor gave me no more than half an hour before I was to deliver him the money, which I sought to borrow with the necessary haste, and it pleased God that I found it and handed it over, so that I escaped his fury. With this benevolence, we continued in our captivity with less trouble than we at first thought

[1] I.e. Arkiko.
[2] A word of Persian origin, originally meaning 'quick', but used for a whip in several languages, *HJ*, 1968, 'Chawbuck'.

we would have, and as for the implementation of the agreement concerning our death, this was not a matter to be decided by this man but rather by a brother of his called the Baxá, further up the coast on another island, from whom they were awaiting orders concerning what was to be done with us.[1] In the meantime the governor extracted from us almost by force more than six hundred *patacas*, both he, taking the largest share and his officers, obliging us to take loans for them, saying that it was the custom to give him some present, and the custom had to be observed. Meanwhile the order arrived from the Baxá that he should send us in some *gelvas* to the island where he was.

On Saint John's day they had us embark in two boats,[2] first making us give them our word that we would not tell his brother of the money he had taken from us, for he said that his brother was so cruel and greedy that he would take from his very own brother what he had got from us, adding that with that present we had begun to pay the ransom for our lives. It fell to my lot to go with the Patriarch and three other Fathers in one of the *gelvas*. A *gelva* is a certain type of a ship having no nails at all but rather wooden pegs. Its planks are sewn to one another with rope. It is one of those ships of which it can be said that the entire ship, just as it sets sail laden with merchandise and all its provisions comes from the palm-tree, so that the planking, mast, rope, sails, wooden pegs, thread with which the planks are sewn together, wine, vinegar, oil, water, cargo of coconuts, dates and something like bread which they call *puto*,[3] and copra, which is also part of the cargo, all these things come from the palm-tree, without any other tree contributing to any part of the ship or its cargo. The planking is made of the sawn trunk, as is the mast; from the leaves, the sails and sacks for the merchandise; from the fibrous outer shell of the coconut, the ropes and the thread; from the inner shell, spoons, cups, flasks, porringers; from the pith inside when still liquid before it thickens, that very sweet, refreshing, healthful water called *lanha*;[4] after it is congealed it becomes the coconut for cargo, and the pulp of it, allowed to dry becomes copra, a great cargo for many parts of India; much oil is also obtained from this copra, which is the principal oil used in India. From the coconut when grated and cooked is made something they call *puto*, which can serve as bread and whatever goes with bread. The wine is obtained from the palm-tree's cluster when the coconuts

---

[1] The Pasha at Suakin, which was the residence of the Beylerbey or governor of the Ottoman province of Habesh (Abyssinia).
[2] Le Grand says they were galleys.
[3] See p. 109 n. 1. [4] See p. 108 n. 5.

279

are about to be formed; by cutting the end of it, they cause a water to drip from it called *sura*,[1] which is very refreshing, sweet and wholesome, and when this substance is cooked it congeals into sugar; when distilled, however, it makes *anipa*,[2] a very strong wine similar to brandy, from which they also make vinegar, also very strong. In my discussion of the *gelva* and what it is, I have digressed to mention the advantages provided by the palm-tree, which each month produces a ripe cluster of forty, fifty or more coconuts. This type of ship cannot sail in heavy seas because of its fragility. It can sail in the Red Sea, however, since there are no severe storms there, and it is well adapted for navigation in that sea with its shoals because its planking, being sewn together, yields when it touches the rocks and does not suffer so much peril as the sturdier vessels with their planking nailed together, which immediately opens up and breaks.

Having embarked in this kind of ship, then, with our Turkish guards, we set our course for Suakin, another island where the Baxá was. The voyage took us forty-five days because of unfavourable weather, this delay bringing us great difficulties because the treatment we received on the *gelva* was that of captives and the arrogance and scorn with which the Turks treated us was what we could expect from persons of their character, religious faith, tyranny and cruelty. Victuals were in short supply and what there was was no more than a dish of poor rice or a sort of cake baked under embers with some dates they called *congos*, the driest and worst imaginable.[3] The *gelva's* sleeping quarters and space in which to spend the days were as uncomfortable and inadequate as they possibly could be. The winds continually blew in the wrong direction, at times, causing us great storms, all the more dangerous since the ship was so fragile, so that during some nights we were in obvious danger of perishing. The weather forced us to seek shelter ashore, where the land was exceedingly deserted, barren and hot. Under a thicket we got through the rigours of the heat and the searing heat of the Arceres or winds which I have mentioned earlier and which seem to have come from the flames of Hell.[4] Because these delays were making our voyage excessively long with consequent lack of food, and because the weather and monsoon which would enable us to embark for India in a ship that was at Suakin was being lost and we could make no progress because of the contrary winds, we decided, with the permission of our Turkish

---

[1] See p. 108 n. 3.   [2] The same as *nepa*, see p. 108 n. 4.
[3] Dates gathered and dried before ripening, Dalgado, 1919, I, 303.
[4] See p. 98 n. 1.

guards, to make use of a very small *gelva* which came upon us by chance, which, because of its small size, could continue up the coast. It was determined that one of us would go in the small *gelva* to Suakin and send camels and food by land for the others remaining behind. I was the one chosen for this journey, and it was with great trepidation that I embarked in a boat manned by Arab Muslims, arch-enemies of Christians and exceedingly treacherous. There were six of these Muslims on the *gelva*, into whose tender care I was delivering myself, placing all my trust in God and paying five *patacas* for hiring the *gelva*. They carried me to the boat on their shoulders and I did not fail to observe the merriment with which they carried me, thinking that this was what they usually do when they want to do something they particularly enjoy, which I believed was to offer me up as a sacrifice to their Mafoma, as I had already experienced with others of their religion, of whom I have spoken earlier, who intended to kill me in this way. However, since I had no other choice on this occasion, I placed myself in the hands of Divine Providence and boarded the *gelva* with them. I found the case, however, to be the very opposite of what I expected, for they treated me as if we were all of the same faith and they devout Christians, and I tried to respond to this courtesy of theirs by giving them some of my poor provisions, all of which consisted of no more than a little flour from which I made a cake baked under embers. We were sailing up the coast in this way, the Arabs now so friendly that they were offering me some of the cargo they were carrying, which consisted of beautiful tortoise shells and pearls. I took nothing from them, however. We reached a place, nevertheless, where we fished for a variety of oysters, both those that grow pearls but are never eaten and others for eating which are as large as any man's head, from which the Muslims obtained so much meat, which they ate, that I am sure it weighed between an *arratel* and a half and two.[1] The ones with the pearls were also large, each one of them being the size of two hands joined together and, when opened, were almost as smooth on the outside as the outer part of a cockleshell and of similar shape, and on the inside they were as beautiful as mother-of-pearl since that is what these shells are. When sailing was not possible, the Muslims passed the time fishing for pearls and in friendly conversation with me, which was all the more appreciated since it was entirely unexpected. We arrived at Suakin, followed by the other companions whom I had left behind in the other *gelva*, also finding seven Fathers already there, who had

---

[1] *arratel* from Arabic *raṭl*, approximately 1 pound avoirdupois, *HJ*, 'rottle, rattle'.

left from Maçuá and had separated from us, sailing for the same island in still another *gelva*, in which they had a little better fortune than ours.

They and we who had just arrived were received by the Baxá with every indication of his ill-will, hatred, tyranny and cruelty.[1] At the time the first group was arriving, he had intended to implement immediately the death sentence he had imposed on them, but he changed his mind after they had arrived and decided to wait for our arrival so that the sacrifice would be greater; for it was a saying of his that he desired no greater glory and honour before God and men than to kill and rid the earth of these *cafares*.[2] The word *cafar* is used among those people as the most abusive, vilest and most dishonourable of all names that can be used to insult a man, for it alone has all of the following meanings: man without faith, without law, without God, infamous, dirty, abominable, and every other word of this kind that can be thought of, for it includes them all. Our lives were in this danger and state when we arrived at Suakin, and after we had disembarked we were again searched in the custom-house for anything that we might be carrying with us. However, the Amir of Maçuá's diligence had been so thorough that he had left us with nothing with which his brother's greed could be satisfied. From there they sent us to a house where the other Fathers were kept in isolation as prisoners. It was a great consolation to see them even though we found them much afflicted by the idea of what could result from the sentence which the Baxá had pronounced concerning our lives, happy, however, to receive whatever fate God had in store for us. Although the tyrant did not immediately implement his decision, it was not because of any lack of will to do so but rather because of his greedy desire to ascertain first if he could get some money from us, since he still had the power, place and time for whatever else he might order concerning us. A few days after our arrival, therefore, he sent us word that his decision was to order us to be killed but that he was commuting our deaths for a good ransom with which we could purchase our lives and which he had fixed at thirty thousand *patacas*.[3] The barbarian came to this decision for several reasons: many *sodagares*,[4] who are Turkish merchants of the Muslim faith, were about to leave for India and doubtless would have to pay heavily in merchandise and in their own persons for the evil he would have perpetrated upon us. Also, by killing us he would make an outlaw

---

[1] Probably Mostarli Mustafa Pasha, Orhonlu, 1974, p. 183.
[2] *kāfir*. See p. 101 n. 2.
[3] Le Grand's text says 30,000 *escudos* (écus).   [4] Persian *saudāgar*, 'merchant'.

of himself as far as those merchants were concerned and would immediately be breaking off commerce with India, for the ships come to his port from India and would be prevented by the Portuguese from continuing to do so. He also would be running the risk that the Portuguese would come with a large fleet to demand an accounting for our lives, which would mean total destruction for him and the rest of them. These considerations caused the tyrant to reconsider his decision and to send us the message referred to above, to which I was the one to respond. I told the messenger that he should tell the Baxá, in the name of all of us, that as captives we did not have that abundance of money he was asking of us nor even a much smaller amount since we had been robbed here of everything we had, were very far from our homelands, and in the land where we found ourselves had no relatives or acquaintances to whom we could go for help, for which reasons, not excusing ourselves from seeking alms with which to give him something as a present, as was customary, his present would necessarily be limited by the means we had at our disposal, and that, as for what he was demanding, it was impossible for him to obtain any such amount from us. The messenger went back with the reply and soon returned with the same proposals, but lowering the price to twenty thousand *patacas*. I however gave him the same reply I had given before, and he again returned, but this time with a message which was much heavier in determination although lighter in the amount of money it was demanding, in which the Baxá told us that he had settled upon fifteen thousand *patacas* and that if we did not agree to this, he lacked neither knives to flay us nor scimitars to cut us into pieces nor stakes on which to impale us. And as we were well aware of the temper, resolve, and practical results of that man's ferocity, all of which had been amply demonstrated to us by fresh examples, his reply did not fail to cause us concern, for he would as easily order a man to be flayed or put on a stake and placed in the sun as drink a cup of water; and whenever he wanted to extract money from the Hindu merchants, he would order them to be put in a house and, demanding so many thousand *cruzados* from them, with no more justification than his own greed, would tell the merchant that he would flay him, and matching threat with deed, would begin with the feet and would continue until the poor wretch agreed to give him what he demanded, whether he had it or not, trusting that he could obtain it through alms. The Hindu Banians[1] are so compassionate that they all contribute to supply the

[1] Hindu traders, especially Gujeratis.

required amount to save one of their people from suffering. This caused us to reconsider the matter, but we concluded that yielding to these threats would not be consistent with Christian valour, even if we were sure that they would be translated into deeds; that, even if we were to accede to the tyrant's demands, his nature was such that he would then increase the amount; and furthermore, that we would not promise something we could not deliver. And although the Hindus and Muslims offered it to us as a loan because they saw our lives in danger, we had no means of paying it back and therefore decided to give him the same answer as before, with the additional statement, concerning his latest threats of torture, that we had placed ourselves in the hands of God, that we were in the Baxá's hands by God's permission, and that he could do with us whatever he liked. With this message the dissatisfied emissary returned to the Baxá while we stayed making ourselves ready for the worst, certain that, at the very least, the tyrant would unleash his fury on some one of us; and since I was the one who was the spokesman in these questions, proposals, replies, and negotiations, I was sure that I would be first.

As soon as the tyrant received word of our resolve, he flew into a paroxysm of rage and would have ordered us to be killed immediately if some of his underlings had not intervened with arguments of self-interest, to which the tyrant was no less subject than to fury and cruelty. They managed to delay his decision for a few days, during which time his determination gradually softened. They also came to advise us to offer some moderate amount and offered to pay it for us immediately provided that we would repay it to them when we reached India. We finally settled on four thousand three hundred *patacas*, which were paid immediately, because the ship was about to set sail, with the agreement that the Baxá was to permit us all to go; for if this were not the case we would not agree to it, to which the Baxá replied that he was accepting the money and that we all could go. After the ransom was paid and we were ready to embark, two hours before we were to depart a message came from the Baxá summoning three *chebir*[1] Fathers, by which he meant three of the oldest and most important of the Fathers. The Patriarch and two other Fathers were obliged to go. He ordered them to be put in a house, after which he sent for the rest of us and had us taken into another house. His steward then came to speak to us, saying in the name of the Baxá that we could embark and that the three companions were remaining as hostages and

---

[1] Arabic *kabīr*, 'big', 'great', also used in several other languages.

would be released when a ship came the following year. And after various arguments and replies concerning the treachery of breaking the agreements they had with us, seeing that there was no way for us to recover the companions, as the Baxá gave us to understand that the rest of us owed our lives only to his kindness, and there was no doubt that we were fortunate to escape safely from his hands, I asked him on behalf of all of us to have them come there so that we could say farewell to them, to which the Amir agreed. After they arrived, as one of them was a Father almost eighty years of age with hair completely white, weary from the weight of years and sufferings,[1] I rose and said the following to the Baxá: 'It is not reasonable, with so many of us here who are stronger and younger that this elderly Father, without any blame of his own, should stay behind to suffer conditions inappropriate to his grey hair and weakened state when one of us can stay in his place; and moreover it is not to our interest for him to remain here as a hostage since he will doubtless die here within the year and the Portuguese will believe that you have killed him and his death will cause them to break off the peaceful relations and trade with you which this port has carried on for many years with India. Choose, therefore, from among those of us here who are leaving, the one you wish to remain and deliver this old man to us.'

The Amir was listening to me attentively and, looking at the Father and seeing his condition and how short a time he could be expected to live, said that he would willingly accept one of us and that we should take the old man with us. I offered to remain there myself, but the others did not consent to it. The lot fell to another of the companions.[2] And encouraged by my success in obtaining the release of this Father, I tried my luck in accomplishing the same thing for the Patriarch, but the Amir interrupted me immediately with an emphatic refusal and obliged us to embark at once, which we did with tears in our eyes and slept that night on the ship.

[1] António Fernandez the elder. Le Grand names the three who were detained. The other two were the Patriarch and Diogo de Matos.

[2] P. Francisco Marques, who stayed behind with the Patriarch, Diogo de Matos, three clerics and two servants of the Patriarch. They were eventually ransomed by a Father sent from Diu in May 1635 and reached Diu on 24 September.

CHAPTER 27

[Concerning our voyage from Suakin to Goa]

Setting sail in the morning, which was the 26th of August, the day of Saint Louis, King of France, and sailing with mild weather, on the 28th I awoke at dawn with a small sore on the little finger of my right hand. Thinking it was hardly anything, I tried to draw the pus out of it, but it grew so poisoned that it became a very dangerous infection, for it quickly spread over my whole hand. There was no medicine on the ship nor any place where I could retire. The pain was excessive, the more so because we slept on the half-deck exposed to the ill-effects of the weather, the worst place on the ship, so that we could say that we were travelling under the Muslims' feet, because all the servicing of the ship was done there, and day and night; the continual work of navigating it had to be done in the same place where we spent our days and nights with no other place to go except to occupy as little space as possible to oblige those who were walking over us. Our beds were the planks of the deck, our pillows some rope, sticks or boards, all of which together was of little help, really very prejudicial to the state in which I found myself, unable to sleep at night or rest during the day with the excessive pain. They soon gave evidence of how severe the infection was, for in a few days the finger was swollen beyond belief. The worst of it was that there were visible signs that the infection was turning into herpes, as those best acquainted with the disease considered this to be, for which there was no other remedy available than a little oil, with which I anointed it and suffered the pain, preparing myself for all the rest that could be expected to follow. God Our Lord, however, never sends a calamity without a means of enduring it, so that, at a time when there was no way whatsoever of stopping its progress and it was at its most dangerous stage, the infection began to diminish until it was completely cured, although my right hand was still somewhat incapacitated, so that I could not move it vigorously; and although the infection was never treated and has not recurred since that time, to this very day I still feel some slight pain in that hand.

The ship carried many people, most of them pilgrims to their accursed, detestable house, by which I mean that of Meca, where

Mafoma is buried.[1] Once these people have visited it, they receive from the Xarifes[2] there an indisputable pass to Heaven; and when they leave Meca in this sanctified state, nothing is more loathsome to them than to meet with Christians, for they believe themselves contaminated if they see or have any dealings with us, so pure in body and soul do they consider themselves when they leave that place. For this reason they very much begrudged our being on that ship, imagining that their purity would be spoiled by our presence there, for they avoided all communication or conversation with us, so that when they arose in the morning and their eyes were unavoidably struck by the sight of us, located as we were in so public a place, they would immediately spit in the other direction as if they had seen the vilest thing in the world, calling us a thousand foul names and heaping curses and imprecations upon us, which continued throughout the day for their amusement as they cleansed themselves, in their way, of the filth they had acquired from the sight of us, considering the abomination in which they held us. In the preparation of some cakes we caused to be made, a little wheat was boiled in a pot of water, in the same manner as one would cook rice, for wheat served us as rice. Because of their dread of being contaminated by anything associated with us, the Muslims would not tolerate having our food cooked at the same time as theirs lest a drop of the water boiling in our pot jump over into theirs, rendering their food unclean and making it impossible for them to eat it. It was therefore necessary for us to prepare our food either before they cooked theirs or after all of them had finished. The Captain, who was a Muslim of a race called in India *Nautea*, one of the worst there,[3] encouraged all of this by the ill-favour he showed us, whether because of hatred characteristic of his low caste and Muhammadan condition or because he wanted to please those of his sect. In any case, he behaved so badly toward us that some Muslims of better natural disposition came to us to express their condolences for the miserable state in which they saw us. In this way we were making our voyage toward the gates of the Strait.

At dawn of the eleventh day of our voyage, we came upon an island which is 14 leagues from the Strait and is a perennially active volcano. It is an almost round high rock, uninhabitable except by birds. Its summit rises to a point and is very steep on all sides. It is always smoking

[1] See p. 89 n. 3.
[2] Arabic *sharīf*, 'of noble descent', particularly a descendant of Muhammad; at this time the local rulers of Mecca were always Sharifs in this sense.
[3] Navayat, Muslims of mixed race from the Konkan and south Kanara, *HJ*, 'Navait'.

at the top and its fire is visible at night.[1] Since we were so short a distance from the strait, where all the danger is, we planned to pass through it at night; for, in addition to the usual risk because of the Turks from Moca who ordinarily have ships in that place to seize the ships entering it, we were warned as we were about to leave Suaquem that we would be awaited in that place by a pinnace and a galley of Turks sent especially by the Baxá of Moca to capture the ship from Suaquem because it had not gone to his port as it had promised to do the previous year. It is customary for those who want to avoid this danger to pass through the strait at night, and if they do so in the daytime, it can be done safely if there is a very good wind. Since we had very little wind, we wanted to ensure our safe passage by taking advantage of an island formed in the middle by the gates. There are two channels, the deeper and narrower one being on the Arabian side, the place where the pirates customarily lie in wait for ships entering and leaving because that passage is the most frequently used; and the other on the Ethiopian side, wider and shallower, with many sandbanks, almost all of which is full of hidden rocks, but leaving a small channel not very much frequented because it is so little known. We took the latter to avoid the pirates who were doubtless waiting in the other one. Although we were sailing with a good wind, and despite our constant watching for the island so as to be surer of having left the danger behind us, we could not catch sight of it until slightly after midnight. And just as we were rejoicing at having sighted it, we suddenly felt the wind die down, so that we spent the rest of the night, with hardly any wind at all, sailing along the two leagues' length of the island. After leaving the strait, we found ourselves, at sunrise, half a league out into the sea, still a very dangerous place, as we shall soon see. The Turks, being serious pirates, kept a sentinel at the highest point on the island. The fellow spotted us and signalled the pinnace and galley, which immediately came after us, the galley being propelled by its oars with the pinnace in tow, for we were then becalmed, there being no more wind for them than there was for us, the advantage, however, resting with the enemy because of the galley's oars, of which we had none. We soon caught sight of their boats, and, since we were totally becalmed, the Turks immediately considered us their prize, which we surely were if God did not come to our aid. The galley was being rowed at full speed, well-manned as it was by eighty white Turks, all of whom were soldiers eager for booty. It had three powerful pieces of

[1] Cf. p. 87 n. 1.

artillery at its prow as well as many other smaller ones on the head rails and bow-chaser. Since they considered us already in their power, they fired the three cannons from a distance, one after the other, as a signal for us to strike our sails. At this time we were all in a very dejected state, for we felt certain that the very best fate we could expect within half an hour, if we should escape with our lives, was to be condemned to rowing a Turkish galley. The Muslims prepared themselves, however, as best they could, to sell their lives dearly with their merchandise and by whatever other means they could find, being virtually certain that they could expect nothing from Turkish mercy. And as we continued in this anguish, with our sails hanging down as the wind left them, for we refused to obey the enemy's signal to strike them, it pleased God that, when our trust was at its lowest and our hopes had all but vanished because our enemies were so close to us, a fresh wind came up, which filled our sails and sent us on our way, putting so much distance between us and the galley that the Turks turned back in despair of obtaining the prize they had thought was surely theirs. And the prize would have been a good one indeed, for, in addition to the prisoners, for whom they would have received a goodly ransom if they spared their lives, the ship carried, among other merchandise, many large chests of gold coins called Venetians, called *Abrahen* by the Turks and Arabians and *sequins* by the Europeans,[1] and many other large chests of Spanish *patacas*, a coinage much used on that sea and which is more esteemed there than any other.

The sea that runs from the strait to the large ocean called the Indian Ocean is 150 leagues in length and is called the Sinus Arabicus. It ends at Cape Fartaque on the Arabian side and at Cape Goardafui on the Ethiopian side, being approximately 50 leagues wide at this its widest point. This Cape of Goardafui is the famous one called the Cape of Aromas, of which I have already spoken. The currents carried us so close to this cape that little by little we came within sight of it. We saw there a remarkable mystery of nature, for which we were unable to find any explanation: in the middle of that sea there were currents as violent as those of any river when it is most swollen and furious, even though there is no land there whence it could come and the rest

---

[1] The sequin was sometimes known simply as the Venetian, *HJ*, 'Venetian'. *Abrahen* represents *ibrāhīmī*, an Ottoman gold coin worth, according to the *Lyvro dos pesos* of António Nunes of 1554, 420 reis. The Ottoman mints sometimes counterfeited the sequin, F. Babinger, 'Contraffazioni ottomane dello zecchino veneziano nel XV secolo', *Aufsätze und Abhandlungen zur Geschichte Südosteuropas und der Levante* (München, 1962–76), II, 113–126.

of the sea is very quiet. This *agoajem*, as it is called, makes a great thundering sound as if it was hurling itself down and breaking over rocks.[1] This violently moving water is plainly visible in the middle of the other water which on either side remains as quiet as if it were a sand bar or *terra firma*. At the foot of this great promontory, we launched a small boat to fetch us a supply of water on land, for it was feared that the supply we had aboard might become exhausted because our voyage was becoming longer than expected. They brought it in leather bags and also simply poured it into the boat, where the Muslims washed their feet in it. With all the dirt and salt water mixed in with it, which either came from the boat itself or was splashed into it by the waves or by the hard rowing, we still would have considered ourselves fortunate to have a little of it, such as it was. However, we were denied this by the Captain, whose steadfast purpose, even in this, was to make our lives as miserable as he could, even though the ship carried a good supply. Since we now had little to lose, and since moderation and humility are of little avail with Muslims, as we had already experienced several times up to that point, on this occasion I said a few words to him concerning what we had experienced at his hands and of how everything he had done to us would have its due reward in Dio, which was our destination. The arrogant Muslim was taken aback and, although he roared with rage, he also understood that he had treated us badly and that he might well have to pay for it all, so that he had to restrain himself and treat us more courteously for the rest of the voyage, which required no small effort of will on his part. The voyage from there to Dio was slow for lack of good winds; for the monsoon was now almost at the Cape. God's will was finally served when, after a voyage of fifty-two days, we arrived at Dio, free of Dutch corsairs, with which the sea was infested, and two of whose ships were coming behind us, passing within sight of the fortress and coming in our wake.

The day after we anchored in the port, many boats, carrying both laymen and Jesuit Fathers immediately came out to receive us, and because they thought the Patriarch and Bishop were arriving, knowing they had been captured by the Turks, the custom-house officials and

[1] The word is now written *aguagem*, meaning a powerful current or bore. 'The East African coast current, as it branches eastward into the ocean southward of Socotra, is very strong in the south-west monsoon period, especially in July to September...Many currents with rates of between 4 and 5½ knots have been reported, with occasional observations of 6 knots and over, the maximum being one of exactly 7 knots. The rates of 6 knots and over are greater than those known in any other oceanic region', *Red Sea and Gulf of Aden Pilot*, 1955, p. 19. It will be remembered that Lobo had left Suakin on 26 August.

a man representing the Captain, Domingos da Camara, who was sick at the time, came out in *manchuas* replete with carpets and silk awnings to give us a joyous and courteous welcome. After they had reached the side of our ship, they made us come down, carrying us in their arms, with joy, amazement and tears: joy, because they saw us delivered from the hands of the Turks; amazement and tears, because of the condition in which they found us and because of the absence of the other Jesuits still remaining in captivity. Our physical condition and our clothing were pitiful; there was scarcely any one of us still wearing a shred of his black cassock; we were barefooted; the white breeches of the few who had them were in varying states of decomposition; our shirts and vests were only such because we called them so; our hair was long; our heads were uncovered; our beards were grown long; in short, we were in the condition of persons who had spent almost two years in constant danger of death, persecuted by the heretics, finally sold, delivered, condemned to death, ransomed from the Turks, scorned and reviled by the infidels who came with us and who, because of their holiness and loathing for us, were unwilling to set eyes on us, considering us as something abominable. Truly, our distressful state would have made a deep impression even on non-Christians. Those blessed with Christian piety, however, discovered in that abjectness and abasement the great worth of Christian piety and the high value that God places on it when one suffers in His service.

When the Muslims aboard the ship now saw us respected and welcomed with such great courtesy by the most important people in Dio, householders, captains and soldiers as well as the king's officials, for the fortress, in the belief that the Patriarch was with us, fired three artillery pieces in our honour as our barge passed in front of it, they were struck with astonishment and now wished that they had behaved differently toward us during the voyage, especially a Muslim *zodagar* who had been prominent as a mediator for our ransom at Suaquem. I stood up and went to find him among the others, and taking him by the hand, a thing which he now considered a great honour, but to which he would not have consented at any time during our voyage 'if I had wanted to do so, because of his desire to avoid contamination, I introduced him to the Custom-house judge, saying how honourable he was and how much he deserved the judge's favour in the Custom-house; to which the judge responded so favourably and kept insisting upon doing him so many favours that he had to be restrained from spending so much for him; but even so, he gave the Muslim more profits than the latter ever would have believed possible, much to the amazement and envy of the others.

We were heading for the wharf which, along with the beach, was crowded with people – Portuguese soldiers and inhabitants as well as an infinite number of Hindus, Muslims and heathen, who live in India and gather there because of the trade and the advantage afforded by the presence of the ships from Meca; and we disembarked on that same beach from which we had embarked ten years earlier for the Red Sea without a thought of our ever being able to return to it. And in truth, the experiences we had in all that time and the knowledge we had of the common experience of others who had exiled themselves to those provinces for that mission certainly gave no promise of our ever seeing Dio again. The vicissitudes of time, however, make anything possible and bring about many unexpected things. The most distinguished people in the city accompanied us to our college with the courtesy and compassion for our sufferings which their piety dictated to them. After we had entered our house, a very fine one we have there along with a church, which is the most beautiful and best constructed of all those we have in India, we rested in the college for a few days, after which we embarked in ships of the Gulf Fleet to go to our colleges in the north. We were distributed among various ships, mine being that of the Captain-Major.[1] All of the ships sailed straight to Goga in order for the Fleet to put a merchant caravan ashore in Cambaya. When we were near Goga, a city of Muslims, a monk died who was one of those who had exiled themselves from their lands, wishing to accompany us in our sufferings. This man was a good monk, nearly seventy years of age, of venerable appearance, very moderate and temperate in his actions, exemplary in his virtue, and so devout and constant a Catholic that, in order to avoid placing in jeopardy his Catholic faith to which he had been converted, he abandoned everything he owned, which was not inconsiderable because of his being Prior of one of their monasteries, an office held for life, not as a public thing but as personal property. He was extraordinarily patient, never showing the slightest sign of resentment in the height of the greatest sufferings in which we found ourselves, enduring everything with admirable equanimity of mind, serenity of face, with a smile on his lips, and, in his speech, the true portrait of a perfect Catholic. He is deserving of this special tribute to his person, and that is why I include it in this narration. God called

---

[1] Lobo was accompanied by Manoel de Almeida, who had recently arrived in Diu from Qishn, Beccari, 1903–17, VII, 329.

him at this time and occasion to give him the reward for his faith and sufferings. We buried this good old man and Catholic, with the grief and tears which were due to him and which were occasioned by the loss of so good and faithful a companion in our sufferings, giving him a resting place where he could await the signal of the wondrous trumpet on the fateful day, at the foot of a tree in an uninhabited place, a land of infidels; although any place is suitable for burial, especially for one who has certain expectation of redemption treasured in his breast, enjoying, as does his soul, the true reward for his faith.

As the fleet continued its voyage, after seeing Goga, we went off course to the coast of Surrate; and passing some Dutch ships anchored outside the cove, we sailed with great care and kept a constant watch for signs of their wanting to come attack us. The Captain-Major, Antonio Mourão de Oliveira, a great soldier and known as such in India, originally from Tentugal,[1] was prepared for any eventuality. We arrived at Damão, where we did not put into port, but lay at anchor just inside the bar awaiting the arrival from shore of a *ballão*[2] sent for by the Captain-Major. The Rector of our college came aboard with another Father, but he was so seasick, from the slight swelling of the sea or because he was unaccustomed to being on the water, that we were scarcely able to exchange greetings. Two days from there, we reached Baçaim, our voyage's destination, where we disembarked and were duly received by our Fathers there. Their Rector had an order to the effect that the Fathers coming from Ethiopia were to stay there until the Father Provincial should make further arrangements for them. In spite of this, it appeared necessary for one of us go to Goa to give the Viceroy an eye-witness account of the state of things concerning that Christian Church and its people in Ethiopia and the situation of the Patriarch and his companions, at the same time obtaining for them the necessary ransom for their liberty. I was the one selected for the voyage, it always being the case that I was considered, I know not why, ready for any adventure, bad or good.

I soon departed for Tana,[3] another of our colleges, and from there for Chauul,[4] where we have another good house. And since one could travel from there to Goa only by sea, I and two other Fathers bound for the same city had to find a boat appropriate to that time, which was when many corsairs were infesting that sea. And in order to avoid

---

[1] A small town in Portugal, on the road from Coimbra to Figueira da Foz, north of the Mondego river.   [2] See p. 44 n. 1.

[3] Thana, a port on the island of Salsette, 20 miles NE of Bombay.

[4] Chaul, now Rewadanda, south of Bombay.

the danger in some way, since no fleet was available to force its way through without fear of them, we took a boat called a Pangim *almadia*,[1] whose only virtue at sea is its ability to flee. It is very narrow, low, with no rail-work at all, and without a keel so as to be lower, swifter and easier to navigate in any depth of water. The 18 oars on each side and the design of the boat make it so swift a craft that it can go fearlessly among any enemy ships and flee from under their bows, for it does not plough the water but rather seems to fly over it. These boats can be harmed only if by chance they are hit by a cannon-ball from some artillery piece or if they are captured in some river or if they risk facing the enemy and the rowers are killed. The latter are seated on boards crossing the entire boat, while the passengers lie underneath. They sail night and day, and are put into some river while the passengers refresh themselves on land. On this voyage, of 80 leagues, we escaped enemy ships on several occasions. On the first occasion, we found ourselves between two ships which were so close together that if they had not all been sleeping it would have been impossible for them to have missed seeing us. On another occasion, a pinnace pursued us closely, but our swiftness of foot, that is to say our oars, served us well as we fled into a river; and when those aboard the pinnace saw that we were escaping from them, they began to call to us as if they were friends; but, knowing they were not so, we paid no attention to their good words. Because they thought we would soon come out again, they waited for us the rest of the night and all through the next day and night. We made two attempts to go out, but because we saw they were still in the mouth of the bar, it was necessary for us to remain in that river for two days to escape them. On the following day, we went out without danger, but we were to come within a hair's breadth of falling into the hands of another corsair; for the bar at Dabul[2] forms two entrances, the larger one to the south and the smaller one to the north, the direction from which we were coming; and in the larger entrance the pirate ship had been lying in wait for two days to attack any boat which might enter there; and since we were completely unmindful of any such danger, we certainly would have fallen into their hands if we had tried to go in by the larger entrance. However, since it was our good fortune that it was high tide at the time and the smaller

---

[1] *almadia de Pangim*, 'Panjim canoe'. Panjim, later known as Nova Goa, is on the south bank of the Mandovi river, about 7 miles downstream from Old Goa. Le Grand says that Lobo made the journey to Thana and Chaul by land because of the danger from Dutch corsairs.

[2] Dhabhol, at the mouth of the Vashishti river, between Chaul and Goa.

entrance had enough water, we went in that way and were unaware of the danger we escaped by not using the other until we were informed of it by the people in the town, who were astounded that we had managed to escape and showed us the enemy pirates who were still there in the morning.

Since the last stage of our voyage was to be a long one and so that we could arrive at Goa in the morning, we left earlier than usual, at 4 o'clock in the afternoon. Seeing that the coast was clear as far as a point of land, we continued our voyage close to the shore, and we saw that many boats were making for the port which was behind the point of land. Since we took them for fishing boats, which most of them really were, we were continuing on our course when, as we were approaching the point, a man, one of the Hindu natives of the country, came hurriedly to the beach and, by shouting and waving a piece of cloth at us, was signalling us to come closer and not to go any further ahead. Although we understood what he was telling us, we attached little importance to it and signalled him to come to us. He quickly did so, throwing himself into the water and swimming for the boat, which we held in place with the oars as we waited for him to reach us. When he arrived he begged us not to go any further because ten praus[1] were waiting for us behind the point and two more were coming craftily among the fishing boats in order to capture us and we would be caught between the open sea and the two at the point of land with no possibility of escape, which was truly the situation in which we would have found ourselves. Now very much aware of the danger, we paid him well for his work and the providential warning, and put up our oars, remaining there very watchfully until nightfall, when, by making a wide detour out to sea, we were able to avoid the danger without being seen from shore. Sailing more carefully and diligently, on the next day we rowed into the harbour at Goa and reached our college at ten o'clock in the morning, where we were received with the Christian love and joy which we always experienced on such occasions. It was the 8th of December, on the day of the Immaculate Conception of the Holy Virgin, and the celebration was in progress at the college, almost all of the members of the Company in that city being present, having come there from the three residences we have there: the Novitiate, the College, and the Professed House, and also the few in the fourth house which is a large, stately Seminary. Incidentally, while

---

[1] *parós*; the word is of wide application in S and SE Asia; it usually refers to a relatively light and fast vessel, sometimes to a kind of galley.

there, I did not fail to note the respect that people in India have for anything from the Kingdom, for, despite the fact that the refectory was well stocked with fruit, which grows in that land all year long, seafood of various kinds, which is excellent and in great abundance because it is so plentiful in the seas of India, and other delicacies and shellfish of all kinds, so abundant in India – all of these delicacies being fish of one kind or another because it was a Friday –, the choicest morsel on the table and the one most esteemed by everyone was a saucer given to each religious with two salted sardines with oil just as they may have arrived from the India voyage, having been soaked in brine for at least a year and being left over from the voyage in the ships that had arrived. Everyone ate these including the bones so as not to waste so good a thing, which was all the more delicious because of what it represented of our Portugal.

CHAPTER 28

[Concerning my report to the Viceroy, my subsequent embarkation on the carrack *Belém* and the pitiful condition of the ship]

After my arrival in Goa, I made an appointment with the Viceroy, who at that time was the Count of Linhares.[1] He heard me very graciously as I informed him of everything I had intended to convey to him. My presentation and request for action consisted of two parts. The first part was a plea for help for Christianity in Ethiopia, so that it would not be completely destroyed, and for the sad state and danger in which the Catholics there found themselves, both Portuguese born there and native Abyssinians as well as the Bishop and Fathers of the Company who had remained there so as not to abandon those Christians exposed to obvious peril of their lives as was soon obvious when the heretics killed two of them[2] and captured three along with the Bishop, who to this very day are still living in heavy irons and harsh imprisonment [*sic*]. The second part was a plea for the liberation of the Patriarch and a few other companions of his who remained as captives in Suaquem as I have already related. Suitable means for accomplishing these two purposes were discussed and the conclusion was reached that a military operation was the only possible one considering the pass things had reached and in view of past experience on many other occasions. The experience of those of us who at such close hand and for so many years had seen the situation and had, so to speak, felt it with our own hands led us to the opinion that a military operation was the most suitable remedy. To accomplish this purpose, a fleet should go into the Red Sea, forcibly take the Patriarch and his companions from the hands of the Turks while at the same time demanding an accounting from the Turks for the cruelties and treachery they had done to us, take possession of the island of Maçuá and establish a Portuguese stronghold there, whereby the Portuguese

[1] D. Miguel de Noronha, Conde de Linhares, Viceroy 1629–35.
[2] Gaspar Pais and João Pereira were killed on 25 April 1635, along with three Portuguese and one Ethiopian, Beccari, 1903–17, XIII, 89.

not only would remain masters of the entire Red Sea but also, because of the very close proximity of this island to the land of Abyssinia and its being the Empire's only seaport, through which all its imports and exports must pass, would make the Ethiopians entirely dependent. This dependency and the great fear they have of the Portuguese would be enough to restore the Catholic faith, permitting the Catholics to live there in freedom, many of whom are roaming the lands closest to the sea in hope of this very thing, awaiting our arrival to throw in their lot with us and to reinforce us and the Catholic side, this closeness being all that would be needed to permit the Catholic faith to thrive without any impediment or fear of any substantial opposition. This enterprise recommended itself not only as a service to God, which was its principal purpose and interest, and as a service to His Majesty, who on several occasions had urged the Viceroys to favour it, but also would be advantageous to the individuals who embarked with the Fleet because of the booty and plunder necessarily to be obtained from rich cities.

In consideration of the reasons set forth for undertaking this affair and to provide a remedy for the difficulties which were occurring, seeing that the matter was of such importance, the Viceroy resolved to undertake it with a sufficient fleet, inquiring in great detail concerning all the particulars of the sea, navigation, enemy ports, forces, ships, soldiers, and everything else that had to be known for successful dispatch of the affair. Since I had experienced and seen all these things so recently, in certain instances I was able to give him complete information concerning everything, apparently to his satisfaction, whereupon he resolved to send a fleet consisting of two galleys, two galleons, and as many as six rowing vessels with sufficient soldiery and his son Dom Fernando as Captain-Major, since it was not possible for him to go in person on the enterprise, as he had told me several times he wished to do because of its nobility and the opportunities it offered for earning fame. In addition to the reasons there were for the restoration of Catholicism in that empire, one which moved me particularly was the prospect of demanding of the two Turkish brothers, the Baxá and the Amir, my former masters, an accounting for more than thirty Abyssinian youths whom they had taken from us, most of whom they had forced to become Muslims, and for the lashes that they had wished to give me on occasion for no reason, as well as the other threats of death and torture with which they honoured me; so that I was now delighted to have a plan which would put both of them in my power. However, just as the enthusiasm for the enterprise was at its height, the whole affair collapsed because the Viceroy was only willing to make a foray up and down the Red Sea, not establishing a force on the island of Maçuá as we asked him to do, which was the key to the whole affair. Although he was willing to take the island, make a fortress on it, and provide it with artillery, he was unwilling to leave soldiers there, saying that the Abyssinians and Portuguese from Ethiopia should come to defend it. And although this affair was thoroughly discussed and I showed him that this procedure could not hope to succeed in making that Christianity secure, which was the whole purpose of it, which could not be done by the Portuguese and Abyssinians of Ethiopia, who did not have the necessary knowledge even if they otherwise would have been capable of it, without the company of the Portuguese from India, even though the necessity of their presence was obvious, the Viceroy resolved not to leave them there, telling me that the state did not have enough soldiers. In view of this, the fleet would be useless; for a punitive expedition from one end of the Red Sea to the other and subsequent return to India, while perhaps easy to accomplish, would only permit the Turks to return once the Portuguese were gone and once again become masters of the same seaports, reinforcing them so as to cut off all access to the Red Sea and all communication with those Catholics, leaving that body of Christians in a worse situation than before. Although I asked him for at least a hundred soldiers to be left in the fortress, it was impossible to get him to commit more than fifty. Since this was obviously an insufficient number, we had to abandon the whole project, appealing to the Kingdom and His Majesty's presence, to whom we would come to present the affair and request the necessary remedy, which met with the approval of the Viceroy, who offered to write letters on the matter to His Majesty in favour of the enterprise while at the same time offering his own services in support of it.[1]

It was then a question of who would go and it was my misfortune to be selected for the task as being the person most accustomed to such adventures. It was then toward the end of January and two carracks were being feverishly prepared for the voyage to Portugal, so that I had to hurry to make myself ready. Most of my task was concerned with the selection of the carrack. There were two of them: one which

---

[1] Le Grand: 'It was agreed that I should go at once to Europe and should represent at Rome and Madrid the pitiful state of the Abyssinian missions. The Viceroy promised, that if I could obtain some help, he would personally command the naval force that would be sent to the Red Sea, and he assured me that he believed he could not employ his life better than in an expedition so holy and of such great importance for the Catholic Religon'.

had arrived that year, *Nossa Senhora da Oliveira*, a beautiful new ship but the one which was to carry most of the people and merchandise going to the Kingdom. The second was the carrack *Belém*[1] which had spent the winter at Goa and, because it had struck the bar on sailing into the port, had already been repaired with the intention of the Viceroy's embarking on it if a successor were to come that year, for the ship was the most beautiful large vessel that had come to India, although ill-fated as we shall see. Made in Lisbon, its first voyage was an abortive one as it had to return to port; the following year, made ready for the second time, it did not leave for lack of favourable weather; the third year, it set sail and reached India, but as it entered the harbour it hit the bar and broke 52 ribs, necessitating extensive repairs;[2] on leaving the harbour it hit the bar again but did not ship water. While the ship was being careened, however, it was found that the blows dealt its bottom as it hit the bar had caused one side of the keel to protrude into the sternpost. Upon being loaded, the ship gave signs of shipping some water. The worst thing was that the captaincy of the ship was promised to a fidalgo who was never able to occupy it, for he died in the undertaking without returning to his home. I did not fail to investigate some of these things I had learned, and for further verification I went to the ship on one occasion to see if it was shipping water, but since it was not yet loaded I was unable to do so.

Not the least of my reasons, among others, for liking this ship were that it was said to be less heavily loaded, that it was a powerful ship, and that Saint Francis Xavier had performed a great and evident miracle by defending it one crucial night on its voyage to India. At anchor on the bar of Moçambique, the carrack was being battered by a furious storm which had broken four of the five cables. Since there was no reason to believe that one could hold where four others had failed, the poor sailors placed all their hope in a relic of the saint, which they lowered into the water with the sole remaining cable. The winds

[1] Properly *Nossa Senhora de Belém*. Joseph de Cabreira, the commander, wrote an account of the loss of the ship and the adventures of the survivors until their arrival at Luanda. This was published at Lisbon in 1636 and reprinted in the third volume of the *História Trágico-Marítima*, the date of publication of which is uncertain. Cabreira describes the ship as the most handsome, best built and biggest that ever made the voyage. He had been in command of the ship, which was admiral of the fleet, on the outward voyage, leaving Lisbon on 6 March 1633 and arriving at Goa on 19 August.

[2] Cabreira says that over forty ribs were broken and that the masts had to be cut down in order to get the ship off the shoal. They were replaced at Goa with difficulty, because the new masts were bigger and were made from puna (see p. 307 n. 2) which was heavier than Flanders pine.

increased in fury and the people saw cruel death before their eyes at every moment, since they were so close to the reefs that they could not have escaped alive if that single cable had not held fast all night long, which the four other cables had been unable to do. What was even more remarkable was that it could do this without any flukes on the anchor, for both had broken off leaving only the shank, as they discovered in the morning when they hauled it up. This miracle was authenticated, announced and celebrated in India with demonstrations of admiration and joy. This reason caused me to prefer this carrack with all its defects and, moreover, the Viceroy gave me a cabin in it, rejoicing that I should be there. All of these things together were working to cause me the hardships I was to suffer later in the shipwreck the future held in store for us. Those troubles could all the more easily have been avoided since there was someone on the other ship who was begging me to accept a cabin and fine food free of expense; for a *desembargador*[1] had decided to go to Portugal and had requested of the Father Provincial that, if any Father were going to the Kingdom that year he would take him at his own expense because of the devotion he and his wife had for the Company. Since at that time there was no thought of sending any Father, he succeeded only in receiving the promise that if any Father were to embark, it would be on his ship; and when he learned that I was to go, he tried to oblige the Father Provincial to be true to his word. The Father Provincial summoned me and showed me the note, to which I responded that I had already promised to go on the other ship and that the decision could not be changed since I had good reasons for making it. What can be stated with most certainty is that this was the way in which my future sufferings and shipwreck were prepared for me. I was soon on the point of departing and did so on the 23rd of February, the day before St. Mathias' day, with such fine weather that, although I usually become very seasick at the beginning of any voyage, on this occasion I did not do so because of the quietness of the seas and winds with which the ship sailed those first days during which my suffering would ordinarily have occurred and was usually so great that if it were to last many days I could not live through it; for the nausea with which my stomach kept churning and vomiting can only be known by those who have experienced it, even vomiting all the various humours, according to the colours by which each one is recognized. Eating, drinking, and all other human

---

[1] Originally a special commissioner assisting the King in the discharge of judicial and semi-judicial business, such as the grant of pardons, licences, etc.; later an appellate judge.

functions are entirely impossible during those days. Finally, there is no other human illness that can be compared with this in the effects, vomiting and terrors it causes. The illness fortunately lasts no more than 8 days and the suffering of that week leaves me with complete freedom from this kind of torture for the remainder of the voyage.

We were continuing our voyage in the two carracks with favourable weather, but we soon began to be aware of the cause of our future ruin, for, although the signs were at first quite minor, they were carefully watched by those who knew of the misfortunes at the bar and who feared that they might result in great harm to us in a time and circumstance when we should be powerless to make the necessary repairs, as was finally the case. Since it was the custom to keep a constant watch for leaks in the ship, because this and fire are the sailors' greatest fears, the pump area was constantly inspected by the calker, who was assigned this task because he was familiar with the condition it was in at the time we left Goa; which was (according to what was afterward reported to me by the sailors themselves but at a time when there was no longer any possibility of rectifying the difficulty) that as he was helping with the loading and stowing of merchandise, after the ship had sprung a huge leak, with the spout of water making as thunderous a noise as if it were that of a fountain, a sailor heard the noise and observed the leak with the aid of a candle, because the place was dark and unfrequented, and for greater certainty he reported it to a companion of his, who verified the leak. They did not dare to say anything about it, however, for fear of the anger of those who had a powerful self-interest in the departure of the ship and because, as the confidence of sailors is great, they never believe they will be brought to ruin unless they were to sail in an 'old basket', as they say, around the Cape of Good Hope, but our ship could certainly qualify as an 'old basket'. Also, since all on the ship had spent the winter in Goa, their desire to realize a profit from their merchandise and to return to their homes was so great that they would disregard anything, risking any misfortune rather than spend another winter in India, and those in highest authority on the ship would be even more unwilling to hear of the condition it was in, for which reason the sailors did not dare to reveal what they had seen even though they too would be the losers and, as it turned out, did indeed lose everything in spite of their trust that all would be well.

When all the cargo was already aboard the ship and the calker went to inspect the pump area, he found three spans of water in it and, measuring it more exactly, discovered three and a half and four spans of water there, whereupon he decided to go warn one of the officers. The officer he warned was so far from thanking him and doing his duty that, heaping verbal abuse upon the poor calker, he forced him to be the one to go break the news to the higher government officials. And although he did so with great fear and trembling, the reply and thanks he received was an oath from this kindly official, who was on land, that on the King's life he would have him hung on the gallows if he found two inches less water in the ship than he had reported. The official went aboard the ship immediately to verify the facts of the case, and the result of his investigation was that the calker was not strung up on the gallows and the very same official ordered the merchandise he had put aboard the ship removed and placed on another ship, according to what I was told later by someone who had seen it and who had stowed it aboard the other ship with much labour. This official was not the Viceroy, for if it had been he, the ship and we who were aboard it never would have suffered so calamitous a fate, but another who was more directly responsible for correcting dangerous conditions on departing ships and who should have prevented the calamity which was threatened in this case.

Setting sail in this condition, we immediately made a false start which, if we did not suffer the miserable fate we later experienced, would have been considered only a foreboding by those more knowledgeable and precise in such things, for the ship veered off course in such a way, putting its prow on the beaches of Bardes,[1] that it seemed as if it were warning us of the misfortune we were to have in the voyage, preferring to remain there rather than continue it. It was, however, put back on course once again, although with great difficulty as the ship was soon adversely affected by the water entering the pump area. We manned the pump daily once each night, for which task the negroes and other prisoners aboard were sufficient. Although the floor-timbers were not covered with water, as I observed on several occasions when I went down and saw them, the pump-well was always full. Since the weather was mild at the beginning and the ship was not leaking any faster, the water not being excessive and there being no urgent necessity of tending to it, the officers of the ship were extremely negligent in not trying to find the cause of the difficulty. If this had been done and the necessary corrective measures had been taken, we should not have come to experience so great a misfortune. The enemy, however, was grossly

[1] On the N bank of the river of Goa, opposite Panjim.

underestimated, which, if one follows the rules of prudence, should never be the case, no matter who the enemy might be; for an enemy is easy to defeat at the beginning when he is weak. If one waits until he has had time to gather strength, he is much more difficult to defeat, as we had occasion to experience. To add to our misfortune, the ship was not well supplied with people. It carried very few passengers, because those who were most cautious and best advised had been unwilling to risk their lives on it. Its officers and crew were much understaffed, there being only 145 of them because of the sickness and weakness contracted by some during the winter season in Goa and the hard work in repairing the ship. There were also others leaving for Portugal with special privileges exempting them from work.

The ship carried two types of pumps in sufficient quantity to serve us well in any contingency provided they were well adjusted and in good repair. The pumps of the old type with hand levers, however, were worn out and were therefore unable to function, which was the case during the whole time we were afloat or had any need of them. Those of the second type, of very recent invention and extremely useful, were not, however, efficiently connected to the windlass, on which the whole mechanism depends, and we were furthermore without a supply of links for the chain since no provision had been made for this. It was also said that the masts were excessively thick and heavy. All of these difficulties contributed to our ruin and our sufferings. As we were reaching higher latitudes, we began to experience stormy weather and with it the ship began to suffer more damage, even though it and the other ships were so large that they resembled mountains of wood, continually feeling weakness in itself just as we felt the effects of how poorly prepared we had left port, the self-delusion we had brought with us, and finally the beginnings of our wretched shipwreck and ruin in the great volume of water with which the ship began to be filled. The officers said the water was from the large casks stored in the hold, which were too poorly constructed to hold their contents. Even if this were the case, it would have been a catastrophe because of the dire straits in which it would have put us, since lack of water is always the greatest lack one can suffer on the sea. In a short time, however, we learned the truth of the matter, much to our distress.

We first began to become concerned about the danger of stormy weather one night when a few signs of the future storm appeared, which, when it overtook us, caused us much trouble because of its fury. It was the last quarter of the moon when it comes out exactly at midnight, which is ordinarily a bad omen for sailors on those seas and latitude in which we found ourselves. To this was added another more infallible omen called a water-gall,[1] which is the foot of the rainbow appearing on the horizon. The colours however are darker and frightful; and when this phenomenon appears, the storm follow so quickly that there is not enough time to strike sail, for which reason the sailors are always on the watch for this warning, all of them shouting 'Strike sail! strike sail!' as soon as they see it, preparing themselves for the furious storm about to attack them. And when, after the appearance of the so-called water-gall, the storm does not appear within 24 hours, it comes with all the greater fury, as it happened with us. Since the phenomenon appeared in the morning, it left us very apprehensive all day; and at nightfall the weather began to become more frightful with the heavy clouds that covered the sky and burdened the air, and with the wind whipping up and the sea growing rough, the expected storm burst upon us. However, as the wind still permitted us to use all the ship's sails, despite its threat of becoming much stronger, we continued with the sails full but with the halyards in our hands and everyone on the alert waiting to see what the weather would do. To the southeast the sky was so heavy, dark and fearsome that it was obviously preparing to break loose against us with great force, which it did so treacherously, however, that, as if it were trying to catch us suddenly and unawares, no matter how forewarned and attentive we were, we were unable to escape the sudden burst of a furious blast of wind called a typhoon or hurricane which came after a sharper wind than the one which had been blowing for some time, which had only caused us to be watchful. The sails kept taking the wind and swelling to the bursting point despite everyone shouting 'Strike sail! strike sail!' Knowing that the foe was with us, we could not escape damage now, and in a moment it tore all the sails in pieces without leaving us a usable shred. The impetus was so strong that, if the sails had not been old and had been capable of withstanding the weight of the wind, the masts and yards would certainly have been smashed to pieces, falling on the ship with all the danger involved in such happenings; but the weakness of the sails was in our favour, and we continued for the rest of the night with the fear of the sudden fury of the wind and the danger in which it placed us and with a wild storm in which we were left after the hurricane had passed, making the seas higher and stirring up the air so that we had much to do the rest of the night to recover and

[1] *olho de boi*, literally 'ox-eye'.

ward off its fury. A terrible circumstance of this kind is difficult to describe, since words cannot convey the difficulties and hardship that have to be undergone in the innumerable occasions for fear and terror in seeing it and experiencing it.

In the light of the morning we were able to verify the damage which the darkness of the night had only permitted us to imagine. We worked to repair it, installing new sails and getting ready for similar ordeals, since we were in a place where we could fear them. As it turned out, we did experience them again. Between the shoals of Pero de Banhos[1] and those of the Sete Irmãas,[2] the wind carried off the main topsail in pieces with the fury of a sudden hurricane enveloped in a heavy shower of rain despite its being furled and well protected by the mainsail. In the work occasioned by this and by the earlier storm we began to suffer from the lack of people aboard and also from the weakened state of the few we did have, as the occasions for hard work kept increasing as we sailed into higher latitudes. For, after this, the wind continued to carry off still other topsails in similar storms; and as these difficulties increased, our fears and the water in the ship kept increasing, and we knew that, in addition to the foes from the outside, we had the more intimate ones, which are usually the greatest ones to be feared on a voyage.

On this occasion and at night, the flagship separated from us, taking a different course. Whether because they forgot to give the customary signals which would have informed us of their change in course or whether we simply failed to see their signals, our two ships had certainly lost sight of each other before sunrise. The flagship, however, made every effort to rejoin us and resuming the course we had been following when it left us, and which we were still following, it found us again toward evening. We were certainly deserving of this effort on its part because of the effort we had customarily made to carry less sail in order to keep ourselves in convoy with the flagship. This effort on our part was necessary because our ship, the *Bellem* was a faster sailing vessel. We here picked up some brisk southeast winds which brought us, at dawn on the first of May, to the island of Diogo Rodriguez, which was uninhabited but sought by sailors because its southern shore was at 20 degrees latitude and from that point they could make a new dead-reckoning.[3] Sighting land caused us great joy, as it usually does

---

[1] Now usually written Peros Banhos. See Boxer, 1959, p. 54, n. 2.
[2] 'The Seven Sisters', the Seychelles.
[3] The latitude of Diogo Rodrigues is 19° 41' S.

for anyone sailing the seas no matter what land it might be, but it gave much greater joy to one of the negroes on board ship, an exceedingly ignorant one, who, already tired out from the two months and several days of sailing we had done up to that time, believed that we had arrived at the final destination of our voyage. His high spirits on seeing the island turned to sadness as he saw we were not landing there, and his sadness redoubled when, toward evening, he saw that the island was already well behind us, whereupon he was so overcome by melancholy that, given over to despair and refusing to eat, he soon ended his life miserably, aided by stout blows administered to him by his master to make him give up that diabolical obsession, which only served to end his sad days more quickly.

Since the winds were so favourable, we had every expectation of being finished with the fears that sailors always have when they are passing the Cape of Good Hope. The flagship, however, following its pilot's course, kept going farther out to sea and getting into higher latitudes so that we found ourselves at 34 degrees, which is almost the latitude of the Cape,[1] and the stormy weather increased as the wind shifted to the northwest and west-northwest, the usual enemies of ships in this locality. Since the winds were contrary, we had to keep our sails furled until such time as the weather should improve. The sea, however, grew much heavier and brought us a storm all the more dangerous since it did not allow us to progress. The continual rolling of the ship because of the huge waves, was greater because of the weight of the large masts, which were made of puna,[2] a wood much heavier than the Flanders pine of which the original masts were made, which were cut off when the ship ran aground the first time at Goa. All this labouring could not fail to cause much damage to the carrack as it struggled with all the weight of its huge bulk, which was like a mountain of wood, and the severe damage that a sound vessel would suffer under these conditions was considerably intensified in our case because of the basic weakness I have already mentioned. On one occasion the ship tossed violently from stern to bow, missing the wave that should have received it and plunging into a deep valley opened up by two waves which it could not surmount any more than it could avoid the hollow into which it had fallen. Since its bow plunged so deeply into the abyss – for the first wave had left it almost in mid-air

[1] The latitude of the Cape is 34° 20′ S.

[2] 'A timber tree (*Calophyllum inophyllum*, L.) which grows in the forests of Canara &c, and which was formerly used for masts, whence also called *mast-wood*', HJ, 'Poon'.

and the other wave did not arrive in time to receive it – when it fell it made such a thud and crashed so deeply into the hollow that we considered it a miracle that the masts were not all decapitated as it made everything in the stern hurtle forward to the bow. We were, however, aware of the considerable damage the ship might receive, because the whole shock was in the bow where the ship was weakest and the greatly increased water in the pump area showed that the ship had been wounded there.

These forerunners of our misfortune and the latitude where we were, as well as the storms we found there, forced us to draw near to the flagship and inform it of our need to sail for shore. We were also impelled by that old pilots' rule that counsels bringing the ship closer to land when in May one finds himself at the latitude where we were, both because of the shelter afforded by the land against contrary winds and because of the north-east, east, and east-north-east winds which are usually found there, which winds would have been as propitious to our voyage as those which were thwarting us where we were, were contrary to it. And we clearly saw the advantage we could have if we were closer to land, because two or three shifts of wind to the northeast close to shore would get us past the Cape. But the wind was now against us, finding us so far out to sea and serving only to carry us to higher latitudes. The advantage of being closer to shore was all the more obvious to us because proximity to the coast would allow us to avail ourselves of the sea-currents which carry a ship to the southwest with such force that, despite the fury of contrary winds, they cause ships to double the Cape, as was the case in 627 when Dom Manoel Pereira Coutinho[1] observed this time-honoured rule of sailors and passed the Cape carried only by the current against continual furious winds beating against his bow. I am mentioning all this to show the causes which conspired to bring us to ruin, for if we had gone closer to shore we would have avoided all the evil that befell us and would have had an extremely happy voyage. The sole blame for all this lies with the one who ordered the course as pilot of the flagship, whose lantern and course we followed, not only because of His Majesty's reasonable order but also because of an instruction issued to us by the Captain-Major to the effect that we should not separate from the flagship under pain of 200 cruzados that each officer of our ship would have to pay.

[1] Governor and Captain-General of Angola, 1630–5.

CHAPTER 29

[How, after many difficulties, we suffered a pitiful shipwreck on the coast of Natal]

In this determination we headed toward land and in a little more than eight days we caught sight of it at a position of 34 degrees latitude. Despite our belief that we would find here the winds which ordinarily run north-east and east, there lay in wait for us, as if in ambush, west and north-west winds which attacked us with a fury which proved to be our undoing. We would sail along yielding to the force of the storm whenever we could not do otherwise; at other times we would lie head to windward, backing the sails, as they say, which means using the mainsail and the foresail against the wind with the bow facing the wind. In the few calms afforded by the weather, the sailors amused themselves by throwing nets into the sea and catching a great quantity of fish – which is the usual recreation of those who find themselves becalmed. The species they caught is, in my opinion, the best in the world, and there was a great abundance of it. However, we never fished for it without being justified in saying: 'adhuc escae eorum erat in ore ipsorum et ira Dei ascendit super eos,' as God's prophet says in the psalm.[1] For we were barely at table raising the first bites to our mouths when the wrath of God descended upon us in the form of a horrible storm, so that we firmly believed our fishing to be a bad omen and we ate it fearfully, but like a child who forgets a beating as soon as his back is relieved of pain, we continued to take this recreation whenever there was a respite in the stormy weather.

At this time, in the first days of June, we were already in a miserable state, because the carpenters and calkers, both regular and supernumerary, were so sick that they could be of no use to the ship in the exercise of their functions. They had embarked in poor health which was prolonged and aggravated by the continuous necessity of straining to the utmost to make necessary repairs. Because the regular calker had to be in the water for so long a time, he became so swollen

---

[1] 'But while their meat was yet in their mouths the wrath of God came upon them', Psalm lxxvii. 30.

that one afternoon he suddenly died. The others capable of doing the work and spending a few hours on rafts outside of the ship were put into the water where they carefully tried to find the leak and did some calking with oakum they had found all dried out. They were never able to repair the leaking, however, because they and the ship were tossed about so much by the waves. This diligence and hard work on their part served only to render them physically incapable of performing their functions on all other occasions.

At this time there was already a great need to make metal rings and valves for the chain of the wheel pump which was the only one that was functioning, and we had to use all the iron rings that were inside and outside of the ship to make links out of them and supply the need as much as possible.[1] Since we also needed a block for the top-mast, ours being worn out, and carpenters and calkers, ours being in the state already described, we tried to get help from the flagship asking it to assist us with these things and much more, so that it would be aware of the state we were in because of the great quantity of water leaking into the ship, which was so copious at that time that we were having extreme difficulty getting it out and we were not always able to do it. I had the responsibility of dividing the people into three squads. The first squad consisted of the sailors under the supervision of the boatswain;[2] the second was composed of the grummets under the direction of the boatswain's mate[3] since he was in general charge of them; and the third squad, in which I had my place was supervised by the steward [4] and comprised all of the passengers. The Blacks formed a supernumerary squad, which was the one which worked most continuously at the pump. Our duties, however, were distributed in quarters, day and night, each squad being on duty for two quarters, one during the day and the other at night, with the squad of Blacks filling in whenever needed. Although at first we were on duty only in the daytime and were hard pressed to do the work, the stormy weather kept blowing and the ship kept opening up more and more leaks, so that the great volume of water coming into the ship forced us

---

[1] Cabreira says that the deficiencies were the fault of the calker. He had taken the place of the calker who had come from Portugal, who was ill. The new calker was also ill and in Goa had been more concerned with loading bales of cinnamon than with what was needed for the pumps. The master (*mestre*) had also been ill and for many days had been unable to come aboard and make proper arrangements. It is evident from Lobo's narrative that he and others were critical of Cabreira's conduct on several occasions. The latter's narrative is sometimes self-exculpatory.

[2] *contra-mestre.* For grummet see p. 339 n. 1.

[3] *goardião.* Cabreira gives his name, Belchior Dias.

[4] *despenseiro.* Cabreira gives his name, Simão Gonçalves Franco.

to continue working diligently and carefully both day and night. The worse of it was that, since the pump was not well adjusted and the chain was big and very heavy, running the machine with great difficulty, it cost us infinite labour to make it work; for eight of the strongest men were needed to make it turn the 15 or 20 times necessary to draw out water, and when they reached the 20th turn, the poor workers were so winded that they were completely out of breath and thought they had exerted themselves to capacity giving so many turns. Ten weaker people barely sufficed for the task, the usual number being 12 working together to turn the wheel with infinite difficulty as I experienced since I did not exempt myself from this exercise, both because of the necessity for everyone to work and so that others would not have an excuse to avoid it.

Our anxiety and the evidence of our danger, with the attendant fears of the pitiful end awaiting us, grew with the increasing volume of water filling the pump area. Since the quantity was so great, we sought help, as I have said above, from the flagship, which, because there were heavy seas that day and the following day, was unable to answer us; and when it did answer us on the third day, it did so with little satisfaction to us. It may have been because what we were asking of it was not convenient. We all wanted the Captain-Major at least to be informed of how great our distress was because of the water we were shipping, which we could say was well up to our chins. However, a person whose opinion should not have carried so much weight ensured our misfortune by saying that it was not a good thing for our ship's condition to be known on the other ship because its loss was so obvious that they would abandon us in order to reach Portugal more quickly so that those aboard could make a better sale of their spices. This advice, which was based only on a self-interested notion, was the cause of total loss, because, since the Captain was so persuaded by it, no one on the ship dared say anything beyond what the Captain ordered, which was only that we needed a few very superficial things. Most of the people aboard were bursting with resentment because of the failure to declare our lamentable state, but their entreaties to the Captain were of no avail. Although the pilot put up a white flag at the stern – a signal of distress on such occasions –, he had to take it down faster than he had put it up, being rewarded for his good work by receiving a stern reprimand. Since the flagship, however, finally became aware of our condition, from the things we were asking of it and from some veiled signals they had perceived as well as from the great volume of water constantly being discharged through the scupper-holes, and from the links, block, and workmen we were requesting of it, they responded that we should send out a boat and they would send us everything we asked for and anything else that we might want,[1] understanding, as they afterward confessed to me, the dangerous condition we were in, but, since we were the most intimately concerned with the welfare of our own ship and did not want to obtain what was needed for it by indicating what our difficulties were, those aboard the flagship did not want to force their help upon us. The Captain of the flagship, however, very intelligently, as we afterward learned and as he himself told me, kept his ship very close to ours, so that he would be able to rescue those aboard if the worst were to happen. With this intention he kept so close to our wake that the flagship's bow-sprit was almost touching our stern and the pilot on duty at night dared to want to inform the flagship of the miserable state in which we were sailing. However, as he wished to be courteous, which he should never have done, he exhibited courtesy toward the person who gave all the orders and sent word to him asking for permission, thereby bringing ruin upon himself and the rest of us; for he was not only refused permission but was also told within my hearing that we were never again to get close to the other ship or to speak with people aboard it and that we did not need any help from it nor did we want anything, when in actuality our need for help was so great that we were soon to have incontrovertible proof of it, much to our sorrow.[2] Anyone reading all this can certainly imagine the esteem enjoyed by the person who, seeing himself so close to a wretched shipwreck and having the power to avoid it was unwilling to do so in the manner that I have described, to which for the moment I shall add nothing except to affirm the truth of everything I have said above. It seems that these were the means God used to punish our sins and the arrogance, ignorance and lack of judgment of the one who gave all the orders, knew nothing, presumed much and was unwilling to accept any advice because it seemed to him to cast aspersions on his judgment and lessen his authority, according to the discourse of one who was quicker to understand things than he.

With this decision, our spirits sank very low as we saw the stormy weather increasing and the water ever rising in the ship, the impossibility

---

[1] Cabreira says that this reply was tantamount to a polite refusal, as it was impossible to launch the boat, which had not been calked. He was in fact asking for a calker. Besides, the block into which the upper mast fitted had split and his carpenter was old and very ill; the spare carpenter was in the same condition.

[2] They now lost sight of the flagship which reached Lisbon on 25 September.

of pumping it out, the tiredness of the people who were already faint from the continual work, day and night, in which they had to participate, tending to the pump which was working very poorly. And when they were working most feverishly at the pump, they would have to run quickly to fasten the sails and then return immediately to their back-breaking task at the pump; and when the water was not getting the best of us, we thought it beyond us to conquer it and had already lost all hope of it, trying to keep ourselves, by main strength, from being engulfed by any more than the many spans of water that we already had, that is, to prevent the water from increasing any more. This ship always responded poorly to the rudder on the starboard side, and now with the weight of the water the difficulty was greater than usual; and since the sea was heavy, five or six men were barely sufficient to man the rudder, in which, since it represented a great share of the means at our disposal to encourage the people who were struggling with it and experiencing great difficulty and were trying to subdue it as if it were a powerful, wild bull, it was no longer enough to steer it with the tiller-ropes, but it was necessary for them to add to it ropes fastened to main-tack in order to make it obey, a necessary but very costly remedy, throwing braces to the main-braces, which are two ropes in the yard-arm extending to the stern bumpkin. We struggled and navigated with that single sail with which we were sailing and yielding to the fury of the winds, or rather the fury of the tempest.

On this occasion the excessive coldness that we experienced, caused both by the furious rain-soaked winds, aided by the high latitude where we were and also the fact that it was winter there at that time, and by our natural faintness because of lack of sleep and food because of the various disagreeable troubles that kept us from sleeping; wherever sleep overtook us we would rest our heads a little, which was usually on the deck, the place most beaten by the winds and infested with water, because it was there that we were continually present to man the pump. One night when I withdrew to a space between two artillery pieces, lying down to rest a little, the cold cut through me so fiercely that I thought I would not last until the morning, and if I had not had the work which I did very vigorously to restore warmth to my body, the cold would doubtless have ended my days. The great quantity of water that came in over the sides of the ship went down through the quarter-decks so that not only were they all dripping but, getting into the sacks of pepper it carried some of the pepper to the pump, with the result that the pump no longer worked as well as before and was failing to pump an amount of water remotely corresponding to the labour we were expending on it. I had to try to remedy the situation by making a pit in the hold so that all the water would collect there and we could pull the water out in barrels of 6 *almudes*,[1] using the capstan to lift them, which is the usual way of coping with such difficulties. Although this was of some help, it was by no means as effective as we should have wished. From Saint Anthony's day until Saint John's day[2] we sailed with the force of these storms and with the excessive labours they entailed for us, and, although the stormy weather abated a very little, the seas remained so high, heavy and swollen that it was, for the ship, a greater torment and danger because of the tossing and rolling it gave and because of its being so broken up.

On Saint John's day, when we were enjoying a little fair weather, as night was closing in a storm whipped up so furiously and quickly that we immediately found ourselves in the worst storm we had had up to that time, just after we were thinking and hoping that our luck was about to change and the winds were finally tired of persecuting us, but it seems that they were preparing to have done with us and, as if provoked at the long time we were managing to stay afloat and oppose their strength, they attacked us with such excessive violence that for the space of two hours it was a Day of Judgment on the poor ship; for the officers were shouting to furl the mainsail, the sailors working everywhere were unable to conquer the impetus of the wind swelling the sail and furiously blowing it in the air at will without permitting them to furl it. The others aboard were working at the pump because the water was increasing at an alarming rate. Everywhere on the ship one heard boatswain's whistles, shouting in chorus, yells, and hubbub, which, with the howling of the wind among the shrouds, the beating of the sail, the confusion and darkness of the night, was fearsome disorder and the very picture of Hell. The work did not let up, but rather kept getting worse all through the night and the next three days, during which time we were sailing alone, for the flagship had become separated from us because of the weather. Because our hopes for improving our condition and having favourable weather were ever diminishing, we discussed, although it was too late and there was no longer any possibility of it, the possibility of either reaching Moçambique or taking shelter in some one of the bays that were there, in which

---

[1] 26 *almudes* = 1 pipe.
[2] I.e. 13 June (St Anthony of Padua) to 24 June (the nativity of St John the Baptist).

we would take refuge while waiting for a better state of affairs.[1] And although this would have been good advice if it were not superfluous at that time since the time for following it had passed, because of the profusion of difficulties besetting the ship, which was already in such dire straits that it could very easily take us straight to the bottom of the ocean at any time and was therefore running a very obvious risk by braving the seas off the coast of Natal, which were very tempestuous at that time; and since it was necessary to brave them in order to make for the head of the island of São Lourenço, we were in danger of perishing in the middle of those seas without being able to reach the place we were seeking. And, even though we might have it virtually in sight and be close to land, the furious contrary winds prevented us from sailing toward the cape in search of the afore-mentioned bay. For this reason and as our fortunes had now sunk to their lowest point, with the seas and winds at their worst and no hope of salvation, we had to seek whatever salvation we might be afforded by the disposition of the waves and the barbarous temper and mercy of so wild a land and so brutal a people as those of that coast. Trusting, however, in Divine Providence and putting ourselves at its mercy, condemned to a miserable shipwreck and the fate which God had prepared for us among the rocks and craggy places which girded the coast and where the sea, to add to our terror and confusion, crashed with great fury and churning, to which we were about to surrender ourselves, we resolved to sail along the coast very close to shore in the direction of Moçambique in order to find there some place more suitable and less dangerous, although the whole coast was very dangerous, where we would take vengeance as much as we could on our miserable voyage and, whenever our misfortune would force us to shipwreck, we would have fewer leagues to walk through the lands of those barbarians, supposing that those who escaped with their lives from the waves, travelling overland to the first land known to us, were to arrive there alive.

With indescribable despair, born of our belief that we were almost certain to die either in the furious waves or on the fierce rocks before our eyes or at the hands of cruel Cafres, we went along the coast with

---

[1] Cabreira says he called together the officers, most experienced seamen, the religious and some other persons to discuss what to do. The purser (*escrivão del-Rei*) administered the oath on the Gospels. It was agreed that the ship was in no state to attempt to round the Cape and that they should make for Moçambique. The master, however, who was experienced, maintained that they could not make the cape at the tip of Madagascar, and must tack because of the persistent and stormy north-east winds.

our eyes on the shore, momentarily expecting the ship to abandon us on the waves or bury us with it in the depths of the sea, for the stormy weather did not stop persecuting us. The water in the ship was increasing, and since the sacks of pepper had already burst open, the pepper collected so much in the pump and the pump-well that they functioned with the greatest difficulty. Unbelievable was the work we did all through the night on a Friday when we made this sad decision. Since there was very little food and equal care to get it, no sleep, and much diligence with which each person was preparing himself for the agony of death and the struggle with the seas, waves, rocks and Cafres, with which we would certainly soon be fighting, the tears and irremediable affliction were enough to break the hearts of any persons who might have seen this pitiful tragedy from the outside. Each one of us who was experiencing the same fate was so full of his own concerns that there was no room in him for pitying his neighbour, although the suffering of each one was increased considerably by the sight of companions of so long a time, sick and healthy, old and young, in the extremity of such great misery, each one weeping over his own misfortune and many weeping over the misfortune of their families, wives and children. I had the responsibility on this occasion for hearing confessions, all of the people wanting to disclose their hearts to me and to have me participate in their afflictions, and in truth I did take upon myself a good share of the affliction of each one, necessary as it was for me to help them all with a happy face, facing my own troubles in the same way and giving encouragement to those who found themselves in such dire straits.

On this night, which was the last one, it was agreed to make a more thorough effort to find the exact location of the place where the water was coming in, which should have been done much earlier and which, if it had been done earlier, would have been effort more profitably and more sensibly spent. Two men went over the whole area of the bow, where our trouble was correctly believed to be located.[1] We soon discovered it, but at a time when neither the seas nor the circumstances nor the volume of water persecuting us permitted it to be rectified. After this discovery of the cause, I myself went to see the place where the water was coming in, crawling on all fours among the bales of cinnamon, getting through there as best I could with a candle in my hand until I hit against the bow, which I found so opened up and

---

[1] Cabreira says he sent one Manoel Fernandes to find the leak. He was a good carpenter and very useful as neither the ship's carpenter nor his mate was able to leave his bed.

broken, with water coming in so copiously that it made the babbling noise of a brook when it is running over stones. We observed, however, that the damaged place was so high in the bow that the pitching of the ship at times brought it up to a point about two spans below the surface of the water, thus allowing the leaking to stop temporarily, which would help if we were able to repair it, although since drugs were stored there and the hole had the knee[1] across it and under it, we were afraid that in attempting to repair the leak, we would run the danger of causing the ship to split apart when we tried to cut away the knee in order to plug the leak, supposing that the knee might be providing support keeping the boards from giving way completely. Although this repair on the inside presented difficulties, there were other ways on the outside surface to help forestall our ruin, and a good carpenter offered his services saying he could easily repair the damage,[2] so that our feeble hopes were revived. This relief and comfort, however, were short-lived; for, when the man in question was coming from the bow, and he was the only one, other than God on whom depended our salvation, and walking along the deck next to the pump-well where two barrels of 6 *almudes* each were constantly being hoisted by the capstan, much to our misfortune he slipped near the opening of the hatch-way and, without anyone being able to help him or his being able to seize any one of the many ropes that were there, he fell down through the opening of the hatch-way, falling all the way into the hold. But since he fell into the water, the impact was not so dangerous as it would have been otherwise as God delivered him in this contingency from two dangers, first from drowning, as he could have done, in the more than 20 spans of water that the ship already had, and the second from landing on a large plank that was over the water and was used to stand on by those who filled the barrels and removed the great quantity of pepper that covered the water so that they could work, for if he had fallen on that plank he would certainly have died because of the height from which he fell. He was so severely injured, however, that we had to give up all hope of any repairs being done by him. We then paid more attention to the state of our souls because of the moral certainty we had that we would not live to the morning because the water was increasing incessantly. The people were

---

[1] *coral.*

[2] This was Manoel Fernandes. Cabreira says he was the only man who could help with carpentry. Usually there were several among the crew who could do so, but the only other one who had come from India on the ship was Thomé Fernandes; he had been bled several times, fainted and fell into the sea.

overwhelmed with fatigue from their labours and unable to continue them and the pumps and well were no longer able to function as the means of emptying the ship of water and bringing it relief.

The dawn came, however, bringing somewhat milder weather, the air thick with fog, the sun overcast, and the land covered with vapours so that we had difficulty telling whether or not the shoreline offered places suitable for our running aground; for our only intent now was to find a suitable place to beach the ship.[1] Since the whole shore seemed very dangerous to us because of the rocks visible there and the pounding of the sea against them, we kept sailing along in the hope of discovering some better place. Although we thought we saw one less dangerous than the rest, where an opening between two rocky places gave the appearance of some river coming out there or of the sea forming an inlet there, we knew that afflicted persons in our circumstances are always affected and often deceived by hopes of this kind and kept sailing on in this way until two o'clock in the afternoon. And because from that point forward, we could see that for a great distance there was no suitable place, the whole shoreline ahead as far as we could see being rocky and unsheltered, and fearing that our shipwreck would occur at night and in so unsatisfactory a place, we began to regret the mistake we had made in not running aground in the place which we had seen in the morning and to which we could not return because of the contrary wind. And with our mind's eye still fixed on it, deciding that that was the place God had prepared to save our lives, and still having its appearance in our minds without understanding why, we drew closer to land a little less than half a league from the beach, which appeared suitable as a refuge for any misfortune because, being all sandy and the sea breaking there with less violence than in the waves, it promised us better protection when, struggling with the waves and very much resigned to the inevitability of our misfortune, we wanted to avail ourselves of its shelter. The sea between the ship and the shore was more and more full of shoals as one drew closer to shore. But since our time had run out and our condition was such that we had to accept whatever God and our luck offered us, we chose this beach as the best place available to us, weighing anchor in that place in order to have time to prepare some rafts for use in getting the people ashore and with two boats which were aboard ship, preparing ourselves as best we could

[1] Cabreira says they sighted the coast of Natal at 32°, which would be south of the present southern boundary of Natal. He says they saw very high mountains which appeared to be divided by a river, and smoke rising as if from settlements.

for the last and most dangerous emergency. At this time I caused to be erected on the stern–castle a beautiful solid crucifix in order to give the people more encouragement to seek and ask God for the salvation of their souls at a time when their bodies were undergoing so much risk. With the sight of this sovereign object, the people were so moved to tears, being already on the verge of tears both because of having made their confessions and because of the wretched shipwreck and calamity in which they saw themselves, that their hearts were breaking with the tears, sighs, colloquies and things they were saying to Heaven as dictated by their grief and affliction. We spent a few hours in this useful manner while the barrels and rafts were being prepared, all of which would certainly be necessary if we were to be saved but were also of very bad augury and signs of our desperate plight since they announced the absolute certainty of our impending shipwreck. We put the boats out so that they would be ready in case of any sudden need.

At this time we descried on the beach some Cafres of that land, a barbarous, savage people, who were loitering about there, coming to take advantage of our misfortune. And because we feared that, in the event of our ship going to the bottom, those who escaped with their lives would have to make for the shore arriving there wet, weak and spent from the cold and fear of death, and it would be easy for them to become the prey of those savages, it seemed appropriate that a goodly number of our people should go ashore first and, taking a good military position, should set themselves up there with their weapons in a strong posture of defence to serve as a shelter and refuge for those who, thrown up from the sea, would later come ashore, thus affording them protection against the barbarousness of the Cafres, with whom those who had arrived first could deal more effectively, reaching land dry and with their arms in their hands and in a state of readiness. For this first challenge, forty men were chosen, who wanted me to accompany them; and because the danger was the same for all of our people, if it was not greater on land, I had to please them by accompanying them.[1] And leaving the ship in a small boat with about an hour and a half of daylight left with the intention of returning for more people after the first group had been put ashore for the purpose I have stated, we thought it well to go first to observe that place and location which

---

[1] Cabreira says that the majority wanted to run the ship aground, but he forbade this. He ordered the boat to be launched and took with him the boatswain's mate (*guardião*), thirty-seven men armed with muskets and matchlocks, a barrel of powder, shot and rope, but no food as there was not time. Lobo asked to come too and he also summoned the chaplain, Fr. António.

we had seen from the ship. And as it was nearly a league's distance away, even though we rowed with six oars to arrive in time and by daylight, we were unable to do it, nearing shore with so little daylight left that we could not recognize the danger we were getting into; for, as we reached the edge of a sandbank that came out into the sea on the northeastern side, we quickly found ourselves in the surf and swirling water in such obvious danger of perishing that we considered it an extraordinary favour of Heaven that we were able to get back out of there. And finding a place to anchor in the mouth of the river, we cast anchor since it had become completely dark, waiting for the morning when, being able to see, we could decide what we should choose to do. We spent the night, each of us seated wherever possible, for there was no room for us to lie down. There was no shelter other than what all of us huddled together could provide one another, which was rather necessary especially as the night progressed, for the cold was so biting because of a north wind between two high rocks close together. This wind, funnelled to us after blowing over the sea and being bathed and penetrated by the sea for a great distance, cut through us in such a way, in our weakened state, without sleep, with debilitated stomachs for lack of food.[1]

.   .   .   .

on us with such weight of water that if it had hit us squarely with all of its body it would have buried us lifeless at the bottom of the sea, shattering the boat into pieces. But God willed that it only enveloped us with a part of itself and, even so, it caused us great destruction, I and the Captain with whom I was coming to the rudder, experiencing the first impact, which was so furious that it threw everyone in the boat down, broke oars and rudder, and destroyed everything, making a large hole in the boat, flinging it closer to the beach on the other side of some shoals, which was the cause of our salvation because, with the boat lying crosswise, three waves were coming immediately one after another and would have hit the boat squarely on its side if they had not been prevented from doing so by breaking first against the shoal.[2] With the slaves, however, who exerted themselves enough to carry the boat closer to the beach and because by this time all of us

[1] A leaf of the MS. is missing at this point. Cabreira relates that for a whole night they made unsuccessful attempts either to disembark or to return to the ship until, Lobo having led them in an act of contrition, they turned the prow towards land and entrusted themselves to the waves.

[2] Cabreira says that the boat was saved because of the skill and presence of mind of a sailor called Antonio Domingues who was steering the boat with an oar and next to whom he was standing.

were ready to swim, now that the essential goods could present no obstacle, since the boat was already full of water, we had to surrender ourselves to the mercy of the waves, among and under which each person as best he could, because we were not in the rolling sea, tried to get to the beach, in whatever order each of us could get there according to his fortune with the waves. It was God's will, however, that no one perished, nor did a noble lady who was coming there with her husband run any greater danger of perishing than the rest, since the bravest and strongest came to help her just as they did afterwards, for the weaker men.[1] Two of them came to my rescue. When they reached shore and found me missing, they came back into the sea where I was struggling against my fortune, but when they reached me, I was already in less danger, and all three of us close together, because the greatest danger is when we reach land, for the waves that break on the beach and flow back again take the sand away from under one's feet and, causing the poor shipwrecked person to fall, envelop him in it and with the water carry him back out to sea, not letting him regain his footing, both because of the force and volume of the water and because of the more or less weakened and fatigued state in which he necessarily finds himself as he reaches the beach.

[1] The lady was D. Isabel de Abrantes, her husband Estácio de Azevedo Coutinho. Cabreira says she had herself worked at the pumps.

CHAPTER 30

[How the ship came to run aground near the beach and how we began to deal with the Kaffirs. A report on their customs and on the fruitfulness of the land]

After this miserable occurrence, we all arrived, true shipwrecked persons, most of us in shirts and white breeches, on a deserted shore of a land and people more barbarous than any other known to us, more than three thousand leagues from our native land, totally ignorant of everything we were seeing, without any possibility of repairing our ill fortune, without clothing with which we could cover ourselves and recover, with no food whatsoever except for a small quantity of biscuit which I happened to take from the cabin when I embarked on the boat and took with me.[1] The peril, however, which we left behind us and our escape from death, which we had struggled against for a long time, made that deserted shore seem to us as if it were the shore of Lisbon. We thus embraced one another, we thus kissed that unfamiliar sand, we were thus delighted with those mountains, groves of trees and land as if it were our own native land, all of us on our knees and our hands raised, with our eyes bathed in tears, with grateful and humble though sad and afflicted hearts, giving due thanks to God Our Lord for bringing us alive to that place. And because those aboard the carrack kept us constantly in view, observing all of our actions and what happened to us, since it was they who were expecting us to bring help to them, when they saw us enveloped in the waves being driven to shore where the sea was breaking so furiously, they were so sure we were lost that, pitying our sad fate, the master gave a signal with his whistle, as is the custom and ordered them to say the Lord's Prayer and a Hail Mary as for the dead which they thought we were, and in truth we were not far from being so.

The first thing we did was to shelter ourselves from the sun, because

---

[1] Cabreira says that they retrieved the powder which was in a sealed barrel and was still dry. The boat itself was half broken and full of sand.

Plate IX. Scene near the mouth of the Umzimvubu River

it was then out, in order to regain our strength while the clothes dried on our bodies, for we could not be so immodest as to take them off, our clothing consisting of shirts, white breeches or drawers.[1] We then began to look for drinking water, because that is the thing most worried about on such occasions, for hunger can be allayed and remedied in various ways, while thirst can only be quenched with water, the lack of which is so much more desperate and unbearable that such pejorative words as gluttony and greediness are used only with respect to food and not water. We found excellent water at less than a matchlock-shot's distance from a brook or spring, fresh, cold, sweet and perfect, this being the first of the favours that God Our Lord did for us afterwards on that coast until the time when he finally brought us to the lands where we were born.

All of these happenings both with respect to the ship after it came closer to land and with respect to the boat, were witnessed by the Cafres closest to the beach, poor, wretched people, shepherds with little cattle, who lived on the shellfish they caught. These Cafres then, seeing us now scattered about and safe on the beach, having watched us until then from a high mountain that descended abruptly to the sea, came down little by little until they were on the beach, but with their backs to the mountain and at a distance of a quarter of a league from us, and all of them seated in a squatting position, somewhat as if they were holding a council on what they should do. There may have been as many as forty of them. We unfortunate shipwrecked people were in a similar state of indecision, waiting to see what the barbarians would decide to do, and, not at all unwilling to establish friendly relations with them, we nonetheless waited to see what they wanted of us. They got up a few at a time and gradually drew nearer to us, sitting down and resting from time to time. We imitated them, drawing nearer to them and sitting down in the same way as they did until, we and they being a stone's throw apart, they all rose and, clapping their hands and dancing in time with the sound and singing in a barbarous but moderate voice and tone, came toward us with great celebration and signs of joy. We did the same, going toward them, also clapping our hands and singing, not failing to dance in time with our singing and clapping until all of us were together seated in a squatting position on the ground and each group astonished on observing the manner and dress of the other. The Cafres gave signs of great wonderment as they saw what they had never seen before, and we pretended that we too were amazed because their

---

[1] Cabreira says that wood was plentiful and that they all lit fires.

dress consisted only of a very soft hide of wild animals of the forest, which hide had been softened by watering and had been made into a small cloak going from the shoulders almost to the knee and was tied about with a sash of the same kind of hide, a hand's breadth in width, from which hung another piece of hide, which covered, both in front and in back, what reason and decency teach even people as savage as these. Some of them wore on their heads some small pointed half-hoods, also of hides; others had their hair loose, so dirty, greased with butter, with a thousand dirty things hanging from it, which were nauseating, because there was not a trumpet-shell, small shell, bird's foot, wing and head, and some whole birds, small pieces of iron, brass, copper, and everything else that pleases them that they do not endure. Their faces are blackened with charcoal, making them even darker than they are naturally, except that some of them add red clay. On their ears they wear similar pendants and large copper ear-rings with little strings of small red beads. They wore larger ones of the same kind at their necks, their king being distinguished from the rest of them by his wearing a greater quantity of them and larger ones and by the addition, in his case, of a certain part of a lock from a chest that he perhaps found on the beach, as if it were a jewel of great value. On their arms they wore many copper bracelets and they carried in their hands some sticks the width of a finger and the length of a *covado* with the shaggy tail of a dog or some other country animal set in both ends, which serves them as an elegance, amusement, fly swatter, and handkerchief with which they clean their eyes and anything else they wish. Their weapons are some assegais, each one of them carrying two in his hand. I have treated the dress of these barbarians in such great detail in order to give a report of it once and for all and to avoid further mention of it, supposing that it is that of all of the inhabitants of this vast region.

After the first inspections were over and the initial fear was allayed, we tried to make ourselves understood by using signs. And since our whole trouble and greatest need was to satisfy our hunger, we so informed them, asking if there were chickens, sheep, cows, whichever one of us who best knew how to do it imitating the sound of a chicken until, by this means, they finally recognized what we wanted. Others of us forming horns on our heads with our arms and bellowing like an ox or bleating like a sheep, declared what we had in mind, to all of which they answered us that there were many farther inland. And because this discourse and conversation had already been continuing for more than an hour, they got up and went away, one going off to see our shelter that we had already chosen at the edge of the beach under a large thicket of trees, which had within it so much room that it sufficed to provide shelter for all of us, protecting us overhead with its branches and shade and on all sides with the trunks and undergrowth, so that it served as a safe though rustic dwelling place and protection as it appears, from the Cafres and the wild animals, as if it were made specifically for that purpose. The Cafres refused to take with them one of our companions who was willing to risk going with them in order to have knowledge of their thatched huts and to see if he could negotiate for some food. They did not fail, however, to take some presents which they received with much delight, namely some old nails and three or four keys, [which were of no use to us] because there was no longer anything to lock up.

After the departure of the Cafres who left us as pleased with seeing them and with their friendliness as if they were people already known to us, we tried to learn what happened to the ship, which we had left in the state described earlier, and on which the following occurred: after we had left, and seeing that we certainly could not return to it that night, those who remained there tried to correct the difficulty of water in the ship with better sense than earlier; for, observing that it was all coming in at the bow, some of our people were saying that we should relieve it of the weight by loading the stern so that, rising, the opening through which the water was entering could come up out of the water and would thus receive a lesser quantity while at the same time permitting part of the great quantity of water already in the ship to be cast out and at least prevent it from increasing. And although I myself gave this same advice to one who was in a position to implement it, it was our misfortune that they did not accept it, to the surprise both then and afterwards of those who saw how easy was the remedy and wondered at the secret judgments of God, who by such means was disposing our ruin, using us ourselves, who were to suffer this ruin, as the instruments of His will. They turned their attention, then, to alleviating the bow and all together and with one accord they threw into the sea everything that was in it – goods, a great quantity of chests, as well as artillery pieces – so that they were probably experiencing some improvement or at least their plight was not worsening and they had been able to keep themselves afloat until the next day at the time when we had just finished talking with the Cafres. At this time everything on the ship was already in disorder, split open and destroyed, each person aboard treating both his own belongings and those of others as one would do thinking that the ship was to be swallowed up by the sea and become the booty of the Cafres and of the waves. It is certainly true that the disorder was excessive, for there was much that could have been done to improve matters, but the absence of the Captain caused great disorders, these and many others, just as his presence occasioned those which I have related up to this point and others which I do not mention.

Aware, then, that we were not coming, rather thinking us dead, and still mindful of the good shelter they had noticed in the mouth of the river that we had gone to reconnoitre, they discussed making for it and running the ship aground there, and, attempting to put their words into action, they cut the cable and put out the main foresail, many of them working at the helm, for the ship was now responding very badly to it. It was their misfortune that when the sail unfurled they found that a sheet had been cut so that the ship was being carried willy-nilly and with force by the wind, which had become brisker, toward the rocks, without any remedy because they were very close and there was no rudder to cause the wretched ship to head back out to sea and no sail to fortify it. The poor sailors here gave themselves up for lost and in the little time they imagined they had to live, which was at most seven or eight minutes, they prepared themselves for death, each of them also making ready to struggle with the waves, resorting to barrels, boards and anything else that could help them in that conflict. In the meantime, the mariners were shouting continually as they tried to put the ship on course, but all their labour was in vain. The cries, tears, acts of contrition, reconciliations, and pleas for God's mercy of those who imminently expected to find themselves wrestling with the cruel death of the shipwrecked, crueller than any other, since it is always very ugly; and because I saw this and other kinds of confrontation with death on many occasions with my own eyes and struggled with not a few of them myself, I can give personal testimony as to which is ugliest and most fraught with difficulties. In this dire extremity, God came to relieve the affliction of those pitiful, wretched people with His mercy, causing the ship to go away from shore just as it had got so close to the rocks that it was almost touching them, but since it was moving without any steerage whatsoever at the discretion of the winds, they found themselves in equal danger, because heading out to sea, it sailed with the force of the wind which was already very brisk and the further from land it got the greater was the danger of death in which it placed those it was carrying on board, carrying them further out to sea and making it impossible for them to be saved on shore. Here they found themselves in greater affliction because sometimes they were in greater peril because of being very close to land and other times because of being very far out to sea, which was the greater danger, so that, powerless to do anything more, they went wherever the discretion and impetus of the wind took them. In this fashion they passed before us, as we observed them from shore, and although they were not very far from shore, they were so involved in working the rigging of the ship that they did not notice the signals we sent them. However, as they were close to the mouth of the river which they wanted to approach and they were fortunate enough to have the tide rising, the force of the water carried them where they wanted to go, for if it had ebbed as much as it rose, they would doubtless have perished that night being swallowed up by the sea along with the ship, which was already barely managing to stay afloat. Sailing in this way, then, to the mouth of the river, as they ran into shallow water, the ship touched bottom and with the few bumps it made, the rudder broke off and the ship came to rest wretchedly on the sand in a depth of 4 *braças*.

This event which would normally cause great affliction because of their finding themselves in the utmost distress as victims of a shipwreck on the shore, which plight I have just now described, came to them as a relief, for it seemed to them that they would end their lives not swallowed up by the sea, with the work of struggling with the waves, but on land and with more time and means to render an account to God even if they had no hope left of saving their lives. That evening they did not leave the ship, making themselves ready to do so on the following day, in the meantime preparing rafts and another small boat that was aboard the ship, up to that point having no knowledge of us, although we were very close to each other, and although we had all seen what happened to the ship because we had kept following it with our eyes and kept a continual watch on it from an eminence until we observed that it had already run aground in the sand. We thereafter returned to our den or thicket and turned our attention to sustenance, gathering some mussels on the beach, which were to be found there in great quantity and which were very good. We collected a great supply of them as a group, and I being the one who divided up the poor supper among them, I gave each one a dozen mussels and as much biscuit as each one could hold in his hand, afterwards putting the rest away in a safe place, for we did not know what need we might have of it. This meagre supper had to make up for the two preceding days, during which we had not eaten, the more diligent of us, however, adding some stalks of wild fig of India of which there was a great abundance in the bush, and all that is good about them is that they are sweet and non-poisonous. However, we made a very good fire, since there was plenty of wood, and, each group of us making its own fire, we lay down next to it so that the warmth of the fire would supply that of the mattresses, which were sand, and that of the covers and bolsters, which were none other than the air and foliage of the thicket. And although our stomachs were not much satisfied, neither this lack nor that of beds prevented us from sleep because we had gone for days without any.

The dawn came and we began to set our poor, miserable lives in order. Some went to inform those on the ship of our whereabouts and situation;[1] others stayed, awaiting the visit of the Cafres, prepared for any event, good or bad, especially since we saw them appearing already on the hilltops little by little, wending their ways by different paths according to the location of their thatched huts with relation to where we were. They were coming now more in order, all of them with their assegais in their hands.[2] And as it appeared to be a custom for them to be accompanied each by a little dog, all of the dogs with their tails cut off, and the day before they had told us that there was much small cattle in the land, our need and desire made us believe that those animals were goats, which in reality were dogs.[3] We were already making ourselves ready to appease our hunger, looking upon the goats as a good augury, and we were dividing them up according to our desires, and since we saw so many of them, we were already permitting ourselves to discuss what was to be done with the hides, each one of us planning to use them in the manner which seemed best to him. The truth of the matter, however, was soon apparent to us as the Cafres drew near to us and we could see that the animals were dogs, which saddened us considerably, but if they gave them to us dead and said they were goats, there is no doubt that we would have to eat them as such. For greater precaution we received the Cafres in this way: I was seated in the middle of the sand on a high place where they were heading, with

[1] Cabreira says that before daybreak he sent the boatswain's mate, Simão Franco, and fourteen others, all armed, to help those who had come from the ship.

[2] Cabreira says that eventually there were more than 300 Kaffirs.

[3] Cabreira says they all have little dogs with their ears and tails cut off, with which they hunt wild pig, deer, buffaloes, elephants, tigers, lions and many hippopotami. There were partridges, wild chickens, small domestic fowl, green pigeons and parrots, which were very good eating, of which the Portuguese killed many. There were also rabbits, hares and genets which the Portuguese caught in snares. There were, of course, no tigers or rabbits.

8 or ten men accompanying me; the Captain with the others distributed in posts with muskets and swords in readiness, all however concealing their readiness to use their weapons. As the Cafres arrived, they thrust their assegais in the sand at a distance from us, and without any weapons at all were coming happily and confidently toward the place where we were. There must have been about two hundred of them in all, and we were little more than twenty people, for the others had gone to the carrack. For barter they were carrying with them a small leather bottle containing about two *canadas* of sour milk, some small quantity of millet, which I estimated to be three quarters in all.[1] The trading was done near me, since I was in charge of bartering our goods, which consisted of some old nails. The trading began, and after the small pieces of iron were spent, the keys became the objects of trading. These were much valued by the Cafres, particularly the females, who whistled when they saw them, and so, to make them even more impressed with them than they already were, I would whistle first with a thing which caused them laughter and amazement, and when they too tried to make a whistling sound with it, they couldn't do it. Finally they came to the conclusion that the keys were talking and that that was sorcery, although a 'sorcerer' among them means 'a wise man' and is thus held in high esteem, as I shall presently relate. The trading lasted for several hours, the time being spent partly in selling and partly in seeing and conversing, with which we were not at all annoyed, because it served to familiarize them with us and to make them favourably disposed to dealing with us. They did not fail, however, to notice, and told us so, that, whereas they had laid down their weapons, we were not laying ours down, and this was certainly malice on their part, because, since there were so many of them, they could easily take them from our hands and do anything they wished with us, since there were more than six of them to each one of us. We replied to them that it was our custom never to lay down our arms, with which answer they had to seem to be satisfied, whether they were or not. After this, they took leave of us, but with malice, for, although we believed they had left, many of them remained hidden in ambush, as I shall presently relate. We withdrew to our den after the barbarians had gone, and I began to distribute dinner to all our people. The dinner consisted of the same ration of biscuit, two dozen mussels, a handful of millet for them to toast and three spoonfuls of sour milk, except that the first ones served took the curds and the last of us served had three spoonfuls of whey, which was, however, good luck for some and bad luck for others. The

[1] Presumably of an *alqueire*, which would be a little less than $2\frac{1}{2}$ gallons.

bad thing was that when we sent a boy to fetch water in the brook the Cafres caught him unawares and after hitting him several times on the neck, they took what he was carrying away from him and fled. The booty which these people obtained, which consisted of a knife, a copper pot and a pewter vessel, inspired such envy in the rest of them that they were determined to get something for themselves. We ran to the boy's aid but were too late to be of any help. We tried to lay a trap for the others who were hidden by putting a large cauldron in the spring and hiding close enough to it so that we could rush in and catch them. One of them was lucky enough, however, to dart in like a young deer while our backs were turned and, seizing the cauldron, disappeared before we could do anything about it. We laid a second trap and a third one. Although they came, they took nothing because we were now very much on the alert and it would have cost them their lives if we fired our matchlocks at them in earnest. However, we certainly did not want to kill any of them, for in so doing we should have offended them, and we had good reason to believe that we were to stand very much in need of them. The day was coming to an end and the Cafres increased their numbers with the intention, taking advantage of the darkness of the night, of coming to attack and rob us of whatever they could, as they did. We, however, placed ourselves in an order of defence, distributing our people with their weapons, and although they fell upon us from various directions, finding resistance everywhere, they did not enter because of their fear of the firearms. They tried, however, to drive us from the den by hurling clods of earth at us and pelting us with them. Since we were protected by the trees of the thicket they did us no harm, although we could have been badly hurt if they had used stones. And because one of them was daringly coming into the thicket and was fired upon with a musket, they left us alone until the morning, as we kept a continual watch, sustaining ourselves with the mussels now in greater abundance. As soon as it was daylight, we departed thence for where the ship and our companions were, leaving the place to the Cafres who came in in infinite numbers in our sight, looking to see if we had left anything there, and taking an anchor from the boat, which we had left buried, a writing-desk, a keg of musket-balls and powder, which was of no use to them, looking like hunting dogs which with the scent of a rabbit run about in a very lively fashion, darting in and out of the thicket.[1] Such were

---

[1] Cabreira says the Portuguese began carrying a barrel of powder with them, but because of their physical weakness, the arms they were taking with them, and the sand

these people, wretched, barbarous and fierce to the highest degree, and they did not fail to discover the boat, which they broke in pieces in order to get the nails from it. When we had got within sight of the ship and, some of our companions were already going on land, as they realized that we were not dead, and as we had observed their danger and good fortune, we all rejoiced as much as our wretched state permitted. Since we are all now in the same place, I shall give a description of the land, the latitude occupied by the place where we shipwrecked, how well we were received by this land all the time we were there, its qualities, and the barbarity of its inhabitants.

We underwent our pitiful shipwreck at the end and first land which they call the land of Natal, which is at slightly less than 32 degrees at the place which modern maps, made since the shipwreck of the carrack *São João*, call River of Ants because of the many ants there are in the land as soon as it rains, as we experienced, the name being given to it by those who escaped from that shipwreck.[1] The coast and the interior are inhabited by barbarous pagans, for these people have not yet been infected by the Mahometan sect which has spread so much through all of Africa. These pagans are generally of good disposition. They do not adore any idol nor do they have any temple or prayer-house. They recognize, however, that there is something up there in Heaven which governs this world and from whom they hope for the good things of this world, for they are completely unconcerned about those of the other life and are ignorant of their existence. Some, however, are more barbarous than others, more ferocious, thieving and cruel. And the division of the people is the same division which is made in the land by this river where we were, for those who inhabit the land from here to the Cape of Good Hope and all the rest of the coast as far as Angola are the worst people who populate this region.[2] Those who live from this river to Moçambique are tractable people, obliging and of good disposition.[3] It appears that they take the good and bad qualities they have in their nature and disposition from the quality of

which was either loose or pebbly, they decided to bury the powder in a thicket where they later recovered it.

[1] The *São João Baptista*, Captain Pêro de Morais Sarmento. For the narrative of this wreck and the adventures of the survivors, Boxer, 1959, pp. 188–271. The shipwreck took place south of the point where the *Belém* reached land, apparently near the Keiskama river; the River of Ants is mentioned on pp. 231–2. P. da Costa notes that Cabreira estimated the distance of his landfall from the Cape at 170 leagues, and identifies the River of Ants with the Umzimvubu, or St John's river.

[2] Apparently referring to the Khoisan peoples.

[3] Cabreira says they are lean, erect, tall, handsome in appearance, well able to endure toil, hunger and cold. They live for two hundred years in good health, keeping all their teeth, and are so light-footed that they run along crags like deer.

the land, because that which runs as far as the Cape of Good Hope for the space of 160 leagues, which is the distance involved, is rugged, barren, more or less mountainous and wilder. That which runs as far as Sofala, however, for the space of 170 leagues, is fertile, level and rich in food.

These barbarians live in two styles: those who are closest to the sea live in extreme poverty and wretchedness, more like savages than rational people. They sustain themselves with milk from a few cattle they have, by hunting and gathering shellfish, and by scratching in the earth and sowing some millet, gourds and watermelons. Those in the interior live in an abundance of cattle, crops and breeding of domestic animals and have their villages and houses of straw, timbers and clay.[1] Each village has its own person whom they call King and in their language Lord *Musungo* Great *Muculo*, great *muculo* meaning great lord to distinguish the king from the others honoured by the title *musungo*, distinguishing the one they call king with the particle *muculo*.[2] Among them live some people they call sorcerers, a word which they use to

[1] Cabreira says that they cover themselves with cow skins, softened till they are like velvet, which reach from the shoulders to below the knees. Their wealth is reckoned only by the number of cows they have. They carry in their hands sticks two spans long the end of which is like a fox's brush, which they use as a handkerchief and as a fan. They have round sandals of elephant hide which hang from their hands; he had never seen them on their feet. They use assegais with broad, well made iron tips, and small shields of elephant hide, made like *adargas*. The rich use other things. The women do all the sowing and tilling of the soil, harvesting a coarse millet as big or bigger than linseed. They sow large and very good water-melons, beans, gourds of many kinds and sugar canes, though they brought few of these to the Portuguese. They rely principally on cows which were the handsomest and most docile Cabreira had seen anywhere. They curdle the milk and make it sour, which the Portuguese did not like. They eat a root resembling spurge flax which they say gives them great strength, and another with a tiny seed which grows underground and which they eat with great pleasure. They also eat tree resin and waste none of the forest fruits. This was of great use to the castaways whom they helped to support for many days, though the fruits were quite unlike those of either Portugal or India. The women do not bring dowries to their husbands, but the latter pay cows to their fathers-in-law. The wives are like prisoners. The husband will select one from six or seven each month and this causes no jealousy. The jewellery, consisting of copper or bone bracelets and earrings, belongs to the men.

[2] Both these words are Bantu and occur in slightly different forms and with varying meanings in a number of languages. However, no word like *musungo* occurs in the Nguni languages, which are those spoken in the region in which the shipwreck seems likely to have taken place. The language in which words like these most nearly have the sense which Lobo assigns to them is Chopi, spoken between Cape Corrientes and the mouth of the Limpopo. Here *musungu* means 'head', though it is not the normal word for 'chief', and *mukulu* means 'great'. I am indebted to Dr Hazel Carter and Mr David Rycroft for this information.

Cabreira says that when he went among the Kaffirs they called him 'Cananfys, Molumgo, Muculo, Manimusa', all exalted titles. For comment on these 'praise-names' and suggestions of cognate words in a number of Bantu languages see the valuable article by Professor P. E. H. Hair, 'Portuguese Contacts with the Bantu languages of the Transkei, Natal and southern Mozambique 1497–1650', *African Studies*, 39, no. 1 (1980).

mean the same thing as wise men. They ask these people for rain for their crops. They make use of more than a few superstitions in addition to cunning tricks of witchcraft and dealings they have with the devil, for they must not kill a cow to eat it unless it is tied by all four legs, and, with the cow alive and tied in this way, they proceed to quarter it, and before it dies, they open it up, bringing in a sort of priest of theirs, who, putting his hand into the animal's stomach, pulls out a handful of the contents, with part of which he touches the tips of his nose and ears, the front of his head between his eyes, and the instep of his foot, throwing the rest on the ground, stamping on it and rubbing it with the sole of his foot. These blind people believe that these ceremonies ensure that they will have many cows, which up to the present time represents the height of their desires, possessions and joys. With little difficulty it was possible to create a flourishing Christianity among these people, because, since their natural disposition is good and they do not have any sect or superstitions to which they are wedded, they are in effect a *tabula rasa* on which the doctrine which is first taught them can be written and portrayed. For this reason it is distressing to see that, for lack of the necessary effort, so many millions of souls redeemed with the blood of Christ are lost. And we can say of them that they are like children dying of hunger because there is no one to distribute to them the bread of the doctrine of Heaven, the only true sustenance of souls. In the midst of this barbarity, they enjoy the best soil and land climate that I have seen, for most of it is black and of fertile quality. The grass grows to the height of a man, and food crops would grow in the same way if they were sown. I know that we planted a grain of corn found by chance among the rice and that I soon counted nine ears that sprouted forth from it, and what is more, the soil was not of the best but was sandy, being right on the shore.

The tree cover is as perfect as it can be, covering mountains, valleys and plains, as verdant and luxuriant as the sight could desire, so high, bushy and well grown that very close to where we made our habitation, we could have built many Indiamen, choosing wood to satisfy the desires and choice of those most difficult to please, of varying strengths to satisfy every requirement. And yet amid this tree cover there are beautiful fields free of trees for large plantings of crops. The climate is the mildest and most healthful that I have seen, for not only did we enjoy a perpetual spring for the 7 months we were there but also not one of us became sick and those who arrived in that land in sickly condition convalesced. And although 7 or 8 persons died, it was because they arrived already so wasted by their sickness from the sea that their lives soon ended on land.[1] What amazed us most was seeing the beauty and delightfulness of the flowers that God Our Lord had planted there, so little esteemed by such barbarous people, being such that, in scent, colours, form and beauty alike, they could serve to embellish the finest garden in Europe, especially a tree, of which there were many among those of the wooded areas, which gives forth nothing but beautiful bunches of flowers so well fashioned, of a perfectly pyramidal form, that art cannot improve upon their composition. I caused many of these to be cut to decorate the altar, and they could have done the same for any of the most elegant altars in the world. The sight which the tree affords when it is laden with these bunches of flowers (which at the bottom are about the thickness of a person's two hands together and more than a span in length) is the most charming I have encountered in any of the parts of the world I have travelled.

The land does not produce domestic fruits, for lack of their cultivation, of which there is none among the Cafres, who have no interest in it. In the wooded places, however, we found some wild fruit, namely: cabbage palms; a kind of fruit like unripe cherries; another kind like dates but smaller and yellowish; another like immature fruit the size of walnuts, very sweet tasting but with little pulp; carandas like large nuts as hardy as cherries of Cintra and in colour an extremely fine scarlet, of an excellent taste, whose flower, in scent and every other aspect, is like that of the orange, without yielding any advantage to it in colour, leaves, size and fragrance.[2] Water abounds in rivers and cool, pure, healthful, sweet springs. The winter is like that of India, which begins in June and continues until October, but not so troublesome with rains and cold as that of Europe, nor is it a hot winter like that of India. In conclusion, I say that I have not seen a more temperate land or one with a better climate than this one and very few as good, for I can say that it is always delightful springtime.

In so much forest, and all the more so since it is in Africa, there is sure to be a multitude and great variety of wild animals. Those about which we were able to have information are the following: elephants, wild buffalo (which were very wild indeed), lions, tigers,[3] ounces, wild

---

[1] Cabreira says that four or five died in the first five or six days. They were buried in a selected place below a cross, as it was thought many people would die. 'It moved us to great grief and enhanced our great homesickness to see our companions buried where no feet had trodden but those of brute beasts and those native savages that are hardly distinguishable from wild animals'.

[2] The flora of South Africa is, of course, of great beauty and variety, but Lobo's descriptions are too vague to permit precise identifications.   [3] See p. 59 n. 3.

boar. There must be many others further into the interior. A great variety of birds, but all different from ours except for the partridges which are in every way the same as those of Europe, although somewhat more ash-coloured. Chickens are numerous but small. We made vegetable gardens with some seeds that there were in the land: millet; very large, sweet, red watermelons; three or four varieties of Guinea gourds; two or three of those called calabashes,[1] beans, and others of this sort. Beyond all this, considering the quality of this land in all that which extends from the said Cape as far as Sofalla, this was the most suitable place for remedying our misfortune and wretched shipwreck that we could find, bringing us, as it appears, by the hand to this place so that we should not all perish, putting us in a good port with a beautiful, delightful river, for, bordered on both sides with very high rocks densely covered with large, luxuriant trees, it presented so beautiful a view that if it were relished and enjoyed by people less tormented by suffering and more at leisure, it could be considered a rare treat, but in the condition of shipwrecked people in which we found ourselves it did give us some comfort.

[1] *abóboras...das que chamão de Carneiro.*

CHAPTER 31

[How we salvaged what we could from the ship and obtained food through the good offices of a man who had stayed there from another shipwreck]

It was on a Monday when we appeared in sight of our ship already run aground and of our companions, who were beginning to come to land. As we appeared at the top of a mountain, with the river separating us from them, the joy in all of us was great and equal on both sides of the river, as in companions who had experienced together so many sufferings and dangers, they having already given us up for dead, we who were to be most loyal to those who were about to come and for whom we made ourselves ready. We descended the mountain and while the *balão* was being prepared to take us to the other side, we appeased our hunger with many mussels, with which the rocky parts of the shore were covered, and it was no small banquet for people who needed some remedy for hunger. I well know that, if it were in another place where there were greater abundance of food, that someone certainly would have persuaded us of the great harm that so much poor food would do to us, but there was no one who paid any attention to this or to whether they were well or badly cooked, each of us thinking that harm could come to us only from what we did not eat. When we had got to the other side of the river, we found a good place within sight of the sea, enclosed by trees at the side, where we decided, until we should have better counsel, to make our dwelling-place. Straw and branches served us for the huts which were soon constructed.[1] We next turned our attention to water and food, resolved until then to

[1] Cabreira says he divided the company into three squads to maintain a continuous night watch, with their arms in their hands, calling to one another at regular intervals so as to prove to the Kaffirs that they were on guard. Though the latter came to look several times they never ventured to attack. The grummets slept in the *balão*, which was moored in the river where it was sheltered from the storms. One night the Kaffirs tried to cut the cable, the grummets fired two musket shots, which roused the camp. Cabreira took ten men with him and went to the *balão*, whereupon the Kaffirs hid in the bush.

336

travel by land back to Moçambique, waiting first to see what would happen to the carrack, from which we were beginning to remove some things, as it was continually opening up more and more. Water was what worried us most, because all we could discover there was a stagnant pool between some mountains, containing water that had run down from them during the time of rain, which, in addition to being stagnant and impure, served both us and the wild beasts of the forest not only as a drinking place but also as a place where they came to bathe. There is no doubt that it would have been very injurious to our health if we had continued to use it. Although we had found much good water at our first site, it was too far away, being almost a league's distance from where we were now, and for two hundred and fifty-two people, men, women, children, old people and youths, sick and healthy, for there were a great many in all these categories, it was a great inconvenience. We sustained ourselves for a few days with the water from the stagnant pool, and we were already feeling the effects of it when we discovered a fresh spring of very good water next to a rock, on seeing some rushes in that place. With this spring we were well supplied with water, although we turned our attention to food, and because God favoured us by preserving the *balão* for us, we began to use it to remove some food from the carrack, consisting of rice, biscuit, salted meat, salted fish, some wine, and sweetmeats. Because there was so much food carried on the ship, we could have removed enough to keep us free from distress for more than two years.[1] However, a lamentable lack of order in this matter resulted in there being brought to shore only eight hundred bales of rice,[2] each containing approximately three *alqueires*. Experience has shown that the dissension and bad behaviour which prevail in situations such as this cause serious and unfortunate consequences when the distribution of these things is not handled by a person who is generally respected. They all agreed with the Captain to ask me to assume the responsibility of distributing the food to everyone. The Portuguese are certainly impatient by nature and even more so when galled by sufferings such as those in which they found themselves on this occasion, and they insult one another and anyone who deals with them. However, since I knew them well

---

[1] Cabreira says that it was often impossible to reach the ship for three days together because of the heavy seas. He went to bring off the sealed royal letters, the powder, shot and rope, and the remaining arms which had already been crated on his orders. This he did with great risk. He had had the precious stones, amber, musk, bezoar and pearls unloaded and kept by the officers until they could be registered and handed over as they later were in Angola.

[2] Cabreira says 640 bales, already wet, but they were able to dry it.

and they loved and respected me and thought I could be of great help to them on this occasion, I accepted the work and received everything as it came ashore. As I say, it could have been a very great quantity if there had been more order and if, when the ship was still afloat but in danger of sinking, so many items of food as well as merchandise had not been so recklessly pillaged. I put everything together in one pile, paying no attention to names or marks on the items, whether they were those of the Captain or of common people, the pilot or other officers. And because greed, even in that wretched state in which we found ourselves, blinded the poor shipwrecked people so much that it made them forget the very things they needed most in order to stay alive, busying themselves in removing from the ship the clothing and merchandise which we would probably have to burn on the shore. Even if we were to be travelling through known territory inhabited by Christians, we should consider ourselves signally favoured by God if we were to escape with our lives. It was necessary, therefore, to make those who were rowing the *balão* swear that they would bring me only rice, which they did for a whole day so that the *bangaçal*,[1] as the storehouse of food was called, increased very much.

One of the most remarkable of the various favours we received from God in this whole wretched shipwreck was that no one died in it except for a poor youth from Vizeu.[2] After he was safe on land and well rested, he was courting his own fate and unfortunate death, for one day he got it in his head to go back to the ship, and none of his friends could dissuade him from it. It happened to be on a day which was clear and pleasant in the early morning but which clouded up so much after mid-day that a big storm was threatening. Those who had gone to the ship and others who were already on it, about 60 people in all, seeing the indications of a storm and fearing that they would surely perish that night, for it appeared that that was when the storm was threatening to strike them if they slept on the ship, they signalled to us to come to their aid. It was impossible for us to do so, however, because it was high tide, the sea was very rough, the sandbank at the mouth of the river was in a heavy sea, and risking the *balão* as well as the lives of the people who would be going in it, which was the only hope of salvation for the shipwrecked people, would have been the height of imprudence. We therefore informed them that we could not come to their aid and that we believed the danger was not so great as they

[1] A warehouse, *HJ*, 'Bankshall'.
[2] Viseu in central Portugal, about 50 miles SE of Oporto.

imagined, for it was only a threat to them and, as it turned out, it was not what they feared it would be. In any case, fear impelled them to make a raft of timbers, boards and beams well tied together with ropes, and they all got on it with some shovels to guide the contraption into the current which would bring them to shore. The waves, as I say, were large, and each one that struck them covered them completely, all of them clinging to the timbers and rising to the surface of the water so late that it caused them great anxiety while they were under the water, which happened because the raft was heavy and carrying many people. It happened then that the poor youth, although in the middle of all of them, was snatched away from their midst by a wave. It took no one but him, and it drowned him. The rest of them, some swimming and others on the raft, reached shore, where we gave them the kind of reception deserved by people whom we had seen escape such perils. Better luck was had by others for whom there was no room on the raft. One of them jumped into the water to swim sooner than he should have, and, as the tide was going out, it carried him out to sea. Everyone thought he was drowned, but, since he was a good swimmer and was strong, he kept himself above water until the tide came in again, bringing him in with it, and delivered him safely to the shore. Another boy, 12 or 13 years old, threw himself into the waves with a bolster under his arms, and, with the bolster, his courage and the good luck he had, braved the rolling waves and misfortune and appeared safely on the shore when we least expected it. Some made use of kegs, which are very useful for such a task. Another, however, had better luck than all of them, which was certain to be the case because of the method he chose to use. Making a cross with some cross-pieces for a hammock, he embarked on it to save himself, in which he was not mistaken, for if the true cross is the ship that carries us over the stormy sea of this world to the safe port of blessedness, the poor imitation might well bring about similar results, as this poor lad experienced, whom we received in safety on the shore. Two others, of those on board the ship, were the victims of no small misfortune. When they found themselves on the stranded ship and saw that everything aboard was at the disposal of anyone who wanted it, two grummets[1] lunched on a beautiful jar of preserved ginger from China, which is the best made in the Orient, and, to counteract the heat caused

---

[1] *grumetes*. 'They were apprentice seamen, not necessarily boys, though most of them were probably in their teens. They did all the hardest work aboard the ship', Boxer, 1959, p. 9, n. 3.

by the ginger, they seized a keg of brandy. Since this was like adding fire to fire, the mixture of both things was so harmful that it caused one of them to die right away, and the other became so miserable and incapable of any human activity that he was the same as if he were dead and was the object of much pity. These two cases were the last of our calamities resulting from the shipwreck.

At this time we began to plan more sensibly for our future needs. We had already been living for six or seven days in our thatched houses without the negroes of the land coming to us with cows to sell; for, although a few had come, they had raised the price for the cows so that we thought it better to conceal our hunger and craving for fresh meat rather than pay too much for it, because, although they were asking for old nails, keys, and some brass rings, all of which would come to a value of six or seven *vinteis* for each cow, it was important for us to barter more advantageously in the future, so we let them go without buying any cattle from them, and our eyes followed the cows longingly as they left. I was the buyer because if each one tried to do it for himself, in addition to causing confusion, our bartering would be extremely expensive. And since no others came for several days afterwards, we decided to go up the river in the *balão* to discover land and see where we could attack some cows and take some if that should become necessary. With 12 persons in the boat we went a few leagues up the river, discovering on both sides of it beautiful forests, delightful meadows, many plantings of millet and large herds of horned cattle. We then came back, carefully hiding our interest in the cattle and giving no indication of our intent, well aware of the Cafres' readiness for any attack and knowing that they would make every effort to hide and flee with the cattle if they had any idea we were planning to attack them. We came back in peace, however, reserving our intentions for a better opportunity. When we arrived just before nightfall, something better than we could ever have imagined happened to us, because the reason for the Cafres' not wanting friendship with us was that they were persuaded that we ate people and would surely do so with them, as if there were no better meat and fish than the flesh of a filthy black Cafre. It was God Our Lord's will that there had grown up among them a Christian *cabra*[1] from India, who had stayed there from the wreck of the ship *Sam Alberto*, whose Captain was Nuno Velho Pereira, 48 years earlier.[2] God had preserved him for our salvation. At the

---

[1] Strictly the child of parents, one of whom is a mulatto, and the other a negro or negress.

[2] The *Santo Alberto*, Captain Julião de Faria Cerveira, was wrecked on 25 March, 1593. For

present time he has been there for more than 60 years, having been left there as a very small child because he was unable to accompany the rest of the people. His Christian name was Antonio, but he is now called Mangabome, meaning 'man like God'.[1] He had this name because they thought that he was something great and that he gave them rain. With this and other deceits, he got the poor Cafres to hold him in high esteem and he lived there with the reputation of a great sorcerer and was wealthy according to the standards of that land. When this man, then, heard of our shipwreck and the place where we were, he wanted very much to see us, but the Cafres' opinion of us made it difficult for him. He had, however, so much credit and authority with them that he persuaded them that they should come to see us and deal with us because we were all relations of his and behaved well toward other people, which in the final analysis they did not find to be an accurate description of us, as I shall explain further on, nor did poor Antonio find his due reward, as I shall also relate. The king of the land, for we can say that each span of land has its own, made up his mind to come in company with Antonio with 8 very beautiful oxen and cows, one to give as a present and 7 to be bartered. Several hours after our departure [to reconnoitre the possibility of obtaining cattle by force further up the river], the king being accompanied by as many as 50 Cafres, and because they signalled that they wanted to talk with us, the *cabra* Antonio saying a few words in Portuguese which he no longer knew very well, our people felt confident enough to have one of their number swim across the river, for we had taken the *balão*, to find out what people they were and why they were coming. Informing them of the Captain's absence, he persuaded them to remain there until our return, which they did. While we were still in the boat we received news of the people awaiting us, so we rowed to the other side where the petty king and Antonio were. As they were all descending the mountain to receive us, Antonio, seeing our boat already landed, hurried ahead of the others shouting joyfully: 'My Christendom, my Christendom,' words he was using to express what was uppermost in his mind and to announce who he was, forgetful now of other words that would have been more appropriate. Our joy in receiving him was equally great, for although badly pronounced, the sound of those familiar words in so distant a land was music to our ears, and the joy

a narrative of the shipwreck and the fate of the survivors by J. B. Lavanha, see Boxer, 1959, pp. 106–186. Pereira, who had been Captain of Sofala, was a passenger.

[1] Mr David Rycroft informs me that there are no words in the Nguni languages which bear a meaning resembling this.

in many of us was accompanied by a few tears awakened in us by our plight and our remembrance of other lands. Antonio was in all ways similar to the rest of them except for the love and the few familiar words with which he greeted and embraced us and the love we had for him as if we had known him for a long time, as our minds, even then, were in anticipation of the benefits God was to grant us through the instrument of that poor fellow, providing in him the remedy for our wretchedness. The petty king and the others arrived and we gave all of them the courtesy and entertainment required on such an occasion. Staying there for a short time, since it was already dark and they wanted to remain on the other side of the river with their cattle, we went back to our huts to have supper prepared for them. On bidding us good-bye, Antonio had asked us to get him some sweetmeats and biscuit, because he had only the remembrance of all that and had a great longing for it.

When we were back with our companions we happily celebrated the gift of that new and budding friendship, hoping that because of it we could barter for cattle for our sustenance without danger of offending the natives by using force against them, which was what we had decided to do as a last resort. I arranged for our new guests' supper and for satisfying Antonio's longings. Providing some of what he wanted for the others also, we had two large cauldrons of boiled rice prepared, and in addition to this, to please the king as well, a cloth full of biscuit and a bowl of citron syrup which we happened to find in an earthen jug. When these gifts of food reached them, there was great rejoicing among the barbarians, who were at first in doubt as to how they should eat the rice which was thrown on a large platter placed on the ground. They were all crowded around the platter with no distinction between king and servant, and they all thrust their hands into it, trying to outdo one another in grabbing handfuls of the rice so as not to be left with a smaller share of it. One, however, more astute, perhaps because he had hands that were small or not as large as he would like, or because in that tumult and confusion he could not get as much as he wanted no matter how many times he put his hand into it, made use of a better stratagem, which was to take off one of the sandals he was wearing, made of raw buffalo hide, almost as wide as they were long, and oval in shape, which they wear so wide in order to protect their feet from thorns, overlooking the inconvenience of having footgear so poorly adapted to their feet. He took one of these sandals, then, in his hand, and paying no attention to whether it was clean or dirty, used it as a spoon, putting it in the plate in all confidence. His companions saw no objection to this, but rather showed their approval of the stratagem since they saw the advantage to be derived from it in the larger amounts that could be got at one time in the proportion that each one's sandal was larger than his hand. Availing themselves of the device, they all hurried to take off their sandals, and using them as spoons, quickly disposed of what was on the platter with their vigorous shovelling, each of them afterwards putting his sandal back on as if it had not served him as an implement for eating. After this action was over, the king was already staying with the fruit syrup and Antonio with the biscuit, all of which he reserved for himself. The king, after drinking what he wanted, did not trust any of those present to put their mouths to the bowl because of the risk of having it all disappear. He therefore made use of a good stratagem, which was to moisten the palm of his hand in the syrup and by putting it flat on the palm of the nearest person to him, moistened his palm with some of the syrup, after which the king would lick his own, the second fellow put his palm on that of another and, after licking his own, again pressed it against the king's palm which was now without any of that ointment. And with these touchings and lickings the bowl was being emptied with much merriment, and our own was certainly no less as we watched them from the outside, amazed at the barbarousness and boorishness of such wild people. After the banquet was over, which was more notable for the happiness and celebration that accompanied it than for the food, we went back to our huts and the Cafres withdrew, both of us waiting for the morning when they were to cross the river to see our thatched huts. We waited for them on the shore and we brought them across as if they were visitors in a foreign land. They were the best of that land and we had great need of them. In the meantime I prepared the present for the king, which consisted of several items, to wit: a few keys which were no longer of use to us, some brass rings, ornamental pieces of brass for locks on writing desks, and things more or less of this kind. I also distributed some of the same things among those who were accompanying the king. As a special gift and as an item of great value, I presented the king with a little bell which could very well have been used for a pack-mule. It was strung on a red woollen cord which set it off very nicely. I rang it first and then put it over his neck. The petty king was astonished and grateful for its workmanship and value and kept saying that it was talking. He kept shaking his body to hear it. There was never a cat or a donkey-colt that was more pleased with its bell than he was with his. We then crossed to the other side to barter for the cows, for which purpose I had the pieces of copper into which I had caused the ladle used for loading the bombards to be broken up. Each one of the pieces was probably a little larger than the palm of one's hand, some large and some small. And so that they would think the more highly of them, I had a Portuguese carry them in his bosom wrapped up in his cape and, keeping apart from the others, keep very much to himself, bringing out each piece very slowly and deliberately, as he did with great skill and greater success, because with that I bought the seven very beautiful cows, with a few pieces still left, which I gave to those present in order to please them and gain their approval of the bartering we had done and our liberality. To others I gave nails and other things of this kind, the price I paid for the 7 cows being approximately 12 *vinteins*. The worst part of it was that they thought they had put one over on us, and such ingenuousness on their part caused us much merriment. With this, that day's celebration came to an end, and we returned to renew ourselves with fresh meat, killing an ox, of which nothing was wasted, for in addition to the meat, which was approximately one *aratel* for each of us, the feet were distributed separately as well as the blood, the liver in slices to the sick, the heart by common agreement was always the butcher's honorarium, the tripe and lights were given specifically to the black people, and from the hide leather thongs with which to tie the roofs of the thatched huts. Finally, of the whole animal there was little left for a few dogs which had escaped the shipwreck with us and had accompanied us aboard the ship. As long as we had little cattle, we killed only one cow on Saturday. As the supply increased, we killed others on the other days of the week, finally reaching the point, when they were in greatest abundance, where we would kill two or three each day.

CHAPTER 32

[How the order was given to construct boats and the means by which this was accomplished]

We decided at this time to make boats for us to sail in, in consideration of the elderly, weak and sick who were still with us and who were certainly unable to accompany us if we were to travel the 170 leagues or more that we would have had to traverse to reach Sofala by land. As we were starting to make plans for the boats and to remove from the *Belém* what we needed in the way of cordage, sails, tar, gum-mastic and benzoin with which to daub the ships, the devil threw us in such a state of disorder that, if he had been successful in what he prepared for us, it certainly would have gone very badly for many of us. The fact was that some were ill content with the treatment they had been accorded by the Captain during the voyage, the shipwreck, and the time we were on land and, since their courage would not endure many delays in that bush country, trusting in their relative youthfulness, health and good strength, they all began to discuss travelling by land.[1] And even though the Captain could have calmed them down with good treatment and words, he did not do so, but rather, following some very bad advice from people to whom he listened more attentively than he should have, he let his anger get the better of him, and, instead of encouraging those who needed it so much, he did the very opposite and ordered it to be announced that to all those who wished to go by land he would give arms and merchandise for trading and that they could leave immediately. The people rejoiced at this and since they were already dissatisfied because of some words uttered by the same Captain on several occasions affirming that he was going to make a single ship for himself and for his friends, leaving the rest of them to the mercy of their bad fortune in that bush-country, with this and with his conciliatory remark one day, when all the people were together, in

---

[1] Cabreira says that they were inspired by what had happened to the survivors of the *S. João (Baptista)*, but that one João Ribeiro de Lucena, who had been one of them, warned them of the great difficulty of travelling by land.

which he promised that he would give a gold chain to those who would leave, the people became so angry that they resolved to travel by land, more than 80 men signing on immediately, those who were the strongest and healthiest among the shipwrecked, and doubtless some others not of this opinion, in good or mediocre health, would have gone with them to avoid remaining and perishing there in utter abandonment. The only hesitation was concerning who was to serve as their leader, for, if they did not have a person for whom they had respect and to whom they would defer, they were certainly courting disaster. For this reason, of one accord they sent word to me that in any event they wanted me to go with them and be their commander, promising to obey me to the death on all occasions on which I should give them orders, promising further to carry me on their backs whenever I should be tired. They would certainly do everything they promised because of the great deference they had for me and the love and respect they had conceived for me. After the message had been given to me, and, weighing well what a suitable course of action would be in the matter, I answered them that it would be improper both for them to leave and for me to accompany them, since they would be leaving more than 100 persons to their deaths at the very outset, since the old, weak, and sick would be unable to make even the first day's journey, and since God had given all of them life in such a wretched shipwreck and danger of losing their lives, it would be an evil thing to abandon so cruelly such good companions, knowing that there was hope of our having another way of saving all of us, that even if there should prove to be none, the way by land would still certainly be available to us, or in the event that the Captain were to do what they feared with respect to the ship and even though I were very much opposed to going by land, that I would then go with them as a brother and companion and not as their leader, and for these reasons it was not fitting that I should do so now before seeing how things would work out.

At this time the decision that the people had made had already come to the Captain's notice, and, seeing the danger he and the others were in, since he was one of those who could not travel by land, repenting of the announcement he had issued and what it had caused, he tried to smooth everything over, and unable to dissuade the people, who remained determined in their intention and dissatisfied with him, he asked me to conciliate them in any way I could since he saw the harm that would ensue for the majority of those poor shipwrecked people.

I took this opportunity to turn heaven and earth, as they say, to impress upon him how badly he had acted in not taking the advice, when I gave it to him, not to issue the announcement and other considerations touching this matter. But since all that could be done now was to find a remedy for what was done, I talked with the people and, although with difficulty, I persuaded them to accede to what was desired, with some conditions without which they would not desist from their intention. And since these conditions were not prejudicial to the common good, it was my duty to propose them to the Captain. Since it happened to be night-time when I did this, some of the conspirators took the opportunity to verify what I was saying and what the Captain was answering, by placing themselves behind some thickets next to which we were walking and discussing the matter. And as I believed I was being heard only by the Captain, criticizing him again for his behaviour and impressing on him the risk in which he had placed the neediest of those poor people, I added that they would all give up their plan to go by land provided that two ships would be built in which all of the people could embark. The second condition was that they had to begin and continue working on both ships at the same time so that no deception would be possible. The third condition was that the Captain was not to be in command of them in the work, nor was he to have anything to do with them in any distributions or dealings, other than to be content with the title of Captain, but that everything was to be entrusted to me, so that I would be in charge of them and would assign them their work, for they would agree to do anything if it were commanded by me. The final condition was that all the people's food should be in my control, for they trusted me, and I should distribute it and they should receive it from my hands. The Captain heard all of this, approved of it and agreed to comply with all of it and would have gone much further if they had asked it of him, for he was ready for and very much in need of whatever was required to appease them. And since they had heard the whole proposal and reply, little was needed to acquaint them with their purport, all of them immediately agreeing to remain. However, so that the Captain would see how determined they were concerning the plan to travel by land and the people they were, on the following day they handed him the list of names they had made, adding, however, that they were abandoning their plan in view of what I was telling them on his behalf.[1]

[1] Cabreira says that his announcement enabled him to tell what everyone was really thinking, and he found that there were some religious among those who wanted to go

After this was over and now that the Captain was in a prudent state of mind until another time, we turned our attention to emptying the ship and to making plans for the two pinnaces that we wanted to make. And hurrying to remove the most necessary things, on the eve of St Mary Magdalena's day,[1] we removed cordage, sails and a barrel of tar along with some other things of that kind. Many people went to the ship that morning and turned the storerooms[2] upside down for anything that could be of use. After they had all returned to the shore, it happened that at midnight we saw the unfortunate *Belem* blazing in flames. We had no more knowledge of what had caused it than the suppositions of a few people discoursing on it or the possibility that it had been set alight purposely by persons interested in the loss of the ship; for, since they bring much merchandise for which they are responsible, taking their chances, as they say, with the ship, as was the case with this one, even though it was shipwrecked it stayed on the water nonetheless for twenty-two days, during which time those who so desired came and went at will removing from it what each one prized most, those who had mercantile interests could have difficulty with their creditors concerning the uncertainty as to whether or not they had saved the merchandise they were bringing, and, to free themselves of any uncertainties they could explain that the ship had burned, so that nobody could take any action against them. This, however, was the opinion of the strictest, most prudent among our people, but it did not have any currency among the worst elements of the shipwrecked group. Another reason, and it must have been the true one, was that, when they were in the storerooms, they must have accidently left some fire there, which, igniting the large quantity of materials in the storerooms, became so intense that it very easily burned up the whole ship. Whatever the cause may have been, the ship burned, and our lamentation was great not only because a ship as beautiful as it was unfortunate ended its days consumed in flames but also because the kind of affection one has for his own home was how we felt about that ship, on which we had spent so much time and which certainly deserved some affection from us, and also because we were losing in it many things which would have helped save us from our wretched plight. At sunrise the carrack was already burned down to the surface of the water. After dinner some people went to it and, stepping aboard what little

by land. However, he makes no mention of their approach to Lobo, or of Lobo's nocturnal interview with him.

[1] The Feast is on 22 July.

[2] The text reads *pagões*, a copyist's mistake for *paiois*.

was left of it, found many nails, which were of great use to us. Some hatches from the carrack began to wash ashore, providing us with a great supply of nails for the building of the ships, for the construction of which, according to our prior decision to make them, we had to move further inland at the edge of the river, choosing a suitable place which would serve us better in expediting our work and which would give us more protection, since we realized that we were going to be there for a long time. For this purpose we found a beautiful, level field surrounded by mountains, with tall, thick trees all around, and open only in the direction of the sea. The place was excellent in itself and of great convenience to us because we had firewood, water and timbers for construction so readily available that we could properly and truthfully say that we had everything at our doorstep.

And since the location was so fresh and cool and so desirable a place, we had to reckon with great numbers of hippopotami, of which there were many in that river, and because from time immemorial they had been sole proprietors of that site, to which they came out to graze and sleep, it being their custom to spend little time in the water and most of their time on land, we had a fair amount of work, if not recreation, dispossessing them of that place, for which purpose we now and then chased, wounded and disturbed them until on one occasion we killed an enormous animal, the mother of another smaller one which escaped from us even though I exerted myself mightily to ensure that it would accompany its mother. I became involved in chasing it because it happened to come in my direction. I was pursuing it with another young man who was pricking it with a lance he had in his hands. However, the hide of these animals was and is so tough that he could never wound it no matter how much strength he put into thrusting the lance, and I was even urging him on to greater efforts with words of encouragement, for we had all the time in the world because we were pursuing it for a very long time, always keeping it between us, since it does not run very fast. And because I kept about 4 paces away from it as I went along, there was no danger in having the beast so close because it never veers to one side or the other. Even when it is maltreated it attacks only in a forward direction and tears to pieces whatever or whomsoever it finds in front of it. And because I knew about this peculiarity it has, I was not afraid to go along so close to it. Because of our respect for its forward attacks, it escaped us by plunging into the water, so that the mother paid for both of them, having been felled by a musket-shot which struck her in a weak spot that could be pierced by the shot, after receiving many others in the other parts of her body without sustaining any serious injury. With this and the hunt being so incessant and with our constant presence in that place, we had to drive them away willy-nilly.

We then concerned ourselves with the construction of the ships, for which we had very few skilled workmen, as follows: There were three carpenters, of whom the best one was so sick that, as he was finishing drawing a plan of the ship and making three models of the ribs for it, he promptly died. The second one was so old that he was of little help to us because of his age, weakness and sickliness. The third carpenter was the only one with some vigour, and he was the one who, on the carrack, fell down the hatchway.[1] Of blacksmiths we had only one, who was sickly, weak, and minus one eye which was a great help since he had much work to do. There was just one calker, so bloated, encumbered and in such poor health that we believed his life would not last long. There was not one sawyer among us, a trade so necessary for our work; everyone, however, had good will and great need and desire for saving us from disaster, and we were resolved to do our best to carry the work forward to a successful conclusion, trusting in God's favour, which did not fail us. And thus, according to the agreement we had made, I assigned all the people to the various tasks as follows: The strongest to cut down the timber in the woods and rough-hew it; others to haul it to the shipyard where the ships were being made and where there were some more skilful people helping with the planing as best they knew how, with the carpenter giving directions to all of them. A goodly number of the most important and distinguished people served in the shipyard helping to set in place and remove the planed wood; some served only to bore holes and drive in the nails and bolts. The one who did this best was a confectioner, who, being very skilful and practised in making sweetmeats, had excellent qualifications for the new trade I gave him. The calker was assisted by a few people practising his trade, and the blacksmith also had the help of some others who were more skilful than those helping the calker. For sawyers I selected a dozen of the strongest men, for they certainly would have to put their strength to much use sawing the great quantity of planks we needed. And because it was not fitting for any persons to be idle while all the others were working, and certainly the time and circumstances did not permit such a thing, I made the Captain be of assistance in the shipyard, being a place of greater esteem than others,

---

[1] Manoel Fernandes, who had now recovered from his fall (Cabreira). See p. 317.

on condition that he would not be lacking the necessary skill for the work. For the service of everyone and to go fetch water along the river, the *balão* was manned with six sailors for rowing and a master, who also were to go out to the sea with those who went fishing and to ferry from the carrack to land, which would have been before the carrack burned. The old and sick who were still able to do something were assigned to making oakum from old ropes for the calking and cordage which we made later; two more were assigned to cutting firewood and making charcoal for the iron-forge, and six were to be herdsmen for the small number of cattle we already had and for the great number that we hoped to have. The negroes, who were numerous, were assigned, some to serving their masters who were busy working, the others, and when necessary all of them, to hauling the wood. I had the task of distributing the food to them and visiting them as they were performing all these various kinds of fatiguing work in order to give them encouragement and consolation. Four other religious who were there were assigned to the service of the church, tending also to the spiritual well-being of all the people. In addition to my own share in this last task, all the sermons were necessarily given by me because there was no one else to do it.[1]

After everyone had been assigned his work as I have related, we first had to busy ourselves making dwellings better made and roomier than the first ones, because we were to live in them for a longer time, although both the first ones and the new ones were of the same material: straw and wood.[2] It is very true that we had ideal conditions and every material at our disposal, which facilitated our work considerably. I took responsibility for the church, making it large enough to hold more than 200 people, supported by timbers and covered with straw, beautifully adorned with an altar-piece and pictures, for there were many of these things like flotsam and jetsam on the shore, because, as the ship was splitting open, it threw out all the spices, clothing, merchandise, pieces of furniture and baubles it contained, which were many and the kind of things that customarily

---

[1] Cabreira says nothing of Lobo's part in all this. He says they went to a sandy beach and there drew plans for the ships, which were to be in the style of Seville boats, with a keel of sixty spans, ten round the bow, nine from the deck to the bottom of the hold, and a beam of twenty.

[2] Cabreira says that he had a sawmill made with a stream and sufficient space to stack the cut timber. He cleared the area of bushes so that there should be no hiding-place for the Kaffirs. He chose for his own dwelling a small hill which everyone else avoided because of the snakes they had seen there. It had the stream in front and the river at the side. He did this with his own slaves and at times the help of a grummet.

come from India, the shore being so cluttered with all of these things that it was a pity to lay eyes on them; so that the people cooked their food with cinnamon bark, this being the fuel they used for the fire. Since I was disturbed about this because there was an abundance of firewood nearby, I did not consent to their burning this, each mess-group, in which there were 4, six or eight persons, having one or more bales readily available for burning. We first devoted all our labours to setting up the iron-forge, both because of the problems in creating it and because all the iron tools for every procedure in the work of building the ship had to be made in it. Everything worked out well in making the forge, and we made the anvil from one end of a block from the main topmast. The forge was easily devised. The bellows, however, gave us trouble and work, but a piece of leather that I had and used as a bed in Ethiopia and took with me, which they called *nete*,[1] five spans wide and eight spans long, made of six tanned sheepskins, red in colour, was used for the bellows since there was nothing else available at the time. With these makeshift bellows attached to two pieces of large chest lids, two musket-barrels served as the air-tubes through which the bellows supplied wind to the fire. The use of musket-barrels for this purpose was at the suggestion of a Capuchin friar who was with us, had been in the shipwreck of the carrack *Sam Gonçalo* and had seen the manner in which they were made in another urgent circumstance similar to ours.[2] Having advanced this far, we began to work the forge, making axes with which the necessary timber was brought to the ground, to be immediately planed by those designated for that work and then to be hauled by others so assigned to the edge of the river, whereupon we began the construction of the ships, preceded by two ceremonies. The first one was as follows: We all went to the woods, and reciting the litanies of Our Lady, the Chaplain, who was a monk of the third order of St. Francis, blessing that whole place and the trees that were in it, we selected the first tree to be struck by the axe, which was done by the Captain, who gave the first blows, and with the others continuing, we soon brought it to the ground, whereupon it was planed. The second ceremony was as follows: Taking a seasoned piece of wood which had washed ashore from our ship, adapting it for a keel and setting it on the stocks, we all came barefooted and in procession from the shore to that place, and, with the Chaplain Father blessing the keel, we named the ship *Nossa*

---

[1] See p. 147 n. 2.

[2] The *S. Gonçalo* was wrecked on the return voyage from India in 1630. The survivors built two small boats, one of which reached Moçambique; the other was rescued by a Portuguese ship near the Cape of Good Hope. The Capuchin was Frei Francisco.

Senhora da Natividade, offering it to her if she would take us in it to some Christian land, and imploring her favour and protection for continuing, completing and profiting from our work and construction for the purpose of coming out of that exile.[1] The ceremony was certainly celebrated with much devotion and many tears, considering the state in which we found ourselves and how much our lives and salvation depended on that piece of wood, upon which, after God, we founded our hopes, liberty and escape from so much misfortunes seemingly foreseeing in our hearts the contingencies and misfortunes, we were to endure on that piece of wood and the difficulties it was to have in order to save our lives, fighting the fury and boisterousness of the storms of the formidable Cape of Good Hope.[2]

With our reputation for liberality, acquired from the manner in which we bartered for the seven cows, the desire on the part of the rest of the Cafres for similar gains increased, and they came to us with their cows. And, realizing now that we did not eat people, aided in this by our faithful Antonio encouraging them to bring many, they did indeed bring us a great quantity, so that we were now losing our fear of hunger, as a beautiful corral was being filled with good cattle, so that we were now herdsmen on a grand scale, with the Cafres becoming so familiar with us that they now came to see us and bring us their cattle with no fear whatsoever, which was an invitation to us to go to their villages also, which we did on various occasions, bringing back cows, chickens, very badly made clay cauldrons, various gourd and bean seeds for our gardens, hides from which they made their clothing and from which we made shoes, which to a great extent made up for our lack of them, although most of the people made sandals out of the hides from the large rice bags. And since there were practitioners of all trades among the shipwrecked, we chose tailors and shoemakers whose only tasks were to repair the clothing and footwear for the rest. When our people made these excursions inland, they always took our Antonio with them to inspire more confidence and assurance, because of the credit he had with those people of his, whereby the Cafres

[1] Cabreira says that on Saturday 20 July they went to a wood and blessed the trees in the name of Our Lady of the Nativity, vowing that if they reached a port beyond the Cape of Good Hope in safety, they would sell the boat, take the proceeds of the sale to Portugal, and give them to the nuns of St Martha where her image was. However, 20 July 1635 was not a Saturday, but a Friday, and it was not St Martha's day which falls on 29 July. It is possible that Martha is a mistake for Mafalda, the daughter of Sancho I, who reformed the covent of Cistercian nuns at Arouca, where her embalmed body is preserved.

[2] Cabreira says that they had only three serviceable axes, one saw, and two carpenters, Manoel Fernandes, who was excellent, and a grummet attached to the regular carpenter.

came to have so much confidence in us that they asked us to give them rain. Unfortunately, we had a few pranksters among us who promised it to them, increasing their liberality in proportion to their powerlessness to give it, while the poor Cafres were more than ignorant enough to believe them. On one occasion, however, this foolhardiness of theirs turned out very badly for them, because, as it was getting dark in a Cafre's village with a few houses in it, as night was already closing in and a thunder-clap resounded, threatening a great rain, which did indeed come, they asked the lord of the village to have a house given to them in which they could take shelter. The Cafre, who could not have been the most rustic or stupid fellow in those woods, answered very haughtily: 'Don't you say that you give rain whenever you wish? You can also prevent it then, so just order this threatening rain not to fall, and it will doubtless obey you, so that neither will you need a house nor will I have the trouble of going to find it for you, nor will its inhabitants have the inconvenience of getting out of it for you'. And if he said it well he did it better, for, grabbing the door, he shut it in the guests' faces, leaving them to the rain for them to experience, as they did, the strength of the influence or authority they had with God.

As we were spending a long time there and there were many mouths to be fed, we were more and more conscious of a grievous but irreparable mistake we had made: We should have brought more rice and foodstuffs from the carrack and fewer rags and useless items, as we could have done. And because we still had many months ahead of us, we were reducing the portion of rice and increasing the portion of meat, because the cows were increasing in number, not only the ones we bought but others that were born of those purchased, so that we were coming to have a good herd of calves and an abundance of milk, enough for the majority of us, but it could have been enough for all of us if the person on whom this depended had been fairer. The bad part was that the poor people whose work was heaviest were the only ones cheated, the others being able to enjoy this small treat, which for that place was a great one, some being very successful in raising chickens, for we had ample time, leisure and opportunity there for all this. And because we also took advantage of the sea, we caught an abundance of fish by two methods. One of them was that, on the calmest days, the *balão* went out to sea and caught many fish, especially sea-bream,[1] since they were extremely abundant on that coast and so

[1] *pargo.* Dr Greenwood suggests that either the mussel-cracker, *Cymatoceps nasutus*, or the red Roman, *Chrysoblephus laticeps* is meant.

large that any one of them provided 8 companions with enough to eat. This fishing and the distribution of the catches were carried on in such a way that they certainly were of great benefit to some, but with little method as far as all our people were concerned, for, if it were not for this lack of order, we all would have been feasting on fish. This disorder had its origins in the boldness of some people by whom the Captain had allowed himself to be so dominated that he dared not contradict them, and so, as they went out to enjoy themselves, though also to work, the others did not remain idle but rather were engaged in heavier and more laborious work, so that it was only reasonable that the catch be distributed among all of them, since the work of those who remained behind was for the good of all; but it did not happen that way, since the unfortunate neediest ones often remained comfortless without anyone giving them any relief for this. For this reason they had recourse to another method of fishing, which was as follows: After a dragnet had been made, we went out at night to places we thought to be most propitious, starting from the bar at the mouth of the river and going inland, and, throwing it in, we caught varying quantities according to changing conditions, but always enough so that our work was never in vain. The relief afforded by this extended to everyone, because the catch was distributed by the day, with each group of messmates getting its share.

On one of the days when it was my turn to fish with the dragnet and when I was on the other side of the river feverishly engaged in the fishing, lo and behold, we suddenly saw our village burning, and surely, being made of straw, a material susceptible to any disaster, the whole village would have been consumed along with those poor belongings we had in it, particularly the food which was what we were most worried about, if they had not hurriedly stopped the fire, which still gained ground and left a few of our people with only what they had on their persons. Aid was brought to these people immediately, as I conducted a collection among the rest, each person giving a part of what little he had, so that disaster was avoided for them for the time being and for that calamity. Another similar fire occurred on another day toward evening, causing us more obvious danger because of the fury with which the fire raged aided by the wind, and if a certain house had caught fire, which seemed sure to happen, all the others would have burned. God Our Lord delivered us, however, taking pity on our misfortune and not permitting it to increase in that way. My fishing suffered to no small degree from the first fire; for, although we had already put a few draughts of fish in a safe place, we let the rest of them go because of our haste in running to help avert the catastrophe threatening us all and the fear each of us had in particular for his own thatched hut. Although, for the time and circumstances, we lived contentedly enough in those huts, we still experienced various frights in addition to those occasioned by fire because of the material which was so inflammable. These other frights were caused by the many snakes with which that place was heavily infested. And although we killed many in the beginning, driving still others away with the presence of so many people there, some still visited us, however, in our houses, extremely fond of going to our beds, where we found them. And although they were all harmful, the worst ones were some called spitting cobras, one of which I killed in the middle of our living area and in the place where my group had its mess, more than two *covados* long and the thickness of an average wrist, with two extremely long teeth in its mouth, which were as sharp and as fine and slender as a thorn. And God willed that, when I killed it, as it was about to spit upward and certainly would have harmed me because of my nearness to it, it rather whipped around to bite and spit on the blade with which I had pierced it and nailed it to the ground. Its colour is beautiful, but its poison is refined. I have seen this species of animal only in Africa and do not know if they are found elsewhere.

[Concerning how we were helped by the Kaffirs and the injurious treatment accorded them by the Captain]

While we were busy working on the ships, our Antonio brought a Cafre to us, named Domingos, one of two from the carrack *São João* who had remained there to live with the others, and, being a person with good qualities, he was so pleased with our way of life, as one who had been first reared in it, that he was unwilling to be parted from us ever again and was very useful to us in accompanying our people who went into the interior of the land, since he was thoroughly acquainted with it. Very unfortunately, however, after being with us for a long time, he drowned in the river while trying to swim across it and never reappeared. After this the other one came, named João, whose propensities nature tried to indicate to us by giving him one squinting eye as an outward sign of his treacherous nature, for he soon left us. And after we had departed in the first pinnace, with no further knowledge of him, it fell out that he died at the hands of our people, whom he was attempting to betray; for he came, after our departure, to join the people of the second pinnace,[1] of which I shall speak later, who, from 118 in 34 leagues' journey, had all died at the hands of the Cafres and from hunger except for 17 who managed to get back to this same place, where, trying to recuperate from the fatigue of the journey in order to continue, they were not helped by the arrival of this Cafre, who came as a spy with his father; and after two days the father left him with our people for better security, and since our people suspected what it might be, they killed him one night by striking his head with a stone and crushing it, whereby they caused him to continue the sleep he was enjoying, but making it the eternal sleep of death. What happened afterward showed that their decision was justified, for the father came the next day with many Cafres to attack our people, but, not receiving the spy's countersign, they turned back without putting their plan into effect. This was the fate of these two Cafres. Antonio's

[1] *pataxo.*

357

was better, if one can consider being doomed to eternal damnation as a better fate, for he never agreed to come with us no matter how many times we begged him, giving as a reason the fact that he had a wife, children and grandchildren, some of whom he brought to us there, and since he was married to two women, in the manner of the heathen of the land, his sins held him captive, rendering him unworthy of being reformed and returned to the land of Christians through the grace of God.

Even though this *cabra* was very useful to us, he still received the payment ordinarily given by the Portuguese, especially when they find themselves vexed by troubles, as we were; for they began to argue with him and say that he was stealing from what we gave him to buy some things with, all of which amounted to no more than four old nails and a few pieces of brass and copper. And because the Cafres were now forgetting to come with the cows for barter, either because they were already tired of the things we gave them, or because they wanted to alarm us a bit so that the price would be raised, or because they took offence at some instances of mistreatment we gave them in their villages, the Captain and I became fearful that we would be lacking the necessary food in the future for so many people, and the others thought that Antonio was causing the said estrangement. And because they were already offending him by their words, we wanted to test his fidelity in secret, for which purpose we secretly gave him the price of 12 cows so that he would go inland and, after buying them, would bring them to us on a certain day, which he did as punctually as if we had asked him to fetch them from our herd. As he was appearing on the other side [of the river] with the cows we had contracted for, they began in loud voices to speak badly of the poor fellow, saying that while he was away from there, the cattle would then come and the bartering would continue. We did this secretly so that if he returned we would disabuse the people of their error and if he did not return we would be apprised of his intentions toward us, but the people were not aware of this, and they were certainly confounded when they learned that he was the one who so faithfully had gone and returned, and they were much more so when they saw him returning in the same way a few days later with twenty or more cows. As things finally turned out, however, they had offended him so much that he stayed away from us for some two months before our departure.

The work on the ships was progressing and our desire to see them completed, so that we could leave that exile, was becoming more intense, but, since the work was extensive, it required a very long time, during which we diverted our minds from our vexation by going out sometimes into the interior of the land and at other times along the shore. And one time among others, I went with a few of the men who were there to a part of the shore we had not yet visited, a little more than a league away, to see if the sea had washed up on the shore we were traversing something we could use, and we found quite a few things. The first was the unfortunate Loureiro, a bombardier, who had drowned on the raft and whose body was completely emaciated and cast up from the sea on the beach. We buried him in a place so far away from his native land, but suitable enough to receive a dead body, because for this purpose the whole earth is one's native land, and he surely will hear there the final trumpet of judgment when he arises from there, and until that time we shall have left him there covered with sand and stones with a cross at the head of his grave. And that was perhaps the first Christian grave-marker with such a symbol seen on those shores, although we later made still others for some people who, as we have already said, were to die. The beach we were traversing was all strewn with the riches of the Orient – spices, clothing, gilded objects, and quantities of chests and boxes –, causing us considerable pity as we thought of the great pains and trouble with which they are acquired in India and how easily, and with what little care for such things, everything was ruined here. And the Cafres surely do hold these riches in very low esteem, for we found beautiful chests and boxes of angely-wood, sideboards, beds, and writing desks from China and Japan ripped to pieces by the Cafres so that they could remove from them a small piece of iron, a lock, and any other thing of this kind, which are the only things they prize. We reached an inlet which the sea makes into the land like a river when the tide is high, which we found to be extremely rich in all kinds of gilded objects from Japan, side-tables with drawers,[1] writing desks and many other pieces of furniture and items of jewelry. And because, staying there for a while lamenting the total ruin we had before our eyes, we saw smoke from a thatched hut not far from the edge of the water among the trees, we went to find out what was in it and found a Cafre with a cauldron on the fire boiling pieces of raw leather from a leather bag which he had at the door of the hut and had brought from the shore, leaving the cinammon that was in it in the same place where he had found the leather bag because, distressingly, the cinnamon was coating the

---

[1] *bofetes.*

leather on the inside. The Cafre gave himself up for lost when he saw us, and, in the hope of securing our goodwill, he hastily pulled out a piece of the half-cooked leather he had in the cauldron and courteously and generously offered it to us, continuing to eat the rest with much relish and no less amazement on our part, considering how satisfied that barbarian was with so wretched a life that he deemed it a rare treat to eat a meal of raw leather boiled in water, which, from what we saw, was not very tender since he had great difficulty chewing it, and also considering how little he cared for everything so highly esteemed by human greed, since from so many riches that had been cast up on the shore, in the river and readily available to him, only a little raw leather caught his eye and his fancy. Although we thanked him for his goodwill, we did not accept the offer, because, although he was giving what was available there and what he had, we preferred our ration of cow-meat and half-measure of rice which we cooked together in the same pot, making a *brinje*.[1] From the river, however, we took the pieces of furniture which best pleased us, according to the desires of each person. I had four beautiful side-tables with drawers from Japan carried away for my thatched house, each of which was worth a great deal of money, with which I adorned my hut; I made a table of one, I ate on another, I sat on another to avoid sitting on the ground and I used another to lean on, each one of them being fit to grace the wardrobe of any great prince. I used them, and they stayed there when we embarked, there being no place on the ship where these things could be put.

Although we lived in this exile in the peace and quiet permitted, the devil did not fail to perturb us with some troubles partly caused among the Portuguese, a very common thing in similar misfortunes, but there could have been many more if God had not been served by their being checked because of the good understanding the people had with me, partly, also, stirred up among the Cafres,[2] who, seeing people of their own colour, land, inclinations and features, yearned for the freedom albeit barbarous, which they could have among them, esteeming it more highly than captivity in a Christian land with the means for their salvation it provides, so that some of them began to flee, not only Cafres but *cabras* from India as well. The first, either because they found a good welcome and free acceptance into the society

---

[1] The word is found in the dictionaries as *brinie*; it is from Persian *birinj*, Turkish *pirinç*, 'rice' and evidently means a pilau.

[2] I.e. the negroes who were with the Portuguese as slaves etc.

of the native Cafres or because they died of hunger and bad treatment, were never heard of again, nor did we ever learn what happened to them. Others, who were the majority of those who attempted to flee on different occasions, were treated to such a reception by the Cafres that they came back in a very few days, more content and less incensed with life among us. One time, however, there were suspicions, whether well or ill-founded I shall not dispute now, the result of which was that, it being affirmed that there was a general conspiracy among most of the Cafres who served us to flee, with other circumstances much more in our disfavour, which were that they would come at us with a multitude of the natives of the land, for which purpose, like thieves in one's own household, they were familiar with the ways in and out and the place where we had our entire supply of gunpowder, and would thus take it so that we could not harm them with our firearms. This cost many of them much flogging and various other punishments, and the one they said was the leader, which I do not believe was the case, was put to death by hanging, and he was the only person who lost his life in that place with a violent death. And it truly would have been better for us all to depart without making this wretched man pay the penalty for the rest, for he had served us the whole time until his death, which amounted to some months, and had served us very well. It was not possible, however, to persuade the Captain not to kill him, and his death so terrified the others that not another one of them fled. The reason may have been, however, that the little time remaining after this did not afford an opportunity for anything else.

There was an incident, however, which I shall not fail to relate with great sorrow, because I was much aggrieved by the outcome of it. A young *cabra* of the Captain's ran away from him one time, like the others, carrying off a mortar pestle which he stole from him. The Cafres took it from him and made him a herdsman of cattle, in which occupation he found himself so out of favour that after a few days he came back to us, looking like the very picture of death. And after a long time, he repeated his escape, taking two tin plates, at which the Captain was much grieved. When, however, we were about to busy ourselves with preparations for our departure, about two months before it, the Captain wanted people to go in search of his mortar pestle and his two plates, ordering a brave man with ten others to go out and perform this illustrious exploit, as though some of our good name would be lost if this were not done or as if these items were more valuable than the good friendship we were losing with people from whom we had received so many evidences of friendliness. The risk these men were incurring, of returning in a state of mortification or being in dire trouble without bringing back what they were going to look for or committing some injustice by killing the Cafres, from which much harm could ensue for us, and the responsibility for it all was to be borne by the adventurers. They were cunningly being ordered to go without any clear instructions about what they were to do, whether to fight or return empty-handed. And since the one who was giving them the order was unwilling to take sound advice, I advised the leader of the adventurers that they should not leave without an express order as to what they were to do in case they were not given the priceless items which they were going out to seek. And although they tried to find out what the will of the person who was ordering them to do these things was, he would not declare it to them until, pressed hard at the last moment, he told them, which he should not have done, that they were to fight or bring the items back to him. After their departure and arriving at the kinglet's house, they asked him for the items, to which he fearfully answered in the affirmative, and his manner of looking for them was to have all the people of the land called together, which they do by shouting from the hilltops so that one informs another and in less than a quarter of an hour the alarm is given for many leagues around, the people coming together and rushing to the place to which they have been signalled to come, understanding already from the tone of the shout that it is a call to battle. The Cafres were gathering by groups of six and ten according to how they met, and because our men began to become suspicious about what could happen, they tied the poor kinglet's hands behind his back and, coming out of the thatched hut, placed themselves in an open field, very much on the alert and with their weapons in their hands, relieving those present of theirs, which consisted of assegais, and doing the same with all of the new arrivals, of which they made two neat piles. And since the shouts on the mountains were continuing, as was the flood of new arrivals, already numbering two hundred not counting those they saw coming along the paths, and also the unfortunate kinglet had not succeeded in giving satisfaction with respect to the mortar pestle and the two plates of tin, they decided upon the greatest barbarity they could commit, because, without any other right than that of violence and satisfaction of a foolish whim, one of them cocked a matchlock and killed the wretched kinglet, knocking him to the ground, pierced by two balls, in repayment for the kind treatment he had accorded us during the 7 months we stayed in his lands. The reasons there were for not doing so idiotic a thing to a poor people who, although barbarous, had not wronged us in any way, are so obvious that I shall not stop to rehearse them except to say that the motive was so patently insignificant and, if that were not enough in itself, should have been sufficiently considered in relation to the wretched state in which we found ourselves and the respect and gratitude we owed to a land which, receiving us as we were cast from the waves of the sea, treated us as benevolently as if it were our own homeland, for us not to stain it with the blood of the poor Cafre, of whom and of whose subjects we could still stand in great need; and providing for our own necessitous state and situation was surely a more compelling motive for action than the loss of two plates or the discredit that could result from it, which was the cloak that was thrown out to cover such great disorder. The difficulties that could and can still result from this, and did result from it, are great, because the risk in which those ten men put themselves, or were so ordered – the risk of all or some of them perishing, which would be a great misfortune and loss – was obvious, and the necessitous state to which we could be reduced as a result of this, by no longer being able to barter for cows, also was obvious, and, as it turned out, they never brought us another one. We also were running the risk of having all those pagan people descend upon us, and, even if they could not harm us at all with continual assaults and wound or kill us in a thousand places with their assegais, they could lie in wait for us and keep destroying us a few at a time, because we necessarily went out for water, firewood and many other things we needed. The most important consequence is the state of open warfare that will be faced by the people on any carrack that experiences our misfortune and shipwrecks there, for the Cafres now remain outright enemies; and if it were only to preserve the friendship and goodwill of these people for the calamities that befall our carracks in that latitude where the kinglet's misfortune occurred. The first was the carrack *São Alberto*, with Nuno Velho Pereira as Captain,[1] whose people travelled overland and traversed Kaffraria to come out next to Melinde[2] with good success because they always carried their weapons in their hands, and our

---

[1] The Captain of the *S. Alberto* was Julião de Faria Cerveira. Nuno Velho Pereira was elected commander by the castaways after the wreck, Boxer, 1959, p. 118. For his distinguished record, *Ibid.*, p. 109, n. 1.

[2] The *S. Alberto* was wrecked near the mouth of a river which was either the Bashee or, more probably, the Umtata, Boxer, 1959, p. 114, n. 3. The survivors did not walk to Malindi, but to Delagoa Bay.

Antonio was of this company and stayed there as a tired, sick child;
2nd was the galleon of Manoel de Sousa de Sepulveda, whose people,
wanting to travel by land, all perished because they abandoned their
weapons, the Captain and his wife dying in a state of utter helplessness
in the most pitiable circumstances and the most wretched shipwreck
ever seen;[1] 3rd was the carrack *São João*, whose people left by land
in the direction of Moçambique and only 23 of 279 escaped with their
lives;[2] 4th was the carrack *São Gonçalo*, whose people, not daring to
travel by land, made two pinnaces in which they brought themselves
to safety;[3] 5th was the carrack *Belem*, which is this one, of which I
have been speaking, whose people took the advice and made ships, one
of which with 118 person can be considered the 6th, for it ran aground
in the same latitude after three days' navigation, and since the Cafres
were so recently offended, they destroyed most of them as they
traversed 34 leagues to reach the place where we had been, so that
scarcely 14 of them were able to reach the land of Christians, which
was certainly the result of this idiocy.

After the poor kinglet was dead, the Cafres scattered in terror and
our men, taking the two piles of assegais, set out again for our dwelling
place, which must have been about three leagues from there. However,
as the Cafres saw that our men had gone, they came back to see what
the matchlock-shot had done to their king, and, seeing him dead, set
up a great clamour, especially a brother of his, and inciting one another
to vengeance and led by the brother, they attacked our men several
times, who had difficulty driving them away from them. And because
the people kept increasing in number and our ten men were hard
pressed, one of our men put his musket to his cheek, well loaded with
musket-balls and grape-shot, and felled the dead man's brother, tearing
off half his head, whereupon the rest of them withdrew, abandoning
the pursuit, and our men cautiously continued their journey. The Cafres
went, however, to lie in wait for our people at a narrow pass with steep

---

[1] This refers to the wreck of the *S. João* on the African coast in 1552; a few survivors
eventually reached Moçambique. The narrative of the wreck is the first item in the *História
trágico-marítima*.

[2] The *S. João Baptista* was wrecked in 1622 somewhere near the mouth of the Keiskama
river. The narrative of the wreck, by Francisco Vaz d'Almada, was included in the *História
trágico-marítima*, and is translated and annotated in Boxer, 1959, pp. 188–271. Lobo's figures
are inaccurate. According to d'Almada's narrative, of the 279 who began the march along
the coast, four remained at Sofala and twenty-seven reached Moçambique.

[3] In 1630 the *São Gonçalo* sprang a leak off the Cape of Good Hope; some of those on
board landed on an island and built two boats, one of which reached Goa, and the other
the bar of the Tagus. The ship itself sank with the loss of all those who had stayed on board,
James Duffy, *Shipwreck & Empire* (Cambridge, Mass., 1955), p. 130.

sides and when they saw them engaged in it threw rocks down at them from the hill so that all our men found themselves in immediate danger of being killed. And, if they had not taken a short cut by which they reached the top of the hill without being seen by the Cafres, it is hardly possible that they could have returned to where we were waiting for them in a state of suspense and worry concerning what the outcome of so just and honourable an undertaking might be. Because the Cafres saw them with an advantage equal to theirs as far as their location was concerned and a better advantage in weapons, since ours were firearms, they abandoned the position, allowing our men to pass and be able to reach the place where we were. When we learned what had happened, we gave thanks to God for delivering our companions, again reprehending the order that had been given and that we had been unable to prevent, despite our fearful premonition that the result would be as disastrous as it in fact turned out to be.

The time was now growing very long for us in that exile, our supply of rice becoming so depleted that we were already reduced to half a measure, an extremely small portion for people who were working and had no other delicacy; and what is more, much of it became spoiled and rotten with the continual bad weather and rains which had come upon us, and, since it was not a time to scorn such food and our situation certainly did not permit us to do so, since we would have run more of a risk by not eating it than by eating it spoiled, we continued to make use of it all. And although the meat was fresh, eaten without bread and at times without rice, our constitutions came to conceive an abhorrence for it, and the delicacy with which we chased our squeamishness consisted of some piths of wild palm-trees abounding in the wooded areas. We were so hasty, however, in bringing them to the ground to obtain their piths that we were soon unable to find any palm-trees for two leagues around. Also the great abundance of oysters found in great quantities in the river fed our appetites as we sent for them in quantity or went to eat them at the river's edge for greater entertainment in the evenings, on Sundays, and on holidays when work was not in progress, availing ourselves of this form of rest and recreation. Another thing that happened was that, as the sailors are so devout and are so grateful to Saint Francis Xavier, especially those of this carrack because of the favour received and the miracle that happened, as I have related earlier, when his feast-day arrived,[1] they wanted to commemorate it with the greatest celebration possible, as

---

[1] December 3. See pp. 300–1.

they did, putting up a mast 15 days before the feast-day in the middle of our village with a written challenge promising a prize to the person who would come out with the best poem in praise of the Saint, to the one who would set up and decorate the best altar in his street, because the village had several with their names taken from familiar streets as a way of relief and consolation for our homesickness, to the person who would produce the best monologue, dance and intermezzo. All of this was done and prizes were given, with bull-fighting the preceding day, a beautiful sort of enclosure of wooden poles having been made for it, and it happened that the 'bulls' that were ridden at were cows without horns. In the morning of the Saint's day there was a mass and sermon. In the afternoon there was a comedy presented very beautifully by the sailors, for persons and clothing were readily available for every need. We had the celebration for two days and were wonderfully entertained for passing the time and relieving our cares, there being no lack of riddles and enigmas and the prizes for them, poems, altars in the streets of our poor village, some of the Cafres who still came to see us coming to the celebration and being thoroughly amazed and more open-mouthed than usual at what they saw, this wonderment of theirs contributing still more to the merriment of those who most availed themselves of the opportunities for amusement and relaxation from the many troubles we had had there.

A short time before we became more actively engaged in immediate preparations for our departure, we had an incident with the hippopotami that might have cost many of us dearly. In that river there were a great many, and we would encounter them when we went out in the boat. One time when the boat was making for shore with about 10 people in it, it reached the place where its occupants saw I know not how many of these wild beasts, which could not retreat inland because the mountain was very steep and were equally unable to seek refuge in the water because we were in their way. As the beasts were in this state of perplexity, the people in the *balão* fired a few shots at them causing them to scatter. One of them appeared to be the mother of another smaller one that she had near her, and, with the thunderous noise of the matchlocks, she noticed that her offspring had disappeared. Since she recognized that the harm had come from us, she attacked the *balão* with savage fury and the first thing she did was to try to seize the nearest one of us in her teeth, which the speed with which she hurled herself at him would have enabled her to do if she had not suddenly thrown herself at another part of the boat. But seeing that he had escaped her, she tried with equal fury to get into the boat. Unable to do so and hindered by the oars, she caught one of them and smashed it to pieces along with the tholes it was in, and she did the same to a strake of the *balão* with great fury and, getting under the boat, she tried to raise it up with her back to see if she could turn it over. In all this time our people could not make up their minds what to do, because going to shore was obviously dangerous and heading for the sea was much more so. In the midst of their danger and confusion, the wild beast must have caught sight of her offspring, for she went away, having taught us the lesson never again to become entangled with these wild beasts on the many occasions when we met up with them.

CHAPTER 34

[Concerning how we embarked on the boats, and the great storm we experienced until reaching Angola]

In these labours and occupations we were continuing our life on those sterile, deserted shores, putting our hope first in God and secondly in our two ships or barks called *Sevillans*,[1] until, in the beginning of the month of January, having been detained in that place for seven months we were to put them into the water, which we did, with the help and favour of God Our Lord, more easily than was promised by the little equipment we had for the task, our supply of oakum and tar for the ships' bottoms being completely exhausted. Since we lacked pitch and tar, we used fine benzoin of almonds and another kind of fragrant benzoin with some frankincense which made an admirable mixture and a costly, sweet-smelling, excellent tar, for nothing is so ingenious as necessity. And since we were very impatient to be gone and to experience our final fortune, whether good or bad, we worked feverishly to make the ships ready for the voyage, because we were already much disturbed at finding ourselves in that place for so long a time and also because we did not have enough rice, of which we selected 80 bales in the best condition and agreed to reserve them for the voyage.[2]

There were some who spoke disapprovingly of our leaving so hastily, giving two reasons for their disapproval. The first was that winter had not completely left that place, so that we could fear contrary winds and storms at the Cape of Good Hope, a very dangerous thing to contend with in such small vessels. The bad part was that the validity of this reasoning and fear was borne out as I shall presently relate by what we in fact experienced. The 2nd was that the people were

---

[1] See p. 351 n. 1.

[2] Cabreira says that *N.S. da Natividade* was launched before Christmas, and *N.S. da Boa Viagem* on 8 or 10 January. The ship's master Miguel Jorge managed all with great skill. Ballast was put into the boats and they were brought under a cliff which could serve for a derrick in fixing the masts. Cabreira appointed a sailor called Antonio Alvares as master of the *Boa Viagem*.

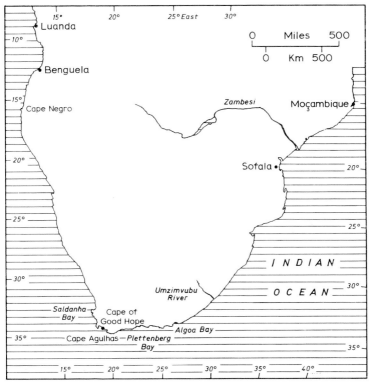

Map 4. Southern Africa

thoroughly exhausted and weak from lack of food, and because from that time forward the crops were to be harvested, there were those who believed that for this reason also we should delay for a month and a half or two so that the people could avail themselves of the abundance of crops, which were millet, and recover their strength; for we had already observed a place where we could get an abundance of it in the event that the Cafres should be unwilling to sell it to us. With this we could supply our immediate needs and provide ourselves with sufficient food for the voyage in order to avoid the shortage and wretchedness we experienced later, when we had ample opportunity to verify that this second argument also was well-founded. It was not accepted, however, along with many other pieces of advice of various kinds, which were given on the occasions which presented themselves and which demanded them.

Resolved then to set out on our voyage immediately, we bent all our efforts toward this end, assigning the people to the two ships, making *Nossa Senhora da Natividade* the flagship and *Nossa Senhora de Boa Viagem* the admiral. The latter happened to be assigned 137 and the flagship 135. However, there was a difference between the two, because the Captain took the best people with him, the best officers and sailors as well as the most vigorous people, allowing his self-interest to prevail over fairness and the good of that whole community, while necessity dictated that they be divided equally for many reasons, especially so that they could cope with the troubles which should have been prudently feared and cautiously forseen. And because the greatest danger was our being unable to continue the voyage and, with the two ships separated from each other, each one taking its own chances and utilizing the land route, there would not be enough people to travel by land without obvious danger. All of this came to pass and almost all the people in the other ship lost their lives travelling by land, because of the lack I have mentioned and shall touch upon again. Of the five religious, three of us went on the flagship: one belonging to the third order of St. Francis, another a Dominican,[1] and I. A Capuchin and an Augustinian went on the admiral.[2] The bulk of the baggage, the small amount that had escaped the shipwreck, was all loaded on the flagship because the most important people were there, which was also of great inconvenience to us, as I shall presently explain. For lack of

[1] Both were called Fr. Antonio (Cabreira). Domingos Lopes was appointed pilot.
[1] Cabreira appointed Estácio de Azevedo Coutinho captain of the *Boa Viagem*. He was accompanied by his wife, D. Isabel de Abrantes. The pilot was Manoel Neto.

baggage, the admiral was extremely light-laden and rode too high in the water, carrying little more than provisions and people. And since the ships were so small, we tried to put water aboard them according to their capacities, for which purpose, estimating 48 days of navigation and counting the people embarking on each ship and giving each person a half-measure of rice and half a *canada* of water per day, we supplied each ship with 40 bales of rice and sufficient water according to this distribution. In addition, each person was given a leg of cow so that, cut into slices and dried in the sun, it could help him eat his small quantity of rice. Salt was one of our greatest lacks, for the fish and meat brine we used was already gone. We boiled sea-water in a copper kettle until it was congealed into salt, yielding a handful, equivalent to the bulk of two fists, from an *almude* and a half of water. Unfortunately there was only one kettle, which was loaned in turn to each mess-group, so that we made quantities of salt which, if not sufficient for our needs, were enough to be helpful to us.

With this preparation we planned our voyage for the twentieth of January, but thanks be to God it was not implemented on that day. At the time, we did not understand the signal favour God was doing us by preventing us from it, but on the 22nd of the same month at nightfall there appeared in the sky approximately to the south of us a sign they call 'ox-eye,' and the darkness was not completely upon us when there erupted the wildest, most horrendous storm that I have seen or experienced on the sea, for it seemed as though the winds had come out to challenge one another and do pitched battle among them or that by common consent and with concerted effort they wanted to show their fury and ferocity by combatting the sea and the land with everything in their power, creating such frightful agitation in the sea that it seemed as if they intended to overwhelm the land with the force of the water. And on land they were attacking the woods and trees, breaking and shattering to pieces everything that offered resistance to them, with frightful noise and terrifying impetus. The night was getting gloomier and darker with a rain so heavy and continual that it seemed more like the flood than a rainstorm that would pass, especially the continual horrendous thunder-claps and the sky-cleaving thunder-bolts and flashes of lightning, so frequent that it seemed as though Heaven was threatening to consume with fire everything that might escape the water and the wind. The force of this storm lasted about two hours, the most terrifying I have had or seen among all those I have experienced. We withdrew to our small chapel, imploring God's favour and protection, asking for His mercy, and offering up our thanks to Him, remembering that if we had embarked two days before, as we had determined to do, the force of the storm would have caught us in the most dangerous part of that coast, where we all would have perished with no possibility of saving ourselves somewhere along the coast between where we were and the Cape of Good Hope. After the fury of the hurricane was over and daylight had returned, we agreed that we would depart on the following Saturday because it was a day dedicated to the Virgin Our Lady, whom we had taken and were taking again as our special advocate and protectress for this very dangerous voyage of ours. The flagship was as small as I have said, having a keel 62 spans in length, being eight spans deep, which was all the space there was from the deck to the bottom of the ship, and 20 spans wide. And since the capacity inside was so small with what little baggage there was stowed there, the provisions of water and bags of rice filled up all available space so that there was no room for any of us under the deck. We all had to be above, from the stern to the mainmast and on the bow, each one finding whatever place he could. In the stern, however, two small cabins were made on either side, for the Captain and for me, built on thin planks and covered with raw leather. Mine was only large enough to accommodate my body lying down and only slightly higher than what was needed to permit me to be in a sitting position. On Friday they all confessed and had communion, some bidding farewell to those who were embarking in the other ship, shedding many tears as if in their hearts they already knew that they were never again to see them in this life, which turned out to be the case, since after so long a time in constant company sharing so many varied and troublous happenings, we boarded the ship that night so as to be ready to depart in the morning. We left nine cows on land in a safe place so that, if by chance we should have bad luck in our departure and should be wrecked, there would be some resource on land to sustain our lives until we could arrange for our sustenance by some other means. The Cafres, as if they had been spying on us, suddenly appeared in great numbers on the top of the rock overlooking the river and were shouting at us from there. I know not whether or not they were hurling curses at us, which we well deserved because of the legacy we had left on land in the two deaths among their people, which we had inflicted and which I have reported earlier. And because we delayed until eight or nine o'clock without deciding to depart, some others had time to go down to our thatched huts. With admirable diligence they scurried in and out of the huts looking for some nail or piece of old iron on the chance that some such thing might still be there. And although they did carry off something, they could not find the most important piece of hidden treasure, which, if they had found it, would have indeed been a treasure for them, namely the cauldron in which we mixed our concoction for tarring the ship's bottom, which was too large for us to take with us. Giving it to them was out of the question, for they did not have the wherewithal with which to buy it, and, what is more, God Our Lord was already planning to use it to help the people of the other ship, as I shall presently relate. We, however, with no other intent but to keep it from the hands of the Cafres, put it in the deepest part of the river, which happened to be in the very place where we were. As soon as we determined that we could not set sail because the tide was not high enough and there was no wind from the land, we postponed our departure until the following Monday. And because the Cafres were still totally engrossed in searching through our thatched huts, some of our men went ashore to attack them, firing their muskets at them. The poor wretches found themselves in considerable danger, for the firearms were very effective at long range. They entrusted their lives and safety to their feet, however, and, although some shots were fired at them, none of them, fortunately, reached their mark. Our purpose was to drive them off so that they would not find the cows we had in reserve, and thus they were held at bay by fear, no longer daring to go into the village, as they had done at first, until after we should depart.

With the arrival of the 28th of January, a Monday, at 7:00 in the morning, after the *balão* had been sent ahead to sound the bar and place buoys there, we cut the cable and, setting sail, we began our difficult voyage with the *balão* in tow. And not the least of our dangers was at the bar, for the water there was only 8 spans deep, which was almost what the ship required to stay afloat, and if we touched anything on the bottom, we ran the risk of being stranded, having all our work go for naught, going ashore again, and having to try to reach safety by land; for, in anticipation of such an eventuality we had left the surplus cows, had hidden ammunition and gunpowder, and had kept the other ship behind us so that in case we did not succeed in crossing the bar we could all travel by land. And all of this misfortune was a very real threat to us, for the pinnace did hit the end of the sandbank and received four severe shocks, pushing the rudder up but, through God's mercy, not causing it to break off, although one of the shocks broke a few boards that were above the gangplank support, a matter of little consequence. We finally crossed the bar with no more damage than I have reported. The second ship came in our wake and, although it had better luck in the beginning, it ended up very disastrously and very differently. Both ships now found themselves on the open sea, already on course and sailing along the coast in the direction of the Cape of Good Hope. Ours was certainly unsteady on the water, with so many people in one pea-pod, the tiniest boat ever to cruise the seas of that stormy promontory and risk fighting its waves and tempests. At that time we had a gentle favourable wind so that we had only to sail before the wind aided by the currents that were running in our favour from northeast to southwest. We were delighted with such good weather, but we no longer needed the *balão* and even if we did have some need of it, towing it behind us made it difficult to keep the ship on a steady course, so that the harm it could cause us was greater than any advantage if offered us, although it had served us well. Because of this and since we no longer had any intention of going ashore but were entrusting ourselves to whatever fate God had in store for us on the sea, we cut the cable with which it was tied to the stern, whereupon it was left to the mercy of the waves, which would soon carry it to be smashed to pieces on the rocky shore.

It was about three or four o'clock in the afternoon when we began to realize how little importance we should attach to the things of this world, for the Cape of Good Hope began to threaten us with its furious rage, possibly because of our boldness, since we were daring, in our ludicrous weakness, to defy its ferocity, having experienced how tempestuous it is and the helplessness of those mountains of wood, such as the *Bellem* was, against its tempests and waves. And a storm was thus whipping up, which not only deprived us of the favourable wind we had but changed it into a contrary wind after we had sailed a little more than ten leagues. The weather forced us to turn about again and sail back in the direction from which we had come, but, so as to lose as little headway as possible, we pulled in our sails and were sailing with the lower foresail, with the other ship following us and sailing in the same manner. The rest of the afternoon and all night we were sailing with the same wind, although the weather was not such as to cause us more concern than we felt because of the contrary wind and our fears that it would get worse. With the return of daylight the weather relented and permitted us, with the wind turning in our favour, to continue our voyage again in the direction of the Cape. The joy with

which we resumed our course, however, was of short duration, because
it was not quite four o'clock in the afternoon when we noticed a fish
which the sailors call *orelhão* because of a fin that it thrusts out of the
water like an ear,[1] and when this creature appears, looking like a shark,
it is usually a sign of a tempest, and was immediately promised as such
by the boatswain, who saw it and was extremely conversant with things
of the sea. The fears and signs were followed by what they portended,
for the wind suddenly changed to a northwest and west wind with such
impetus and darkening skies that we were promised a great catastrophe
if God did not help us with his favour. The most discouraged among
us, those who evaluate things by the way they turn out, did not fail
to condemn our setting sail and braving the dangers of the sea, so certain
in that latitude, in a pea-pod so hard to keep on course and so well
and badly loaded, approving the opinion, desires and constancy of some
who wanted to travel by land, and considering its dangers easier to cope
with and less severe than those of the sea. And although these people
kept their mutterings to themselves, their murmurs did not fail to reach
the ears of the rest and cause in all of us new troubles in addition to
those we already had with the menacing weather, which made it
necessary for us to reverse our course, sailing only with the lower
stern-sheets and with some of them furled, all so that we would not
fall back too far in the direction of Moçambique. The other ship was
going ahead of us, which we judged to be because it was better under
sail than ours. Both ships were sailing with equal sails until it was dark,
but before the darkness closed in completely we saw the other ship
unfurling the mainsail, going farther out to sea, and sailing right before
the wind with great determination in the direction of Moçambique.
Meanwhile the darkness settled upon us and we sailed in it with
tolerably good fortune and with the desire to find ourselves once again
in the river of the shore we had left. And if we were to find it in the
morning there is no doubt that we would run the ship aground, go
ashore and make our voyage to India by that other way. However,
when morning came we found ourselves without the other ship and
above the place where we wanted to be; and although we made every
effort to find it we were never able to do so. It seems that God had
resolved to bring us to safety in a port and country of Christians by
a surer means than the one we were thinking about and wanted to use.

The wind favoured us again and for the third time we tried to set
our course for the Cape. It now appeared that the devil decided to

---

[1] Portuguese *orelha*, 'ear'. The fish is the sun-fish, *Mola mola*, Lin.

utilize all the strength and abundance of his wickedness, undoubtedly offended by our perseverance and ashamed of how powerless he had been to destroy us completely. Sailing as we were with the wind and currents in our favour, and having sailed, in a little over thirty hours, a number of leagues that we would have believed impossible if the sun's altitude, when we took it three days later, had not verified it, so that we came to believe that we had either doubled the Cape or were very close to doubling it. However, because of the contrary wind and furious storm having driven us for two full days during which we had gone once again, not sailing but flying, in the direction of Moçambique, we now found ourselves, after so much voyaging, only slightly beyond the mouth of Alagoa Bay.[1] After we had been sailing, then, in this good weather, the wind suddenly shifted to the northwest, then to the west-northwest and then to the west, blowing in different directions, swelling the seas, burdening the skies with such heaviness and darkness that we soon found ourselves with our hopes completely dashed and plunged into seas so swollen and turbulent that they were like mountains from all directions conspiring to send us to the bottom of the sea. We placed our trust in God and, allowing a small part of the lower foresail to be filled with air, we let ourselves be carried by the full fury of the storm. The danger we were in soon became more clearly evident as we found ourselves in the midst of waves swollen into high mountain ranges of water coming from every direction. Since our salvation depended upon skilful manoeuvering of the rudder, the four best sailors and helmsmen were assigned to steer it. The poor little ship was undoubtedly like a hare fleeing from speedy greyhounds pursuing it, except that, as the seas were attacking it from every direction, it had to swerve away in every direction, turning its stern to them and in such a way that, with 4 greyhounds attacking the frightened fugitive hare, it would veer now in one direction, now in another, swerving away from all the directions from which the enemies were attacking it. This little power against such vast ones had to be continually alert and immediately responsive to every threat, for as soon as it would turn its stern to the wave that was attacking it on one side another larger one was threatening it from the other, and when it was trying to escape from the latter it was hitting against still another swollen mountain of water coming to send it to the bottom. In the middle of this labour, which was on the feast-day of Our Lady of the Candles,[2] the second

---

[1] Algoa Bay.
[2] The Feast of the Purification of the Virgin, Candlemas.

of February, already despairing of our lives, we tried to prepare ourselves for the other life in the best way permitted us by the state in which we found ourselves. I confessed everyone as briefly and in as few words as I could, preparing them all for death with the best words I could think of at the time, with litanies and acts of contrition. The deck was swimming in water, the waves coming in on one side and going out on the other. We had the hatch-way shut and well calked so that the ship would not be completely filled with water. All the people were placed on the fore and stern-castles, commending themselves to God and awaiting death, fully expecting to be in personal combat with it as each wave came in and covered us all. We would come up from under it and thanking God for not taking us to the bottom we would wait for the next one that was coming, to capsize our ship and carry us all to our deaths. I finally withdrew into my cabin, utterly exhausted from waiting for the sinister visitor, although he could be received anywhere. No sooner had I got into the cabin than the harrassed ship was caught with its side to the waves because the impetus of the waves had become too strong for those working the rudder to be of any effect. And because this was the very catastrophe we most feared in our misfortune, when we saw it and saw the fallen sail and the ship sideways to the waves waiting for any wave to capsize it, we were sure that our end had come. Now the shouts, tears and lamentations of 'Lord God, have mercy on us' poured forth as each one embraced his nearest friend. I found them in this state as I came out of the cabin, and judging the danger to be fully as great as was indicated by the people's weeping, I raised my eyes to the sky and offered myself to God in such a death since that was His will. I saw there, not painted but in real life, what has been portrayed for us in paintings of shipwrecks: the sky heavy with clouds, great darkness, the four winds blowing furiously from all directions, the ship with its useless sails torn to shreds, the distraught people, some having climbed up in the rigging, some clinging to the edge, some with their hands raised to Heaven begging for mercy. I saw all of this misfortune of ours in one horrendous picture; but since it was folly to stop everything to weep and lament and a necessity to keep working, so many people ran to work the helm that by the mercy of God the ship turned and again got its stern to the wind and waves while the people were continually throwing into the sea everything that was on deck, each one remaining only with what he had on his person, beds, clothing, and even some bags of rice from our provisions going into the sea.

And although the ship was somewhat alleviated and sailing with greater assurance, the tempest did not abate its fury, continuing thus until into the morning, during which time we had promised God, if He would take us to a Christian land, to make a procession, barefoot and on our knees, from the shore to the nearest church, everyone vowing to do as I should order and each one offering in addition two *patacas* for a silver lamp of Saint Francis Xavier. The weather abated a little more, staying so until five o'clock in the morning, on the Feast of Saint Agada,[1] when it redoubled its fury and again assailed us with redoubled cruelty. We now lost all our courage for many reasons, both because of the past labours which had left us in a state of extreme fatigue and because the winds and seas were more furious, the people weak, sleepless and hungry, afflicted with fear, cold, lack of food and sleep. We finally reached a state where each person chose the least uncomfortable place in which to station himself, and with so many frights and certain of the outcome, we awaited death, grieved that it had not already come and now wanting to hear only of things of the other life where we expected to be momentarily, bidding one another farewell with each wave that came upon us, believing it to be the last one. The ship seemed to be going under the water more than sailing on the surface. The people came to make public confession of their sins not once but many times, asking pardon of one another even for the bad secret thoughts that each one had harboured against those who were there, so that many things were revealed, to which no one paid any more attention than to pardon them willingly. And because many people were repeating their scruples and confessions and the time was too short for so much expansiveness, I made them all get down on their knees and, making them do an act of contrition, I gave public absolution to them all at one time. One, however, who was at a distance and appeared to have two things that were torturing him most, being unable to leave his place to come where I was, shouted to me, asking if I remembered those two things he had confessed to me earlier and if I had absolved him of them, and because I told him that I had, he stayed contented, awaiting death more calmly. It delayed coming, however, keeping us in suspense for many hours, so that there was time for us to offer the whole ship to God, to promise Him that we would sell it, that the money would be given as alms to Our Lady of the Nativity, and that we would scourge ourselves through the city from the shore where we would arrive as far as the nearest church.

[1] St Agatha, 5 February.

With this preparation and these good intentions, our lives were being prolonged. However, if the sea was not taking them from us, hunger, cold and weakness were doing so more speedily and cruelly, and I saw some who had lost their senses and were in a state of dire extremity. Through God's will I had enough biscuit to fill an ordinary napkin, and, although I was as weak as the others if not weaker, I had to come to their rescue, distributing to all of them a mouthful the size of an egg. And because what was weakening us most was the cold which had penetrated our stomachs, for we had not eaten for two or three days nor was there time for it and the hatchway being calked shut did not permit anything to be taken from below and, even if food could have come from there, the tempest would not have permitted it to be cooked on a fire, and also our faculties were so occupied with the immediate threat of death that they could be concerned with nothing else but preparing us to receive it. All of these things together had made us extremely weak. It was God's will that I had a flask of cinnamon-water, from which I gave each person less than half a cup, which, with the mouthful of biscuit I put in each one's hand in the place where he happened to be; for some were unable to get up because of weakness, others so as not to lose their places and not to disturb the rest. Since they were not moving, it was necessary to visit them all, and with this relief they recovered their senses because of the cinnamon-water being warm and good for the stomach. And undoubtedly if I had not helped them many would have perished that night and the rest would have totally succumbed under the work which, thanks be to God, became more moderate with the tempest which began to be less furious, allowing us to regain a little strength as we had time to rest a little, to get something to eat from the hatchway, and to let our clothes dry on our bodies without being soaked again by the waves coming in as had been happening until then. At daybreak there was less cloudiness, but the wind continued to be furious as we sailed taking our chances with it all that day and the following day, the sixth and seventh of February, with steady but slow improvement in the weather. On the seventh in the afternoon occurred the most dreadful circumstance we had experienced until that time, for suddenly as we were sailing close to the land and a small island so covered with sea-lions that it looked all black with the great quantity of them covering the sand that constituted the whole island, there were shouts from the bow that we were about to run up against some shoals which were so close to us and were positioned in such a way that they had us already surrounded on all sides, distributed as they were in the form of a horse-shoe. The pilot gave the order to fall to leeward, but this was now impossible because they had us hemmed in on that side. He wanted to luff, but he was also prevented from doing that by the other arm of the reef which was also encircling us on the other side. In this danger, with no more than a second in which to deliberate, the pilot and all of us resolved to go over them, leaving the outcome in God's hands, as indeed there was no other recourse since it was such a heavy sea there because of the reefs, for the waves would open up prodigious valleys in which we first were buried and then would raise up lofty mountains of water on which we were carried upward. In this danger and affliction we were being guided primarily by God Our Lord who provides succour in the greatest perils and secondly by a sailor in the round-top, who was pointing out a small channel that was there and was deeper, ordering the rudder to be turned now to one side, now to the other, with which we miraculously emerged from the labyrinth, having been brought out of it more by God than by human industry. Toward evening we found ourselves in weather that had already become tranquil, and because we feared another storm with the conjunction of the moon with the sun, soon due to occur, we planned to take shelter in Fermosa Bay,[1] until it should pass, both for the reason I have mentioned and so that we could recuperate. What we noticed in all these events was that when we had already despaired of being able to conquer the difficulties of doubling the Cape and tried to make for some land, we were unable to do so; when we tried to set our course for Moçambique, after a few hours' voyage we would find contrary winds that were favourable for doubling the Cape; and when we were sailing with them on course for the Cape, the wind would change, blowing against our bow, and would oblige us to turn back against our will as we implored God's mercy. And because the time consumed in this conflict was also consuming the provisions we had allotted for a limited number of days, we found ourselves in a state of great affliction.

In the shelter of Alagoa Bay we rested for a day and a half, not going ashore but remaining at anchor. During this time we fished and caught many good fish that abound there. And since it seemed to us that the weather now afforded us more security, we set out to sea again to try our luck, and God willed that it would be with better success; for, with a gentle wind and helped by the currents, at sunset we caught sight of some rocks that appeared to be the Cape. And as we supposed that

---

[1] Plettenberg Bay.

we had passed it, with the night already having closed in, at thirty-four and a half degrees, which is what its latitude was, believing that the reef below Cape Agulhas, which is at 35 degrees, was already behind us, we were confidently sailing along the coast with some moonlight when we were startled by an outcry raised by the sailors: 'Bear up the helm! Bear up the helm! We're running aground!'[1] And this was indeed the case, for two more moments of inattention would have caused us to ram into the shore or the shelf of sand which extends into the sea from that Cape. We headed, however, to the southeast for greater safety and, sailing thus for the rest of the night, by morning we were already past the Cape after 22 days' voyage and occurrences such as I have reported up to this point, although most of what we suffered cannot be expressed in writing. We could not believe the good fortune in which we found ourselves, now leaving all the dangers behind us and heading into gentle seas on the course for Angola with trade-winds which continually blow there with no storms whatsoever no matter how much they may threaten, having 900 leagues to sail before reaching the land of Christians which was so much the object of our desires. We intended, however, to make for Agoada de Saldanha[2] beyond the Cape and to replenish our supply of water, also bartering, if possible, for some sheep, which the Cafres usually give in exchange for pieces of old iron. However, since that bay was frequented by Dutch ships and we were not coming to try our luck in combat, not carrying any of the necessary equipment for it, we did not feel obliged to suffer the only kind of misfortune we had not already suffered, namely, captivity. So as not to run the risk of any of these things, we went further out to sea, losing sight of the land, which we saw again at 22 degrees before reaching Cape Negro,[3] after which we never again lost sight of land.

We were navigating in these seas with less worry about storms but with great concern because our navigation was being prolonged with consequent lack of provisions; for the little treat of the slices we made from the leg of cow given to each person, boiled in salt water and then dried in the sun, was no longer to be available to us, for the meat soon became spoiled, leaving us with the poor half-measure of rice and half-*canada* of water, which was not enough both for drinking and boiling the rice, so that anyone who boiled it did not drink that day and anyone who drank ate the rice raw or cooked it dry over the fire.

[1] I.e. put the helm to windward and change the ship's course to leeward.
[2] 33° 00′ S., 17° 56′ E.   [3] 15° 39′ S., 11° 58′ E.

With these difficulties my stomach became so weakened, as did the others' to a lesser extent, that it could not tolerate rice or any other of the few things that were there. A sailor, however, who still had a little biscuit hidden, gave me a handful of it and a piece of cheese the size of an egg. With this supply of food I passed the next few days sustaining myself with a quantity of biscuit the size of two eggs and two mouthfuls of cheese. The master came to my rescue with three sausages, of which I ate a half of one each day, and after I had already eaten two of them in four instalments, the last one was stolen from me one night, which I certainly took as very bad treatment of me. I was treated equally badly on another night. Since I was not able to drink my ration of water, I would pour it into an earthern jug in the corner of my cabin, and as the cabin was made of pieces of raw leather, there was someone who noticed this and how easy it would be to take advantage of it and drink the water. It happened, then, that one clear moonlit night as I was sitting on the board that served me as a bed, because I was not very sleepy, I saw that a hand was lifting up the bottom edge of the leather and, seizing a coconut-shell that was next to the jug, was taking out water. The first time I permitted him to do it, mindful of everyone's distress. He came a second time, taking a good cupful on each occasion, and this time I again pretended not to see it. I was prepared, however, to catch him if he should return a third time, which he did, and, when he had his arm inside and his hand in the jug about to pull it out with the water, I grabbed it, nearly startling the poor fellow out of his wits by catching him red-handed. I chided him for stealing something from me that he could have had for the asking, but I was unwilling to report him because I knew that he was in a necessitous state. And since everyone was in a similar state, we were sailing more slowly in hopes of satisfying our hunger in the new kingdom of Benguela, a new conquest of the Portuguese, 60 leagues before Angola at 13 degrees, where we could obtain various kinds of meat and other food.[1] We made every effort to reach that land, but on the evening when we sighted it and were almost able to verify the configuration of the shoreline, it was so far after sunset that we could not go in. Waiting to do so in the morning, we lay to during the night, but when morning came we had drifted so much that it was impossible to reach it because of the wind and currents. We were in

---

[1] The Portuguese began the conquest of Benguela in 1617. It is now part of Angola. The position of Benguela city is 12° 34′ S., 13° 24′ E. Lobo's estimate of the distance from Benguela to Luanda is much too low. By the most direct route it would be more like 90 leagues.

an extremely disconsolate state, railing against our misfortune and unaware of the great favour we were receiving from God in being unable to reach that port; for, as we learned later, since the land is very unhealthy and the people who go there arrive from the sea in a very weakened state, most of them die, which was the fate of several ships which had gone there with their people in that condition, leaving some buried on land and others dying when they reached Angola. We had greater reason to fear such a fate, which we surely would have suffered, because of how weak and infirm we were, undoubtedly perishing from the bad climate and the food we would have eaten.

Disappointed that we could not land, we continued on our course, and when we reached the latitude of Angola, at 8 degrees,[1] because we were sailing farther away from land than we should have been, we missed it, being unable to sight it and sighting instead a ship at night which we took for an enemy vessel and were much surer of it when we saw it in the morning sailing ahead of us, and after getting to the windward of us, it reversed its direction so as to be coming directly at us. We got our weapons ready, resolved to meet the ship head on, since this appeared to be the only course of action we could take with any possibility of success and our ship was the better of the two, although the other had a great advantage in the artillery it had since we had none at all. With this resolve and much perturbed by such an encounter at the end of our voyage, with nothing good to be expected from it, we were sailing toward the other ship, and it toward us; but as we were expecting the first signal for battle, we saw that it was going by us and thus went off in the direction of the port of Angola, from which we were sailing away without knowing it, which it had also done, but recognizing the error in the morning, it had quickly changed direction to correct it; and we learned later that it was a ship from the port, which, just as we had done, had taken us for an enemy ship. As we sailed that day, the more discerning of us were discovering a few signs indicating that Angola was ahead of us when in actuality it was already behind us. And as we did not take the sun's altitude that day or the next, through carelessness on the part of the pilot, when we did take it on the third day, we found ourselves many leagues down the coast and so close to the famous Zaire River, so impetuous in its current that, entering four leagues or more into the sea, its current gives sailors fresh water in the midst of the salt waves beyond sight of land.[2]

[1] The position of Luanda is 8° 50′ S., 13° 15′ E.
[2] The Congo. Cabreira says that fresh water can be taken fifty leagues out to sea.

And if we had sailed into this current, it would necessarily have carried us to a place in the sea where we could not have avoided perishing from starvation and lack of water, for neither could we have reached land nor did we have enough to sustain our lives, many of those aboard already having lead bullets in their mouths in order to fortify themselves against the thirst that was torturing them. The worst part of it was that the leagues we had lost in two days could not be retraced in a very long time. In this affliction we drew closer to land, resolved to put almost all our people ashore on rafts that we made, so that they could travel overland from there to Angola, a few staying on the ship, sustaining themselves with what was still there and with a pipe of water that we had reserved for these emergencies. We spent the morning still intending to put this plan into effect, when at two o'clock, unexpectedly and contrary to the way in which the winds normally blow there, there was a peal of thunder and so useful a wind that on the next day in the morning we found ourselves inside the port of the city of Loanda, which is what Angola's city is called, where we immediately became aware of the mistake we had made in thinking that there would be water for those who would have stayed aboard ship while the others went overland; for they would have had to wait a few days trusting in the pipe of water we had reserved for the direst emergency, and we found it completely drained and the water lost.

CHAPTER 35

[How, after fulfilling our vow, I left for the Castilian Indies and was captured by the Dutch]

At anchor in the port, we did not believe it could be true, thinking that what we were seeing with our eyes open was surely a dream. We were congratulating one another, still speaking fearfully of our past dangers and labours from the time we left India and the hopes we entertained for so long, the fulfilment of which we were now enjoying but did not fully believe to be true, finding ourselves in the port we had so much desired and for which we had yearned for so long a time. This day was a Saturday, the day before Palm Sunday, 48 days after we had set sail from the River of the Beach, during which time we experienced the variety of events and the adverse fortune which I have narrated up to this point. We sent word to the shore to report our misfortune to the Governor.[1] And since many of the ship were completely destitute, I offered all who would come to our college we had there a ration of bread flour, the ordinary food of all the people who live there, and fish or meat depending upon what day of the week it was. I felt bold enough to make this offer because of my desire to help those poor people, offering my services to find sustenance for them so that those whom God had preserved in the extraordinary dangers of the sea would not perish on land.

In these speeches and counsels, I reminded everyone of the obligation we were under to fulfil the vows we had made to God and how urgent it was to please Him and not to delay it. And although I found a few resentful at having to do this, most of them placed themselves at my disposal as they had promised, declaring themselves ready to keep their word and do whatever I should order. I then told them that on the

---

[1] Cabreira says he sent a letter to the Governor, who sent water and food. The Bishop gave alms lavishly, supplied clothing to many and took some of the people of quality into his own house. The precious stones were deposited in the Jesuit College in a chest with three keys, one being left with the Rector, one with the Bishop, and one with the Treasurer (*provedor da fazenda*). The Governor supplied him with 800 *cruzados* so that he could prepare for his return to Portugal 'where I expected to be in a few months' time with nearly 40,000 *cruzados* as is well known to the people on my carrack '.

next day I would come to the ship for them early in the morning, which I did; and I found them ready for what I should want them to do, except for a religious of the third order of St Francis, who was the only one to escape me. The others, however, I prepared for the scourging when I went inside the galiot. And since some of them were observing the scourges and did not have any, I had some prepared for them, either of small cords or of bunches of fishing-line, which are very good. The only question was about what the flagellants should wear, and since I was already well-informed, entering my cabin I made a suitable garment out of my cassock by putting it on backwards so that my back was uncovered. To give an example to the others, the Captain also went into his cabin and threw off his coat, remaining naked from the belt upward. There was still someone who was discontent with the attire, looking at it and commenting that that was good for wrestlers, to which I replied that we owed more to God, since we had promised Him this for freeing us from the dangers in which we had found ourselves and that they should remember that we still had vast seas to cross where we would pay dearly for our faithlessness if we failed to fulfil what we had promised to God. And because the Captain and I resolutely jumped ashore to carry out our procession and act of contrition, with some following us with their backs also uncovered, all the rest of them did the same. And as the whole affair was sudden and there were already many people on the shore, it caused all of them great wonder and amazement at the circumstances and state in which they saw us, and much more so when, lined up in order, I in front holding a crucifix in my left hand and the scourges in my right, the Captain on one side and the Master on the other, and all the rest following in two lines, we began to intone the litany and walk toward a church that was on the shore, with the scourges performing their task. The news spread through the city and everyone came down to see us, for there was plenty of time, the church being some distance away, with which we were not much pleased but there was none closer. When we reached it, we found it already filled with people, before whom, right then and there in the same formation and state in which we entered, with our backs well marked by the scourges and switches, I gave a speech to all of them, telling those companions present of the thanks and gratitude we owed to God for giving us time to fulfil the vow, which we were in the act of doing because we were as much obliged to do so as we were grateful for the favour received, declaring to the other people the reason for that spectacle, telling them briefly of the labours and dangers in which we had found ourselves and the particular grace and favour with which God freed us from them. And because what I told them struck them with wonder and admiration and was confirmed by the devotion and rigours to which we had condemned ourselves, with Christian piety and natural compassion working also in helping our cause, they all broke out in such excessive weeping that it obliged us to join them, since they were doing so from seeing and hearing us, as all of our past tragedy was being brought back to our memories as an occasion for rejoicing and praise of God.

With the completion of this act, both of the procession and of the speech and tears, we began the other one, which was for us to make a procession to another church with bare feet the whole way and on our knees, which I ordered and which we put into execution immediately, accompanied by more people than was the case with the first one. And since they were moved by the sight of the earlier procession, little was needed for the weeping to be renewed because of what they saw, considering the affliction in which they had seen us, according to what we had told them, as well as the penance to which we had condemned ourselves in order to escape from danger. Having gone on our knees, then, for a good distance, I motioned for everyone to stand up, as we all continued on foot the rest of the way, which ended at a church of Saint Antonio, where, again declaring to those present the reason for the second devotion and vow, we finished it all by embracing one another in satisfaction, contentment and joy because of how fortunately we had satisfied our vows, each one of us then withdrawing to his house and providing the subject-matter for conversation for many days, concerning both our misfortunes and the praises everyone gave to God because of the mercies He had shown us.

It was the 16th of March when we disembarked on the shore of Loanda, where we remained until the 26th of April when I embarked for the Castilian Indies. Between those two dates, our people tried to ready themselves as best they could for their voyage, the Governor, at my suggestion, giving each of them two *quarteis*, which made slightly more than 20 *patacas* for them to fit themselves out with clothing, and the Bishop helping some by giving many of them food in his house.[1] I did the same in our college for some, and others sustained themselves in houses of friends and acquaintances, until the Captain with many of the people embarked for Brazil to take a ship from there which

[1] The Bishop of Angola and Congo was D. Francisco de Soveral, 1628–42.

would carry them to the Kingdom.[1] Before embarkation, however, our ship was sold at public auction for 540 *milreis*, used to bring sugar from Brazil to the house of Our Lady of the Nativity, which was brought in the amount of 26 large boxes, thirteen of which were donated to the nuns and the other thirteen to the Brotherhood. After this had been done, some embarked for Brazil, others for various parts of the Indies, and I with the Governor, Dom Manoel Pereira Coutinho,[2] for Cartagena of the Indies, since I considered this to be the best route because of the advantage of the Captain's company, the fact that the ship was a large carrack in good repair, and there being no ship sailing directly to Portugal but to Brazil or to the Indies, as we were doing then so that we could make our voyage to Spain in the fleet.

After embarking, as I say, with the Captain, we put out to sea once again with the ship carrying as many as thirty white persons and eight hundred or more slaves as cargo to be sold. We sailed with good weather and the monsoon during the voyage of two months, in which we experienced nothing worthy of note other than seeing the miserable life and unfortunate fate of those poor creatures, put in the bottom of the ship as if they were vicious criminals, with no more guilt to justify such treatment, captivity and misery than their colour and our greed. God seems to be punishing us for it since we condemn to perpetual captivity free people who are driven to such despair that some of them, unable to endure the heat, the lack of room, the foul odour and food, and such a multitude of people in so small a place, being allowed to go out for air only once a day for a short time, when they were able to escape from the clutches of such cruelty, threw themselves into the sea and drowned. Of those who were on our ship, six such desperate people perished in this way.

Our first sighting of the mainland was when we saw the mountains

[1] The Governor provided a caravel for Cabreira and he left for Bahia on 5 May. He took with him the master, pilot, boatswain's mate (*guardião*), purser (*escrivão*), the rope-maker, and some twenty seamen. Some seamen stayed in Angola, others went to Rio de Janeiro or Cartagena. Cabreira took with him the royal letters and letters of the Governor of Angola in which was a record of the valuables from India. He reached Bahia in twenty-six days.

There the Governor, Pedro de Silva, invited him to choose one of three ships which were loading for Portugal. He did so, left on 11 July, and after narrowly escaping Dutch ships, arrived at Peniche on the Portuguese coast on St Augustine's day (28 August). He handed the Governor's letters and the register of goods to the Vicereine and, by her order, gave the letters for the King to Francisco de Lucena, the Secretary to the Council of Portugal.

[2] He was Governor of Angola, 1630–35. Cabreira's narrative names his successor, Francisco de Vasconcelos da Cunha, 1635–39.

called Nevadas[1] because they are extremely high and covered with snow all year long, and although they are thirty leagues inland they looked as high and as close to the sea as if they were at the edge of the water. This sight was a joy to us because we knew that this place was close to Cartagena and because of the beauty of the snow on the mountains. This contentment of ours lasted until the next day in the afternoon, Monday, the day before the Feast of Saint John, when at four o'clock we saw, anchored near the island of Zamba,[2] a ship which we could not identify from afar, but which was judged by the sailors to be friendly. As we drew closer we thought it might be an enemy ship and wondered if the sailors either had failed to recognize it as such or had recognized it as an enemy and had kept silent about it in the belief that, since they were carrying slaves, the enemy, as is customary in such a case, would let the ship go on with them. And as we were sailing with sharp breezes, we soon were at anchor with it in the same waters but to the windward of it and at a distance of a quarter of a league. The pirate ship had arrived there three hours earlier, having sailed from Holland three months before directly to this port, for the Captain of this carrack had been the pilot of the *Pé de Pao* in these same waters, where he had gained much booty two years earlier.[3] And his greed for more of the same had brought him here again, much to our woe; for, hiding his colours until he saw us cast anchor, he then weighed anchor and put his ship under sail, letting a Dutch flag fly in the wind to inform us of his identity. When we finally recognized him, we regretted our mistake in sailing in and putting ourselves in his clutches, from which we now were unable to escape by sea because he blocked our way, continually tacking, now toward sea and now toward land, to make it impossible for us to escape from him. At midnight under beautiful moonlight he dropped anchor so that our ships were within sight of each other, and although he wanted to come immediately to examine us, he could not do so because of the wind. As soon as the sun came up, he resumed the same tacking in order to reach us, but with no success. He launched a shallop to tow the ship by rowing, but he was not able to reach us by this means either, whereupon he again dropped anchor, content with the certainty that we could not escape. In the meantime we were busy discussing the

---

[1] The Sierra Nevada de Santa Marta in northern Colombia.
[2] Off the coast of Colombia between Baranquilla and Cartagena.
[3] 'Wooden Foot', a Portuguese version of Dutch 'Houtbeen', 'Wooden Leg', the nickname of Cornelis Jol, a famous admiral of the Dutch West India Company. In 1640 he seized Luanda in Angola, and then the island of S. Tomé where he died in 1641.

various irksome problems presented by our plight and what, if anything, we could do about it; for escaping the enemy by sea was impossible, the land was unknown to us, and, because there were many people we would die of thirst for lack of water. The nearness of the island of Zamba, however, was very inviting to us, since we were anchored only a matchlock shot's distance away from it, but we did not know whether or not it was inhabited, nor did we have any idea what passage, if any, there would be to the mainland, which in places was less than a league away from the island. The most prudent of us were saying that we should put everything and everyone in the carrack ashore, placing ourselves in the hands of God and fortune, and that, once on the island, we could fortify ourselves, defending ourselves in trenches, and do battle with the enemy if he should fight us from the sea or if he should come ashore and attack us on land. All of this could well have been accomplished and was the surest advice, for we had a day and two nights, which was enough time for us to put everything ashore even including the flintstone ballast, with more than enough water and food carried in the ship to sustain all the people for many days. And because this advice was in the best interests of everyone, our sins prevented it from being put into effect, since those who believed they would not be harmed at all by the pirates beyond being robbed of some little thing they had on their persons refused to do it. Their confidence, however, infected all of us, and because the Governor was so important a person that he was in greater danger and because there was a noblewoman in similar danger because of her youth and beauty, who was there with her husband, the wiser ones advised that they and I, being a Jesuit, for whom the enemy has so much hatred, should be put ashore at night, where we could escape by hiding in the woods and could be rescued. After this advice was given and approved by most of the others, its implementation was prevented by a few timid people, fearful that the enemy pirates would find out that a few of us from the ship had been put ashore, would blame the rest of them for it, and would make them pay for it, saying that we had taken the best of the ship's merchandise with us. It was then decided that we would wait for whatever might happen and would depend upon the piety and courtesy of the thieves, of which these pirates had none. And because, in the morning of the Feast of Saint John, they made great efforts to reach the place where we were and still were unable to do it, we ourselves went to them, after the order had been given for the Governor to be dressed and treated as a poor old man placed in a corner with the others and for his clothing and arms, and everything else that could indicate the presence of an illustrious person there, to be thrown into the sea along with his letters and papers, which was done, putting it all together in three bundles, and, tying a morion to one, the breast-plate to another, and the back-plate to the third one, we threw it to the bottom of the sea. And because I had some very secret and important letters with me,[1] in order to prevent them from falling into the hands of the enemy, I threw them into the sea tied to a bottle of distilled vinegar to carry them to the bottom, which it did.

After this precaution had been taken, we set sail, which was a lure for the enemy to come after us, which he did. When he was within artillery range, he fired a cannon-ball as a signal for us to strike sail, which we did. 10 or 12 of them came out in the cockboat and, reaching the side of our ship, ordered the pilot, Master and Captain to go down with a few other passengers, and then took them to their ship in order to find out what ours was carrying and where it had come from and also to hold them as hostages for those who were to come and pillage our ship, which they did, returning immediately with a boat-load of more than twenty men armed with swords, two pistols each, muskets, and, coming aboard, they began to sack everything there was on the ship. The Captain's cabin, along with everything in it, was appropriated by the enemy Captain, as was the pilot's by the enemy pilot. Some of them rushed to get to me, dressed as I was in the hat and cassock of the Company, in order to see what they could get from me, and, although I had nothing with me, for a few little presents and more important items were already hidden in the ribs of the ship with others belonging to the Captain, they did relieve me of the keys to a chest in which there were some good things. A friar of the Minims of Saint Francisco de Paula, who was with us, was treated very roughly for being unwilling to surrender his cloak to some pirates who coveted it; and, although they took it from him anyway, they punished him further by giving him hearty blows about the neck. My own luck in trying to avoid such treatment was such that, when a youth wanted to take off the stockings I was wearing, which I let him do along with everything else he did, such as frisking my pockets, the drooping parts of my breeches, sleeves, etc., the pilot and the more responsible ones laid hands on him and made as if to throw him into the sea for thinking of doing me that discourtesy, especially the pilot, who began to treat me with familiarity; his heretical nature, however, suddenly caused him

---

[1] Possibly relating to the proposed Portuguese military intervention in Ethiopia.

to become possessed by such rage that he jumped down from the poop, where we were sitting, to the main deck and, so furious that sparks were flying from his eyes, he grabbed a pistol with which to shoot me. Everyone there thought I had reached the end of my days and so did I. I did not move from my place, however, waiting for the inevitable outcome, but his fury suddenly abated and he sat down again, continuing the conversation as before. They spent that whole day plundering the carrack. At night it was guarded by soldiers put on the carrack, who, because of drunkenness and smoking tobacco, set fire to the hold, so that if they had not rushed to put it out all of us would have gone up in flames. On the next day in the morning they devoted themselves to putting us ashore on the uninhabited island, first taking nearly 300 of the sickest and weakest Cafres and then taking us. When the enemy Captain informed me of this, I asked him for my crucifix, breviary, Bible, and cassock, all of which he gave me, but when I tried to ask him for one of a few pieces of cheese that I had, he answered me that all the other things I had asked for were useless to him but good for me, but that the cheese was good to drink wine with and he had no intention of giving it to me. Thereupon he ordered me to embark in the boat so that I could be put ashore. 4 Flemings were in it as guards, with pistols in their hands and more in their belts, ready for any action in self-defence or offence; and they had good reason to be so, for those who were being taken with me intended to lay hold of them and take their weapons away from them, throwing them to the bottom. However, since our people had no weapons and the enemy guards were so cautious and distrustful, it was not possible for them to do as they had intended.

Once we were deposited on the island, there were a number of things that concerned us greatly, the first of which was food, for the enemy had not allowed us to take anything at all for our sustenance. We had gone without food for two days with hardly any sleep, and because our ruin and misfortune had been uppermost in our minds, we had thought little about sustenance. For this reason we came ashore in a weakened state and needed to find food. The island, however, did not have anything on it with which we could supply this need. Our need for water was greater and, because of the extreme heat, was placing us in a very serious plight, from which God Our Lord rescued us by showing us fresh water in the sand, in which we dug down to a depth of one or two spans, as fresh and good as the best anywhere, except that it did not last long in this perfect state, because the heat of the sun kept making it brackish. The ease, however, with which we opened up new wells, which we did by digging with our hands in the sand, kept us from taking it too seriously when the water we had already found became spoiled, for we had no trouble, when the water became brackish, in finding fresh water very close to it.

The island on which they deposited us was about a league and a half long, most of it covered with scrubby trees. And because it was closer at one end to the mainland, we sent a few of the first white men put ashore to find out if there was a way for us to get over to the mainland, and while they went on this scouting expedition, the rest went after them, following in their traces at the slow pace that the effort, weakness and heat permitted us, the Captain, pilot and Master still being held hostage on the enemy ship. When they saw from the ship that the first scouts were returning, and we with them, because we had not found a passage, they appealed strongly to our enemies to give us a boat so that we could cross over to the mainland. And although at first they could not be persuaded, they finally relented and granted it, after we, in the meantime, had got together some poles with which to make a raft on which two or three could cross over to seek help on the mainland for the others. This would certainly have meant loss and death among the rest who would have remained in all the abandonment and intensity of hunger and heat, which was very great. When we received the boat, however, we sent it to the mainland to discover if there were Christians there, to tell them of our misfortune, and to ask them to help us. Meanwhile, each of us was seeking something to allay our hunger. I went off with a few others to hunt for shellfish along the beach, and, as I was going bare-footed, the heat was excessive, the sand was burning, and the salt water itself was very hot, the harm I suffered was greater than what shellfish I caught; for the latter did not amount to much and, of the former, my feet became so inflamed and greatly swollen from the fire that was kindled in them that I could not walk for many days and was in danger of a great misfortune. With all these efforts we caught a few large whelks[1] as big as eggs, two or three crabs, some other shellfish but not much, where upon we came back to where the others were. And because it was necessary to walk more than a league and my feet were now in very bad shape and I was with the Governor, who was more than 80 years old and very weary from all he had endured, we had to remain behind with three other people. Night overtook us at a place where we spent the night, finding that

---

[1] *caramujões.*

we had only one large whelk among all of us who had stayed behind. When it was cooked over a fire it was about the size of an egg. We divided it among the five of us and drank some of the good water we obtained by digging in the sand. Sleeping on the sand, we spent the night, having had only that small bit of refreshment, which was truly all we had had to eat in two whole days. And our share of what we had caught was so small, even though I had caught a little more, because the man who was carrying the whelks and crabs went off with the other group while we stayed behind. Daylight came and brought us happiness because the boat was already back with good news from the mainland that there was a village of Spaniards and some native Christians on the coast. The best part was that we neither felt nor had any stomach trouble in the night from our supper but slept with the light, peaceful, quiet sleep of people who have not over-burdened their stomachs, which was certainly the case with us.

CHAPTER 36

[How, after many storms, I disembarked in Cádiz, and then went to Lisbon, Madrid and Rome and again to Lisbon]

When morning came, about 20 of us got in the boat and crossed to the other side, meeting two *almadias* in the middle of the channel on their way to bring back some of our people, and the people on them gave us a little boiled Indian corn and some fish that had also been boiled, but it was all cold; however, we found both things excellent. After we reached land a Creole Spaniard took us to his village and had us there until I left for Cartagena, which I did after three days during which I was convalescing from the trouble I had with my feet. In Cartagena, I recovered from the ordeal I had been through; and, as the Fleet was waiting there to set sail when the time arrived on the 10th of August, a month and a half after our misfortune, I embarked on one of the galleons carrying silver, it costing me 300 *patacas* for my place on the ship; for the Castilians never give anything away. And although they knew I was poor and robbed, their ever present self-interest and hopes for gain prevailed, and it was necessary for me to borrow that number of *patacas* for my passage.

We left the bar of Cartagena on the tenth of August, and because it is narrow our galleon was in danger of hitting it, and, if it did so, ran a great risk of remaining there, as did we with the difficulties of finding another ship. The whole fleet, however, crossed the bar successfully, and in a little more than 30 days we reached the port of Avana,[1] having experienced nothing remarkable on the sea other than the continual fear of the reefs with which that sea is very much infested, especially of one called the Viper, which is the summit of a rock that rises from the bottom of the sea and barely comes out of the water with a point so sharp that it can scarcely be seen protruding from the water. One can tell where it is only because the waves break over it from time to time and a squirting of water comes away from it as if someone were there with a waterpump. One morning when there was

[1] Havana in Cuba.

394

little wind and the sea was smooth, we were already very close to this reef and would have hit it if we had not discovered it in time; and if it had been a heavy sea we probably could not have seen it. We stayed in the port of Avana for 15 days waiting for good weather and a steady wind because of the dangerous seas for a distance of 40 leagues from that port, for that whole sea is crossed by continual reefs occupying 80 leagues, there being only one channel three or four leagues wide which all the ships get into and run such a risk that, if the wind blows from the northern quarter, which is usually stormy in that place, the ships soon hit against the coast with no hope of salvation, which has happened at times. For this reason they enter it with great fear and their anxiety lasts until they have got through it, although it usually does not take long, from two to four days at the most, the reason being that the currents are very strong there and carry the ships with great impetus, sometimes sideways; and it struck terror into our hearts to see the rocky places on both sides of us as thick as thorns, between which we were sailing. Having left this danger for the open sea and sailing with good winds, we continued to have this fair weather for the whole month of September, on the 15th of which we had set sail. When October came, however, the storms that came upon us were horrendous and fully as bad as those off the Cape of Good Hope. All month long there was not a Thursday in each week that we did not have the Credo upon our lips, prepared to die. There were many of these times of dire emergency, and I shall only say that this was a month of most extreme tribulation for us because the waves were huge, the winds furious, the cold severe, and everything afflicted us so much that, of the 42 ships that left Avana, only seven of us found ourselves able to continue the voyage, some being shipwrecked, others returning to port, and the rest going off course, according to how the wind treated them. With these difficulties we continued to the islands among which and in some reefs called the Foromigas[1] we should have been shipwrecked if God, through His mercy, had not prevented it. The cause of this near catastrophe was that our ship and the whole fleet were almost 300 leagues further along on their course than the pilots thought, so that, in the belief that they had that many leagues to go before reaching those islands, they were sailing without keeping a watch. Other causes for the mistake were the Castilian pilots' lack of skill and the fact that the great storms, most of them attacking us from astern, caused the ship to sail more leagues than were believed possible; so that on a Monday

[1] The Formigas Rocks between the islands of S. Miguel and Sta Maria in the Azores.

at dawn, with the flagship going ahead, as dawn broke, it suddenly discovered the reefs and was already so close to them that it scarcely had time to veer to leeward, signalling to us with one of its guns that we should follow it. And truly, if dawn had come a half an hour later, we should have been wrecked there, and those reefs are ordinarily the cause of such misfortune that none escape who sail into them. They are called Formigas because the tips of the rocks look like ants moving on the water and the water appears to be boiling among them. When we saw this, we realized where we were and were surer of it when we sighted the islands of Santa Maria and São Miguel, ten leagues apart, and sailed between them.

Now aware of our location and the leagues we had unknowingly traversed and having taken a new dead-reckoning, we set our course for the rock of Sintra, which we saw earlier than we expected, again because of some error on the part of the pilots in judging the ship's speed. On All Saints' Day in the morning we arrived at the mouth of the bar [of the Tagus], so close that I recognized everything there: Cascais, Cabeça Seca, the Tower of Sam Gião.[1] And although I wanted to disembark there, it was not possible because, it being a holiday, there was no ship in evidence on the sea. From there we sailed for the Cabo de Espichel[2] and then for that of Sam Vicente,[3] but as we were sailing between the two capes, the wind became so bad for us that none of our ships could pass it. It was the time of the new moon, a dangerous time in those waters, and that coast is the worst there is, because it is all high rocks with certain death for any who are shipwrecked there, nor are there any sandy places on which a ship could run aground, but only rocks on which it would be smashed to pieces. The wind was blowing against us so that all day long, no matter how many times we turned out to sea, we were unable to get up to the Cabo de Sam Vicente. And because night was coming, the wind the worst we could have, increasing by the hour and giving signs of a great storm, and we were being held very close to shore, the flagship, which was going ahead, with us behind it, made one last turn, having decided to pass the Cabo de Espichel in the direction of the bar of Lisbon, reversing the decision it had made two days before not to seek shelter and safety by entering it, which it now desired to do but could not. We were sailing in the wake of the flagship, and night overtook us as we were

---

[1] See p. 15 n. 2. The Tower of São Gião refers to São Julião da Barra.
[2] The first cape south of the estuary of the Tagus, 38° 25′ N., 9° 13′ W.
[3] The SW extremity of Portugal, 37° 01′ N., 9° 00′ W.

a little over a half a league off the coast and about three leagues from the Cabo de Espichel. When darkness had set in, the sky became so heavily and dreadfully overcast that it was a sure sign of the evil it was threatening and the furious wind that was to come from it. This sign caused the sailors to be very watchful and fearful, all of them on the alert in anticipation of our being hit by the sudden storm, when we heard from afar a rumbling which we suspected might be a piece of artillery with which the flagship was giving us a turning signal, as is the custom if they turn. And if we had identified what it was immediately, the hurricane would not have caught us so unexpectedly as it did, for while we were deliberating on what it was, there came upon us the most terrible blast of wind we had ever experienced. Our confusion was as great as the fear which it inspired in us; for, as everyone was shouting, 'Strike sail! Strike sail!,' the sails were so stuck to the mast that they could not come down. There was great tumult and even greater terror of what we were seeing, hearing and fearing, because the wind that was blowing was a confused, horrendous combat of all of the winds together mixed with frightful thunderclaps. The lightning-flashes in the midst of the night's darkness were such that they blinded us, serving only to let us see how close we already were to the coast, where we not only heard but saw the waves breaking furiously on the rocks, on which we surely were to crash soon and suffer a wretched shipwreck, for the wind kept taking us irremediably to the coast and to our final and total ruin.

In this danger and anguish, while the agonized sailors were working, the rest of the people on the galleon were in a most grievous state, weeping, imploring God's mercy, and expecting that the galleon would be dashed against the rocks at any moment. And because of our imminent doom, even though the circumstances afforded little opportunity for it, I gathered the people together for an act of contrition, which was the most we could do in such an extremity, immediately reciting the litanies of Our Lady, with all of them together. Lo and behold, when we were waiting for our destruction, someone came down the hatchway calling for me and asking me for his reward for the good news that the hurricane had ended, the sky was serene, the wind favourable, gentle and at our stern and the best we could hope for. No one would believe it until I verified it for them by going to see it, whereupon each of them returned from death to life with the happiness, easily imagined, of people who had been condemned to a sad cruel death and now found themselves with sure hopes of life. Such were we, as we were left with clear weather, and it was our good luck that the hurricane was mainly on land and we had been hit by only a small edge of it; but even so, it had such an effect on us that, if it had struck us with all its force we should have perished without any possible recourse; for when this fury reached the city of Cadiz, toward which we were sailing, it did so much damage there that it brought even large belfries to the ground. The rest of the night we sailed with a good wind and on the next day we arrived within sight of Cadis, where we lay at anchor outside the port because the wind had died down and we could not enter. Refreshments consisting of bread, pomegranates and melons were brought out to us, for all of which we paid enormous amounts of money; for any ten *reis* loaf of bread was sold for three or four *vinteins*, the pomegranates for two *vinteins* each, and special favour was needed to get them, the melons being beyond price. We stayed out there within sight of the bar for a day and a half, going into port on the 7th of November, 53 days after leaving Avana and almost three months after sailing from Cartagena on the 10th of August. I disembarked in this port and it was the end of the journey, after I left the Red Sea and sailed to get there nearly nine thousand leagues through such various difficult accidents and events as I have thus far narrated, although what I have told has been in broad outline; for the details of the sufferings and the variety of them are as impossible to relate as they were difficult to experience.

I spent a few days in Cadis, going immediately to San Lucar[1] and from there to Sevilha, whence I left for Lisbon. And since winter had already begun, it was very rainy and cold, the rivers were running high with water so that it was very dangerous to cross them. In one that I tried to cross, the current would have carried me away as I was starting out if God had not saved me, since the she-mule already could not withstand the current. In another place the danger was greater, for the river was large with very high water covering the dangerous stones in the middle, on which we would certainly have perished had we struck against them; but it happened that, as we were starting to go into the water, we heard the shouts of a shepherd, who must have been the Guardian Angel, telling us to stop. Immediately coming down the mountain and out of breath when he reached us, he warned us of the danger we were getting into, offering to show us a place further upstream where there was a ford of little water, which he did, and we crossed it without danger with the shepherd going ahead of us, after

---

[1] San Lúcar de Barrameda at the mouth of the Guadalquivir.

which we paid him well for his trouble and for the advice. On the 8th of December I arrived in Lisbon 14 years after I had departed from the same city and 15 years after my first departure, being able to count from the time I left Lisbon for the first time up to my present return there, more than 21 thousand leagues I had travelled by sea and on land in my comings and goings in various parts of the world, not counting in this number journeys of 40 or fifty leagues or so, for there were many of these and I do not pay any attention to them.

On the 17th of January I left for Madrid on business, and on the 26th of March I was again in Lisbon.[1] On the 19th of October I departed for Barcelona, stopping briefly in Madrid, passing through Çaragoça of Aragón, and coming in through Catalunha. I stayed in Barcellona for five months; for His Majesty was unwilling that we Fathers of the Company who came there should embark there, since malicious people were causing our trips to Italy to be viewed with suspicion and there was also the rebellious activity in the Alentejo.[2] After His Majesty had been informed of our purposes, however, he sent us permission. In the meantime I had gone to visit the famous sanctuary of Our Lady of Monserrate and, three leagues beyond, Manrresa, a famous place in our religion because our Father Saint Ignacio had done his first penance there. From there I went to Cardona to see a great marvel of nature there; for, in addition to the mountains being mines of salt, there is one where the salt is found in various colours, crystalline, green, vermilion, red, blue, and yellow; and the fruit-trees reach down into the salt with their roots and do not wither but rather produce the most delicious fruit.[3] The inhabitants of the town venerate, among various relics, a piece of the crown of Christ Our Lord with some thorns, a rib of Saint Ignes, which certainly seemed to be that of a little girl, two ringlets of hair of the Virgin Our Lady, the thickness of a finger, and it appeared that they were decaying. These relics were left in that church by a Cardinal who is buried in it, from the family of the Dukes of Cardona, descendants of the Infante Fortuna of Aragón, the progenitor of this family, who is buried there along with others.[4]

[1] Balthazar Tellez says that Lobo left Lisbon on 20 January 1637 after having presented the business of the eastern missions to the Vicereine, the Infanta Margarida, and that he reached Madrid on 6 February, *Historia geral de Ethiopia a alta* (Coimbra, 1660), p. 583.

[2] A reference to anti-Spanish riots at Évora in 1637.

[3] Cardona is about 55 miles NW of Barcelona. A deposit of rock salt forms a mass some 300 feet high and three miles in circumference. It is covered by a bed of reddish brown clay, rests on yellowish grey sandstone, and is mostly translucent.

[4] The Cardinal meant is probably D. Jaime de Cardona (d. 1466), Bishop of Vich, Gerona and Urgel. The Dukes of Cardona claimed descent from Ramon Folch, a

I returned to Barcellona and, with His Majesty's permission soon arriving, I departed on Easter in the afternoon, and after stopping at several ports in Catalunha for a few days, we crossed the Gulf of Leão[1] in two days and put into port at Genoua. From there we took the road to Rome, traversing Tuscany. I passed through Luca, Sena, Florença, and various cities of the Papal State. On the 9th of May I entered Rome, where I stayed for more than 7 months and saw everything worth seeing in that city, with the 7 and the 9 churches, seeing in them the many things they have that are worthy of veneration. I said mass over the sepulchres of the most distinguished of the Apostles, I saw the famous relics that are preserved in that city as in a sanctuary, a large part of the Holy Cross, the title in Hebrew, Greek and Latin characters, for some of all of these could be distinguished, pieces of the crown and several thorns, the sponge, the lance, Saint Thomas's finger, one of the thirty coins for which the Saviour was sold, the sacred portrait, the one that Christ Our Lord sent to King Abagaro,[2] the sacred staircase on which Christ went up to and down from the Praetorium, the head of the holy Baptist, the Column, the Altar on which Saint Peter said mass, and countless other relics; the catacombs winding for many miles underground with innumerable graves of martyred Saints whose bones were to be seen there. I saw the Pope's palaces, especially that of Saint Peter and that of Monte Cavalo, many other palaces of Cardinals with various, curious and excellent gardens. I went to Napoles, seeing on the way the famous cities in that kingdom; I went to Massa[3] and saw on the way many other cities of that kingdom which are in that part. In Napoles I was shown things of great renown, an infinite number of famous relics, of which that city is another sanctuary, especially three vials of blood: one of Saint Genario or Genuario, which, being coagulated, always becomes liquid when it is within sight of the same Saint's head; another of Saint Patricia, which within sight of a tooth of that Saint became liquid as my companion was saying mass, and I verified first that it was dry and afterwards, when it had become liquid; the third of Saint John the Baptist, which being hard as a stone, as I verified, became as liquid as water as I was saying the mass of his beheading, and I also verified this change. I also saw a piece of the same

brother-in-law of Charlemagne; Fortuna is probably a mistake for Ramon Hugo Folch, Viscount of Cardona, who was accorded the title of Count in 1357 by Pedro IV of Aragon.

[1] The Gulf of Lyons.
[2] The King of Edessa (Urfa). According to legend Abgar V appealed to Jesus to be healed; Jesus wrote a letter, cited by Eusebius. In a later version He is said to have sent His portrait imprinted on canvas. The story may date from the conversion of Abgar IX in the third century.   [3] On the mainland opposite Capri.

Saint's rib. They also showed me a large nail all full of barbs, with which
Christ's feet had been nailed to the Cross, and I had already seen one
from the hands in Rome; two bodies of the Holy Innocents, still intact
with their tiny fingernails and toenails; another Saint, also intact, is a
Franciscan friar named Frey Jacob da Marca.[1] On the way back I saw
the famous monastery of Monte Casino, where I slept one night, and
where the monks showed me great memorials there of their sainted
Father, innumerable relics to the measure of the Saint himself which
is very great; and when each guest leaves they give him a loaf of
delicious bread. I also took mine.

When I was to leave Rome, it was by a different route from the one
I had come by. I traversed Romania,[2] Umbria, entered the Marches,
and arrived at the Holy House of Loreto on the eve of Christmas. I
said midnight mass in the same House that the angels had brought from
Palestine, the one in which Our Lady lived and the Holy Child was
raised. It still has the first door, a window, the chimney, three
porringers that Our Lady, Saint Joseph and the Child Jesus ate from;
I drank out of them. The house inspires reverence and respect and
instills devoutness as one sees and kisses the very walls which were
leaned against many times by the Son of God and within which lived
that earthly trinity, Jesus, Mary and Joseph. I went on to Bolonha and
visited the celebrated monastery of Saint Domingos, where his body
and grave are so much venerated, and in a certain convent of nuns is
the Blessed Catherina of Bolonha, still intact, dressed and seated in a
chair with her body straight and her arms extended, dressed in a nun's
hood, with which they dress and undress her as if she were alive. I
travelled through the Duchies of Parma, Placencia, Modena and
entered Lombardy, travelling through it to Millão, where in addition
to the Castelo of such great fame and its celebrated Domo which is
the cathedral, a very magnificent work of art, I venerated in our
college a famous relic which is a sash in which the Virgin Our Lady
carried her Holy Child to Egypt holding Him at her neck. From there
I passed other famous cities of Lombardy and again arrived at Genova,
where, because there was no other ship, I embarked on a tartan and
crossed the Gulf of Leão in it, with a happier result than could have
been expected from what prudence I had used in selecting the vessel,
for it rather was considered foolhardy of me to board such a ship to
cross that dreaded gulf. With a good voyage I finally reached Spanish

---

[1] San Giacomo della Marca, 1391–1476. He died at Naples and his chapel is in the Church
of Sta Maria la Nuova.   [2] The Romagna.

soil and, bound for Barcelona, I travelled by land, leaving my baggage and curiosities to come by sea; a Castilian, however, to whom I had entrusted them, and who owed me more fidelity because of how well I had paid him, stole it all from me. I saw the ancient city of Girona, arrived at Barcelona, and, to take a different route, set out for Valença, where I soon arrived, and, among the devotional things there is the Holy Chalice, over which Christ Our Lord gave the blessing on the night of the Last Supper. That this is the same Chalice is attested by scriptures and ancient papers worthy of belief.[1] I had it in my hands, kissed it, gave it to others there to be kissed, and put the beads I had with me in it. It is made of a kind of reddish stone called agate.

From there I went to Madrid [This final sentence originally continued with the following words later placed in parentheses and underlined by Lobo with the obvious intention that they should be omitted for the sense of the sentence but that they should be left readable since they conveyed valuable information: 'whence I departed for this city (i.e., Lisbon) where I wrote this Itinerary without finishing it because of the many travels which follow from this point onward and which still remain to be added to it'. The account, as written by the copyist, ended here; but, after deleting all but the first six words of the sentence, Lobo continued the sentence in his own handwriting as follows:], where I stayed for a short time, during which I received the final decision which referred me to the Council in Lisbon and to the Infanta Margarita,[2] the decision being made by the King Dom Felipe, to whom this Kingdom was still subject, although it soon became free of it. The most I could obtain, however, was that the Viceroy, who was embarking for India, should try to carry out the undertaking if he found things favourably disposed and if he could accomplish it to the advantage of the state without serious risk and expense. This decision had little or no effect.

[1] This is still preserved in Valencia Cathedral, the bowl is of agate but the stem and handles are of gold. The base appears to be of shell and is ornamented with gold, pearls and other precious stones.

[2] Margherita, daughter of Carlo Emanuele of Savoy and Catalina-Micaela, youngest daughter of Philip II of Spain. She married Francesco Gonzaga, fifth Duke of Mantua, was widowed in 1612, and became Vicereine of Portugal, an office she held until the revolution of 1640.

Index

This is primarily an index of personal and geographical names. Variant forms used by Lobo are given in brackets in the main entry; they are cross-referenced unless the two spellings would be in juxtaposition. Names of ships are listed under 'ships'. Under Cabreira are references to all notes that include additional or conflicting information derived from his own published narrative of the wreck of the *Belém*. Under Le Grand is a list of the notes which record differences between his translation of Lobo and the Braga MS.